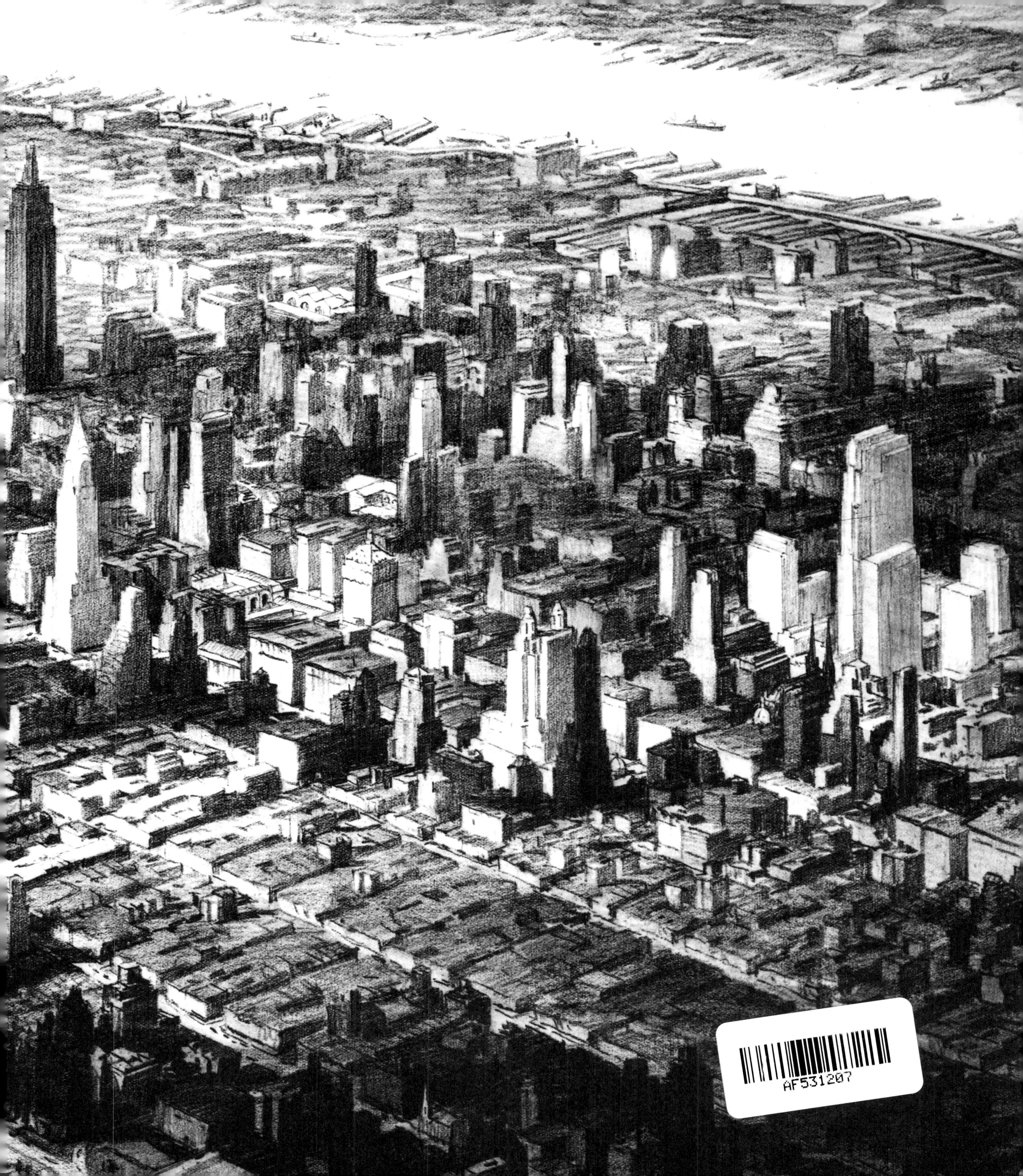

A HOME
TO THE WORLD

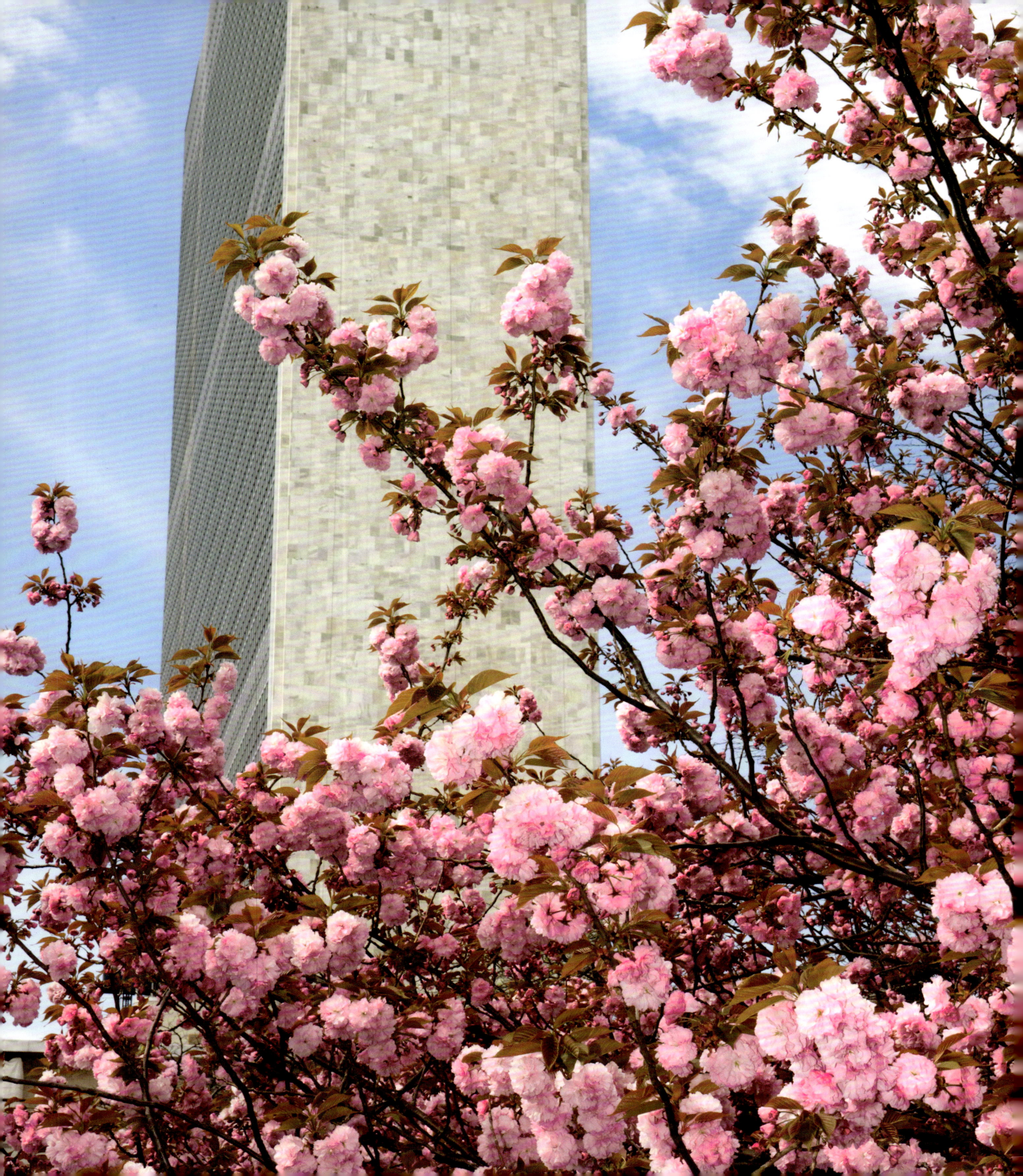

Cherry blossoms in spring at UN Headquarters, against a backdrop of the Secretariat Building. April 11, 2012.

A HOME TO THE WORLD

THE UNITED NATIONS AND NEW YORK CITY

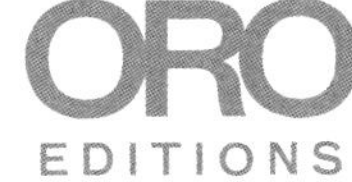

ORO Editions
Publishers of Architecture, Art, and Design
Publisher: Gordon Goff
Managing Editor: Jake Anderson

www.oroeditions.com
info@oroeditions.com

Published by ORO Editions

Book Design: Pentagram
Copy: Raul Barreneche

10 9 8 7 6 5 4 3 2 1 First Edition

ISBN: 978-1-951541-30-9

Color Separations and Printing: ORO Group Ltd.
Printed in China.

ORO Editions makes a continuous effort to minimize the overall carbon footprint of its publications. As part of this goal, ORO Editions, in association with Global ReLeaf, arranges to plant trees to replace those used in the manufacturing of the paper produced for its books. Global ReLeaf is an international campaign run by American Forests, one of the world's oldest nonprofit conservation organizations. Global ReLeaf is American Forests' education and action program that helps individuals, organizations, agencies, and corporations improve the local and global environment by planting and caring for trees.

Cover: On December 7, 1946, the United Nations approved as its official logo an azimuthal projection of a world map centered on the North Pole (a detail of which is shown here) and framed by arching olive branches, all in white, on a bright cerulean blue background. Architect and designer Oliver Lincoln Lundquist, leader of the team responsible for the logo's design, chose this shade because he said blue was "the opposite of red, the war color."[1]

CONTENTS

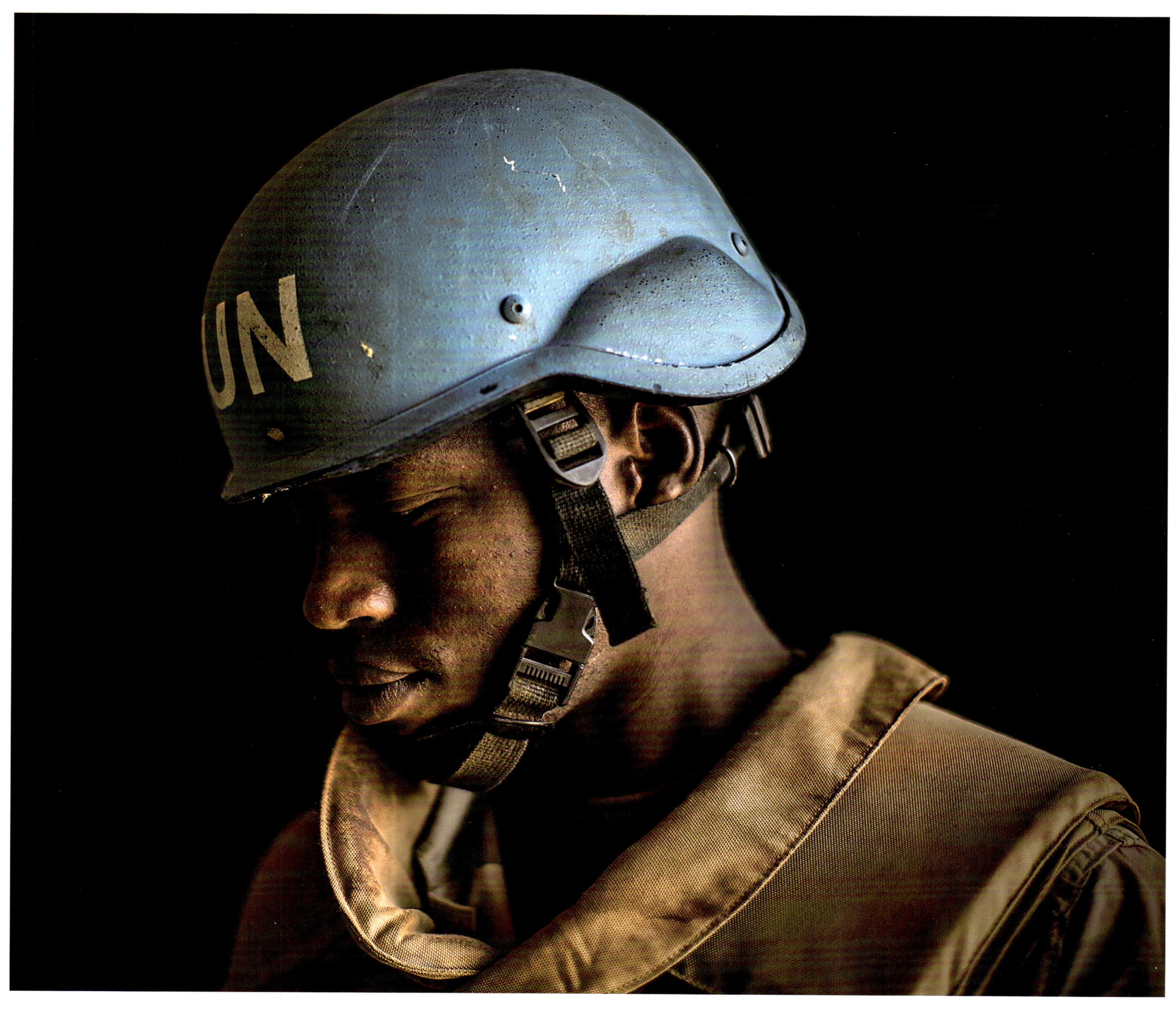

A peacekeeper from Burkina Faso serving with the United Nations Multidimensional Integrated Stabilization Mission in Mali (MINUSMA), on patrol in Timbuktu, Mali, May 2018.

Foreword
António Guterres
Secretary-General of the United Nations

Seventy-five years ago, the United Nations was established with the aim of securing peace, development, and human rights for all. Its creation following the utter devastation of the Second World War showed that wartime leaders recognized cooperation and compromise to be in their national interest. Since then, the United Nations has worked to put its founding promise into practice. A much-feared Third World War has been avoided. Dozens of former colonies gained independence, helping to shape the international community we have today.

Together, we supported the fight against apartheid. We eradicated smallpox, reduced hunger and extreme poverty, and boosted literacy and life-expectancy. We have developed international law and human rights standards. We have fostered global pacts to protect people and our planet—most recently the Sustainable Development Goals and the Paris Agreement on climate change. Every day around the world, we provide life-saving assistance to millions of people. Our peacekeepers and mediators support peace where others cannot or will not go.

And yet, there is still so much to be done.

As we mark our 75th anniversary, we face a confluence of crises. Climate calamity looms; biodiversity is collapsing; and poverty is increasing for the first time in three decades. Hatred is spreading, geopolitical tensions are escalating, and nuclear weapons remain on hair-trigger alert. Transformative technologies have brought new opportunities as well as new risks.

The COVID-19 pandemic has laid bare the world's fragilities. We can only address them together. That message emerged loud and clear from the global consultations we conducted to mark this anniversary.

We need more—and more effective—multilateralism, harnessing the vision and pragmatism that brought the United Nations into existence.

Secretary-General António Guterres makes remarks to a High-Level Meeting on Climate and Sustainable Development for All. March 28, 2019.

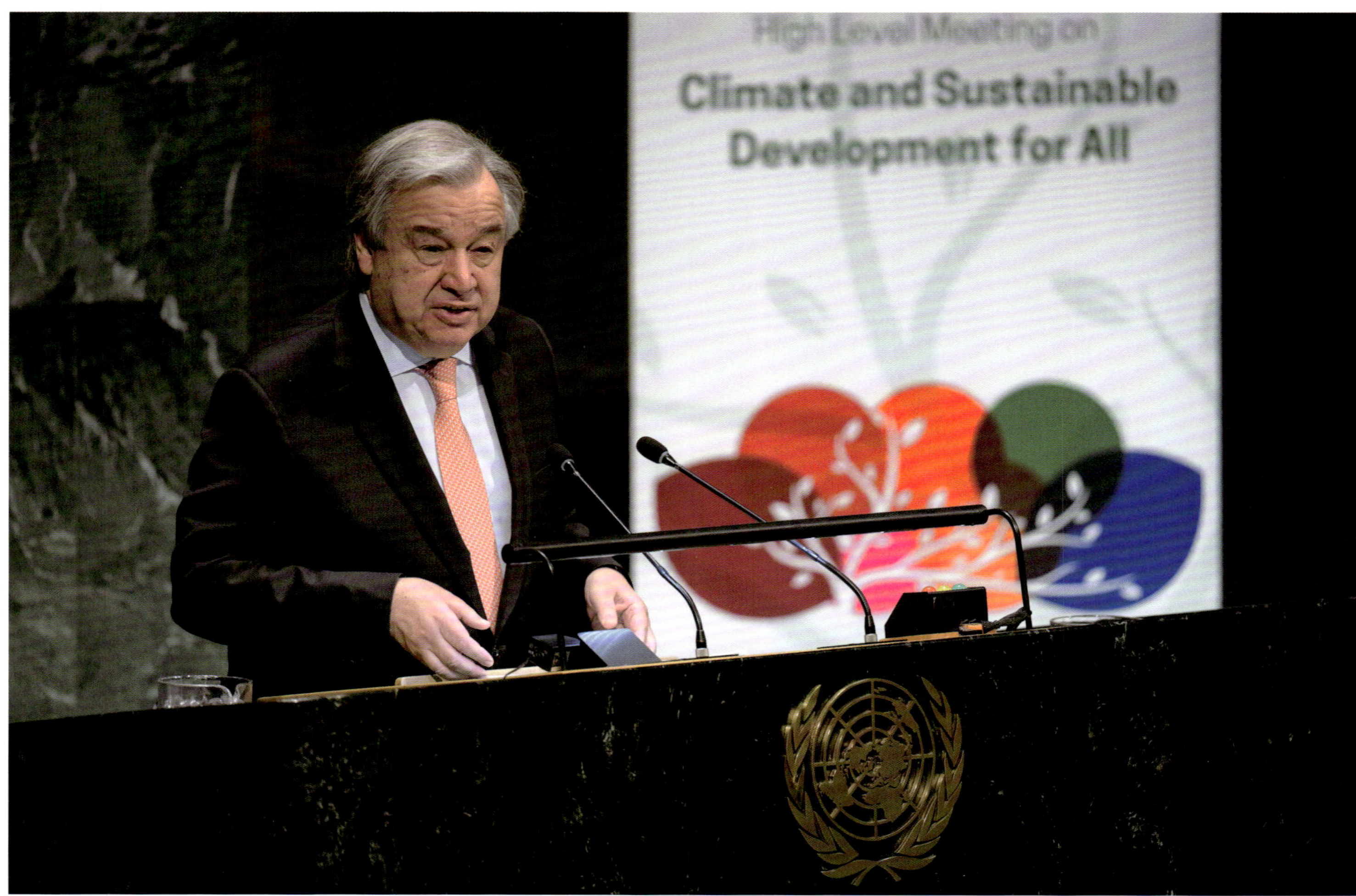

We need a networked multilateralism, in which the United Nations works more closely with international financial institutions, regional organizations, and trading blocs; and an inclusive multilateralism, drawing on knowledge and experience of youth, civil society, businesses, local authorities, and cities.

New York City, diverse and dynamic, has always been a source of inspiration for the United Nations, and I am proud to call it home. For more than half a century, the support of the United Nations Development Corporation has helped us to fulfill our mandates and objectives. This book reflects on the unique relationship between our global organization and this global city, and I look forward to continuing our cooperation.

COVID-19 has upended our world. But that upheaval has created space for transformative action. Recovery is our chance to reimagine economies and societies—and bring the vision of our founding Charter to life for all. By working together, we can build a safer, fairer, and more sustainable future.

A Shared Foundation
By Andrew M. Cuomo

The world has changed dramatically in 75 years. Yet many of the circumstances and principles that spurred the creation of the United Nations in 1945 are still vitally important today.

As the world battles the COVID-19 virus, we should recall the founding ideals of the UN. We are strongest when we work together. Diversity does not have to mean division. When leaders provide people with truth and direction, people respond with intelligence and humanity. New York called upon these ideals during this pandemic, and it helped us contain the virus.

The UN and New York share much in common. We both are populated by smart, tough people striving to change the world—and often succeeding. We both represent the diversity of the world, not just as a matter of circumstance, but as a foundational reason for our existence. We are the sum of our parts: the people of the world. We both are making progress to protect the rights and safety of all people, to provide equal opportunity, and to protect our environment and climate.

We both often face complex bureaucracies and political resistance that stand in the face of that progress. Yet we both fight on, because our goal is to actually improve life for people—not by cursing the darkness, but by lighting a candle.

The mutual respect between New York State and the UN dates back to the organization's earliest days. In 1968, New York State established the United Nations Development Corporation to ensure the UN would have the space and facilities needed for its critical mission. My father, former Governor Mario Cuomo, speaking at the UN, described it as the ultimate expression of the ideas of diversity, interdependence, and family. And he described New York as the diplomatic capital of the world—a fitting setting for such an institution.

Andrew M. Cuomo is Governor of New York.

I cannot imagine New York without the UN. And I cannot imagine the UN without New York. Since 1951, the UN has been a contributor to New York's economy and prestige. But more than that, the UN has become a part of our identity and community.

When I look out of the window from my office and see the magnificent UN complex, I think of what humankind is capable of when we work together. I think of how many of our worst ills are man-made and self-imposed, and I think of how many of our greatest advancements are also man-made, and collectively built. I think of how beautiful it is to see all the peoples of the world under one roof, in one city.

The UN Secretariat Building has become as iconic as the Empire State Building. They are part of a skyline in which all of the structures weave together to write a singular message in the sky: You are welcome here. This city calls out for people from around the world to come here and build a better life, or a better world.

The Statue of Liberty beckons them. The Freedom Tower inspires them. And the UN reminds them that New York is home to all.

A Lasting Partnership
By Bill de Blasio

The United Nations was created three-quarters of a century ago to secure international peace and security through diplomatic solutions. It is hard to imagine a better home than New York City for the institution charged with achieving this ambitious goal, which has served as a beacon of hope for people around the world for generations. The United Nations was born in the aftermath of a great crisis. The Second World War had finally ended and the time had come to rebuild and forge new relationships between nations around the world. This new international organization needed a home that could rise to the immense task at hand. Our city's journey to become that home was hard-won, requiring intense negotiations and a donation from the Rockefeller family. John D. Rockefeller, Jr. understood the importance of locating this important, new "international city" within the greatest city in the world. He hastily arranged to purchase the land—at the time covered by old slaughterhouses and slums—and quickly donated it. The site was accepted by the General Assembly, and now, 75 years later, the United Nations has become part of the fabric of our great city, strengthening our position as a global city, employing thousands of our residents, and generating billions of dollars for our economy.

This year also marks the 50th anniversary of the United Nations Development Corporation, and I would like to acknowledge its tremendous work in our city. The UNDC has long been a great partner in ensuring that the UN and its many programs have the space they need, while also integrating that footprint into the larger community. We are grateful for all their efforts to facilitate a fruitful relationship between the UN and New York City.

I am proud that New York, a global cultural center and home to immigrants from around the world, became a base for the UN's important work. From the financial crises and cultural revolutions of the latter half of

Bill de Blasio is Mayor of New York City.

last century to the dark hours following 9/11 and the devastating COVID-19 pandemic that continues to wreak havoc across the globe, New York City is no stranger to adversity. We have always stood as an example of resiliency, leadership, and collaboration in the face of immense challenges. It is these values that make us a fitting place for world leaders to come together in hopes of developing solutions for the globe's most pressing crises.

The significance of the UN stretches beyond our city's borders and the economic impact it makes locally. The UN community works around the world to promote international peace and security, further sustainable development, and protect human rights. This is critical work—work that has only deepened the relationship between this esteemed institution and its host city. As my administration moves forward in our mission to create a fairer city, the United Nations presses for that movement around the globe. In looking to connect local initiatives to global efforts, we have partnered to help accelerate the impact of the UN's Sustainable Development Goals, designed to tackle persistent inequities and build a fairer society for all. When those goals were ratified by the UN, we incorporated them into our own OneNYC 2050 Plan, geared to secure our city's future by confronting our climate crisis, achieving equity, and strengthening our democracy.

As we look forward to continuing the urgent work of making the world a more equitable, sustainable, and peaceful place for future generations, I am grateful for our enduring partnership with the United Nations and the UNDC. In celebration of the UN's 75th anniversary and the UNDC's 50th, I am pleased to honor their ongoing efforts to achieve our shared vision for a better world.

Introduction
By Stephen Schlesinger

A New Yorker created the United Nations. President Franklin Roosevelt, one-time governor of New York State, who long kept a townhouse on East 65th Street in New York City, was the main proponent for the establishment of the organization. It was he who during the Second World War convinced his two most crucial allies, Soviet leader Joseph Stalin and British Prime Minister Winston Churchill, to support the creation of the global security body. Once they were aboard, some four dozen other nations also followed and all attended the 1945 San Francisco Conference that drafted the UN Charter. It was appropriate that Roosevelt's hometown, New York City, became the site for the assembly.

But the placement of the UN in New York City came about for other reasons, too. Most nations around the globe wanted the body to be in America because its very presence on U.S. soil would guarantee that America would stay in the organization through thick and thin, in good weather and bad. Otherwise, many worried, without that anchor in New York City, the U.S. might be tempted to leave the institution as it had once deserted the League of Nations, undermining its legitimacy and viability.

I have written extensively about the United Nations. My book, *Act of Creation*, tells the story of how the UN came into being. I regularly visit the UN building. Every time I go there, I am awed by the fact that all 193 nations of the world are represented in that slim, classic elegant skyscraper, with their flags flying brightly in the East River breezes. It is a thrill and a matter of pride to enter its premises. The building is an iconic part of the New York City landscape. Passing through the General Assembly and the Security Council is also a hallowed experience—a reminder of all the history that has taken place within these famed halls over 75 years. And we in New York always have a great privilege to have so many representatives from so many diverse countries living in our midst.

Stephen Schlesinger is an American author, political commentator, and international affairs specialist.

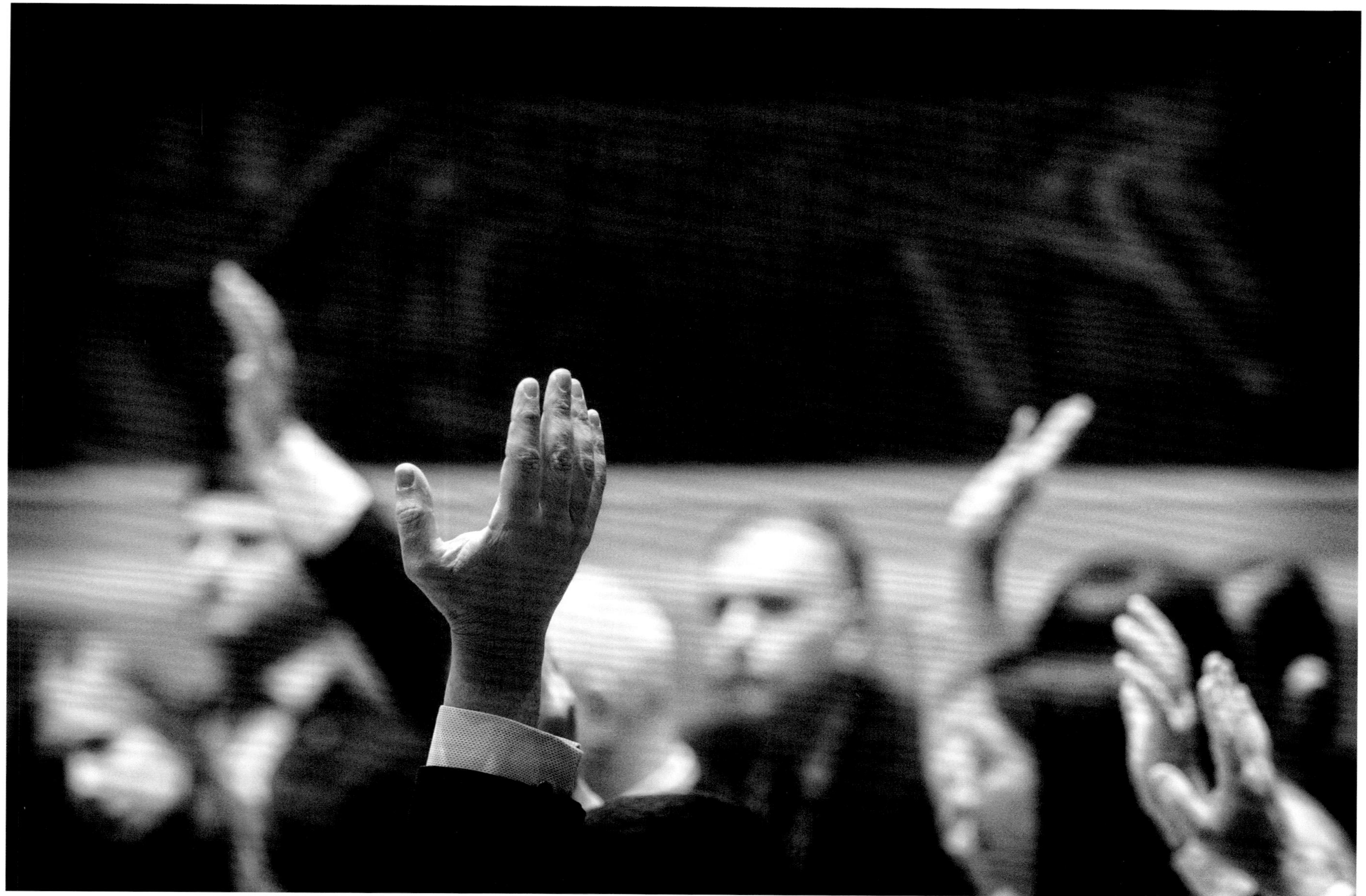

Security Council members unanimously vote to adopt a resolution extending sanctions on those threatening stability in Yemen. The Council also extends the mandate of the Panel of Experts, who assist the committee that oversees those measures. February 23, 2017.

For all its ups and downs, the UN has endured. Given its Charter of unique suppleness and practicality, it has managed to stay relevant and reinvent itself for almost every new season. Even during the worst of the Cold War, when distrust between the United States and the Soviet Union paralyzed the Security Council, the UN took on all sorts of new responsibilities never even mentioned in the original document, including peacekeeping, peace enforcement, cease-fires, election monitoring, constitution writing, nation building, arms inspections, military training, war crimes tribunals, and so on. Through the years it has also brought peace to states like Cambodia, Mozambique, Guatemala, Angola, El Salvador, Serbia, Kosovo, Kuwait, South Africa, Slovenia, Nicaragua, Colombia, Liberia, Cyprus, Bosnia, Macedonia, Croatia, Sierra Leone, and the Ivory Coast.

Innovative UN agencies have sprung up, such as the UN Development Programmme, UNESCO, UNICEF, the UN Environment Programme, UN-Habitat, the Food and Agriculture Organization (FAO), the World Health Organization (WHO), the World Bank—the latter, alone, helping poorer nations build roads and schools and ports and hospitals and so on. Indeed, today the UN is, in many ways, primarily a service organization —almost 90% of its resources are devoted to service. The UN has, in addition, negotiated over 300 global treaties that today provide the rules and regulations for the planet's commerce and for its health and safety and for human rights and for democratic governance. And the UN continues to offer a diplomatic arena to resolve crises, a meeting venue for global leaders, and a 24-hour call center to handle sudden emergencies.

Of course, the framers made sure that in 1948 they drafted the Universal Declaration of Human Rights—led by yet another New Yorker, Eleanor Roosevelt, the president's wife—to insure that such an idea was always in the forefront of all UN resolutions, pronouncements, programs, and policies.

The UN's achievements have come about despite the fact that the organization has no army, has no taxing power, has no legislative functions, has no democratic mandate—only moral authority. Yet, since its founding, our trust in global security has improved broadly over the years. Today we live in a world of democracy, not Hitler's world of fascism or Stalin's world of communism or even in Osama Bin Laden's world of fundamentalism. The UN remains in the forefront of change. It helped spur the extraordinary decolonization of the planet. It has helped expand democracy and human rights around the globe. Lastly, and most importantly, there have been no nuclear conflicts during the UN's reign.

I see the UN as sort of akin to a fire station, sometimes quiet quarters, but the moment a crisis erupts, it comes alive, sirens blazing, ready to handle emergencies and provide the means to end disputes, repair war-ravaged societies, write constitutions, set up viable states. It remains omnipresent in natural disasters. It is the only institution to handle transnational issues like environmental degradation, sexual trafficking, drug smuggling, nuclear proliferation, and conquering medical epidemics like AIDS. It won't necessarily solve the crisis, but it can help dampen it, confine it, limit it, slow it down, initiate talks on it, and prevent it from spinning out of control. Sometimes the UN even serves as a useful scapegoat to compel states to do what they should do but don't want to do. The UN gives them someone to blame. Now that is not nothing!

Let us remember now the famous quote from UN Secretary-General Dag Hammarskjöld, who once said: "The UN wasn't created to take humanity to heaven, but to prevent it from going to hell."

UN MILESTONES AND KEY GLOBAL EVENTS

’40S

The USS Arizona burning after the Japanese attack on Pearl Harbor.

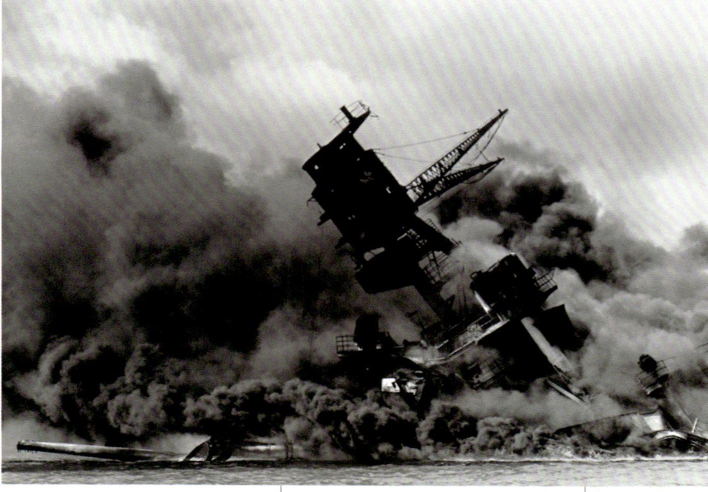

1941

Attack on Pearl Harbor. U.S. enters the war

Inter-Allied Declaration first step toward creating United Nations

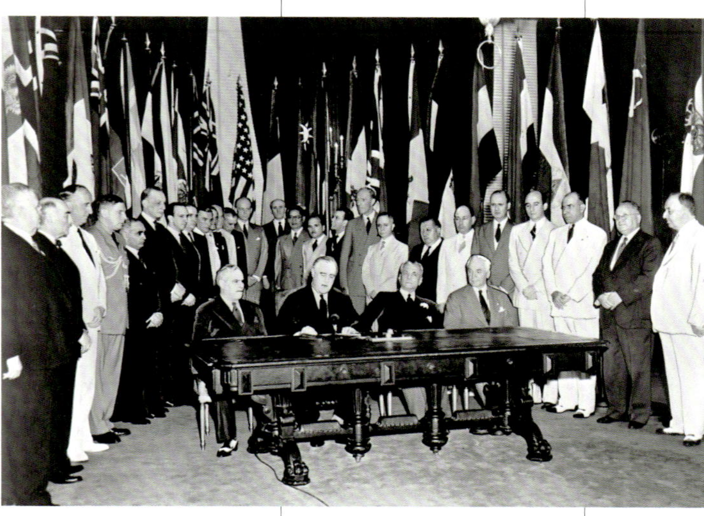

1942

Declaration by United Nations signed by 26 countries against Axis powers

Representatives of Allied nations sign the Declaration by United Nations, a document that contained the first official use of the term “United Nations,” which was suggested by U.S. President Franklin Delano Roosevelt (seated, second from left).

1944

Dumbarton Oaks Conference outlines first blueprint for UN

Rubble and ruined buildings covering the streets after the German bombing of Warsaw, Poland, September 1939.

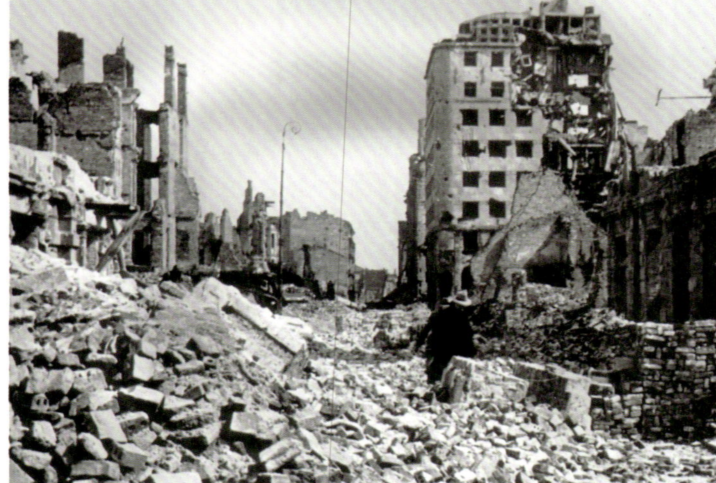

1945

UN Charter signed in San Francisco and later ratified to create the United Nations

End of WWII

1946

UN selects New York City for global headquarters

Nuremberg Trials

Philippine independence from U.S.

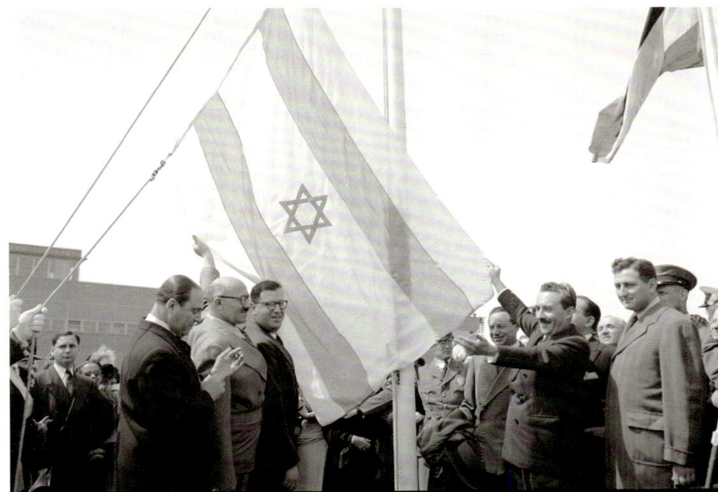

Flag of Israel is hoisted to its place among the flags of the Member States at the UN. Seen holding flag at right is Moshe Sharett, Foreign Minister of Israel. May 12, 1949.

1947

UN votes for the partition of Palestine and the creation of an independent Jewish state

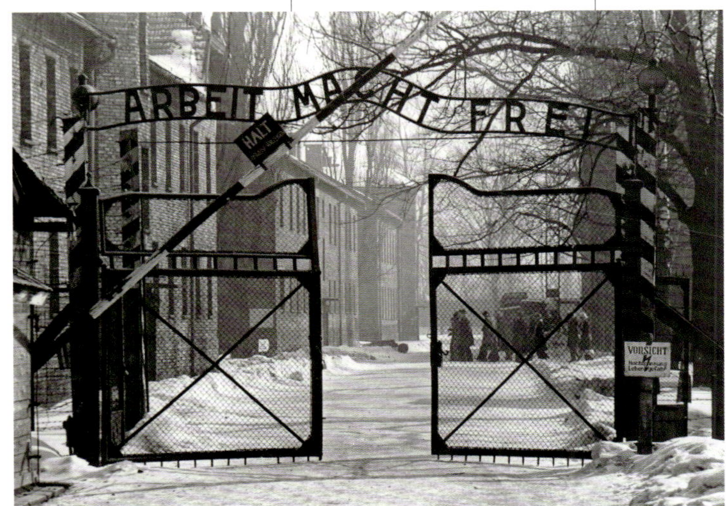

The gates of the Nazi concentration camp at Auschwitz, Poland.

1948

Gandhi assassinated

State of Israel founded

Universal Declaration of Human Rights

1949

People's Republic of China founded

NATO established

Eleanor Roosevelt holding a Universal Declaration of Human Rights poster in Spanish, 1949.

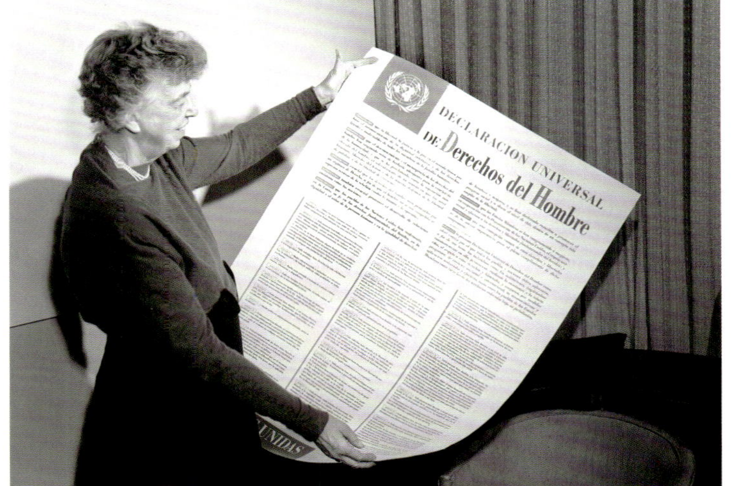

UN MILESTONES AND KEY GLOBAL EVENTS

Trygve Lie (Norway): 1946–1952

Dag Hammarskjöld (Sweden): 1953–1961

'50S

1950

Korean War begins

First human organ transplant

1951

Marshall Plan for postwar reconstruction of Europe ends

Color television introduced

First UNIVAC computer unveiled

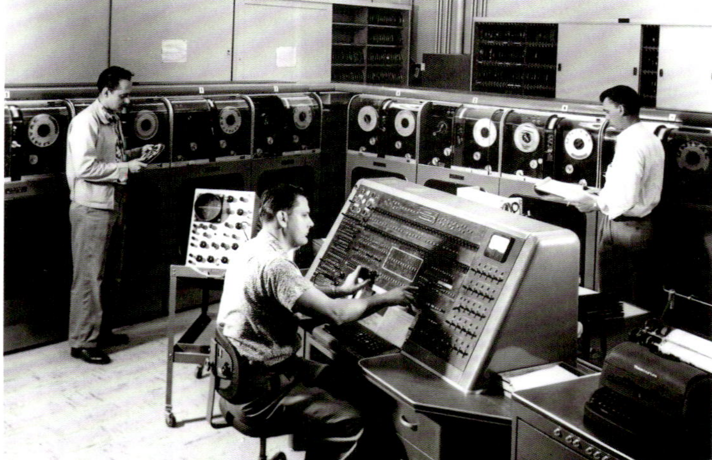

The UNIVAC at Lawrence Livermore National Laboratory, ca. 1950s.

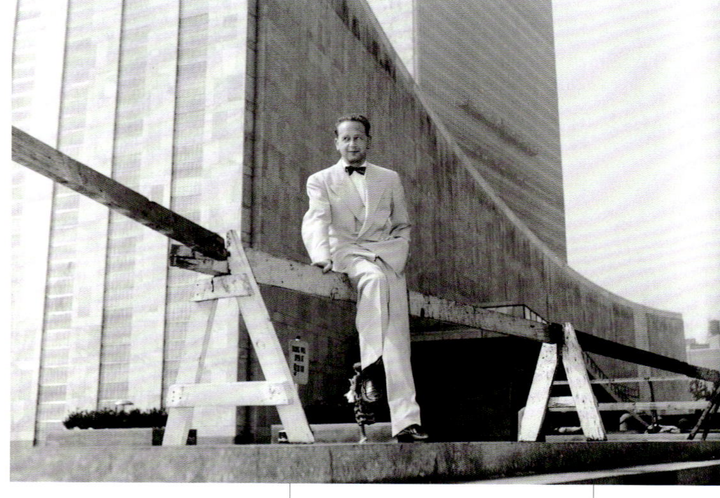

Dag Hammarskjöld, Secretary-General of the United Nations, in front of the newly constructed Headquarters' buildings, June 1953.

1952

UN Headquarters in New York City completed

Lever House completed, redefines modern skyscraper design for a generation

1953

Korean Armistice Agreement signed

Structure of DNA discovered

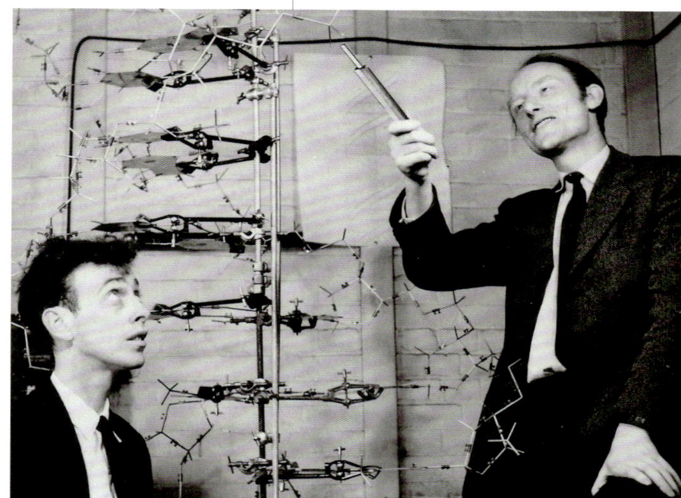

James Watson and Francis Crick with DNA model, 1953.

1955

Vietnam War begins

Warsaw Pact signed

1956

First UN peacekeeping forces deployed

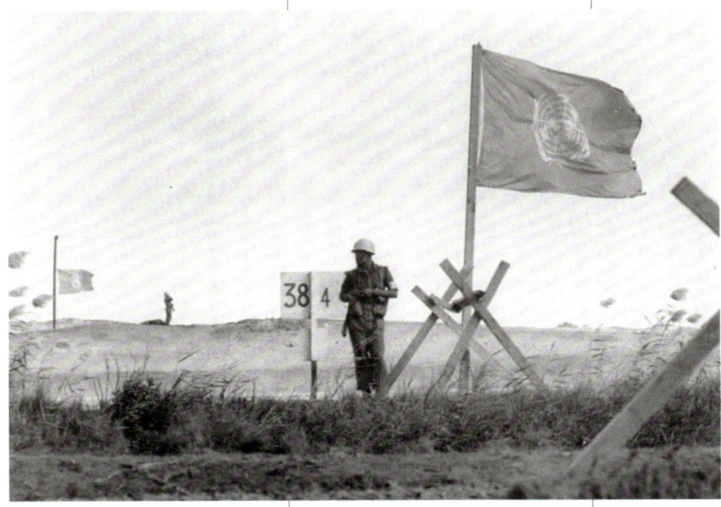

UN peacekeeping troops on patrol in the Suez following cease-fire agreement, 1956.

1957

Sputnik launches

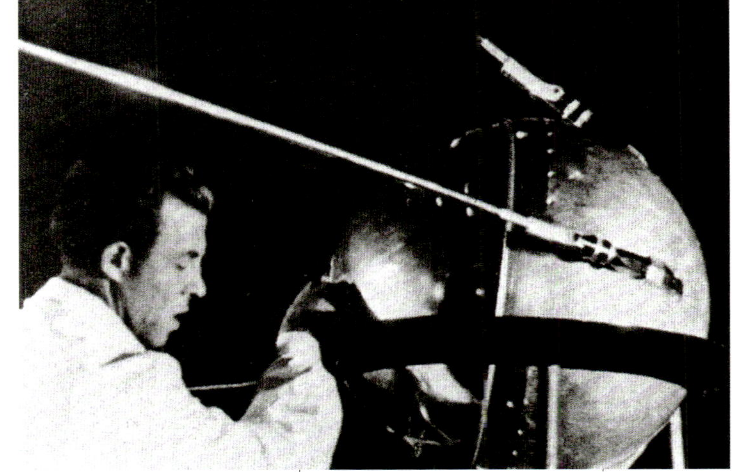

A technician putting the finishing touches on Sputnik 1, the world's first artificial satellite, launched by the former Soviet Union, 1957.

1959

Antarctic Treaty signed

Cuban Revolution overthrows dictatorship of Fulgencio Batista

Frank Lloyd Wright-designed Guggenheim Museum opens

Declaration of the Rights of the Child

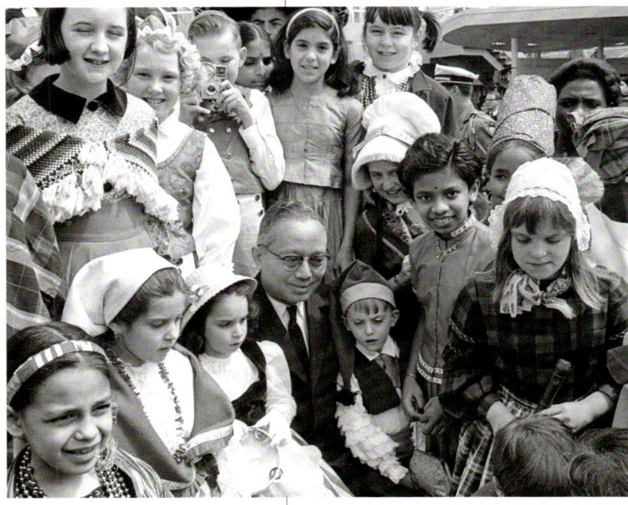

Secretary-General U Thant is seen at the opening of the UNICEF Pavilion at the New York World's Fair, surrounded by children of UN officials, who participated in the ceremonies, 1964.

UN MILESTONES AND KEY GLOBAL EVENTS

Dag Hammarskjöld (Sweden): 1953–1961

U Thant (Burma): 1961–1971

'60S

1960

OPEC created

World's first female prime minister elected in Ceylon, now Sri Lanka

U.S. launches first weather satellite

Xerox releases first plain-paper commercial copier

1961

Dag Hammarskjöld posthumously awarded Nobel Peace Prize

Berlin Wall erected

Peace Corps created

First cosmonaut in space

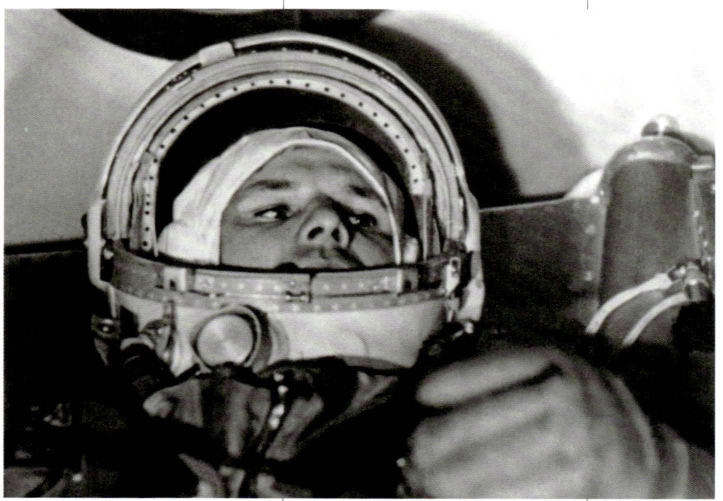

Yuri Gagarin, Soviet cosmonaut and first man in space, in the capsule of the Vostok 1 spacecraft. April 12, 1961.

1962

Cuban Missile Crisis

1963

Assassination of U.S. President John F. Kennedy

Pan Am (now MetLife) Building opens

New York City Department of City Planning votes to demolish Pennsylvania Station

1964

MLK receives Nobel Peace Prize

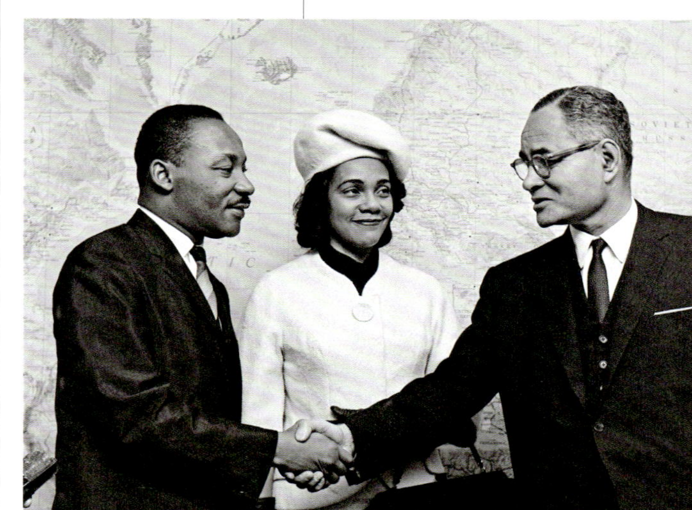

Dr. Martin Luther King, Jr. and his wife Coretta Scott King greeted by Mr. Ralph J. Bunche, UN Under-Secretary for Special Political Affairs, 1964.

1967

400,000 protesters march to the UN against Vietnam War; MLK speaks

First human heart transplant

Men transport a barrel of powdered milk supplied by UNICEF as part of its infant and child feeding program to a village in Guatemala, ca. 1950.

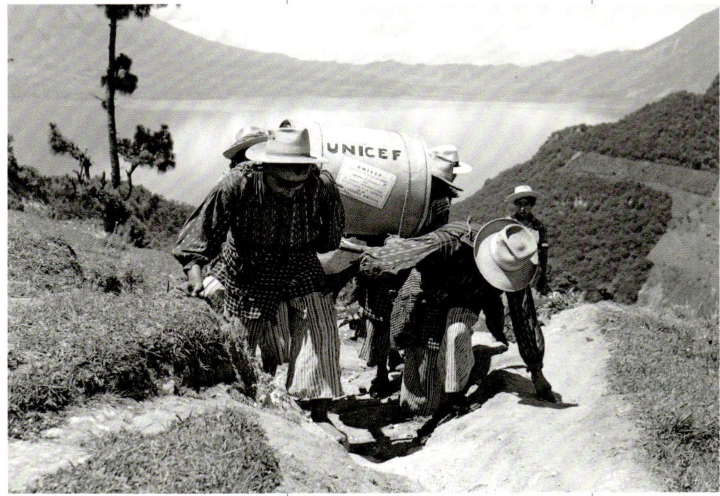

1965

UNICEF awarded Nobel Peace Prize

Pope Paul VI is first pope to address UN, delivers famous "no more war, war never again" speech

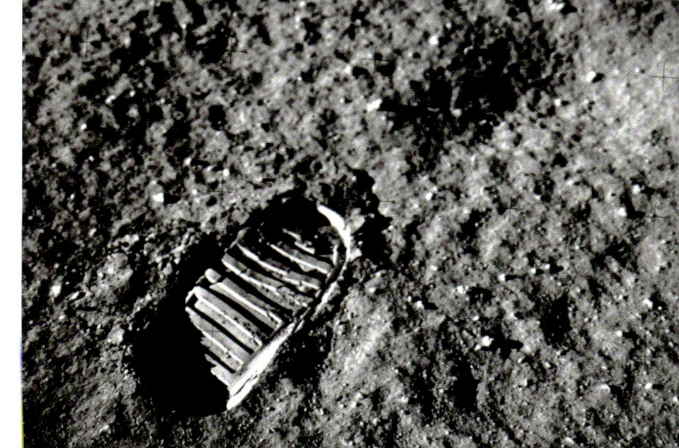

Close-up view of an astronaut's footprint in the lunar soil, photographed during the Apollo 11 lunar surface extravehicular activity, July 1969.

1969

First lunar landing

SALT nuclear weapons negotiations begin between U.S. and Soviet Union

Lincoln Center completed

International Labour Organization awarded Nobel Peace Prize

1968

The Civil Rights Act of 1968 is signed into law

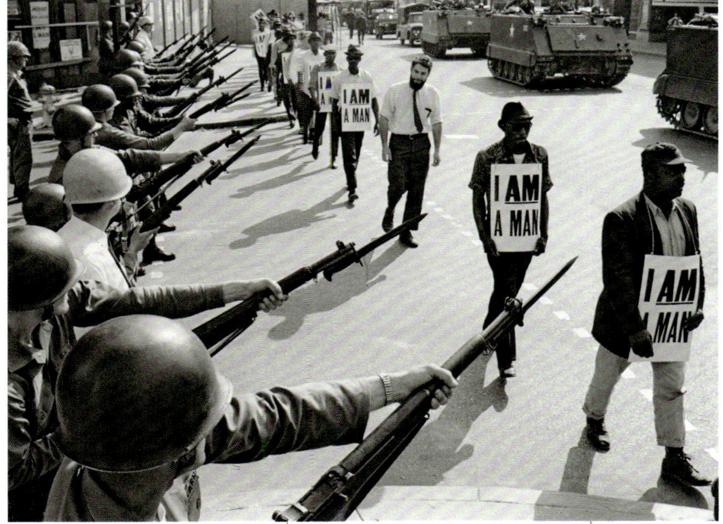

Civil Rights activists are blocked by National Guardsmen while trying to stage a protest in Memphis, Tennessee. March 29, 1968.

UN MILESTONES AND KEY GLOBAL EVENTS

U Thant (Burma): 1961–1971

Kurt Waldheim (Austria): 1972–1981

'70S

1970

First 747 Jumbo Jet enters service

First Earth Day celebrated

Nuclear Non-Proliferation Treaty went into effect

U.S. invasion of Cambodia

1971

People's Republic of China admitted to the UN

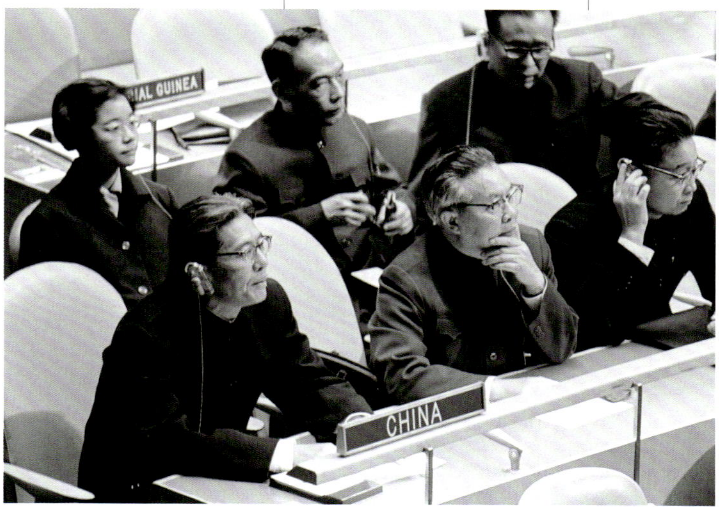

The delegation of the People's Republic of China is formally seated in the UN General Assembly Hall.

1972

Munich Olympics terrorist attack

Nixon visits China

First UN Environment Conference and creation of UN Environment Programme (UNEP)

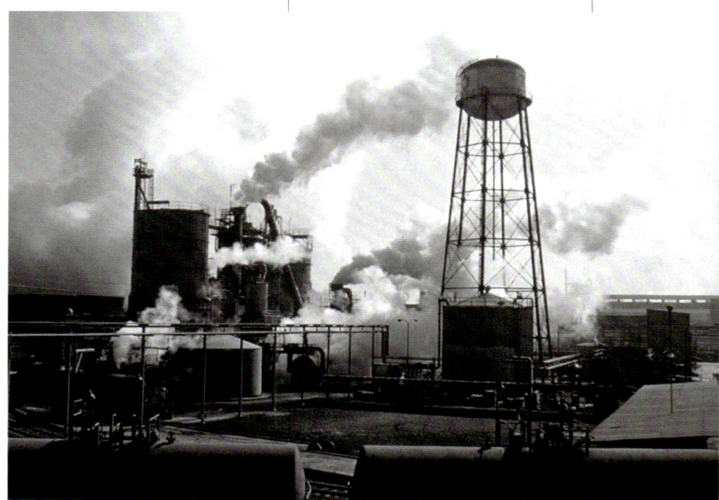

A chemical factory in Mexico City, Mexico, polluting the air, 1972.

1973

Paris Peace Accords

Yom Kippur War

Pinochet coup in Chile

World Trade Center completed

1974

First World Food Conference

Flo Kennedy and several other women demonstrate outside the Tribune, a nongovernmental conference that paralleled the official, UN-sponsored women's conference. June 19, 1975.

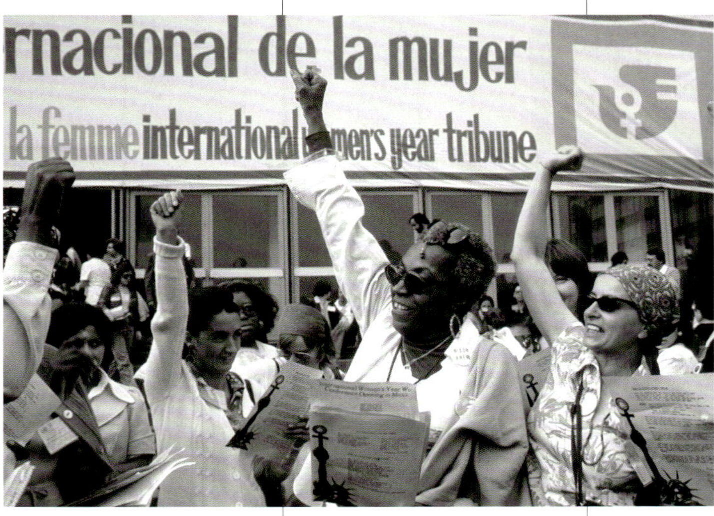

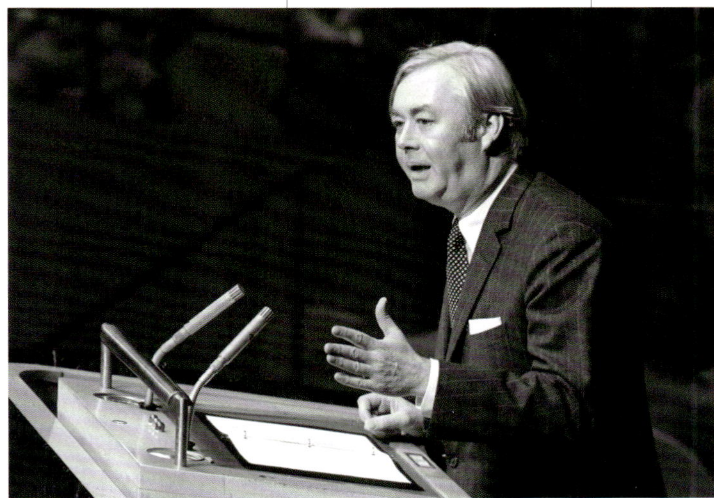

1975

First World Conference on Women; UN begins commemorating International Women's Day (March 8)

Text on Zionism approved by UN General Assembly

End of Vietnam War

Start of Lebanon civil war

Daniel Patrick Moynihan, U.S. Ambassador to the UN, speaks against a resolution that declared Zionism a form of racism: "A great evil has been loosed upon the world... [A]nti-Semitism has been given the appearance of international sanction... The United States...will never acquiesce in this infamous act." The UN revoked the resolution in 1991. November 10, 1975.

1977

Security Council adopts mandatory arms embargo against South Africa

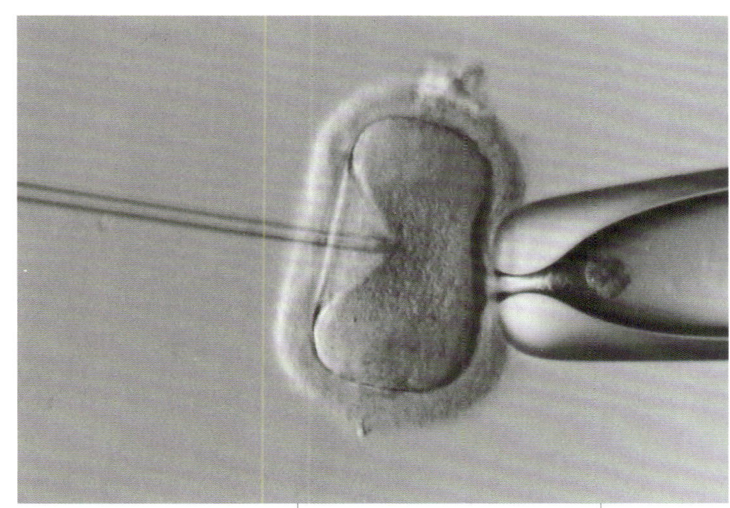

1978

First "test tube baby" born

Camp David Peace Accords

Demonstration of in vitro fertilization

1979

Iranian Revolution

U.S. and Soviet Union sign SALT II Treaty

Soviet Union invades Afghanistan

UN General Assembly adopts "Women's Bill of Rights," the most comprehensive international instrument for protecting human rights of women

UN MILESTONES AND KEY GLOBAL EVENTS

Kurt Waldheim (Austria): 1972–1981

Javier Pérez de Cuéllar (Peru): 1982–1991

'80S

1980

CNN launches

Iran-Iraq war begins

Mariel Boatlift of Cuban emigrants to United States begins

WHO declares smallpox eradicated

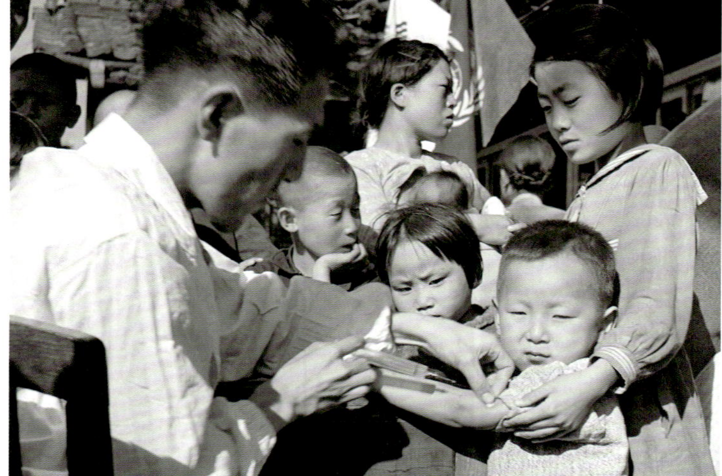

Immunization campaign during the Korean War, ca. 1950.

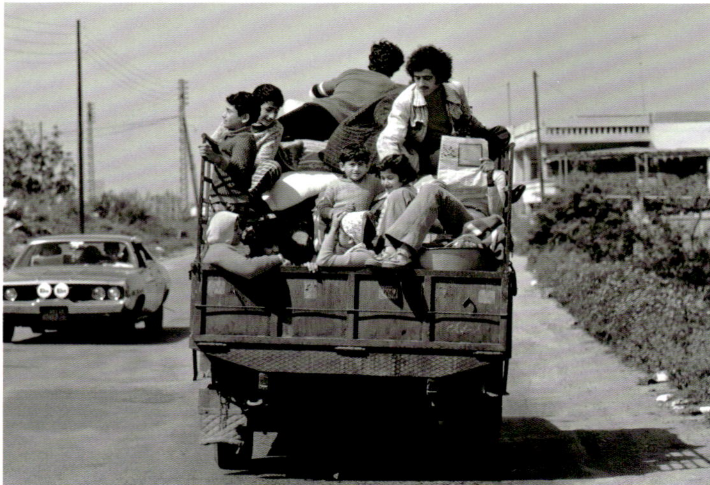

Refugees returning to their homes in Southern Lebanon, 1978.

1981

UN High Commissioner for Refugees awarded Nobel Peace Prize

First PC unveiled by IBM

First clinical report of AIDS in U.S.

Iran hostage crisis ends

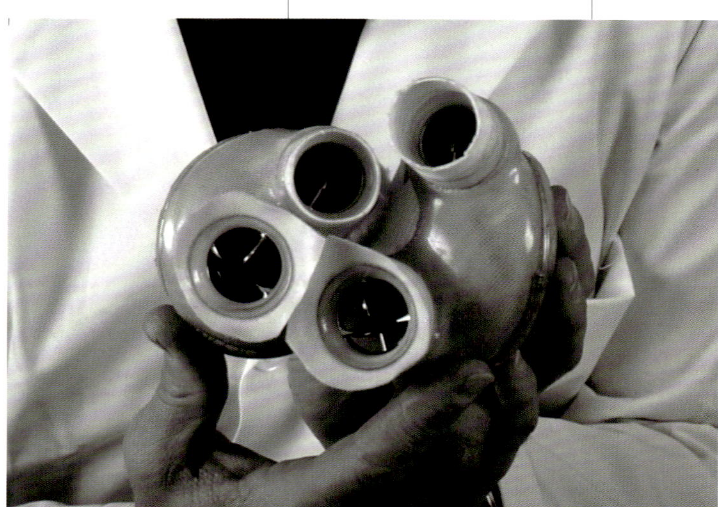

The Jarvik-7 artificial heart used in first human implantation.

1982

First artificial heart implant

Falkland Islands War

1983

HIV virus identified

1984

UN adopts Convention Against Torture

1986

Corazon Aquino elected Philippine President

Chernobyl nuclear disaster

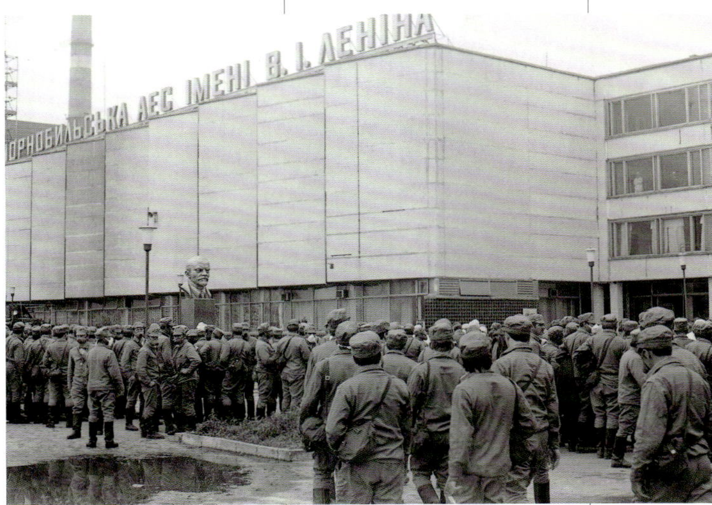

After the accident at the Chernobyl Nuclear Power Plant, thousands of Soviet soldiers assist with the cleanup throughout the 18-mile zone around the plant, including highly contaminated areas near the damaged reactor. Pripjat, Ukraine, 1986.

1988

UN Peacekeeping Forces awarded Nobel Peace Prize

Terrorist bombing of Pan Am jet over Lockerbie, Scotland

Benazir Bhutto elected Pakistan's Prime Minister

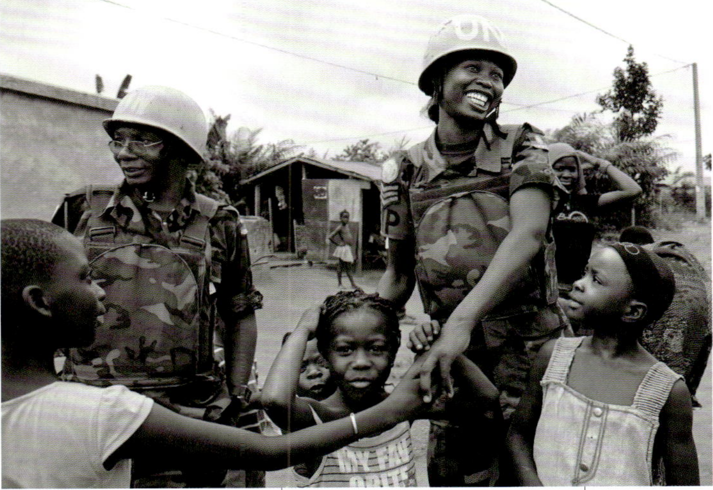

Malawian peacekeepers serving with the United Nations Operation in Côte d'Ivoire (UNOCI) greet children while on patrol. August 21, 2012.

1989

Berlin Wall falls

Tiananmen Square protests

Dalai Lama wins Nobel Peace Prize

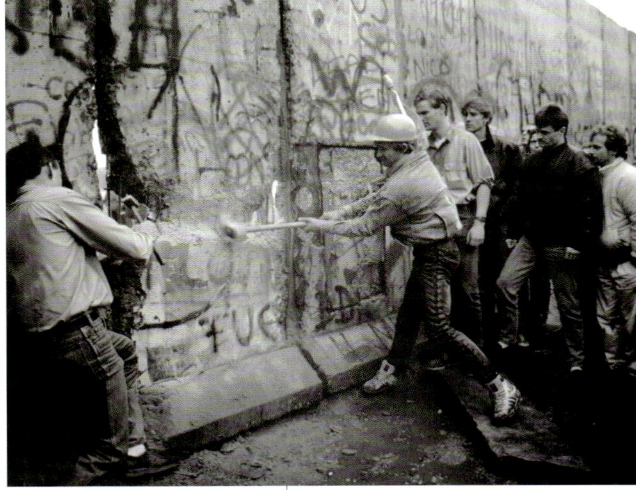

The first section of the Berlin Wall is torn down by crowds. November 10, 1989.

UN MILESTONES AND KEY GLOBAL EVENTS

Javier Pérez de Cuéllar (Peru): 1982–1991

Boutros Boutros-Ghali (Egypt): 1992–1996

'90S

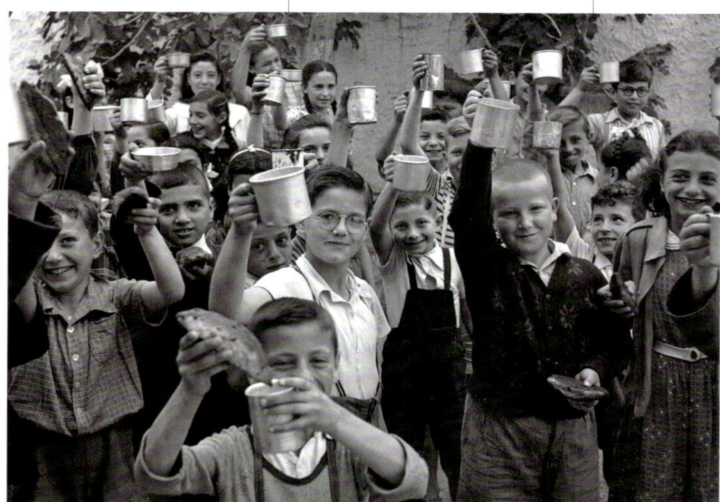

Children in Greece, taking breakfast in a school provided by a joint UNICEF-FAO project, 1948.

1990

UNICEF convenes World Summit for Children

German reunification

Gulf War begins

World Wide Web launches

1991

Dissolution of the Soviet Union

1992

First UN Security Council Summit

Earth Summit held in Rio de Janeiro

European Union created

Bosnian War begins

1993

First war crimes court created for former Yugoslavia

World Conference on Human Rights held

Oslo Accords signed by Israel and PLO

First World Trade Center bombing

1994

South Africa reinstated to General Assembly

Rwandan Genocide

Apartheid ends in South Africa and Nelson Mandela elected president

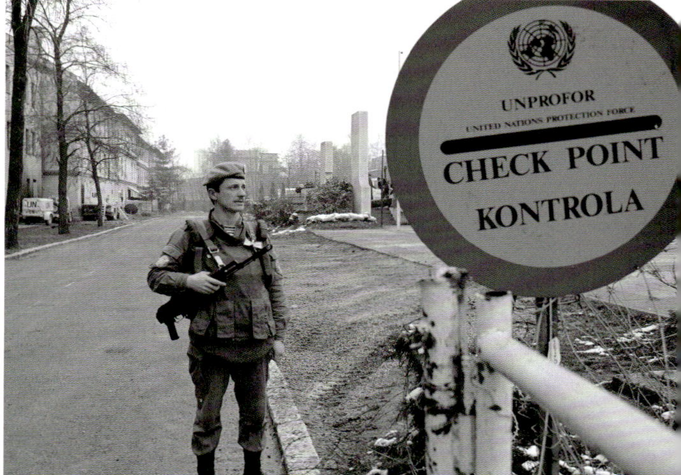

A UN peacekeeping soldier, part of the UN Protection Force in the former Yugoslavia (UNPROFOR), stands guard at a checkpoint in Sarajevo, ca. 1994.

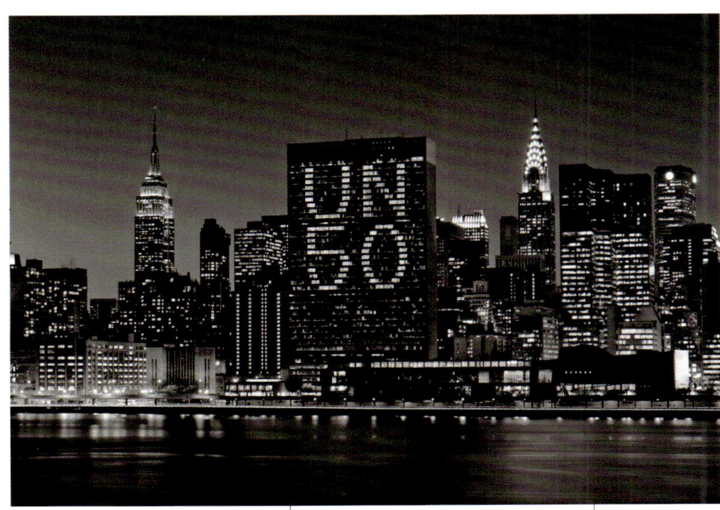

The United Nations, seen from the East River, is lit up for its 50th anniversary.

1995

UN 50th Anniversary Commemorative Meeting

Fourth World Conference on Women held

1996

Comprehensive Nuclear-Test-Ban Treaty adopted

Dolly the Sheep is first mammal to be cloned

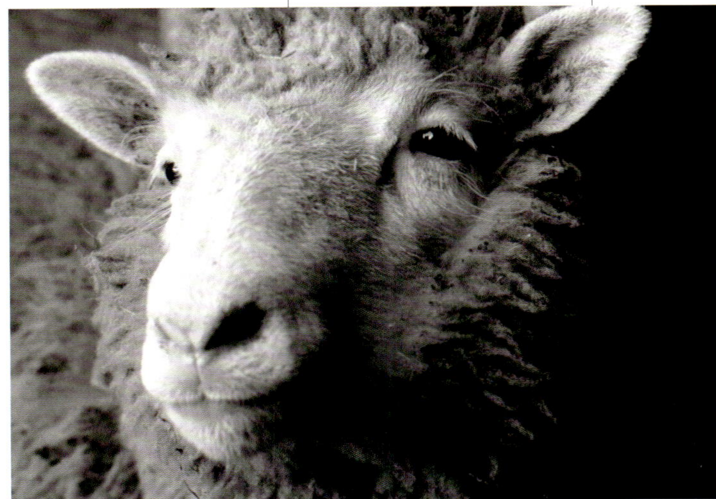

Eight-month-old Dolly, the world's first cloned sheep.

1997

Kyoto Protocol, based on UN Framework Convention on Climate Change, adopted

Britain returns Hong Kong to Chinese rule

1998

Belfast Agreement between Britain and Northern Ireland signed

Kosovo War begins

Kosovar refugees fleeing their homeland. Blace area, the former Yugoslav Republic of Macedonia, March 1999.

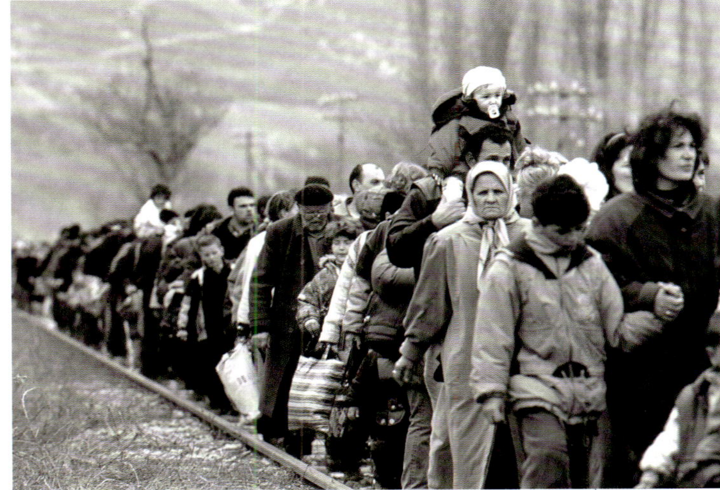

UN MILESTONES AND KEY GLOBAL EVENTS

Kofi Annan (Ghana): 1997–2006

’00S

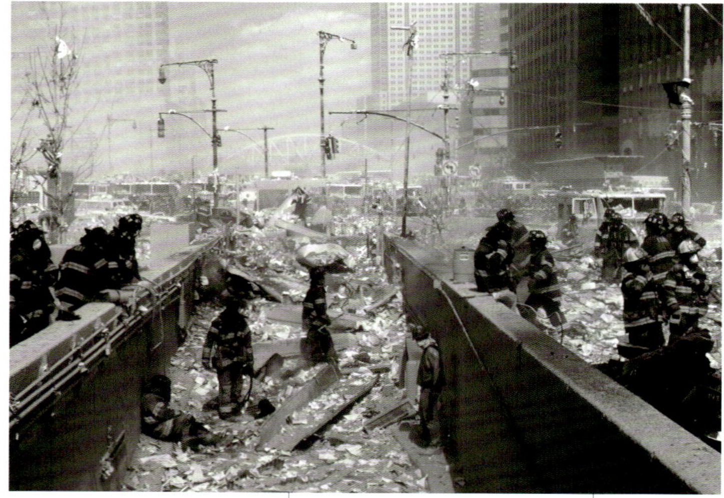

Rescue workers amid debris following September 11th terrorist attack on World Trade Center, 2001.

2001

9/11 terrorist attacks on U.S.

UN Secretary-General Kofi Annan awarded Nobel Peace Prize

2002

Former Yugoslav President Slobidan Milošević goes on trial for war crimes at UN tribunal

Euro debuts in 12 European countries

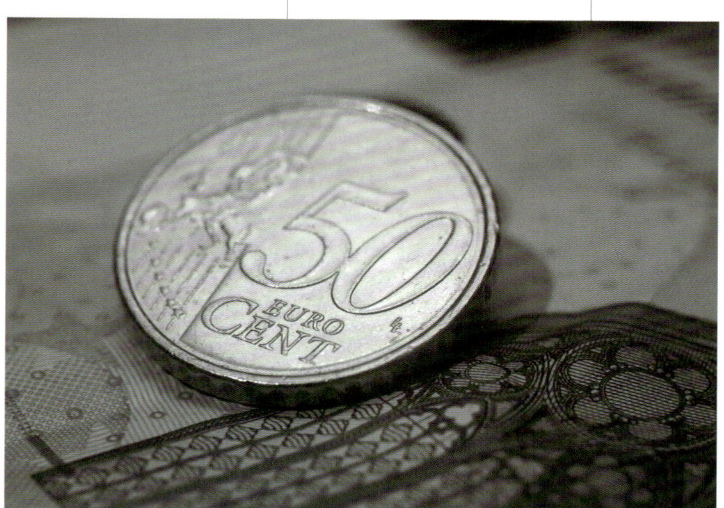

50 euro cent coin

2003

U.S. and UK launch war against Iraq

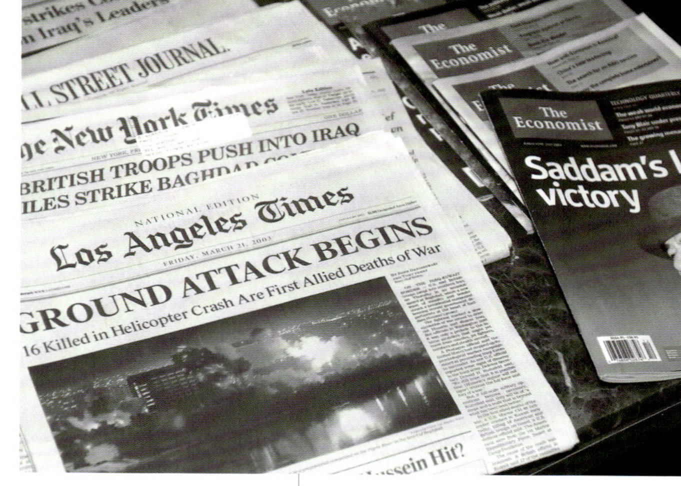

Newspapers and magazines show news of the war in Iraq, March 2003.

2004

NATO admits seven new Eastern European countries

Southeast Asian tsunami strikes

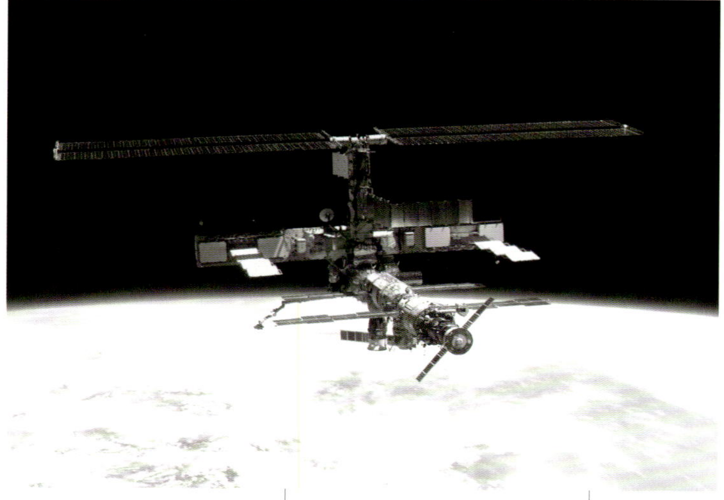

International Space Station following the undocking of Discovery, 2005.

2000

First long-term residents arrive at the International Space Station

Mad Cow Disease hits Europe

Millennium Declaration adopted at UN Millennium Summit

2005

Irish Republican Army officially disarms

Declaration on Human Cloning established

Kyoto Protocol enters force

2006

Security Council calls on Iran to end uranium enrichment program

Human Rights Council established by General Assembly

Human Rights Day event inside the Human Rights Council Chamber in Geneva, Switzerland, 2010.

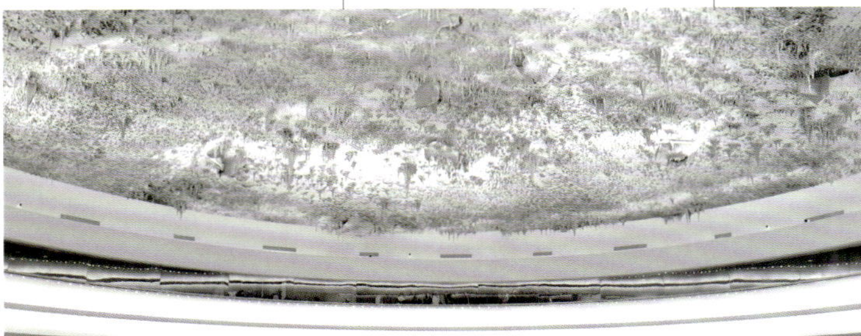

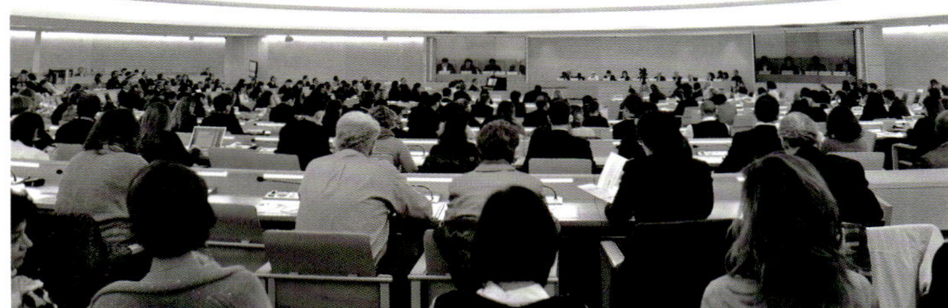

2007

Intergovernmental Panel on Climate Change and Al Gore awarded Nobel Peace Prize

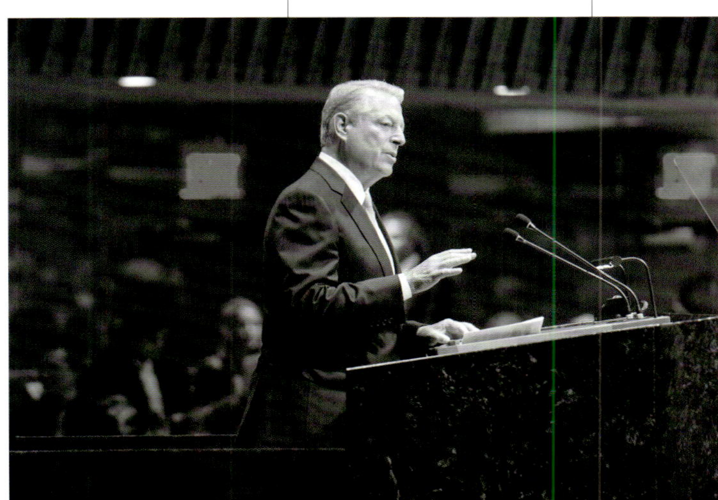

Al Gore addresses the opening of the UN Climate Summit, 2014.

2008

Convention on the Rights of Persons with Disabilities enters into force

Collapse of Lehman Brothers triggers global recession

Barack Obama elected U.S. President

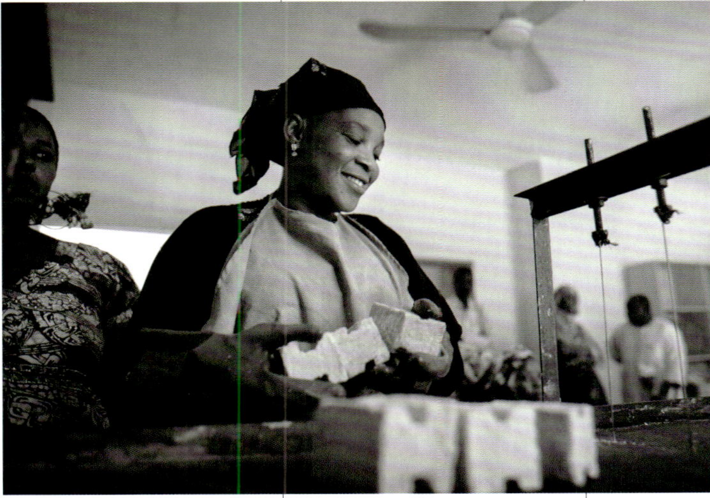

A woman produces soap at a center for persons with disabilities, run by a local association in Mali. The UN supports the programs by providing tools and materials for the production of such goods as soap, shoes, and textiles, 2017.

2009

UN Climate Change Conference held in Copenhagen

H1N1 swine flu named global pandemic

UN MILESTONES AND KEY GLOBAL EVENTS

Ban Ki-moon (Republic of Korea) 2007–2016

'10S

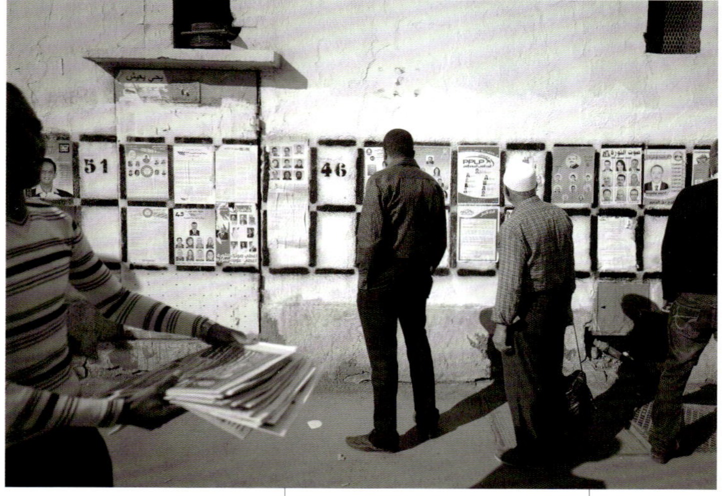

Tunisian men look at a wall covered with posters of candidates ahead of an election. Tunisia, which launched the Arab Spring, will take a historic vote for the drafters of a new constitution. October 18, 2011.

2010

General Assembly created UN Women for gender equality and the empowerment of women

Volcanic eruption of Iceland's Mount Eyjafjallajökull disrupts global air travel

Instagram launches

Burj Khalifa in Dubai becomes world's tallest man-made structure

2011

Arab Spring protests

Japan earthquake and tsunami lead to nuclear emergency

Osama bin Laden killed in U.S. raid

First UN resolution on sexual orientation and gender identity

Republic of South Sudan admitted to the UN as a Member State

2012

Diamond Jubilee of Queen Elizabeth II

Rio+20 Earth Summit held in Rio de Janeiro

2013

Organisation for the Prohibition of Chemical Weapons awarded Nobel Peace Prize

2014

Western African Ebola virus epidemic begins

Russian annexation of Crimea

Malala Yousafzai awarded Nobel Peace Prize

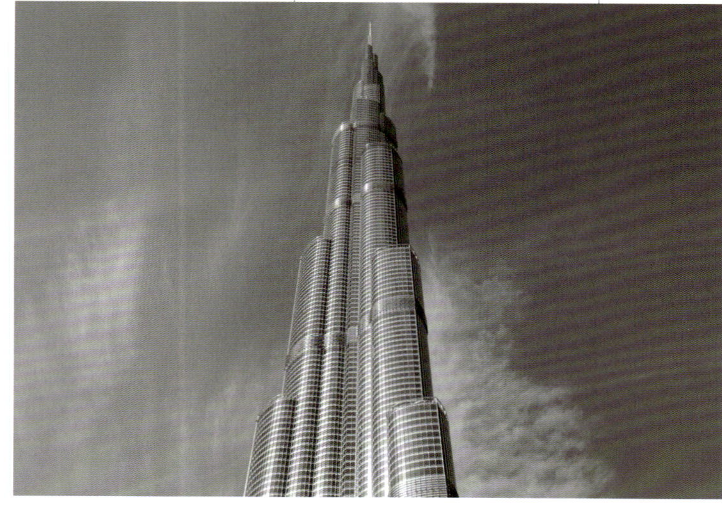

Burj Khalifa, a skyscraper in Dubai, United Arab Emirates, 2018.

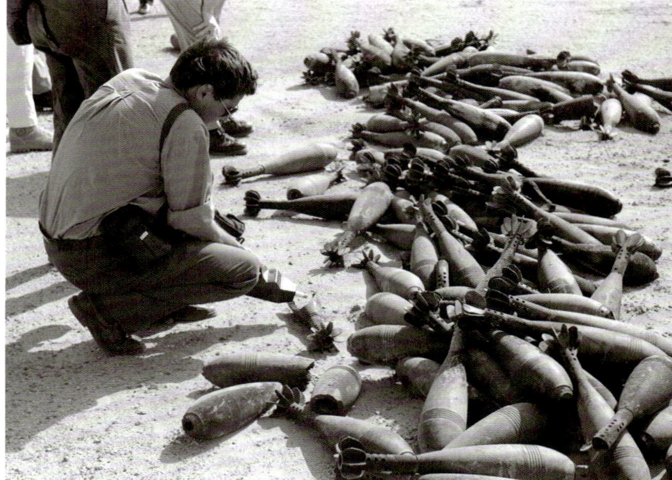

A member of the UN Special Commission verifies Iraq's compliance with the order to destroy chemical weapons and weapons of mass destruction, 1992.

2015

United Nations turns 70

WHO declares elimination of rubella in the Americas

2016

UK votes in referendum to leave EU (Brexit)

UN lifts sanctions against Iran

WHO announces Zika virus outbreak

Paris Agreement ratified

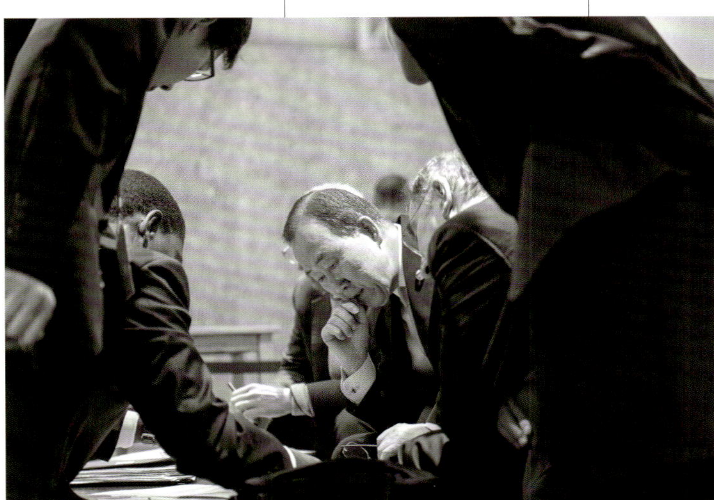

Secretary-General Ban Ki-moon discusses the draft text of the Paris Agreement with his advisors before meeting with the President of the UN Climate Change Conference in Paris, France.

2018

U.S.-North Korea summit held in Singapore

Yellow vest protests begin in France

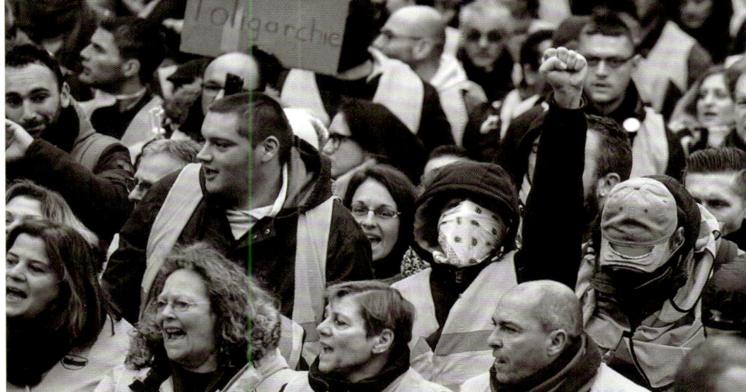

A yellow vest (gilets jaunes) anti-government demonstration Lille, France. December 29, 2018.

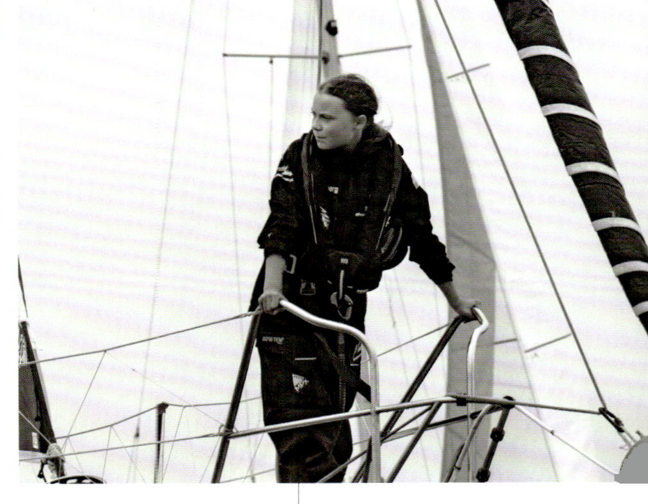

Greta Thunberg, 16-year-old climate activist from Sweden, sails into New York Harbor. She embarked on a trans-Atlantic voyage from Plymouth, England, to New York City on a solar-powered, zero-emission racing boat to attend the UN Climate Action Summit, 2019.

2019

Climate Action Summit called

Venezuelan presidential crisis

Hong Kong strikes

First outbreak of COVID-19 reported in Wuhan, China

CHAPTER 1

NEW YORK CITY BEFORE THE UNITED NATIONS

In the mid-1940s, as the United Nations began its search for a permanent headquarters site, New York's longtime mayor, Fiorello La Guardia, was convinced his city should be the UN's home. "When it comes down to the final analysis," he proclaimed, "it is New York, because there is only one New York City in the whole world, and there is nothing like it."

The UN's first secretary-general, Trygve Lie, had come to the same conclusion. While his official role kept him from publicly discussing his thoughts before Member States took up the matter, he said later he had always believed "the huge metropolis and international crossroads" was where the new world body should be located.

The vision of La Guardia and Lie would be realized in late 1946, with the generosity of a prominent and wealthy New Yorker, John D. Rockefeller, Jr. Referring to the UN as the "hope of the world," Rockefeller donated $8.5 million to the organization to purchase its site on the East River. "If this property can be useful to you in meeting the great responsibilities entrusted to you…it will be a source of infinite satisfaction to me and my family," he said at the time.

As the UN celebrates its 75th year, the longevity of its bond with New York is a tribute not only to the foresight of La Guardia, Lie, and Rockefeller, but to countless others who have worked tirelessly over the years to ensure a lasting partnership between the city and the UN. —**PAMELA HANLON**

Pamela Hanlon is author of *A Worldly Affair: New York, the United Nations, and the Story Behind Their Unlikely Bond.*

2.3 BILLION

Global population at the UN's founding in 1945

7.7 BILLION

Estimated global population in 2020

FIVE

Number of permanent members of the Security Council: China, France, Russian Federation, the United Kingdom, and the United States

51

Number of original Member States in 1945

193

Number of Member States in 2020

Overlooking the East River, the United Nations has stood for three-quarters of a century as a symbol of humankind's noblest aspirations: dignity, peace, freedom, and equal rights for all people. That the institution's aims have been advanced while headquartered in New York City, a vibrant hub of free expression, cultural exchange, and international commerce, is no accident. The spirit of this flourishing metropolis enhances and inspires the work of the global body it hosts.

The enduring idea of the United Nations, as well as its physical landmarks, are inextricably linked to the stewardship of the United States. The generosity of the American people and their commitment to a safer, freer, and more prosperous world has sustained the work of the United Nations for 75 years. As we face a new era of great contests and shared challenges, this generosity and stewardship will sustain the work of the United Nations for years to come. —**KELLY CRAFT**

Kelly Craft is the 30th United States Ambassador to the United Nations.

2011

The year the most recent Member State, South Sudan, was admitted to the United Nations

71

Number of peacekeeping missions authorized by the UN since 1945

110,000

Number of current peacekeeping forces in 13 operations around the world

GENEVA VIENNA NAIROBI

Locations outside New York City where the UN operates secondary headquarters

It may be difficult for New Yorkers today to imagine the blocks between East 42nd and East 48th Streets, between First Avenue and the East River in Manhattan, as anything other than the capital of the world—the headquarters of the United Nations. Since the UN campus was completed in 1952, that riverfront stretch—indeed, the whole of Turtle Bay—has become synonymous with the United Nations. The graceful green-glass slab of the Secretariat rises alongside the solemn curves of the General Assembly Building and the horizontal monoliths of the Conference Building and Dag Hammarskjöld Library, anchoring the East River waterfront and proudly joining the iconic skyscrapers of the Manhattan skyline. Although the dignified architectural ensemble of the UN campus stands at a distance from its immediate neighbors across First Avenue, sheltered behind green lawns and gracious plazas, it is so firmly and elegantly integrated into the fabric of the city that it feels like it has always belonged in that special setting.

As we know, New York City has existed for far longer than the United Nations, and the site on which the organization's headquarters now stands has a history as old and as interesting as Manhattan itself—starting with the name of its Manhattan location. Long before it was a neighborhood, Turtle Bay was an actual inlet, said to offer ships respite from the turbulent waters of the East River. The inlet's name, which dates back to the days of the Dutch settlement in New Amsterdam, has nothing to do with aquatic creatures. Rather, it comes from the Dutch word *deutal*, meaning "bent blade," which locals ascribed to the shape of the small bay.[2] Turtle Creek, also known as DeVoor's Mill Creek, emptied into the inlet in the area of what is now East 47th Street.

In the 17th century, the land surrounding Turtle Bay was verdant countryside. The Dutch colonial governor granted a 40-acre grant to two Englishmen, which they named Turtle Bay Farm. The land grant extended approximately from what is now East 43rd Street to East 48th Street, and from Third Avenue to the East River. By the 18th century, the area began to attract the city's wealthy citizens, who built country houses along the hilly wooded shore. One of the most famous was the elegant Dutch-style estate of Gerardus (James) Beekman, known as Mount Pleasant. Built in 1763 on a hilltop overlooking Turtle Bay, along what is now First Avenue, the house survived British occupation during the Revolutionary War, but not the implementation of Manhattan's street grid. When East 51st Street was about to be paved in the 1840s, the Beekman family moved the house a few blocks away, where it stood until its demolition in the 1870s.

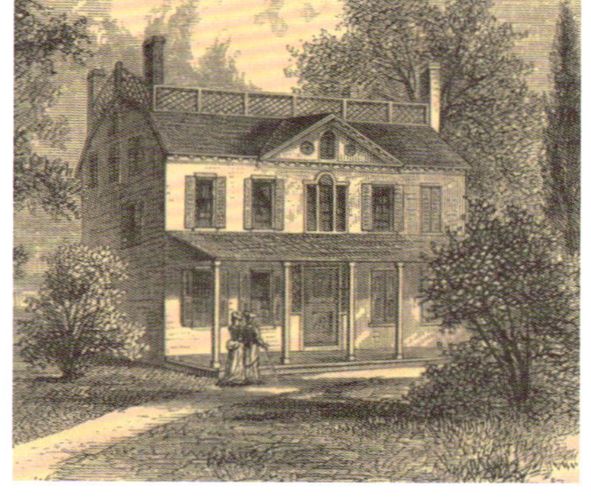

Beekman Mansion.

The American poet and writer Edgar Allan Poe, who lived nearby, chronicled his experiences in Turtle Bay cove for the *Columbia Spy* newspaper, saying, "I procured a light skiff and made my way around Blackwell's Island [now Roosevelt Island] on a voyage of discovery and exploration. The chief interest lay in the scenery of the Manhattan shore, which is here particularly picturesque. The houses are, without exception, frame and antique…I could not look on the magnificent cliffs and

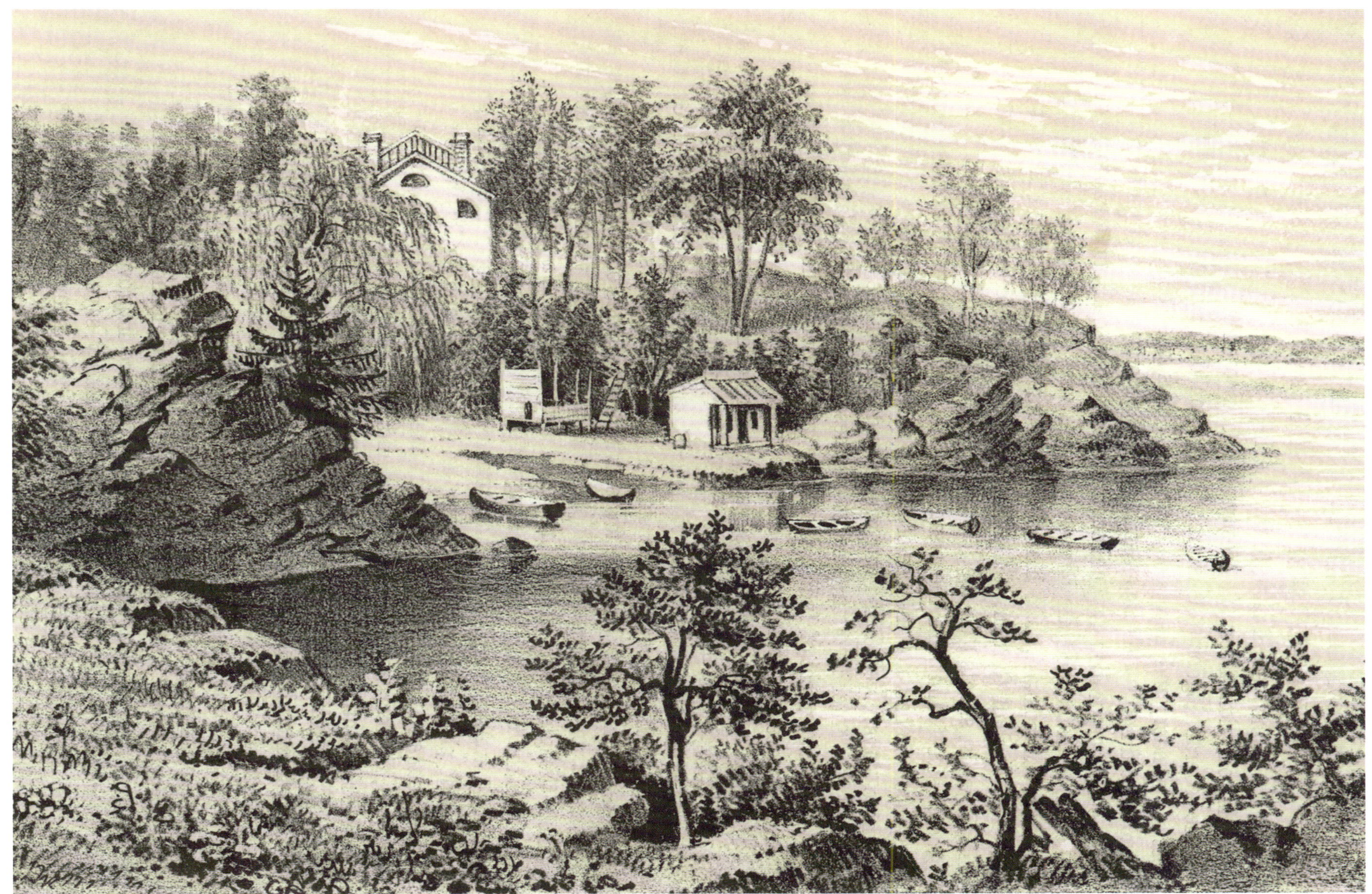

Turtle Bay, East River, New York, 1853.

stately trees, which at every moment met my view, without a sigh for the inevitable doom—inevitable and swift."[3]

Poe could see the impending disappearance of the natural landscape as the end of the Civil War brought industrialization and urban progress. Following the arrival of the paved streets of the city's orderly grid system, brownstones began to crop up to accommodate an influx of immigrants to New York City. By 1868, the actual bay had been filled in, the area sprouting breweries, gasworks, slaughterhouses, cattle pens, coal yards, and railroad piers. By the early 20th century, Turtle Bay was "a riverside backyard" for the city, as the *WPA Guide to New York City* (1939) described it: "huge industrial enterprises—breweries, laundries, abattoirs, power plants—along the waterfront face squalid tenements… The numerous plants shower this district with the heaviest sootfall in the city—150 tons to the square mile annually."[4] The area was also rife with violent crime and thievery, including gangs.

The 1920s brought changes to the neighborhood in the form of ambitious building projects and renovations. Down-at-the-heel

First Avenue, west side, north from and including East 47th Street, from the southwest corner, 1934.

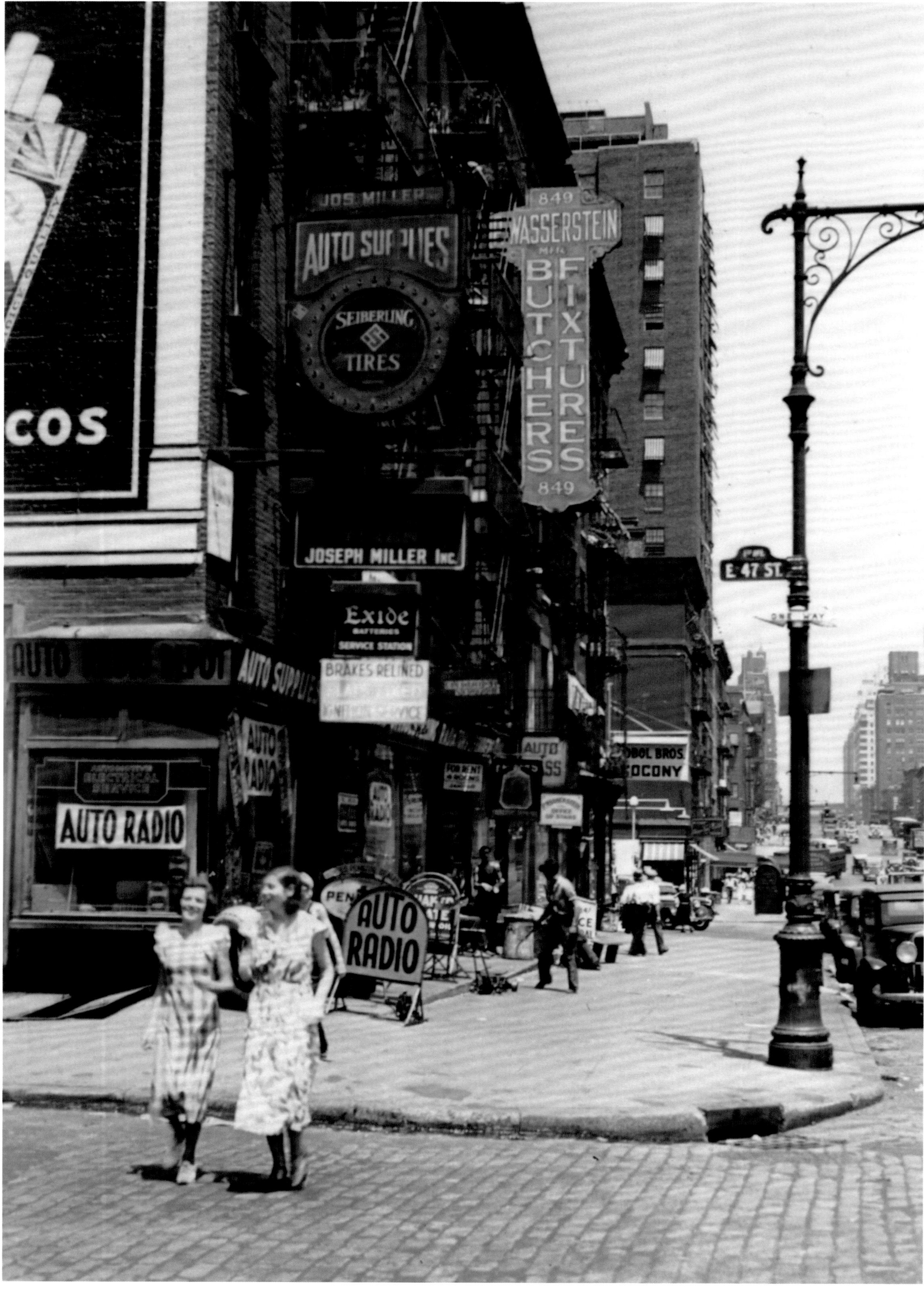

brownstones were converted into fashionable townhouses that attracted New York's literary set, notably the homes on Turtle Bay Gardens, a large communal garden developed in the backyards of townhouses bounded by East 48th and East 49th Streets between Second and Third Avenues. Immediately across from what would become the site of the UN, developer Fred F. French spearheaded the development of the brick apartment houses of Tudor City. But despite such improvements to the neighborhood, the abattoirs continued operating, with livestock brought up the East River by barge and led through the streets to the slaughterhouses. As legendary photographer Ezra Stoller, who attended architecture school nearby, noted, "When the wind blew from the east, the odor was…noticeable."[5] For that reason, several of Tudor City's towers conspicuously turned their backs to the river, offering only small windows to what today are sparkling river (and UN) views. It was only in the years immediately before the creation of the United Nations, in 1945, that the neighborhood was poised for a major transformation, culminating in the arrival of the United Nations' home on Manhattan's shores.

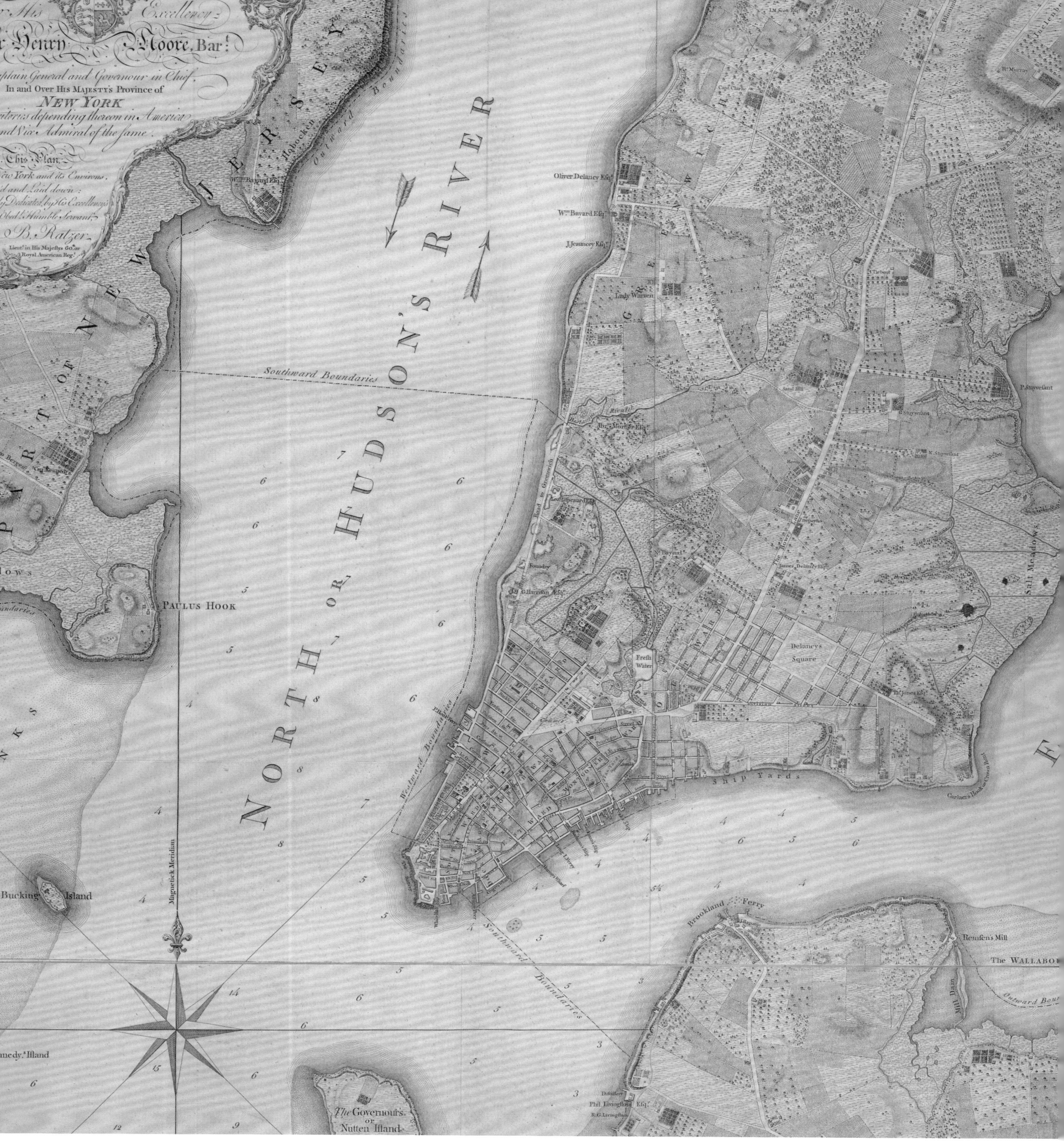

His Excellency
r Henry Moore, Bar!
ptain General and Governour in Chief
In and Over His Majesty's Province of
NEW YORK
rritories depending thereon in America
nd Vice Admiral of the same
This Plan
New York and its Environs
B. Ratzer
NEW JERSEY
Hobocken
Wm. Bayard Esq.
Outward Boundaries
NORTH OR HUDSON'S RIVER
Southward Boundaries
PART OF NEW JERSEY
PAULUS HOOK
Bucking Island
Magnetick Meridian
Oliver Delancey Esq.
Wm. Bayard Esq.
J. Jeauncey Esq.
Lady Warren
Capt. Clarke
Sand Hill
P. Stuyvesant
Salt Meadows
Fresh Water
Delancy's Square
Westward Boundaries
Ship Yards
Southward Boundaries
Brookland Ferry
Remsen's Mill
The WALLABO
Mill Dam
Outward Boun
The Governour's or Nutten Island
Phil. Livingston Esq.

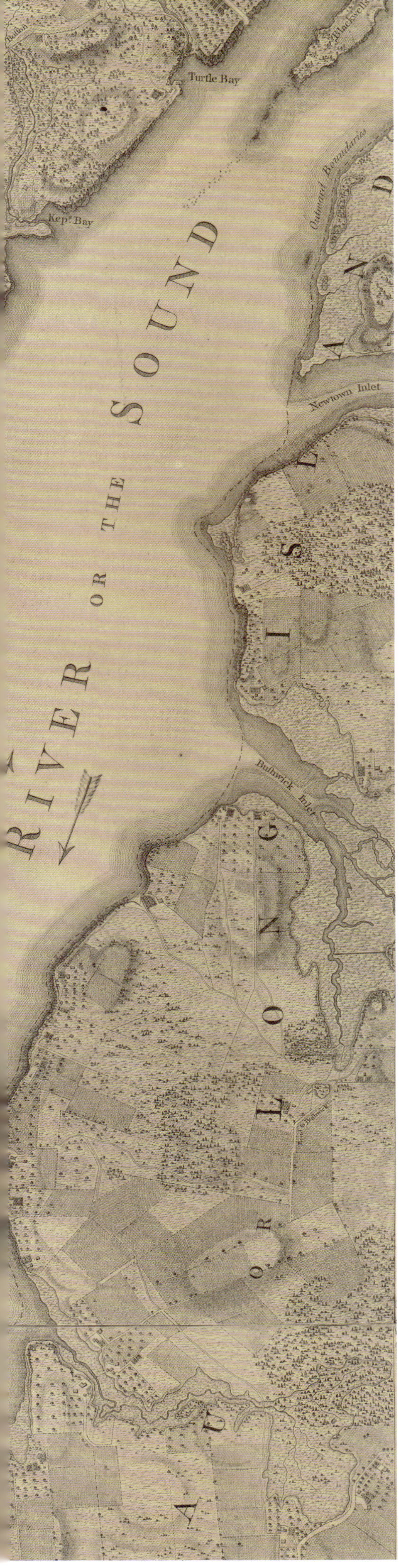

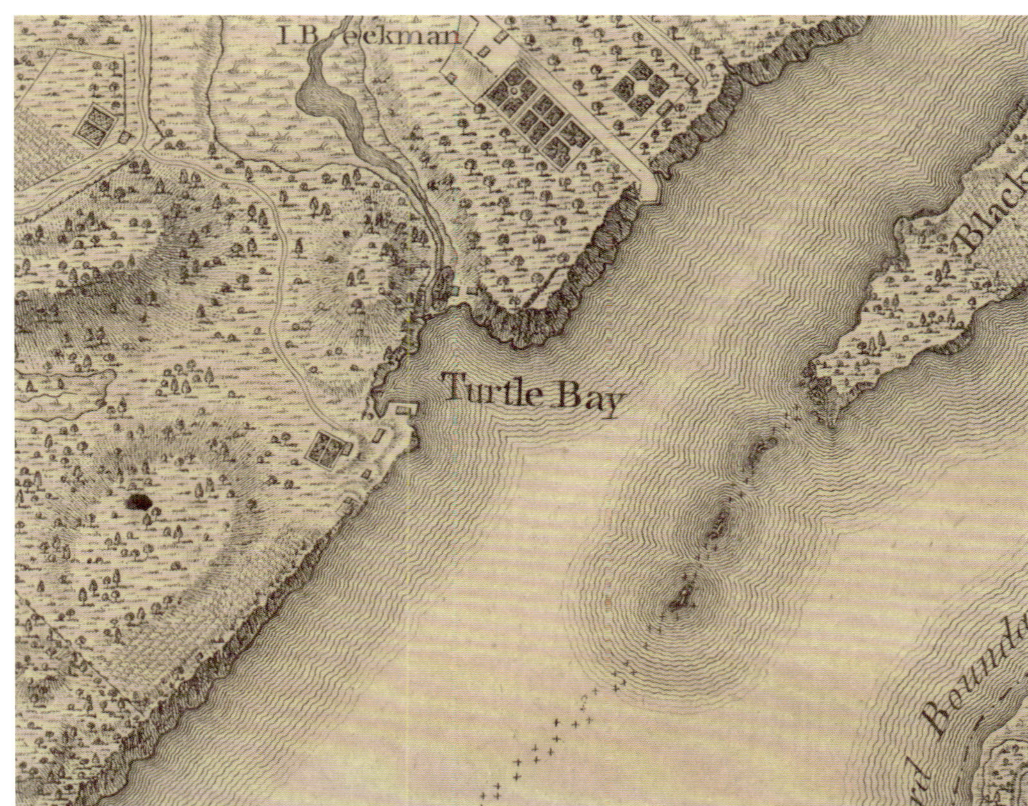

Detail view of the original topography of Turtle Bay.

Plan of the city of New York surveyed in the years 1766 and 1767. The inlet of Turtle Bay is located in the upper right corner.

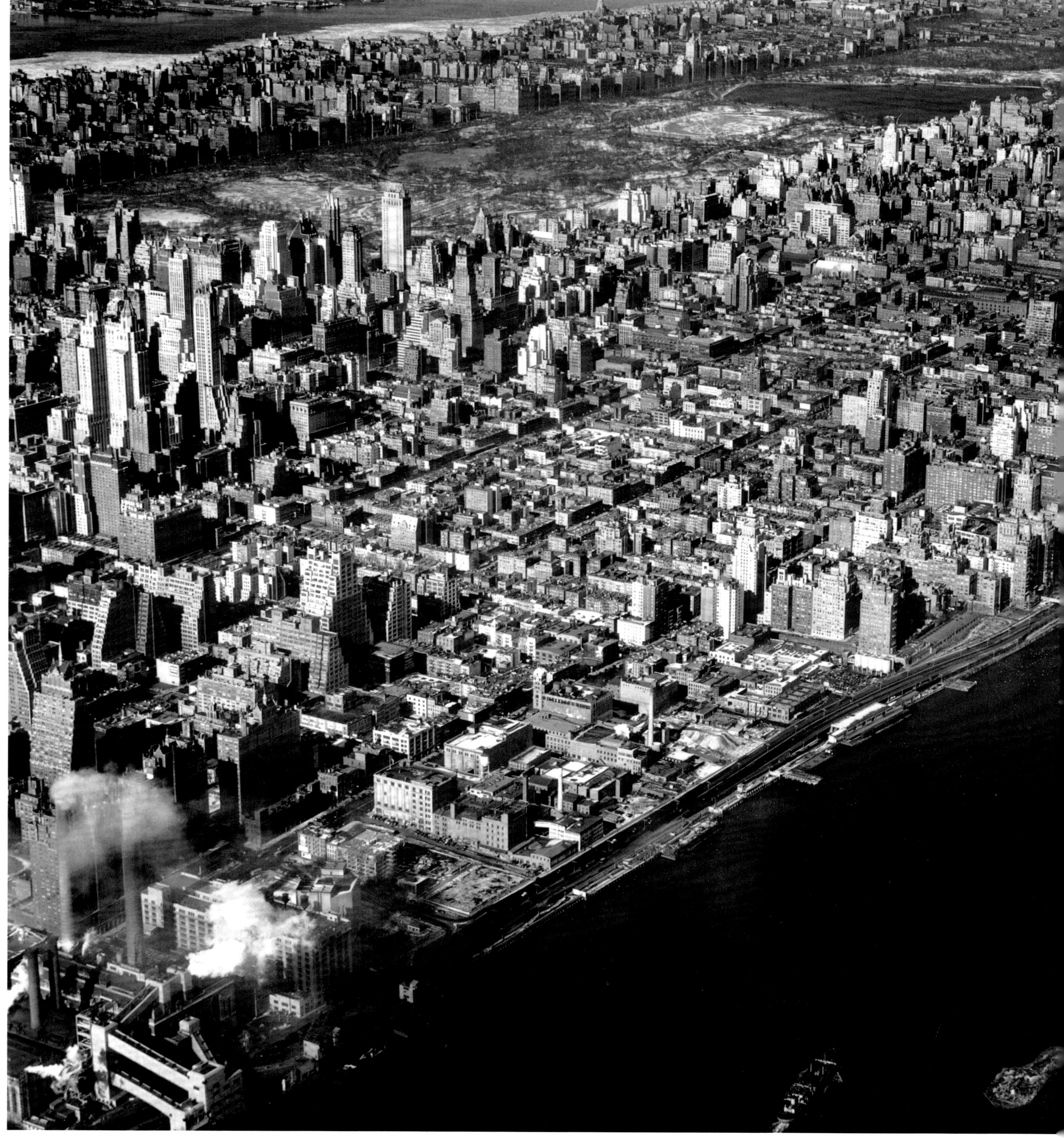

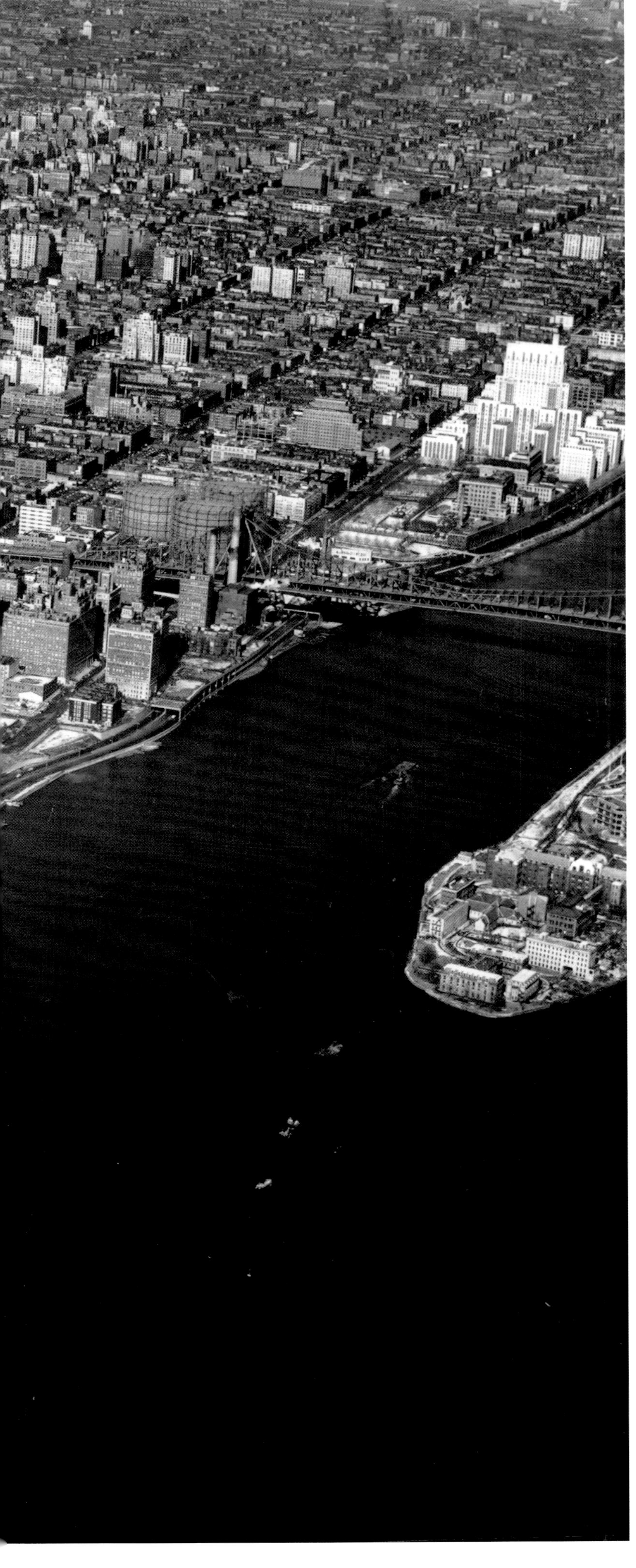

Aerial view of Manhattan and Turtle Bay prior to the construction of the UN Headquarters, ca. 1946–1947.

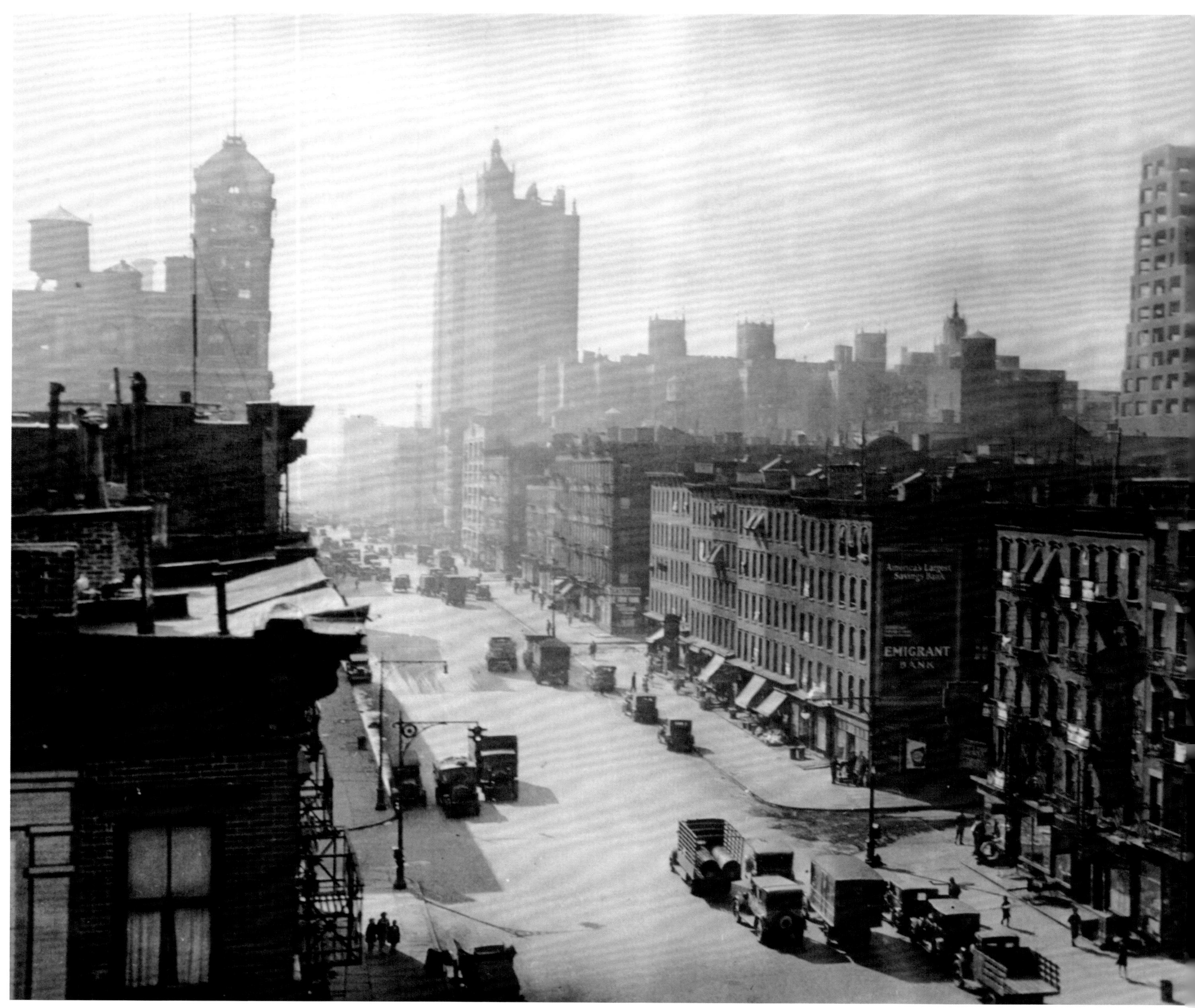

First Avenue, southwest from West 48th Street (right), showing prominently the westerly side of this thoroughfare. Across the top appears the Wilson & Co. building, the Windsor and Tudor Towers in Tudor City, and the Beaux Arts apartment building. To the right of the latter is the vague outline of the Bartholomew Building on 42nd Street, 1928.

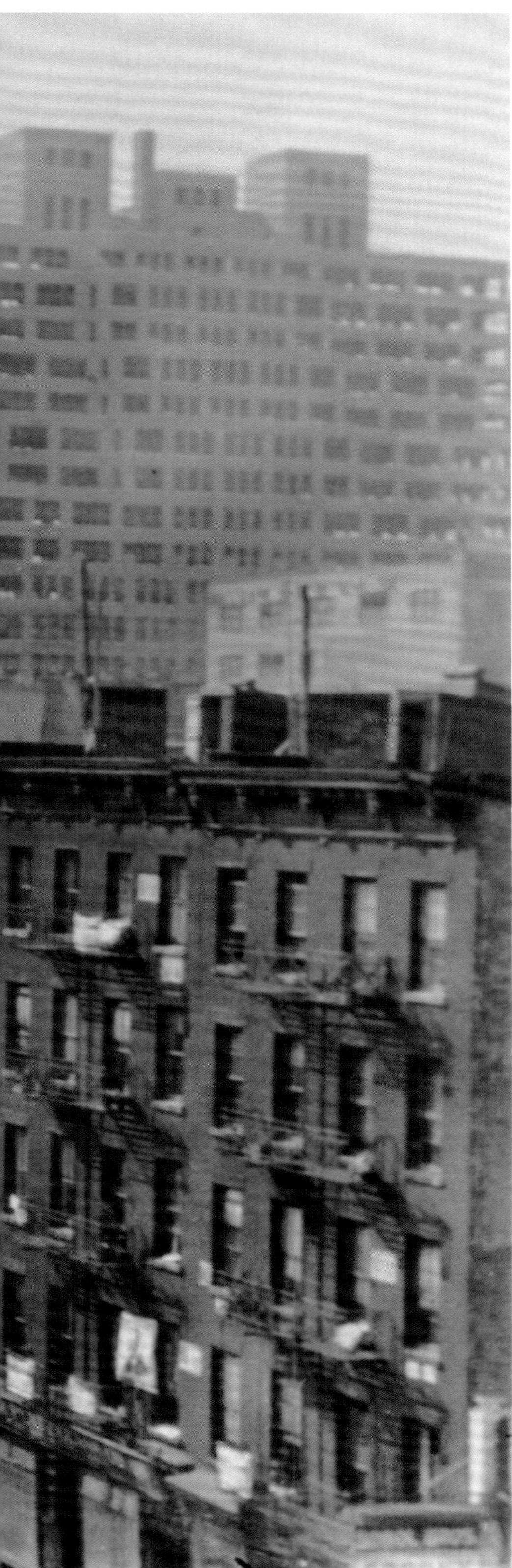

Below: Abattoirs on East 47th Street, adjoining the northeast corner of First Avenue, 1928.

Bottom: First Avenue, at northeast corner of 46th Street. There were many filling stations and garages on First Avenue. Behind the service station are buildings belonging to the meat packer Wilson & Co., 1934.

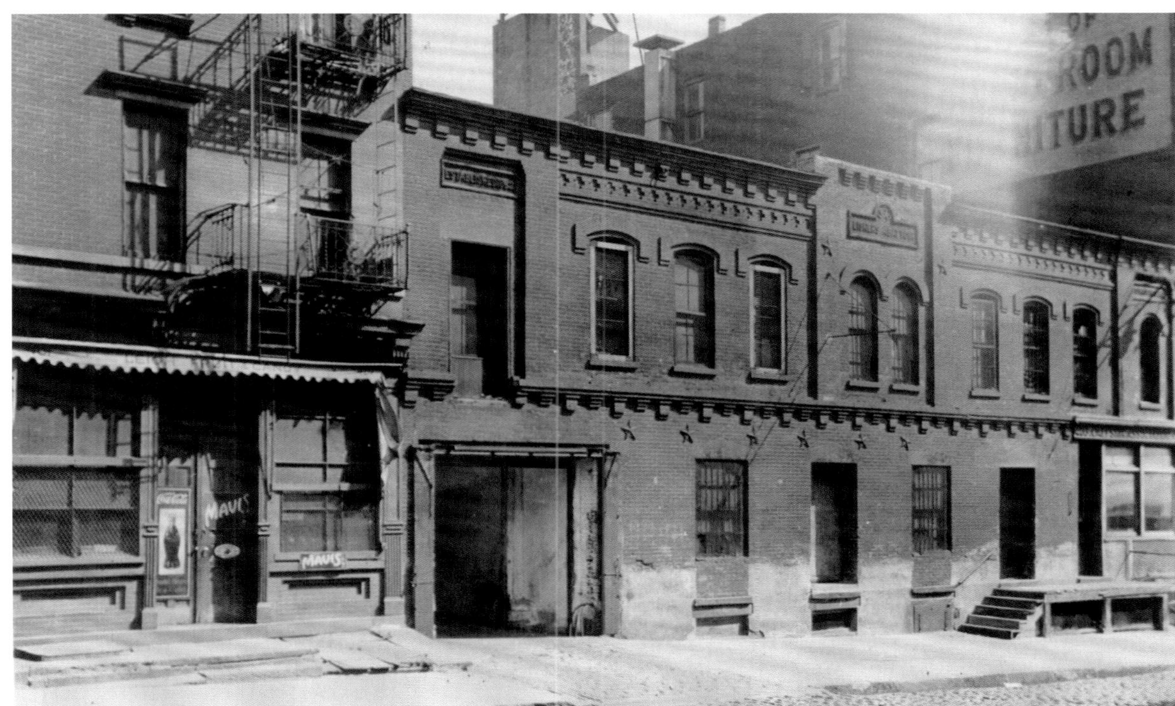

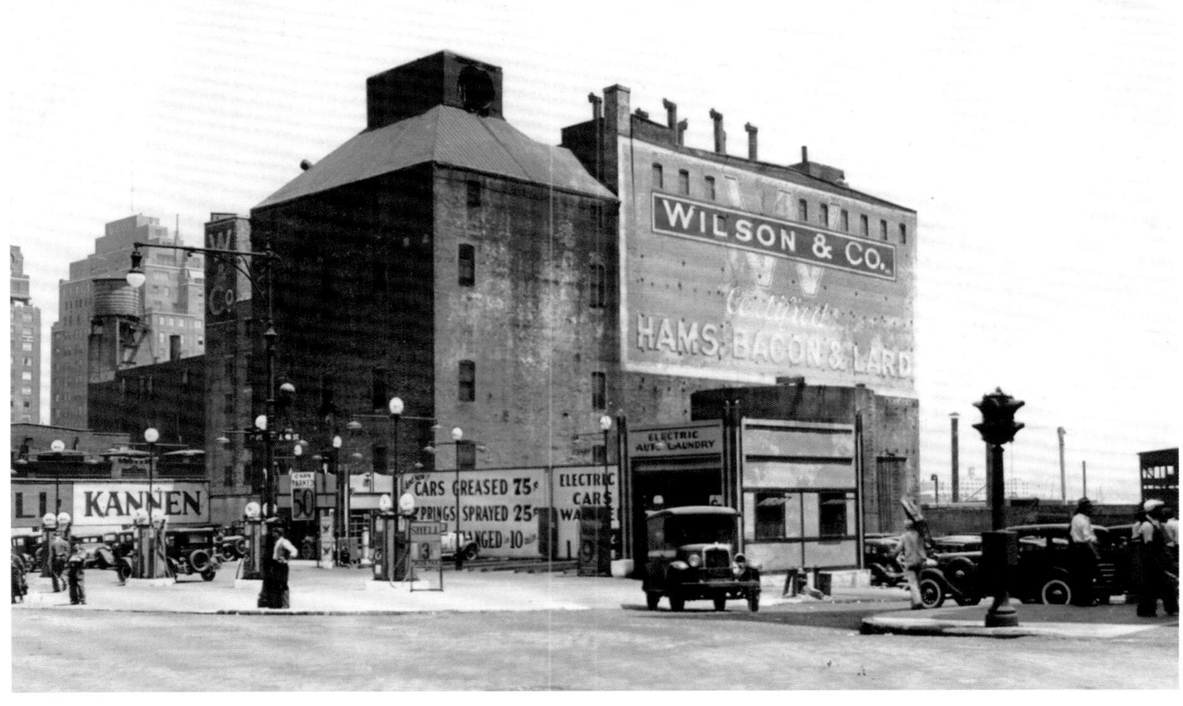

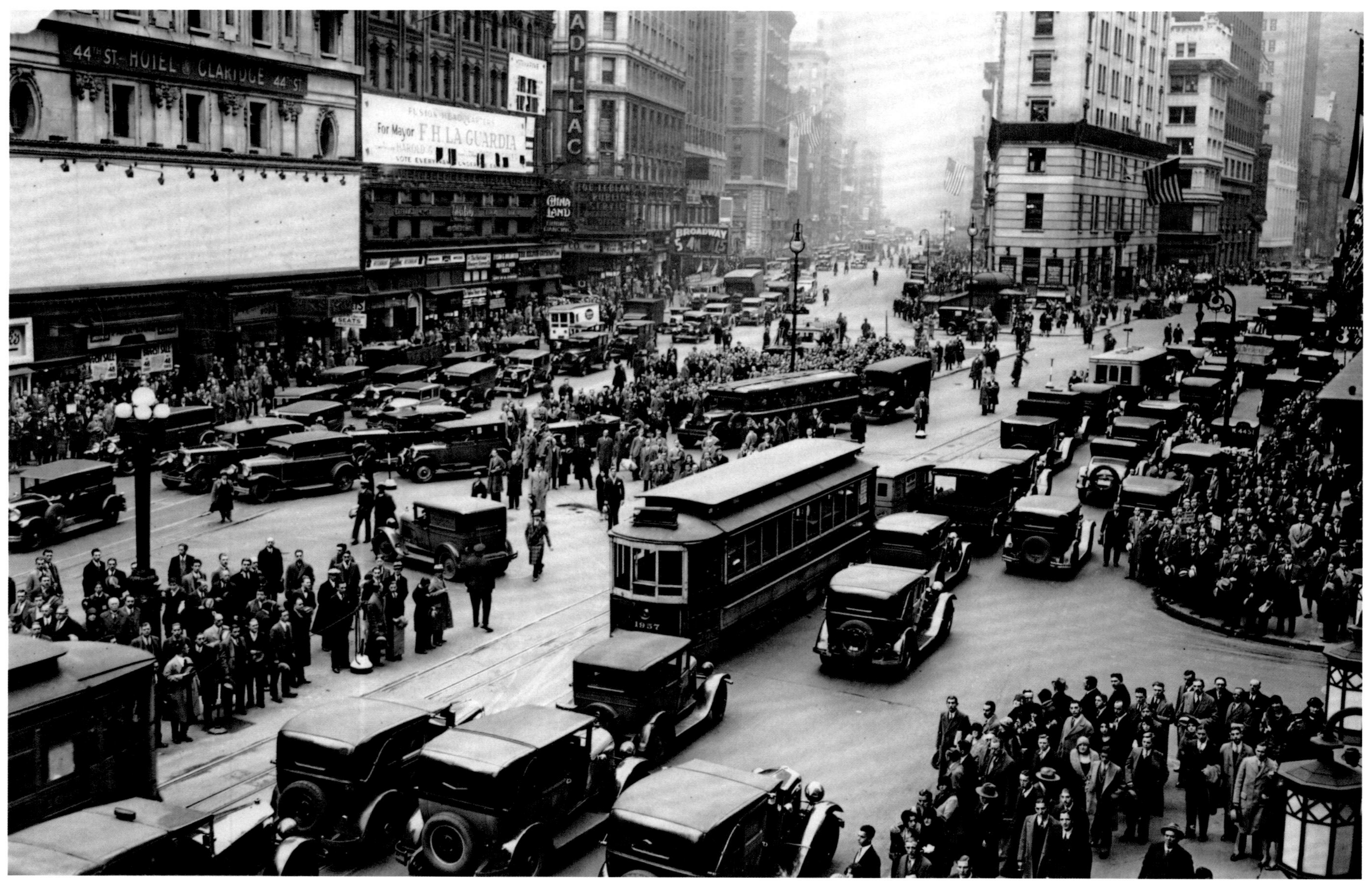

Broadway, east side, south from 44th to 40th Streets. This picture was taken during the two-minute silence on Armistice Day (commemorated every year on November 11 to mark the armistice signed between Allies of World War I and Germany at Compiègne, France), and shows the Times Square crowds standing hushed, the men with bared heads, as a bugler on a balcony of the Hotel Astor sounds "Taps," 1929.

The RKO Building as viewed northwest-ward from West 49th Street, and across the enclosed excavation for the RCA Building. The individuals congregating on the sidewalk are mechanics seeking work. Today, it is part of the Rockefeller Center complex. March 24, 1932.

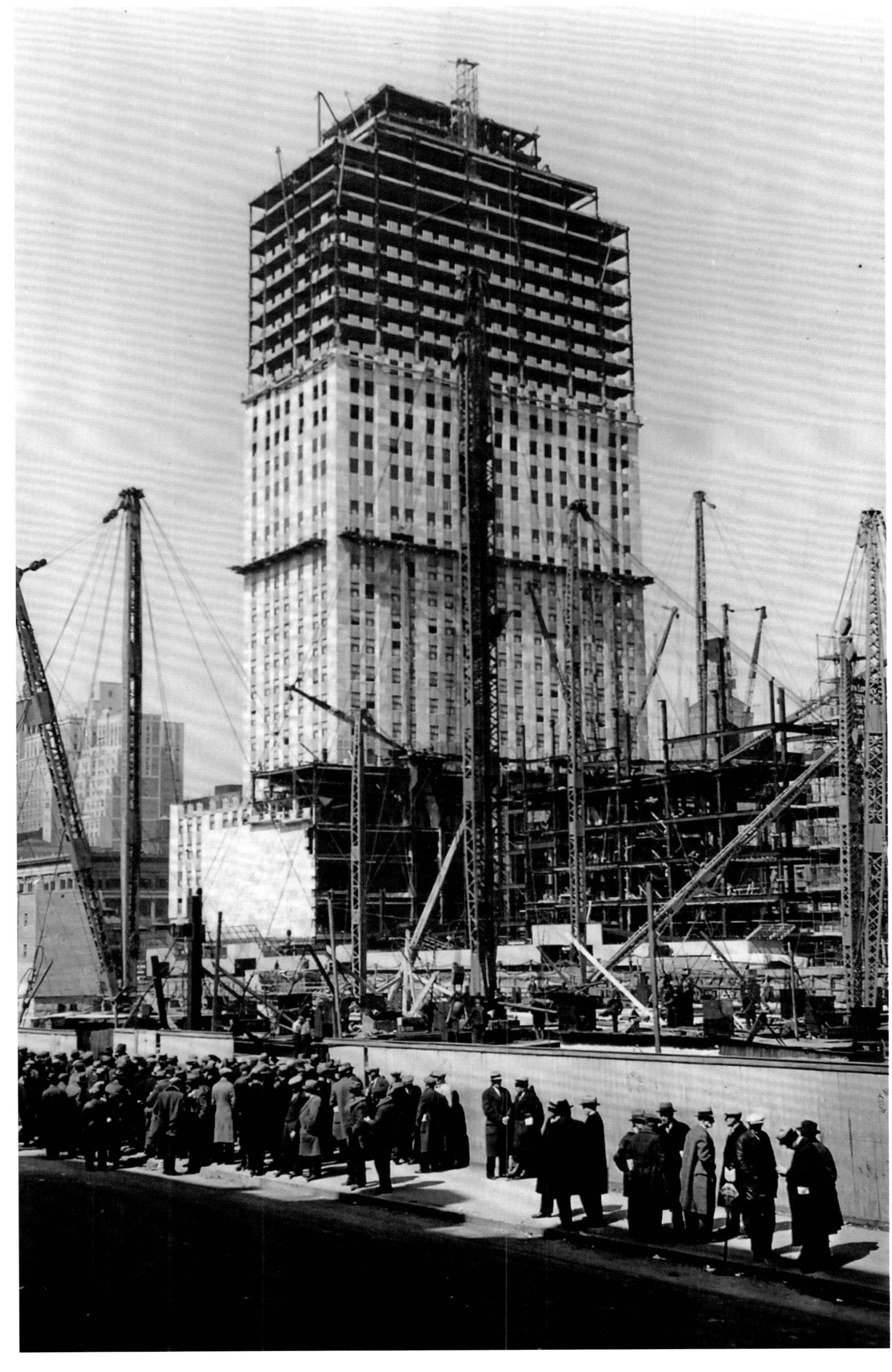

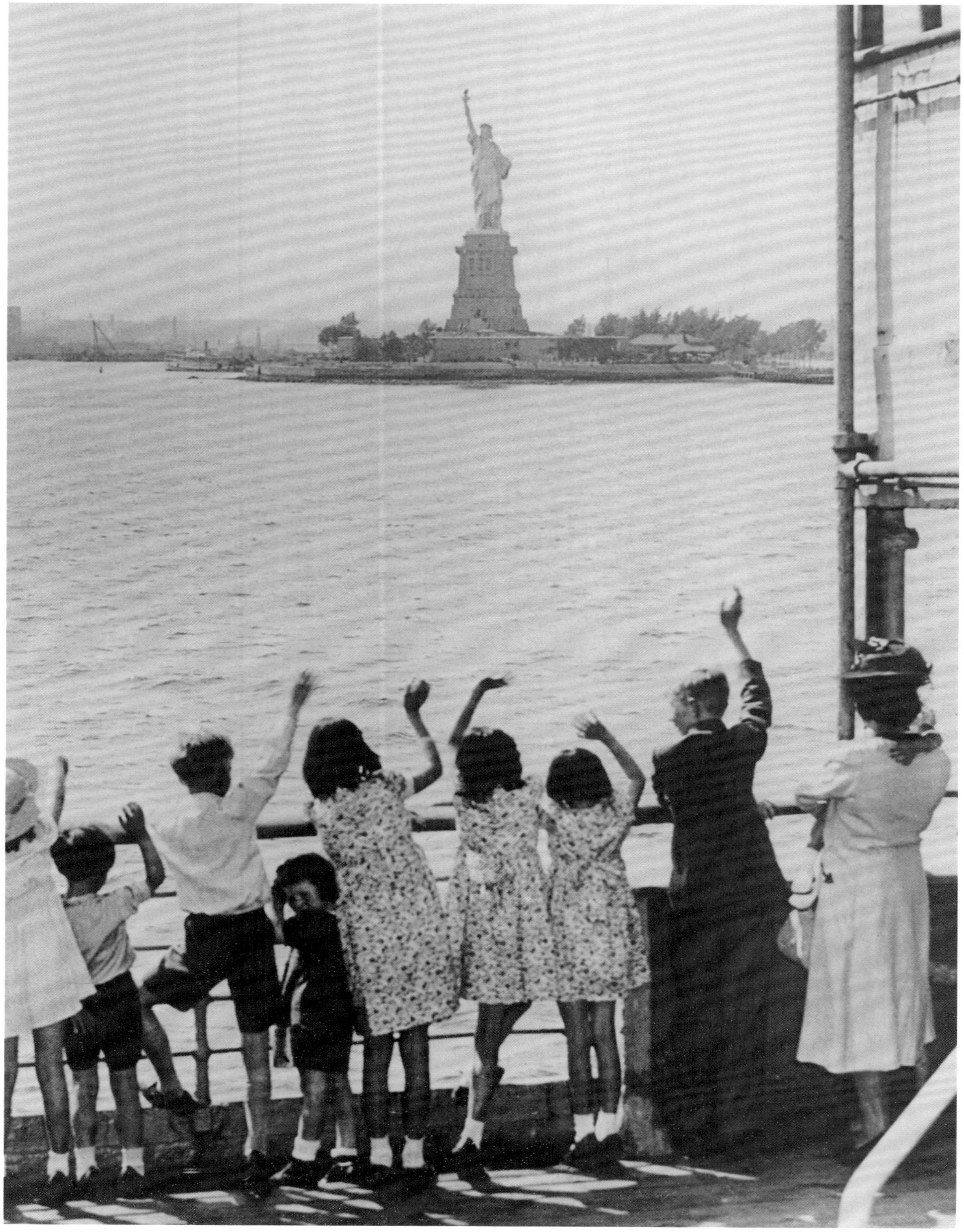

Refugee children from England arrive in New York during World War II. July 18, 1940.

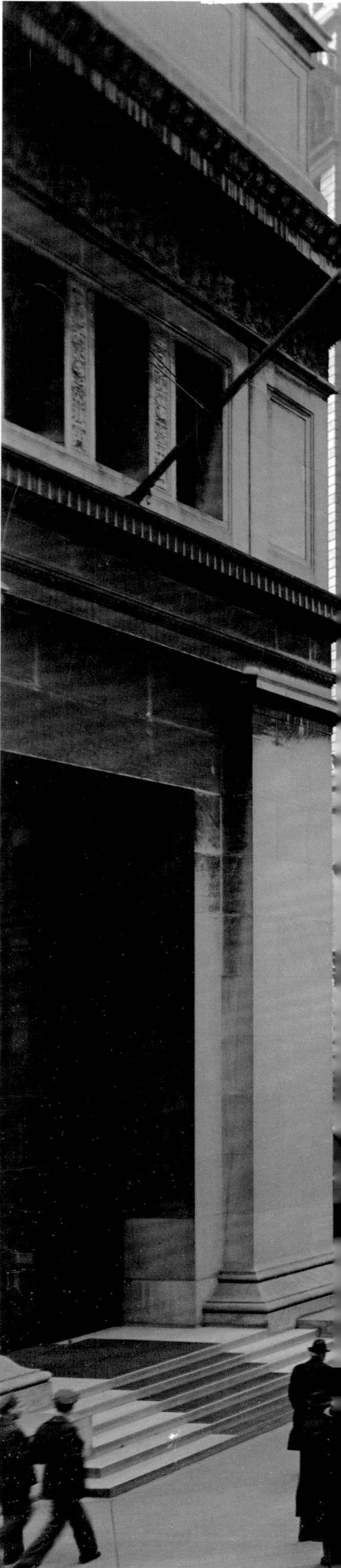

New York Stock Exchange at 18 Broad Street. February 9, 1939.

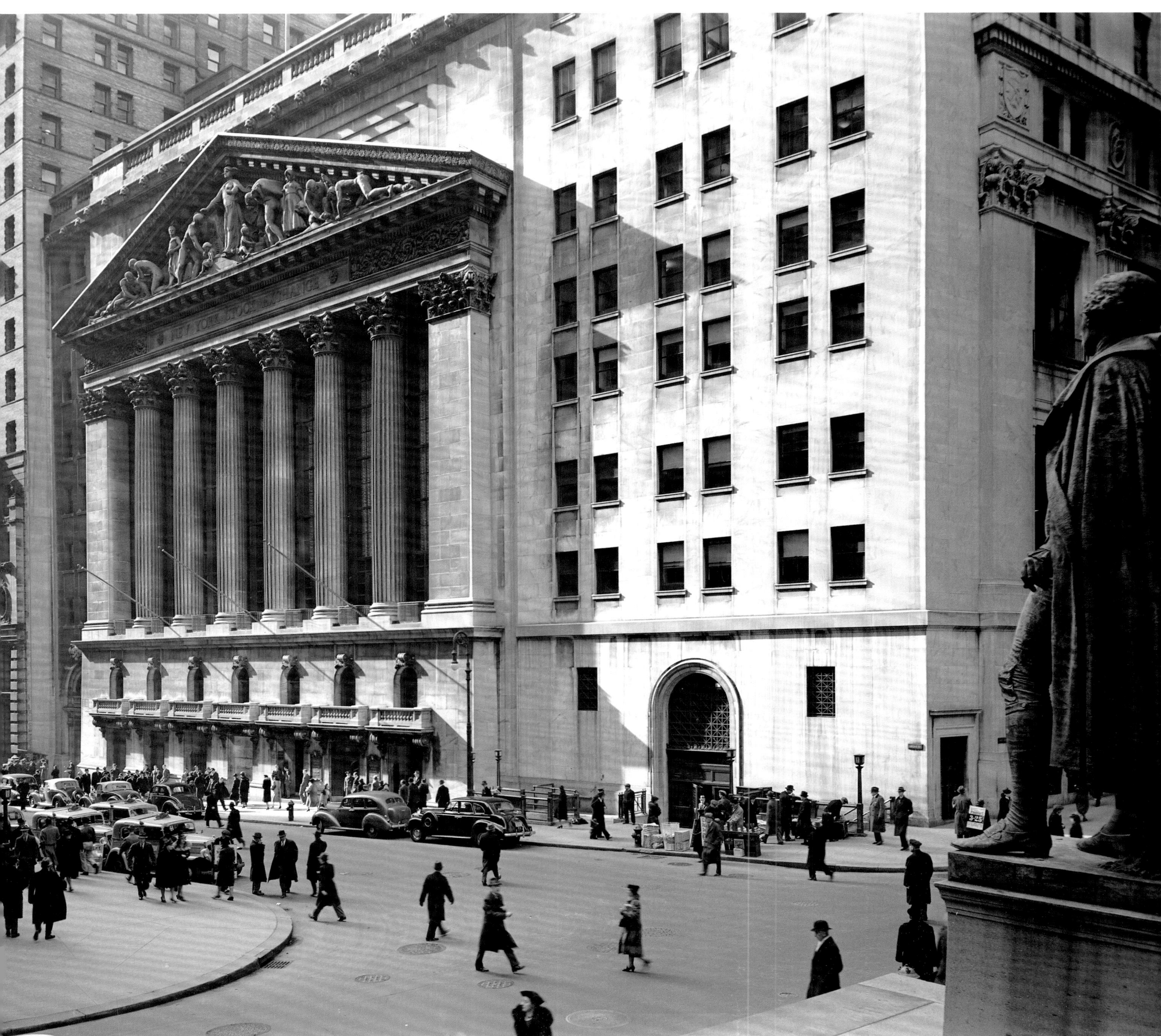

The original Pennsylvania Railroad Station building was completed in 1910 and demolished in 1966. A soldier says goodbye to his wife and infant child in the station before shipping out for service in World War II, 1943.

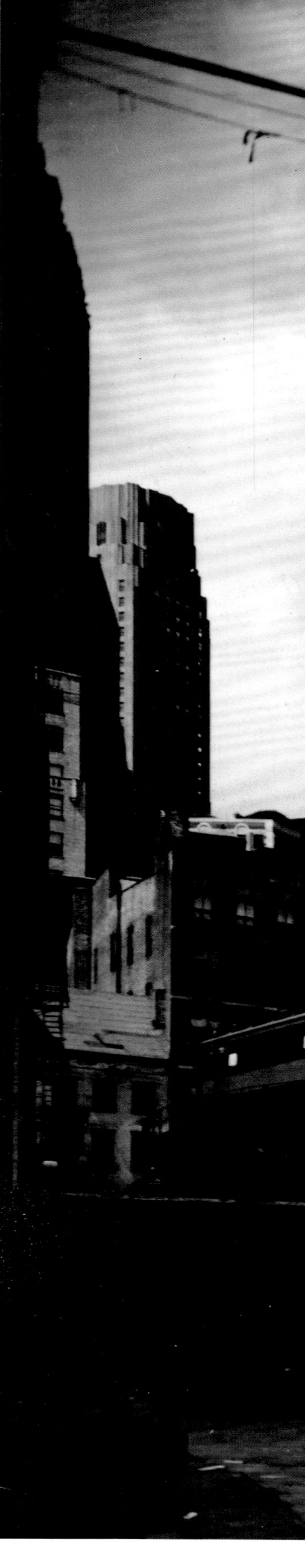

Skyline view of Manhattan's Financial District showing an elevated train line and, at the right, the Cities Service Building (later renamed the American International Building). Also visible are the Bank of Manhattan and the Bankers Trust Building, ca. late-1930s.

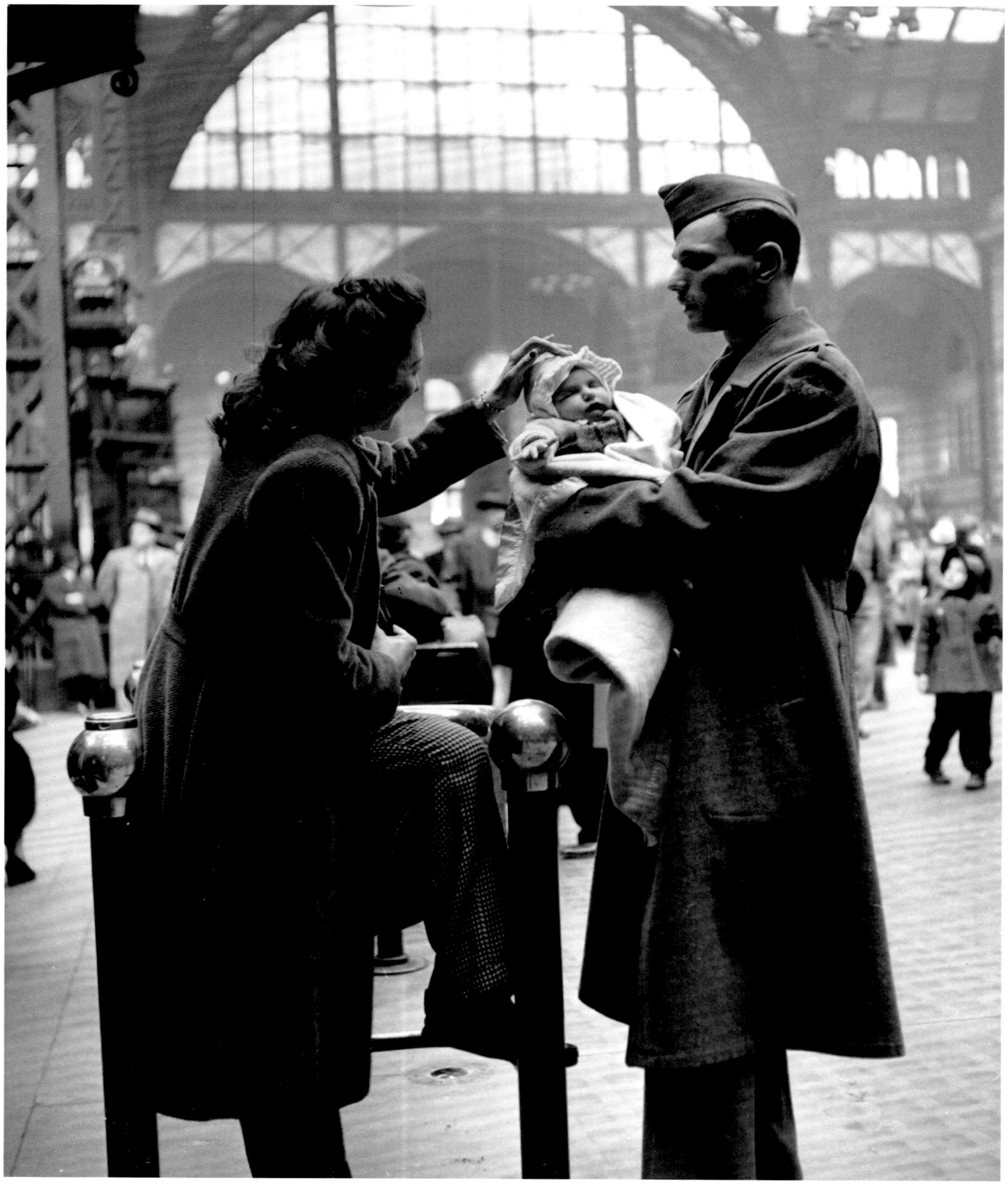

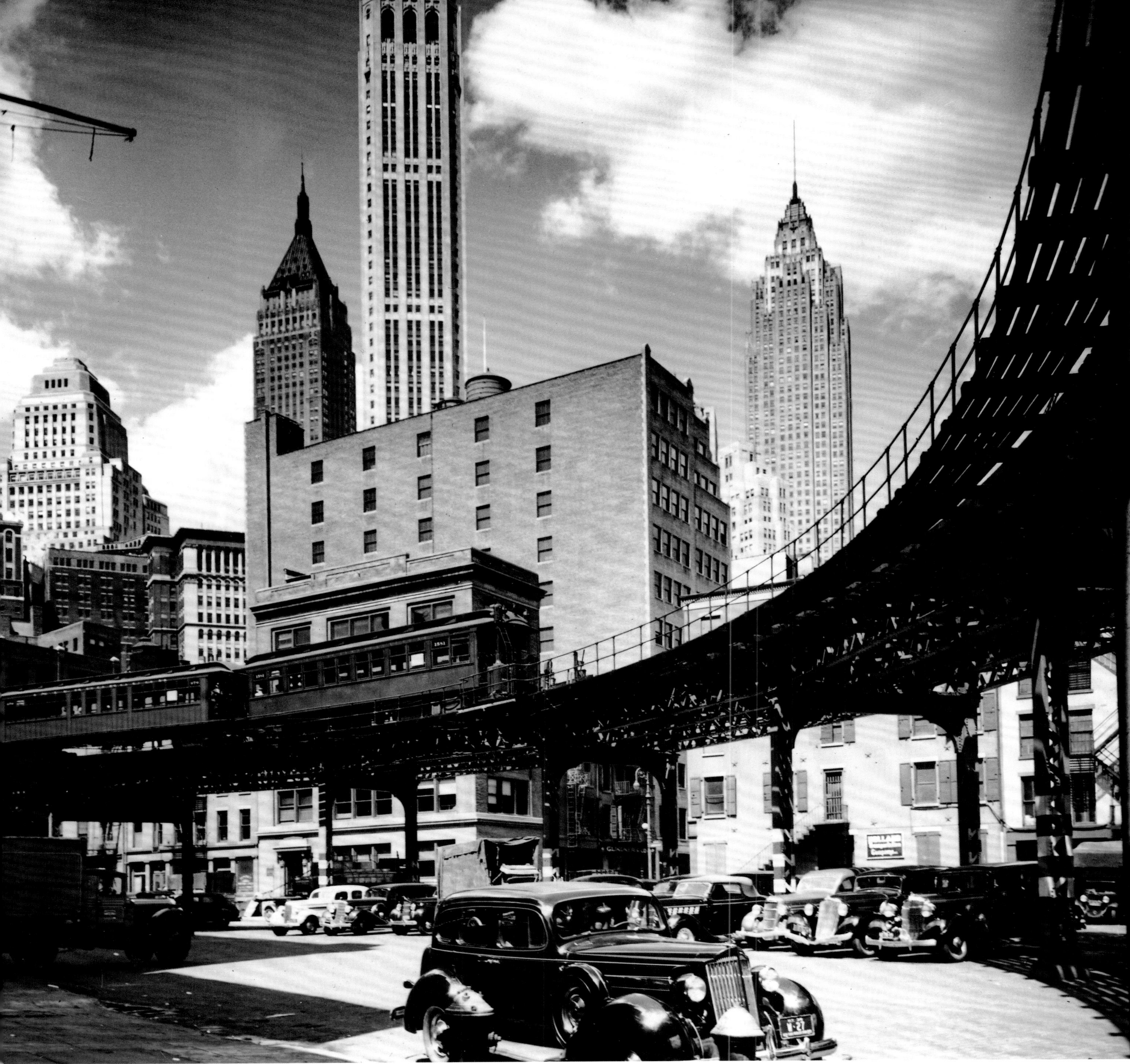

Rowers on the Pond in Central Park, 1929.

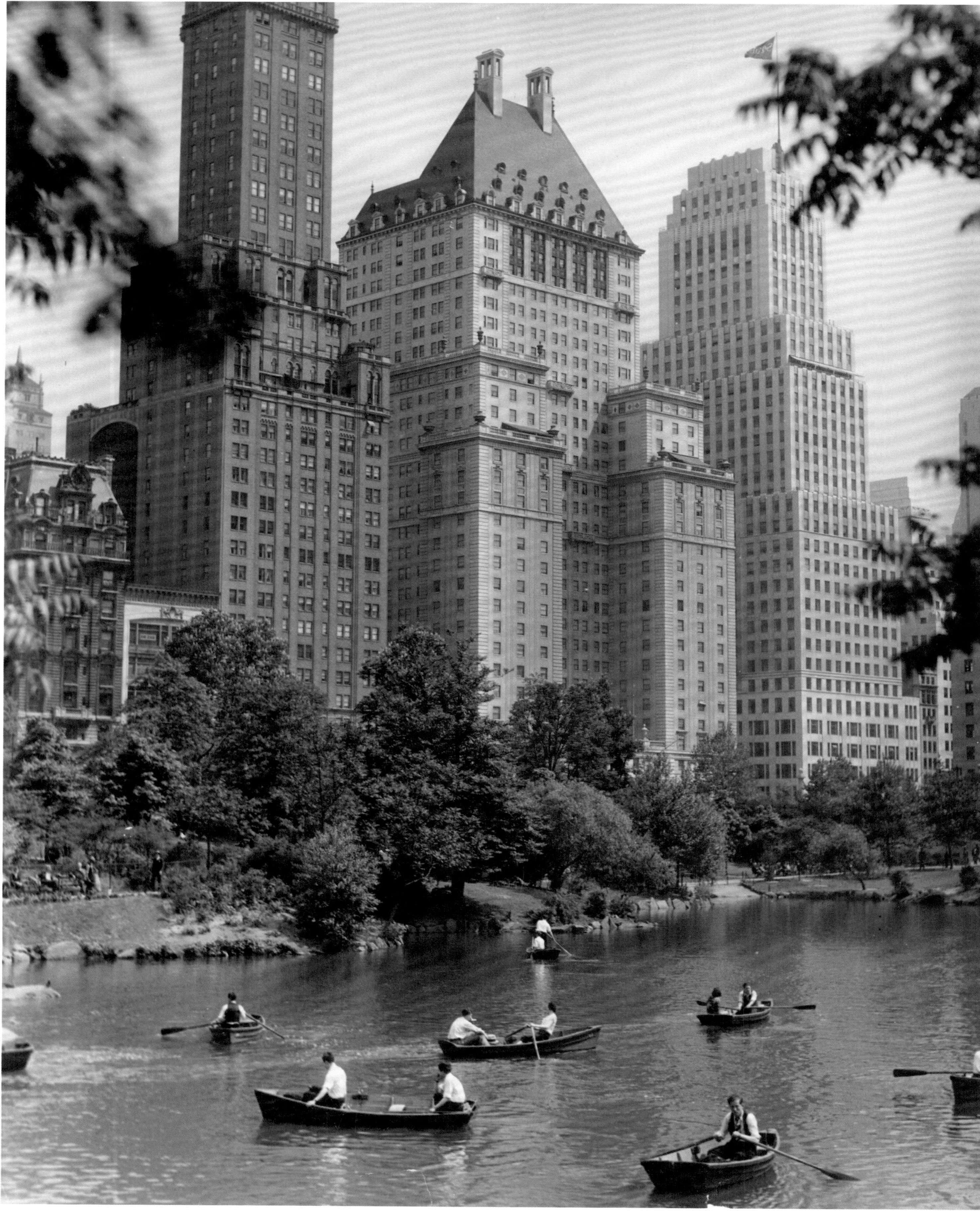

A pizza restaurant in Manhattan, ca. 1955.

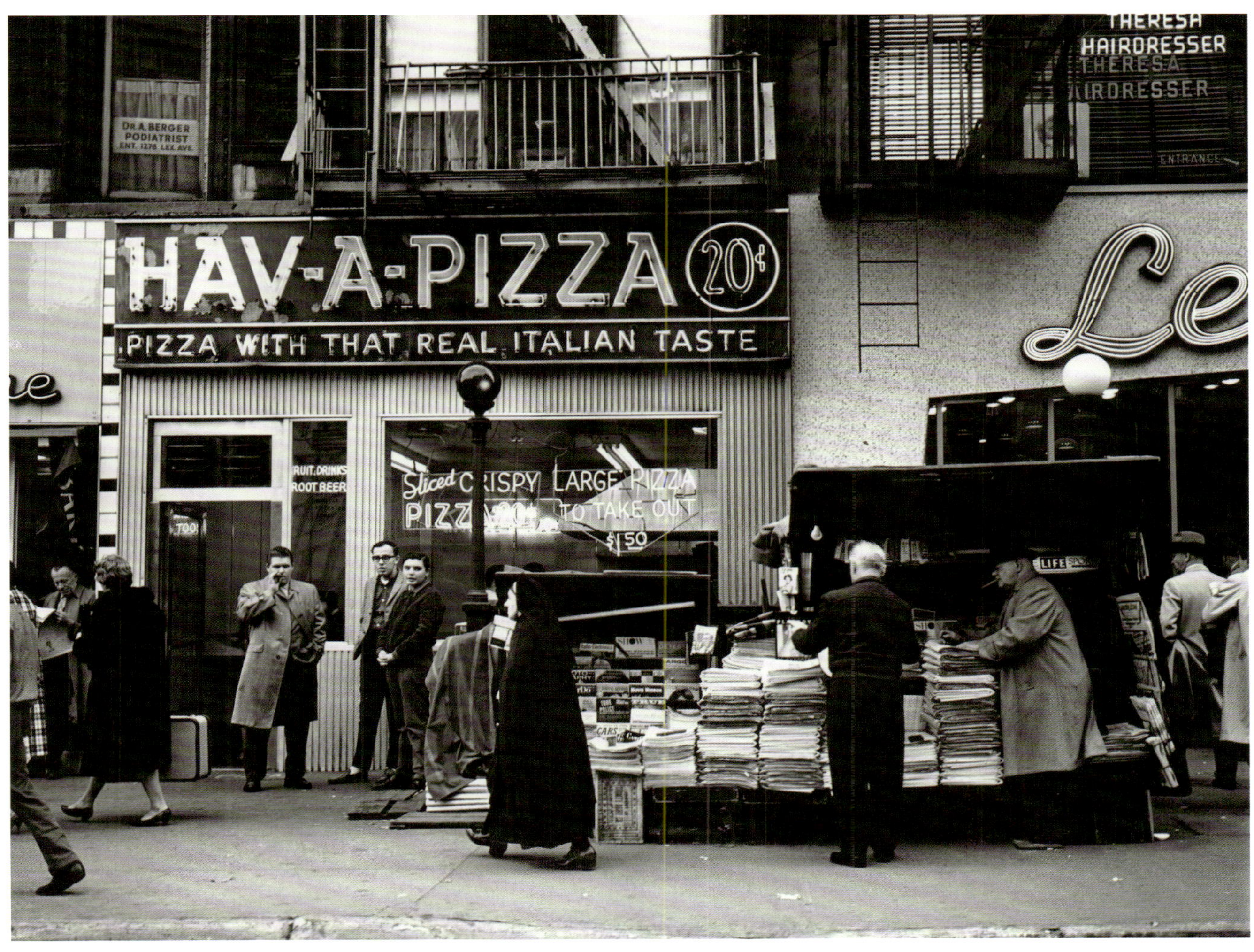

An orchestra performs for dancers at the annual National Urban League Ball at the Savoy Ballroom in Harlem, 1949.

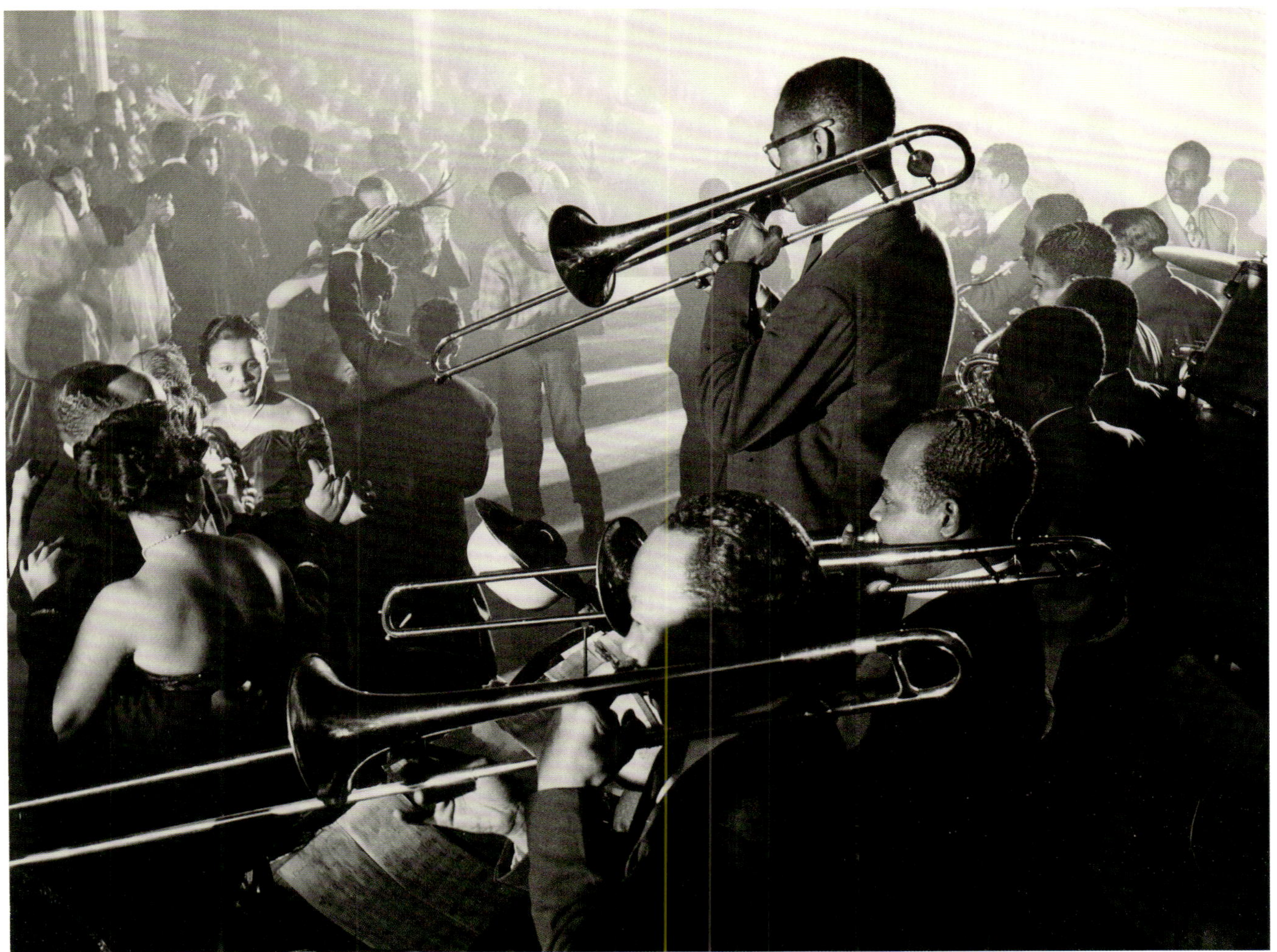

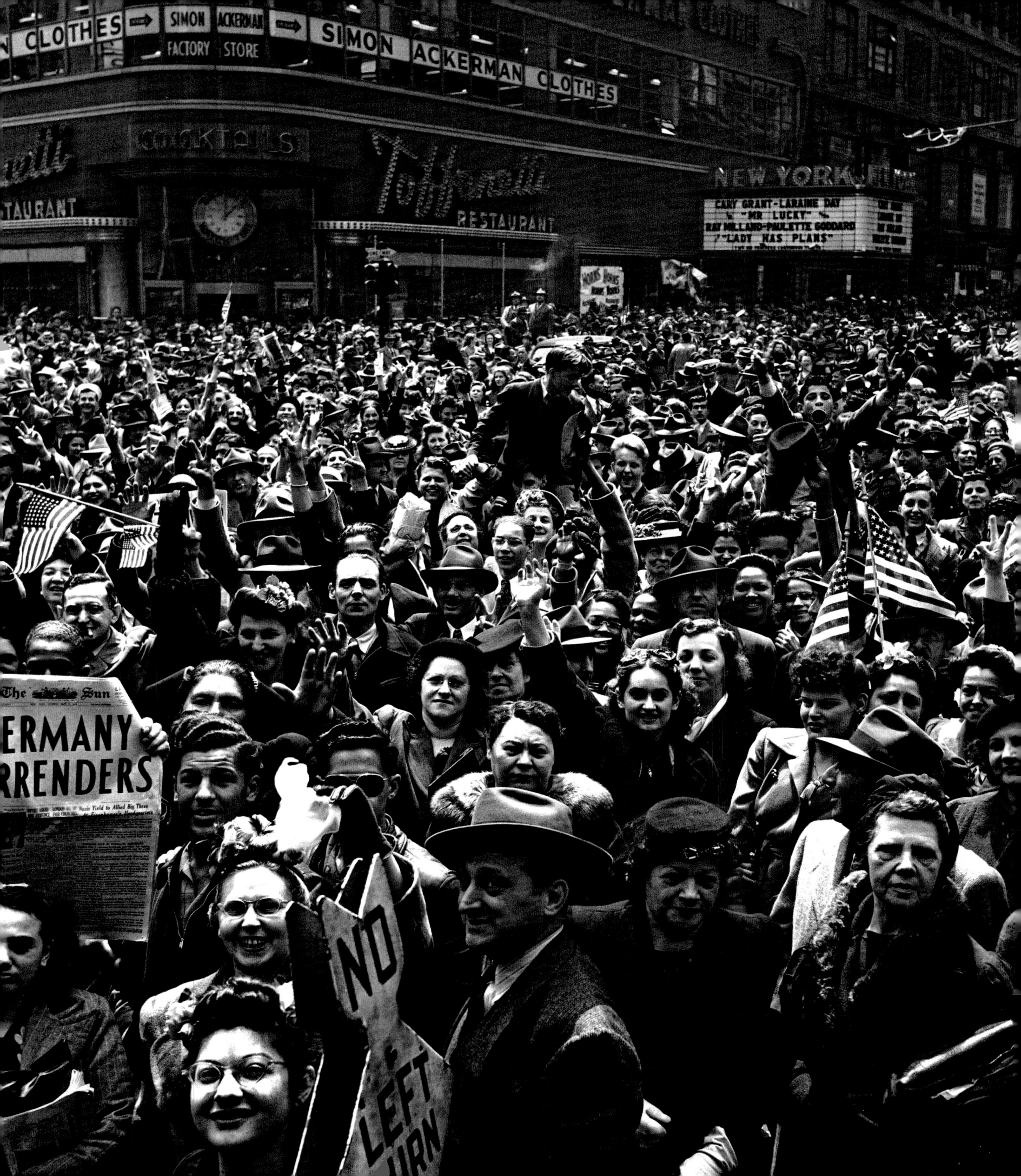
CLOTHES
SIMON ACKERMAN
FACTORY STORE
SIMON ACKERMAN CLOTHES
COCKTAILS
STAURANT
Toffenetti
RESTAURANT
NEW YORK
CARY GRANT-LARAINE DAY
"MR LUCKY"
RAY MILLAND-PAULETTE GODDARD
"LADY HAS PLANS"
The Sun
ERMANY
RRENDERS
Nazis Yield to Allied Big Three
NO
LEFT
URN

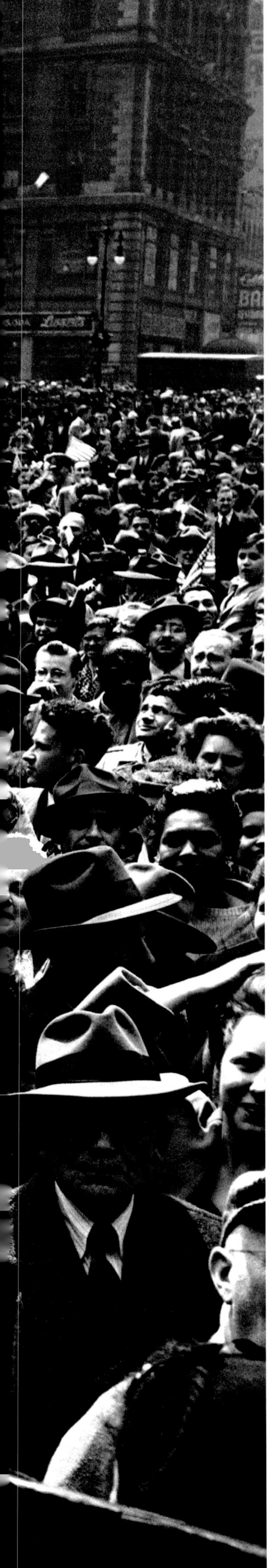

Crowds in Times Square show their jubilation and relief on V-E Day (or Victory in Europe Day), signaling the end of hostilities in the European theater in World War II. May 8, 1945.

A group of men at a coffee stand by the Brooklyn Bridge, ca. 1955.

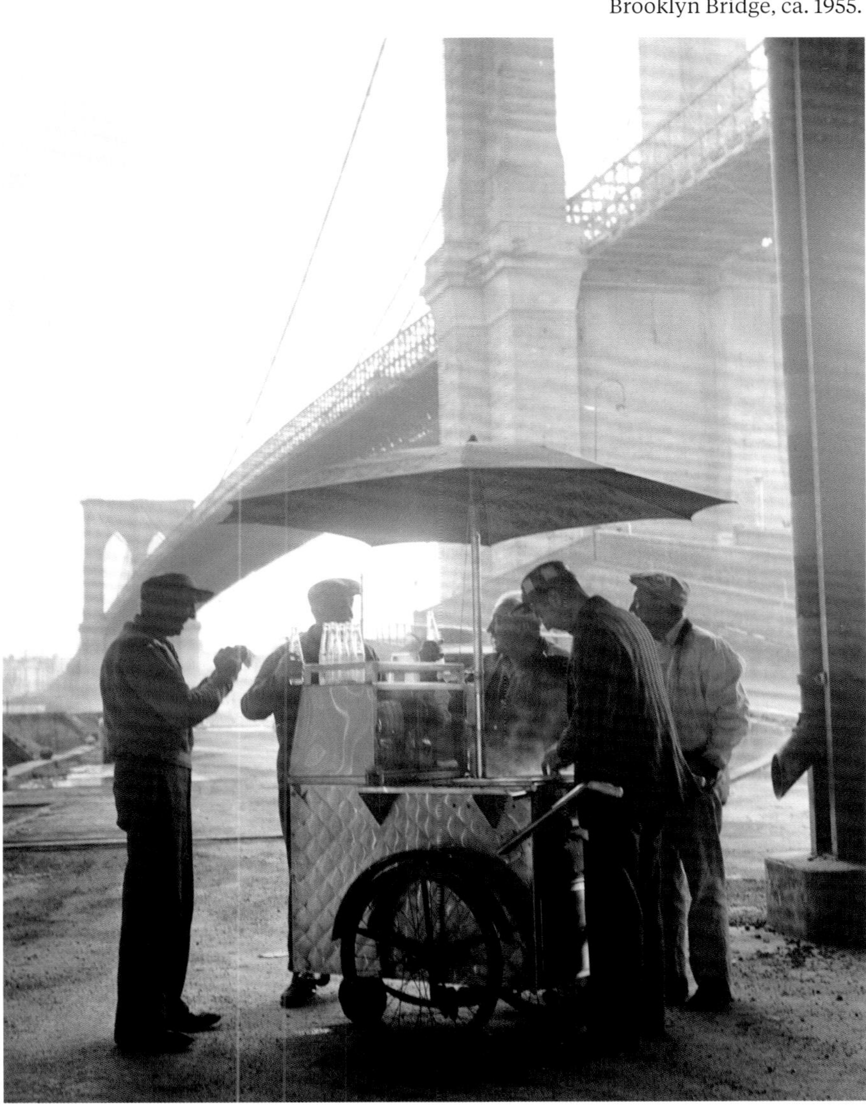

CHAPTER 2

A VISION FOR PEACE

In the vocabularies and aspirations of people around the world, as the world's most visible forum of international communication and cooperation, the United Nations embodies the ideal of an open and connected world.

It is only fitting that the United Nations chose to build its headquarters in a city whose history and culture reflect those same essential qualities. Since the days of the American Revolution, international exchange has been integral to New York City. In the course of its history, the city has become an emblem of freedom and openness. My family and I, arriving as refugees from Germany in 1938, experienced its openness firsthand.

The UN's founding in 1945 inaugurated an era of hope for peace. Seventy-five years hence, we stand at the threshold of a new epoch, which demands that we redefine world order to new complexities in the face of unprecedented challenges. In this context, the UN's work for peace, based on mutual understanding and trust, takes on a special importance.

—HENRY A. KISSINGER

Preamble to the Charter of the United Nations which was signed in San Francisco on June 26, 1945.

Henry A. Kissinger is an American scholar and national security expert who served as Secretary of State from 1973 to 1977.

WE THE PEOPLES OF THE UNITED NATIONS

determined

to save succeeding generations from the scourge of war, which twice in our lifetime has brought untold sorrow to mankind, and

to reaffirm faith in fundamental human rights, in the dignity and worth of the human person, in the equal rights of men and women and of nations large and small, and

to establish conditions under which justice and respect for the obligations arising from treaties and other sources of international law can be maintained, and

to promote social progress and better standards of life in larger freedom,

and for these ends

to practice tolerance and live together in peace with one another as good neighbors, and

to unite our strength to maintain international peace and security, and

to ensure, by the acceptance of principles and the institution of methods, that armed force shall not be used, save in the common interest, and

to employ international machinery for the promotion of the economic and social advancement of all peoples,

have resolved to combine our efforts to accomplish these aims.

accordingly, our respective Governments, through representatives assembled in the city of San Francisco, who have exhibited their full powers found to be in good and due form, have agreed to the present Charter of the United Nations and do hereby establish an international organization to be known as the United Nations.

UNITED NATIONS

PREAMBLE TO THE CHARTER OF THE UNITED NATIONS

ISSUED BY U. N. DEPARTMENT OF PUBLIC INFORMATION

The world has changed in 75 years, and so has the United Nations. This organization, which is particularly dear to France, has lost none of its relevance and modernity. Welcoming all the countries of the world and addressing all subjects, it is doubly universal and an indispensable forum for addressing the world's challenges and contributing to its harmonious development.

The United Nations and New York are now inseparable in the collective imagination. The city and the organization have influenced each other to become what they are today. What other place, so open and multicultural, with its tradition of welcoming others, with its convergence of routes and cultures, could have hosted the parliament of nations? New York has thus become synonymous with the multilateral forum *par excellence*.

And it is a sort of personal pride to see that a brilliant sample of French arts and culture, Fernand Léger's murals in the General Assembly Hall, attend every meeting of the world's parliament. Another French masterpiece, a tapestry of Henri Matisse's "Polynésie, le ciel" witnesses the tireless efforts of the Secretaries-General on behalf of peace, human rights, and sustainable development.

Le Corbusier, one of the architects of the United Nations Headquarters complex, described New York City as "a magnificent catastrophe," its heterogeneous architecture somehow creating a rich and balanced whole. Applying this analogy to the United Nations would be unfair, since the organization carries within it innumerable successes. But the United Nations is indeed like New York City, an eclectic collection of peoples and nations interacting with their environment, a magnificent Tower of Babel. —**NICOLAS DE RIVIERE**

Nicolas de Rivière is Ambassador and Permanent Representative of France to the United Nations.

The United Nations could have been located in a dozen other cities of the world, but its headquarters were built in New York City, underscoring and enhancing the global significance of this place. I am proud that my forebears, especially John D. Rockefeller, Jr. and Nelson A. Rockefeller —my grandfather and my uncle—were leaders in making available the land along the East River for the initial footprint of the UN. They understood what significance it had for New York City to host this post-war icon of future peacemaking, and they understood how much the city—as a place of many tongues and many cultures—could contribute to the vibrancy of the United Nations as an institution.

The UN Development Corporation has played a vital role in helping the UN to expand beyond, but in close proximity to, its East River headquarters and has ensured that representatives from all over the globe could live and work within walking distance. My ancestors would surely smile to see how the dream they helped to initiate has flourished and has maintained so much of its original character.

My own travels to other continents have helped me to understand how vital it is for citizens of one nation to have direct interchange with people of vastly different cultures and histories. The United Nations brings all nations into direct communication with one another and helps to remind us that intelligence and good will are not the sole province of any one culture. —**DAVID ROCKEFELLER, JR.**

David Rockefeller, Jr. is a businessman, philanthropist, and trustee of the Rockefeller Brothers Fund.

The Rockefeller Foundation is privileged to share with the United Nations' philanthropic roots not just a neighborhood, but more importantly an ethos of protecting the world's most vulnerable. We are proud to join many others in honoring the UN's 75th anniversary and its decades of impact on fostering peace and security and its commitment to protecting human rights around the world. We are proud stewards of the Rockefeller family's commitment to the UN and the vision of our founder, John D. Rockefeller, Jr., to promote the wellbeing of humanity.

We also congratulate the United Nations Development Corporation on their own 50-year anniversary. The UNDC is a dedicated steward of the physical space that hosts so many UN activities. We remain, as ever, fully committed to the deep partnership built over decades with the UN and its agencies in our shared commitment to building a safer and more just world for all. —**THE ROCKEFELLER FOUNDATION**

The Rockefeller Foundation is a private New York-based foundation established in 1913.

2.5 MILLION

Number of square feet of space on the UN Headquarters

18 ACRES

Approximate size of UN campus

544 FEET
72 FEET

Height and width of the Secretariat Building

2,000 TONS

Amount of Vermont marble cladding the Secretariat Building's north and south facades

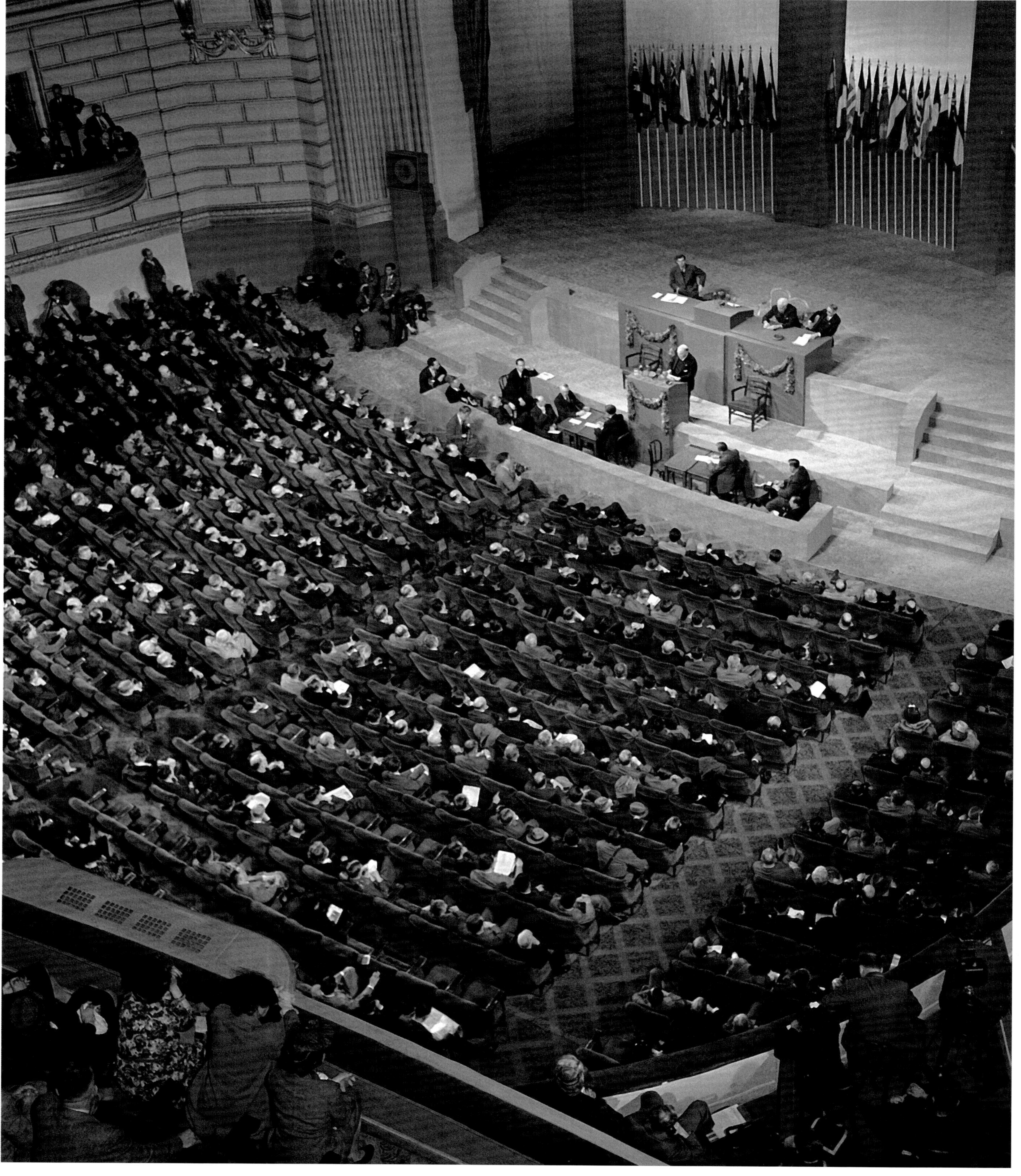

Delegates of fifty nations met in San Francisco between April 25 and June 26, 1945. Working on the Dumbarton Oaks proposals, the Yalta Agreement, and amendments proposed by various governments, the conference agreed upon the Charter of the United Nations and the Statute of the New International Court of Justice. The Charter was passed unanimously and signed by all the representatives. It came into force on October 24, 1945, when China, France, the Soviet Union, the United Kingdom, the United States, and a majority of the other signatories had filed their instruments of ratification.
W.L. Mackenzie King, M.P., Prime Minister of Canada and Chairman of the Canadian Delegation, speaking at the Second Plenary Session. April 27, 1945.

The United Nations took a major step to becoming reality in 1944, when representatives of the United States, the Soviet Union, the United Kingdom, and China met at Dumbarton Oaks in Washington, DC, to discuss a blueprint for a successor to the ill-fated League of Nations, an international organization designed to end war and promote peace, justice, and better living for all mankind.[6] As laid out in the United Nations Charter, the institution's primary governing organs were to be the General Assembly, the Security Council, the Economic and Social Council, the Trusteeship Council, the International Court of Justice, and the UN Secretariat. On June 26, 1945, 850 delegates from 50 nations signed the Charter in San Francisco. It was ratified on October 24, 1945, officially bringing the United Nations into existence.

Almost immediately, the important question arose of where the organization's headquarters would be located. In December 1945, the United States Congress unanimously resolved to invite the United Nations to establish its permanent home in the U.S. During its first meeting in London the following year, the General Assembly voted to establish an interim headquarters for the UN in New York City and a permanent home—a self-contained "international community" on 42 square miles of land straddling Westchester County, New York, and Fairfield County, Connecticut.[7] During 1946, the question of location was revisited, with a subcommittee of the General Assembly's Permanent Headquarters Committee considering and inspecting several sites in and around New York, Boston, Philadelphia, and San Francisco.

While a permanent home to the United Nations was in the works, various locations throughout metropolitan New York City served as temporary homes to the UN and its agencies. The first was the Bronx campus of Hunter College, in 1946. Classrooms were hastily transformed into offices for the Secretariat and a gymnasium remodeled into an assembly chamber for the Security Council.[8] A disused building on the site of the 1939 World's Fair in Flushing Meadows, Queens, which the city's then parks commissioner Robert Moses supported as a permanent headquarters location, was the next home of the itinerant UN's General Assembly. Between 1946 and 1951, the Secretariat and Security Council met in Lake Success in Nassau County, Long Island, in three converted buildings at a former Sperry Gyroscope Company plant.

At the same time that the UN was touring potential sites and considering pitches from aspiring towns and cities from Boston to South Dakota, developer William Zeckendorf was making grand plans. Zeckendorf, of the New York real estate company Webb & Knapp, had been acquiring slaughterhouses and other properties along the East River to build a sprawling mixed-use development to rival Rockefeller Center. Called X City, this monumental 17-acre development stretching between 42nd Street and 48th Street, from First Avenue to the East River, was planned to include two 57-story towers (one containing offices,

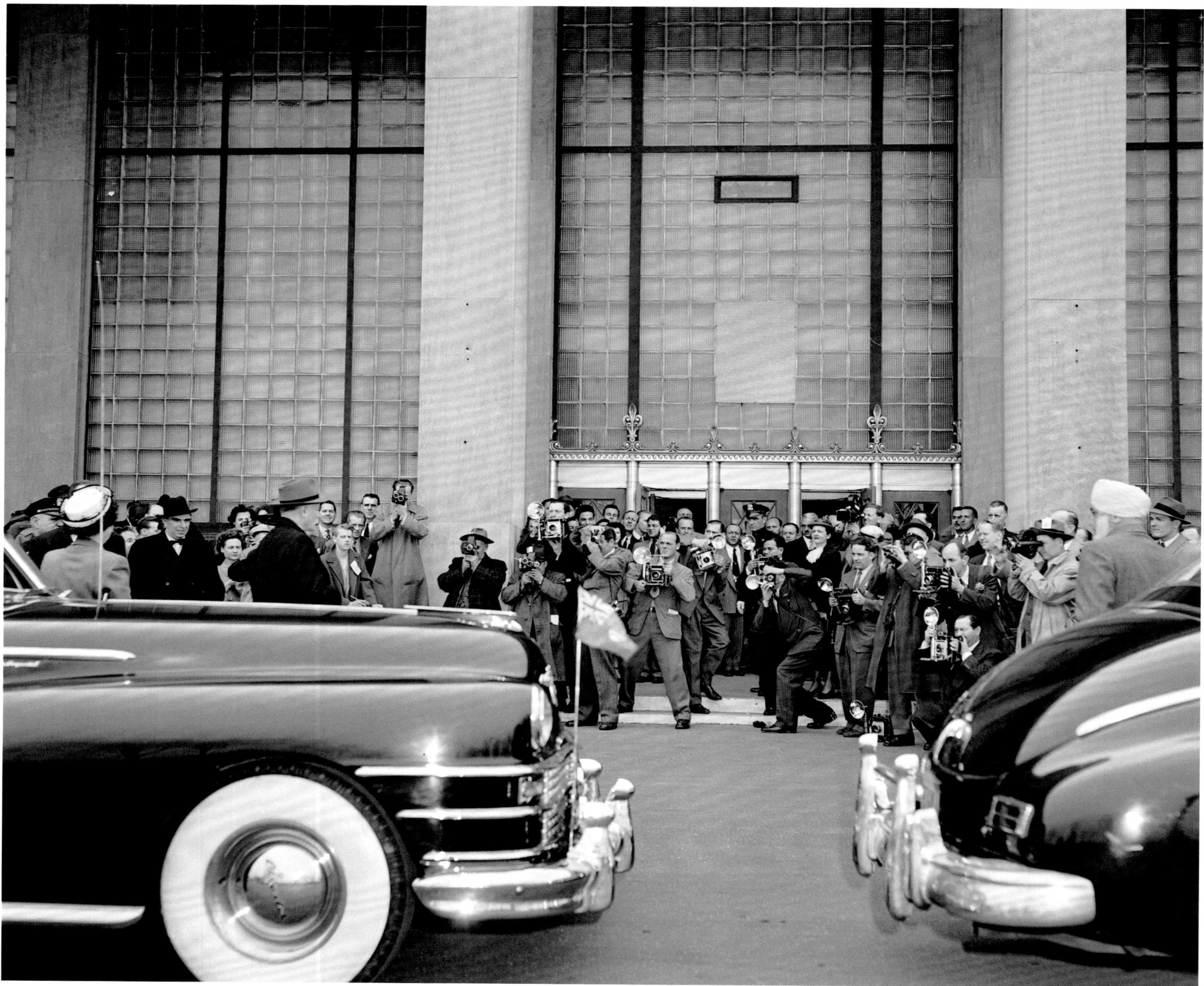

Photographers crowd the entrance to the General Assembly Building to get pictures of the delegates arriving for the opening meeting of the Second Part of the Third Session in Flushing Meadows, New York. April 5, 1949.

the other a hotel), four 40-story office buildings, a trio of 30-story apartment buildings, a concert hall, opera house, shops, parking garage, marina, and a floating nightclub. New York architect Wallace K. Harrison, who went on to oversee the design of the UN Headquarters campus, was to design the entire complex.

While Zeckendorf was seeking financing to build X City, New York's prospects to cement a deal to be the UN's host city were faltering. Robert Moses, the city's planning commissioner, favored refurbishing the former World's Fair site in Flushing Meadows, but UN officials were not enthusiastic. Meanwhile, the Rockefeller family, who were among local power brokers supporting a New York-area home for the UN feared the organization was leaning toward selecting a site in Philadelphia. They initially considered gifting a part of the Rockefeller estate to the United Nations, where they might build a campus overlooking the Hudson River.[9] John D. Rockefeller, Jr. and sons Nelson and Laurance Rockefeller came to the agreement that the Tarrytown property was unfeasible. But Nelson thought Zeckendorf's X City property—which the developer had been discussing as a potential site with UN Secretary-General Trygve Lie, Mayor O'Dwyer, and others—was ideal, if financing was not an obstacle. Moved by Nelson's support, John D. Rockefeller, Jr. presented the UN a last-minute offer in December 1946: a gift of $8.5 million (approximately $120 million in 2020 dollars) with which to purchase Zeckendorf's riverfront property. As Rockefeller himself wrote to the chairman of the UN's Permanent Headquarters Committee, "New York is a center where people from all lands have always been welcomed and where they have shared common aspirations and achievements. It is my belief that this city affords an environment uniquely fitted to the task of the United Nations and that the people of New York would like to have the United Nations here permanently."[10] The General Assembly voted to accept the elder Rockefeller's gift on December 14, 1946, thus assuring the UN's future in New York.

Many New Yorkers saw the price of having the UN in their city as an investment in global security, world peace, and human progress. But not all thought it was a good idea. The Rockefellers received letters and telegrams second-guessing both their financial gift and the appropriateness of the UN Headquarters site with comments including: "Why don't you make such an investment in apartment houses [for] GI's and their families at a fair rental, not...an elaborate building for the UN?" and "Please reconsider the tragic effect of...forcing the United Nations to crowd into an already overcrowded New York."[11]

New York City contributed additional sites to complete the full UN parcel from East 42nd to East 48th Streets and from First Avenue to the East River, as well as funding the clearing of the land at a cost of $5 million (roughly $60 million in today's currency). The city also committed $23 million (about $325 million today) for improvements around the UN site, including the widening of East 42nd and East 47th Streets and the construction of a tunnel beneath First Avenue.

When ground was eventually broken in September 1948, New York City Mayor William O'Dwyer declared in a public ceremony, "... [Here] will be established a plan for peace so that the little children of today and those unborn will know no war." Acting Secretary-General Benjamin A. Cohen added, "[W]e establish our roots on strong soil, where we'll have our own home in a great metropolis. New York City is an example of people coming from all over the world to live in peace and harmony."[12] But before the UN dream could become a reality, another monumental battle had to be waged: designing its headquarters.

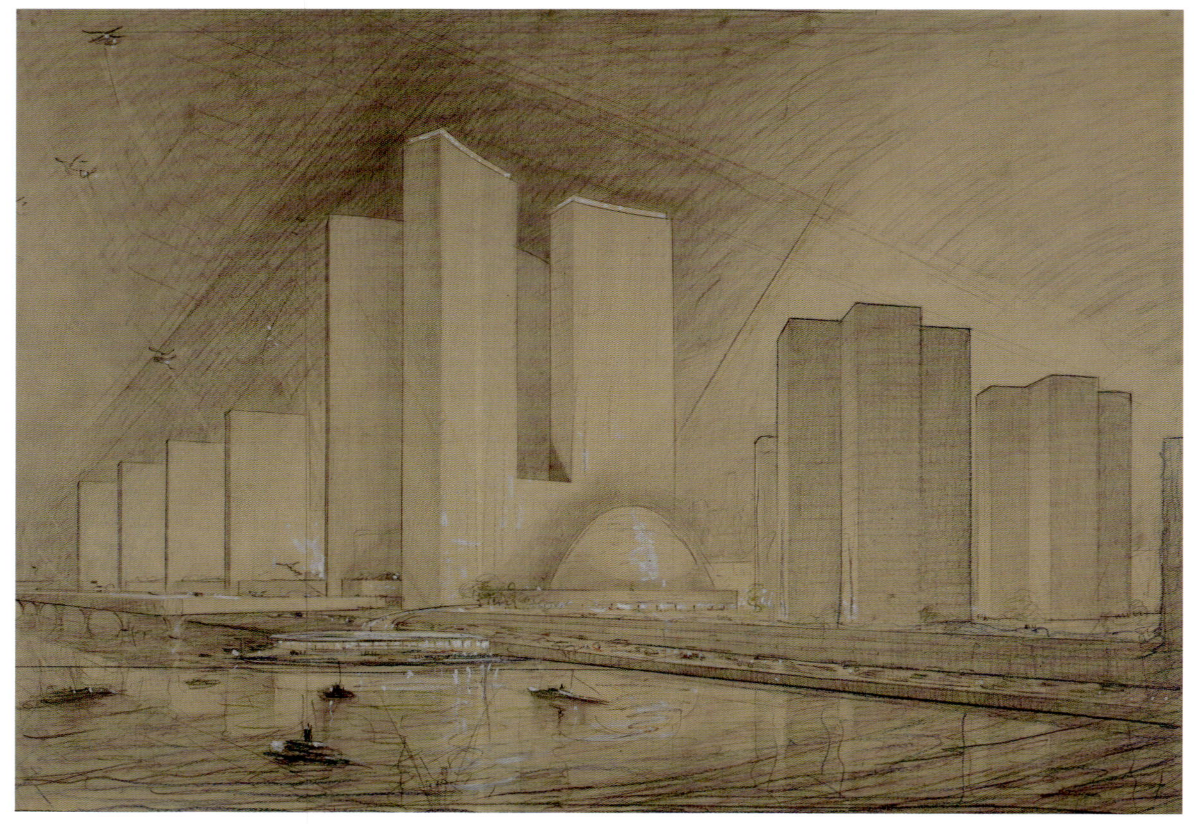

In 1946 the big-thinking developer William Zeckendorf assembled most of the land between First Avenue and the East River from 42nd to 49th Streets. Mr. Zeckendorf never made little plans, and for this site he envisioned X City, a megaproject unlike anything that had yet been seen in Manhattan's private sector.

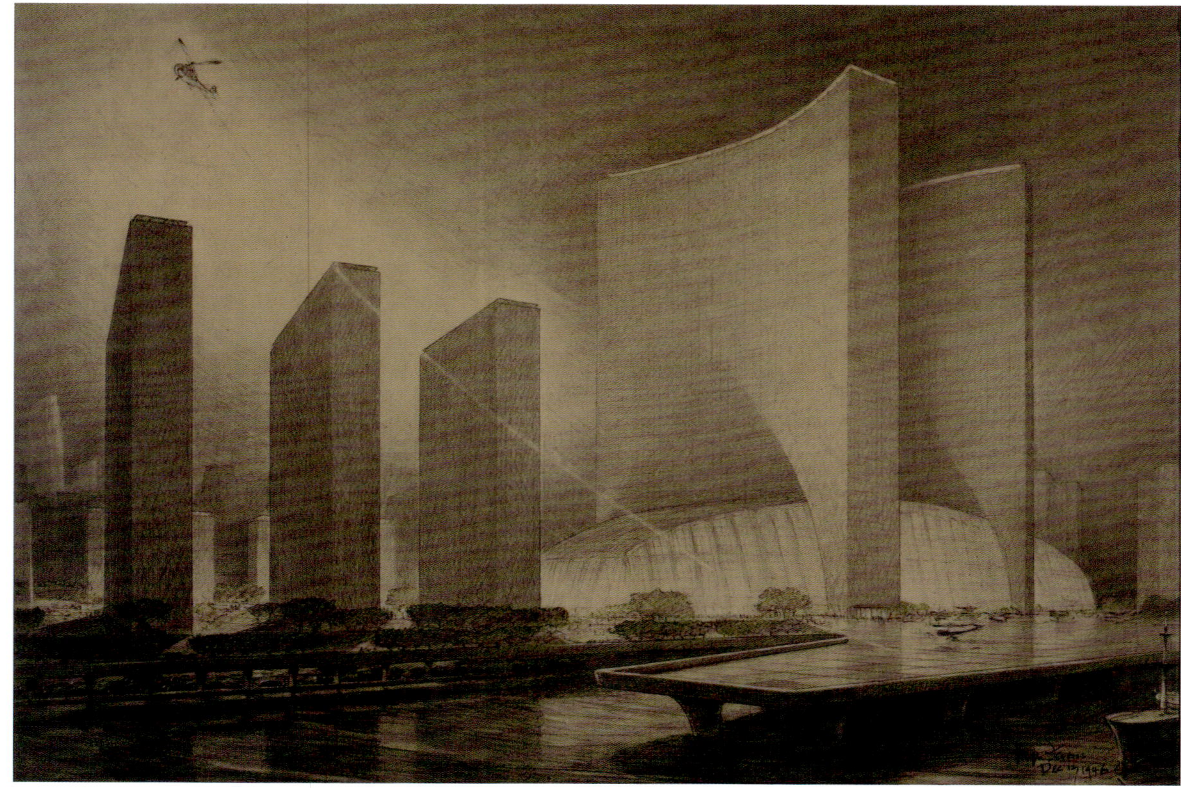

In late 1946, John D. Rockefeller, Jr. optioned Mr. Zeckendorf's site for $8.5 million, intending to donate it to the United Nations. To inspire the site-selection board, Mr. Zeckendorf had his architect, Wallace K. Harrison, modify his X City plans to include a low-curved assembly hall straddled by two towers.

On behalf of his father, John D. Rockefeller III presents Secretary-General Trygve Lie with a check for $8,500,000 to purchase the six-block East River site where the United Nations would build its permanent headquarters. Mr. Lie exhibits the check during a ceremony at the Empire State Building. March 25, 1947.

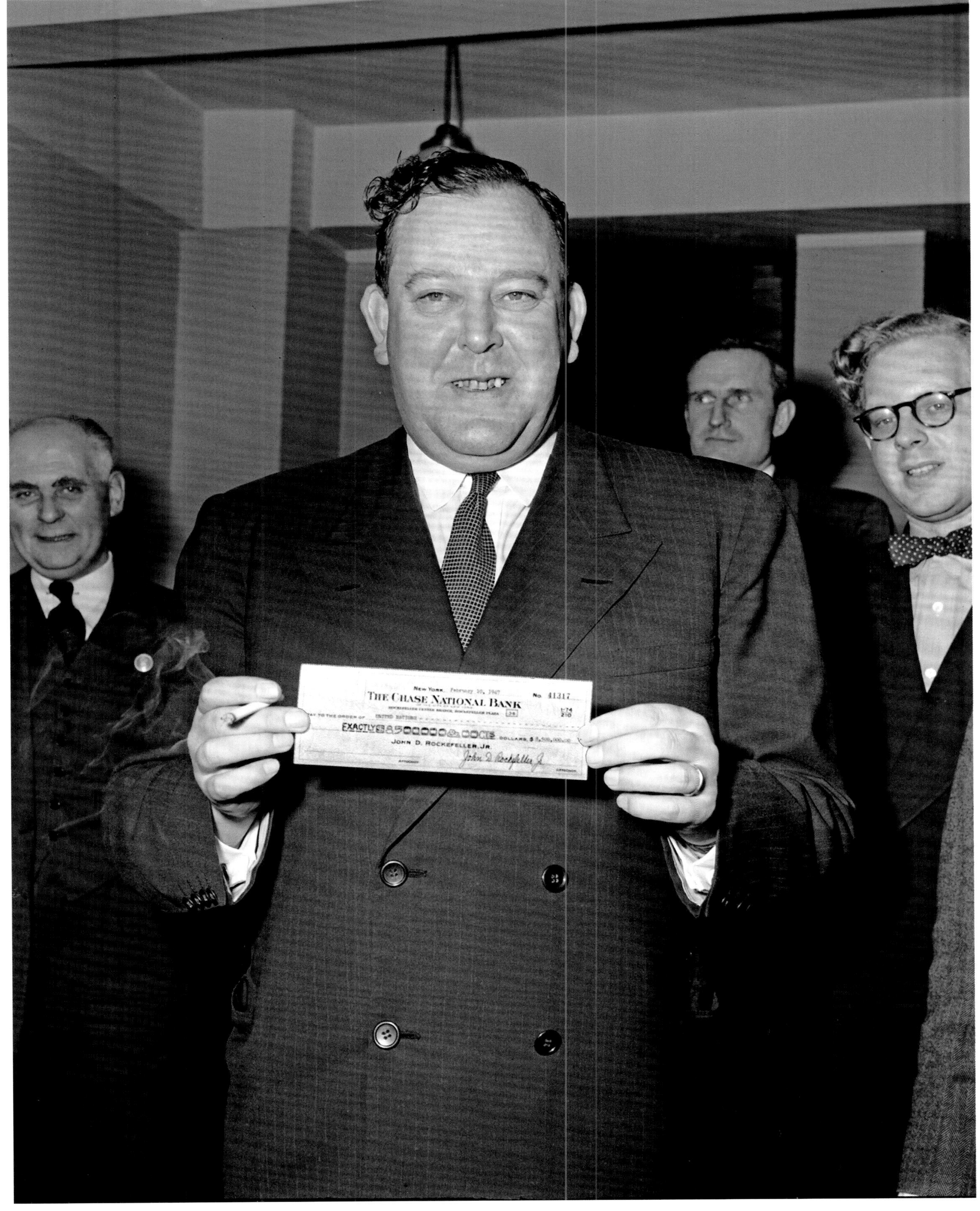

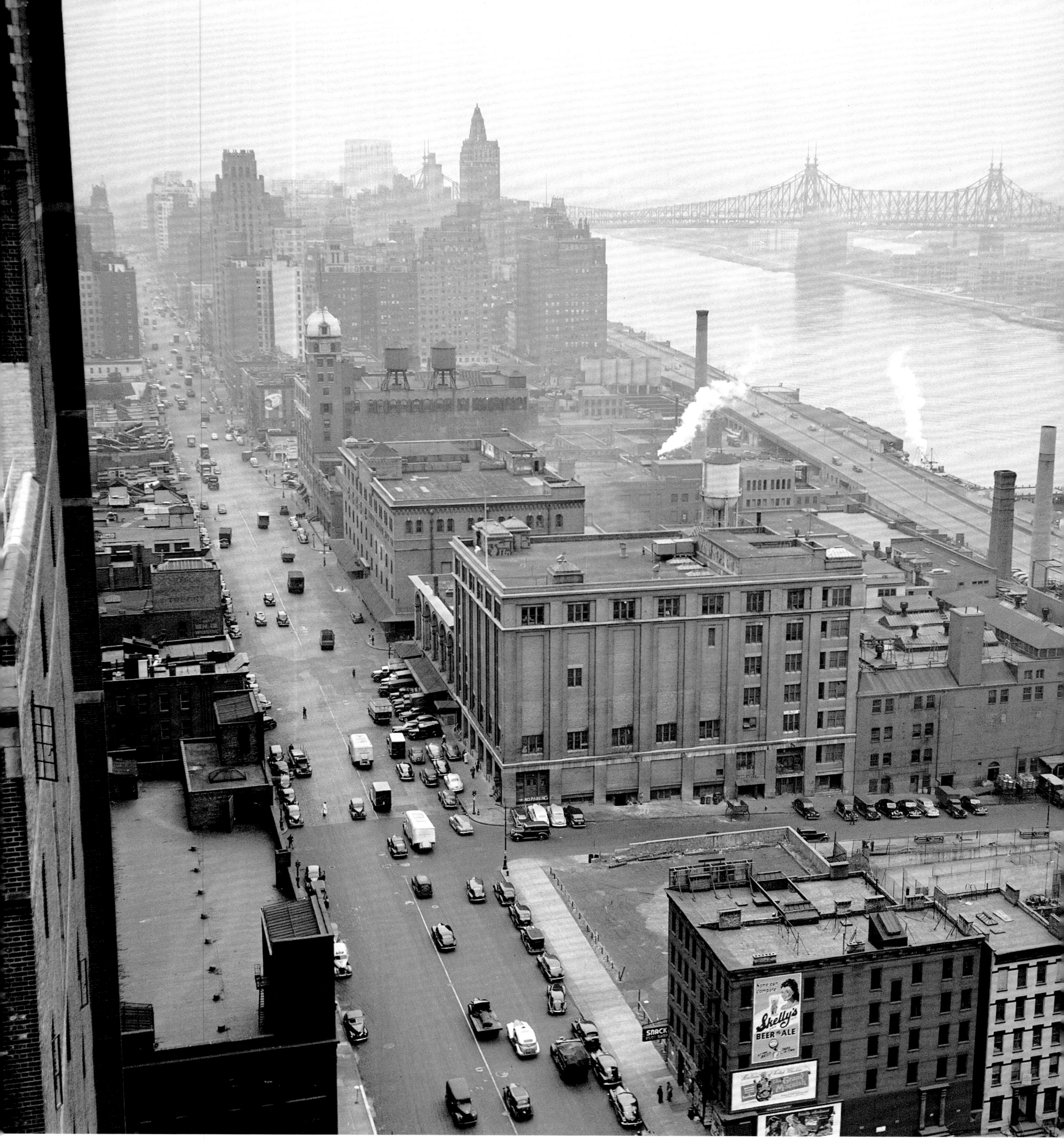
SNACK
Skelly's
BEER ALE

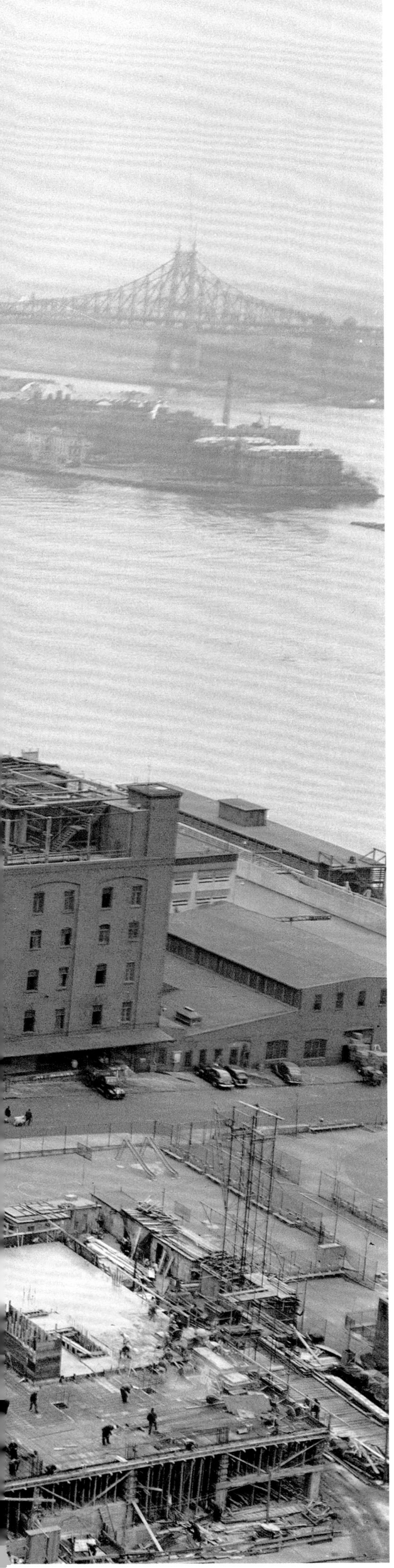

View of the future site of the United Nations Headquarters looking northeast toward the Queensboro Bridge. December 12, 1946.

Demolition ceremony for the United Nations Headquarters site. Byron Price, UN Assistant Secretary-General for Administrative and Financial Services, far left; Hugo Rogers, Manhattan Borough President, center; and William O'Dwyer, Mayor of the City of New York, remove the first dozen bricks from a boarded up five-story tenement building. July 8, 1947.

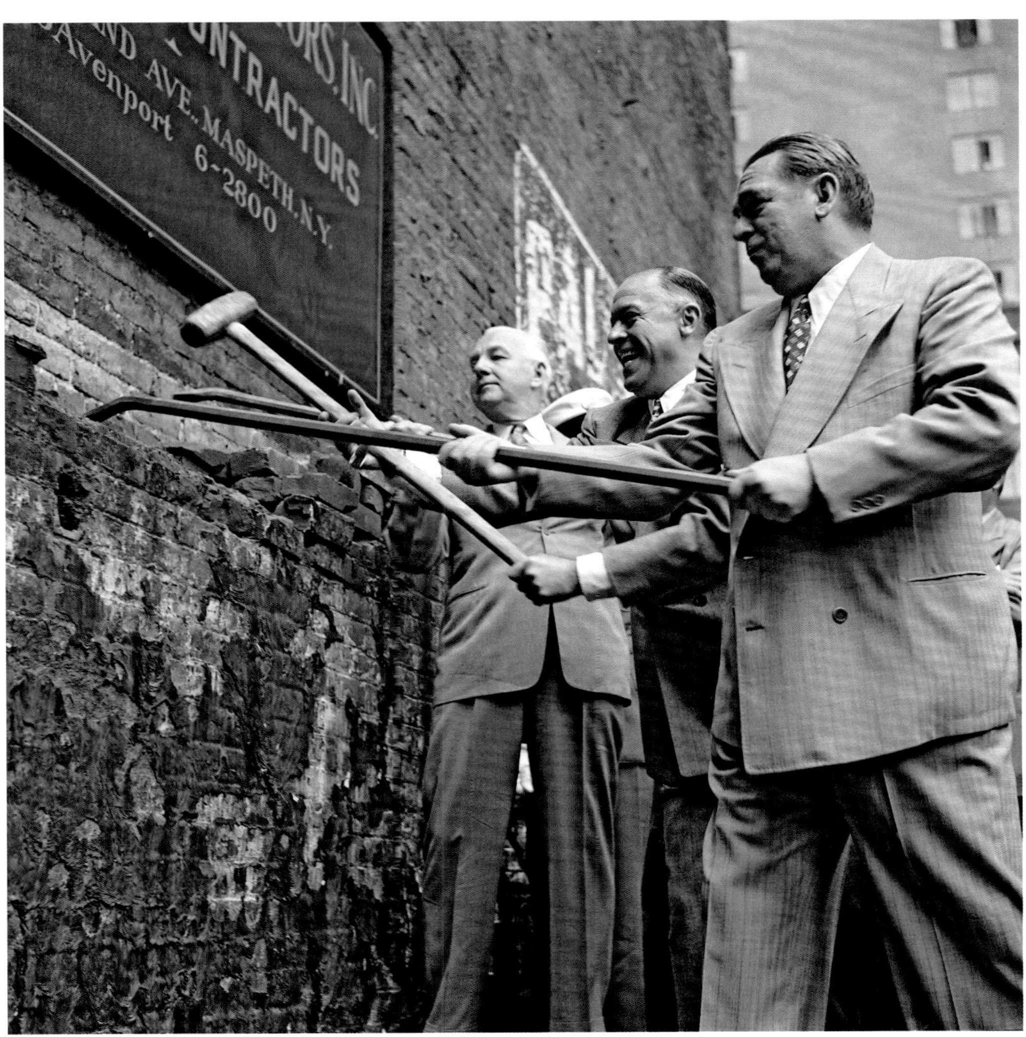

Demolition work in progress on the United Nations Headquarters site. Here, a wall of the building formerly occupied by the meat packing company Swift and Co. on 46th Street is being torn down. July 23, 1947.

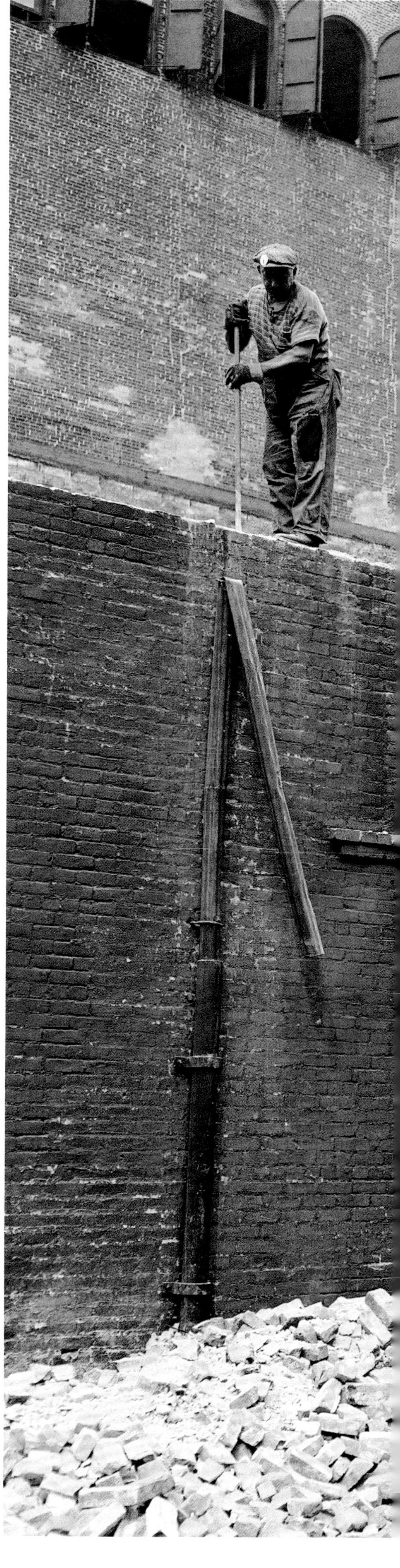

Workers wash themselves on 45th Street after a day spent demolishing structures on the United Nations Headquarters site. The leveling of the site is expected to take four months. August 21, 1947.

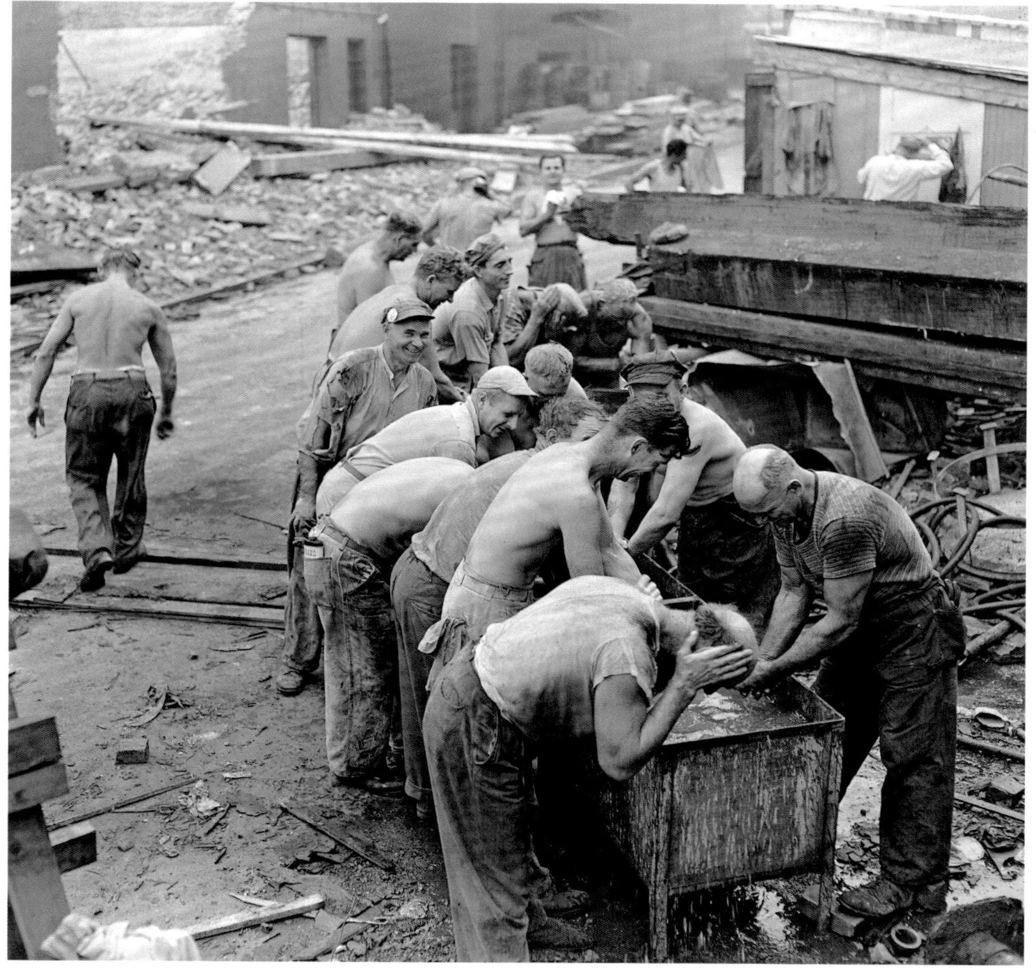

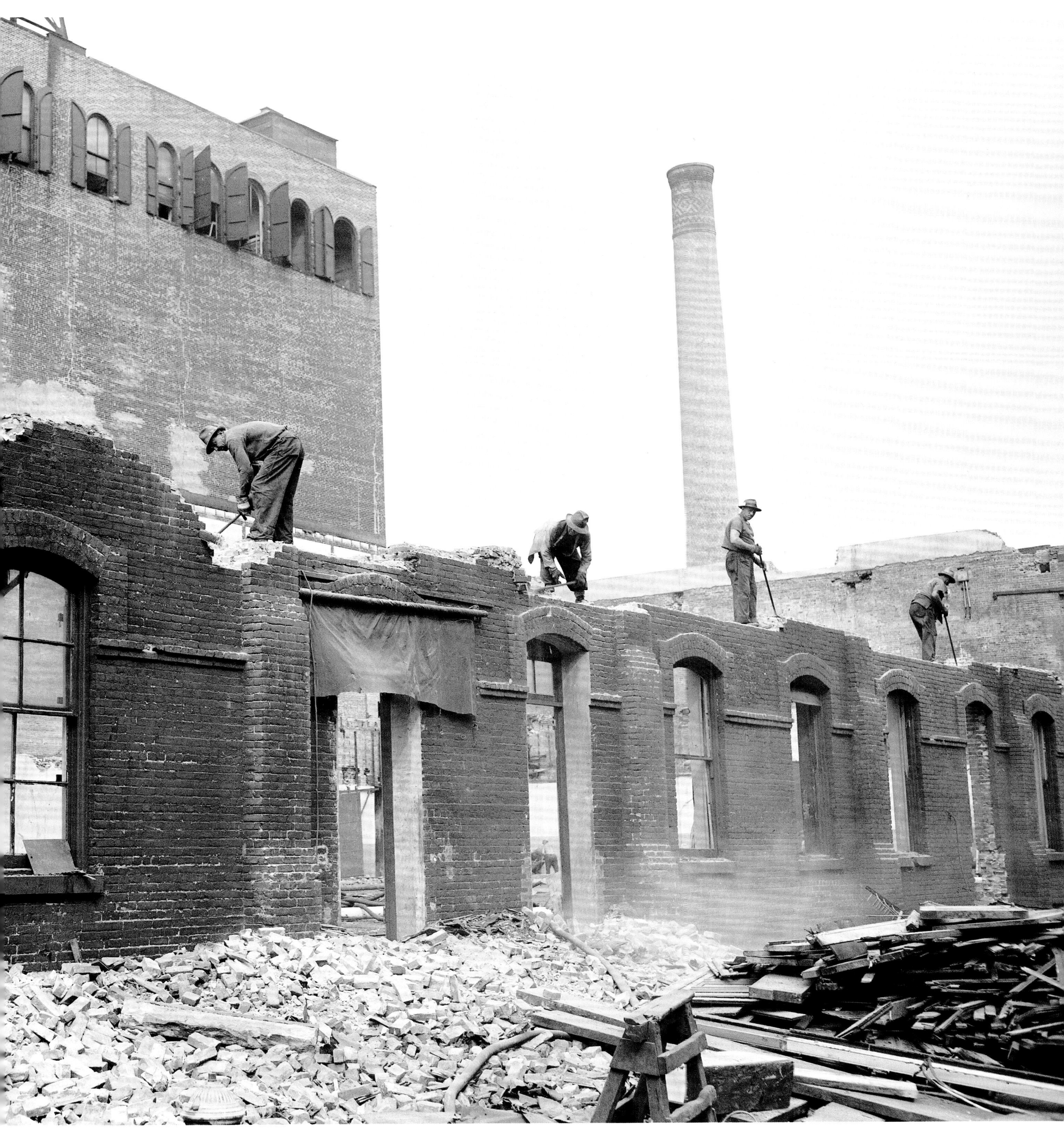

CHAPTER 3

THE UN RISES

Serving as the United States Ambassador to the United Nations was the honor of a lifetime. Of course, moving to New York City from South Carolina was a big adjustment for me and my family. But it was well worth it for the chance to represent America to the world—to uphold our country's principles and defend our interests.

One of the best parts about having the United Nations in New York is that the American story is on full display. The representatives of other countries are literally surrounded by a city that shows the strength and staying power of freedom. In days gone by, millions of people from across the world came through New York Harbor in search of the best shot at a better life. In the present day, the city is a testament to the opportunity and prosperity that freedom brings. No wonder America is the example that so many countries still want to follow.

I was glad to renew American leadership during my time at the UN. I was also proud to call on the UN to renew its commitment to its founding values of human rights, peace, and security. At a time when tyrants the world over are corrupting and abusing the United Nations for their own evil ends, America must continue to stand strong and show a better way—one that moves beyond the decades-old debates of the past and looks toward a brighter future. When the United Nations is irrelevant or worse, it does not serve America's interest. But a relevant and principled United Nations is squarely in America's interests, and my hope is that the United States continues to lead it in the right direction.

—NIKKI HALEY

Nikki Haley was United States Ambassador to the United Nations from 2017 to 2018.

MAINTAINING INTERNATIONAL PEACE AND SECURITY

PROTECTING HUMAN RIGHTS

DELIVERING HUMANITARIAN AID

PROMOTING SUSTAINABLE DEVELOPMENT

UPHOLDING INTERNATIONAL LAW

Since my first UN high-level week in 1998 and throughout my career as a diplomat, I've come regularly to New York—and to the center of global diplomacy here at the United Nations. Those visits were always exciting. The vibrancy of the city made a mark on me.

Then I came to live in New York. Walking into my first Security Council meeting felt like arriving at the Olympic Games, for diplomats at least. Taking a seat in a room rich with history was an honor as well as a test. Addressing the General Assembly from the famous green marble podium and looking up at the majestic golden dome always made me reflect on the important debates and decisions that have gone before and will come after.

New York is a world city, a global melting pot of people from every part of the globe. Unlike other places, where belonging takes generations, everyone who lives in New York is readily accepted as a New Yorker. That common identity unites.

In the same way, we representatives of our countries, the Member States of the United Nations, are unified by that common membership. We tackle common threats and problems. We have to overcome fundamental differences of approach, ideology, values, and interests along the way. But we work together to make our world more peaceful, prosperous, and secure.

The success of the United Nations rests not on its past, but its future. The UN needs to be at the heart of the problems the world faces today and tomorrow. It must adapt and reform to do so. In that regard it mirrors New York, a city that is always ready to reinvent itself. —**JONATHAN ALLEN**

Jonathan Allen is Deputy Permanent Representative of the United Kingdom to the United Nations.

25,040

Estimated number of full- and part-time jobs in New York City attributable to the presence of the UN

15,890

Number of people directly employed by the UN in New York City

1 MILLION

Average number of annual visitors to the United Nations in New York City

8,000

Number of meetings held annually at the United Nations Headquarters

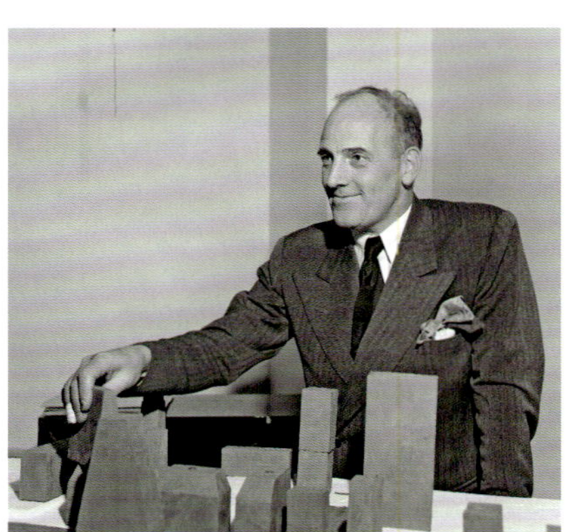

Wallace K. Harrison, Architect and Director of Planning for the United Nations Headquarters, 1948.

With the question of where to build its headquarters settled, the UN could turn to the even more important issue of *what* to build. In January 1947, UN Secretary-General Trygve Lie appointed architect Wallace K. Harrison, a confidant of the Rockefeller family from his work on Rockefeller Center, who had also collaborated with William Zeckendorf on his X City project, as the UN's Director of Planning—in essence, its chief architect. Harrison would oversee the new UN Board of Design, a team of esteemed architects from around the world. Max Abramovitz, Harrison's partner in the architecture firm Harrison & Abramovitz, was to serve as deputy director.[13] The architects represented a broad geographic range, but a unified Modernist esthetic: G.A. Soilleux of Australia, Belgian architect Gaston Brunfaut, Oscar Niemeyer of Brazil, Ernest Cormier of Canada, Liang Sicheng of China, France's Le Corbusier —the most renowned among the group—Sven Markelius of Sweden, Nikolai Bassov of the Soviet Union, Howard Robertson of the United Kingdom, and Julio Vilamajó from Uruguay.[14] To the UN, the idea of an international group of architects working together in harmony was important from a public relations perspective. Photos of the design board were part of a public information campaign "aimed at presenting the design as the unanimous product of a meeting of the minds of the world's best architects."[15]

Harrison and his colleagues were charged with designing a general assembly hall for large gatherings of delegates, a conference building including meeting halls for the Security Council, Economic and Social Council, and the Trusteeship Council, and an office building for UN Secretariat employees. Initial plans also called for additional buildings with space for diplomatic missions to the UN, agency offices, and housing for UN staff.[16]

Early in the process, Le Corbusier sketched a slender, slab-like skyscraper rising from a low horizontal volume containing the general assembly and conference functions.[17] The concept drew from the architect's provocative concept of the *Ville Radieuse* or Radiant City: urban districts composed of grids of identical glass skyscrapers rising from parkland. Later, Niemeyer sketched a breakthrough scheme that built on Le Corbusier's design, but with the General Assembly, Secretariat, and Conference Building as separate structures. George Dudley, an architect at Harrison's firm, described how this new direction captured the team's imagination: "In Niemeyer's refreshing scheme the site was open, a grand space with a clean base for the modest masses standing in it," as compared to Le Corbusier's "intersecting spaces in [a] unitary block." Harrison supported this new concept, announcing to the board, "I conclude the only scheme that gets complete satisfaction is an early idea of Le Corbusier, as carried out, drawn up, by Oscar Niemeyer. This seems like a good compromise to me."[18] So it was that the Board of Design proceeded with an assertively modern campus.

The final design embraced the International Style esthetic, with bold, dramatically scaled forms. Such architectural language was deemed suitably optimistic and forward-looking for a global institution founded on the promise of peace, not to mention free of classical forms that might be associated with Western colonialism. (However, Harrison did add a shallow dome to the General Assembly Hall when advised that the U.S. Congress might be more likely to authorize an interest-free loan to finance construction of the campus with such a traditional nod.[19]) Towering above the low-slung volumes of the General Assembly and Conference Building, the Secretariat would rise 550 feet, or 39 stories, clad on its broad east and west sides with green-tinted glass and 2,000 tons of Vermont marble on its shorter north and south facades. It was the first building in New York to be constructed with an all-glass curtain wall, and it heralded a trend that would come to dominate the city's skyscrapers in the coming decades.

The design was approved by the General Assembly in the summer of 1947, after trimming some $20 million from the initial $84 million building estimate, mostly by reducing the height of the Secretariat from 45 to 39 stories. Construction was financed by an interest-free loan of $65 million from the United States Government (more than $775 million in today's currency). Clearing of dozens of tenements and slaughterhouses on site began shortly after approval of the architectural design, with dignitaries including New York City Mayor William O'Dwyer taking sledgehammers to bricks in front of official photographers. Only one existing building was left on the UN site: the offices of the New York City Housing Authority, which would serve as offices for UN workers and the UN library until its demolition in 1960. In its place, Harrison designed the fourth major campus building, the marble and glass Dag Hammarskjöld Library, which was financed with a $6.2 million grant from the Ford Foundation.[20] The library opened in 1961.

Official groundbreaking on the new campus took place on September 14, 1948. At a dedication ceremony that was part of a special open-air meeting of the General Assembly on October 24, 1949—a date henceforth celebrated internationally as United Nations Day—Harrison and Secretary-General Lie sealed a metal box into the cornerstone of the Secretariat Building, inside which were copies of the UN Charter and its Universal Declaration of Human Rights. Among the 16,000 diplomats, dignitaries, and guests were Mayor O'Dwyer and U.S. President Harry S. Truman.[21] Harrison and Lie formally announced the completion of the United Nations Headquarters on October 9, 1952. Several days later, the General Assembly welcomed delegates from its then 60 member nations—the first of countless important global meetings to be held beneath the silvery dome of the UN's home.

Architectural planning of United Nations Headquarters. Members of the Board of Design and consultants appointed to assist them pictured before preliminary models. In the foreground, from left to right: Liang Sicheng, China; Oscar Niemeyer, Brazil; Nikolai Bassov, Soviet Union; and Ernest Cormier, Canada. In second row, from left to right: Sven Markelius, Sweden; Le Corbusier, France; Vladimir Bodiansky, France; Wallace K. Harrison, United States; G.A. Soilleux, Australia; Max Abramovitz, United States; Ernest Weissmann, Yugoslavia; John Antoniades, Greece; and Matthew Nowicki, Poland. RKO Building. April 18, 1947.

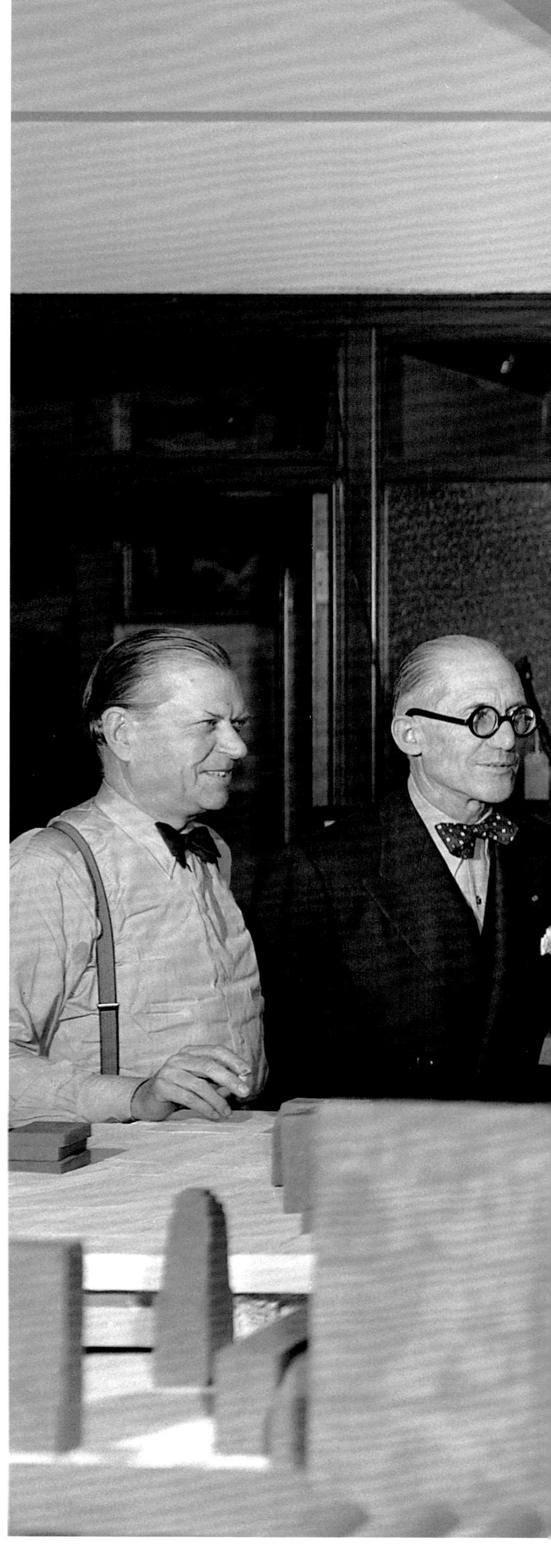

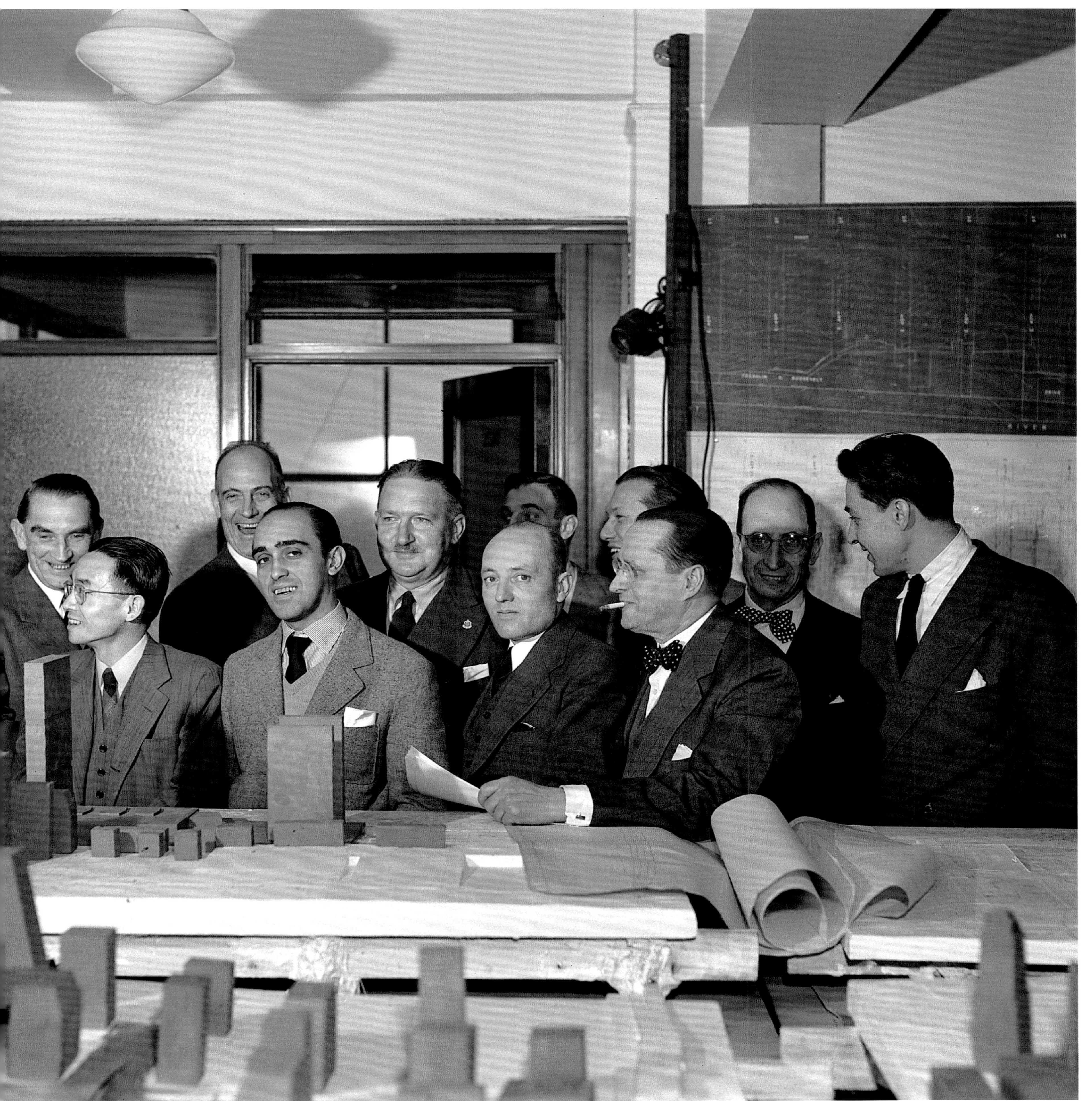

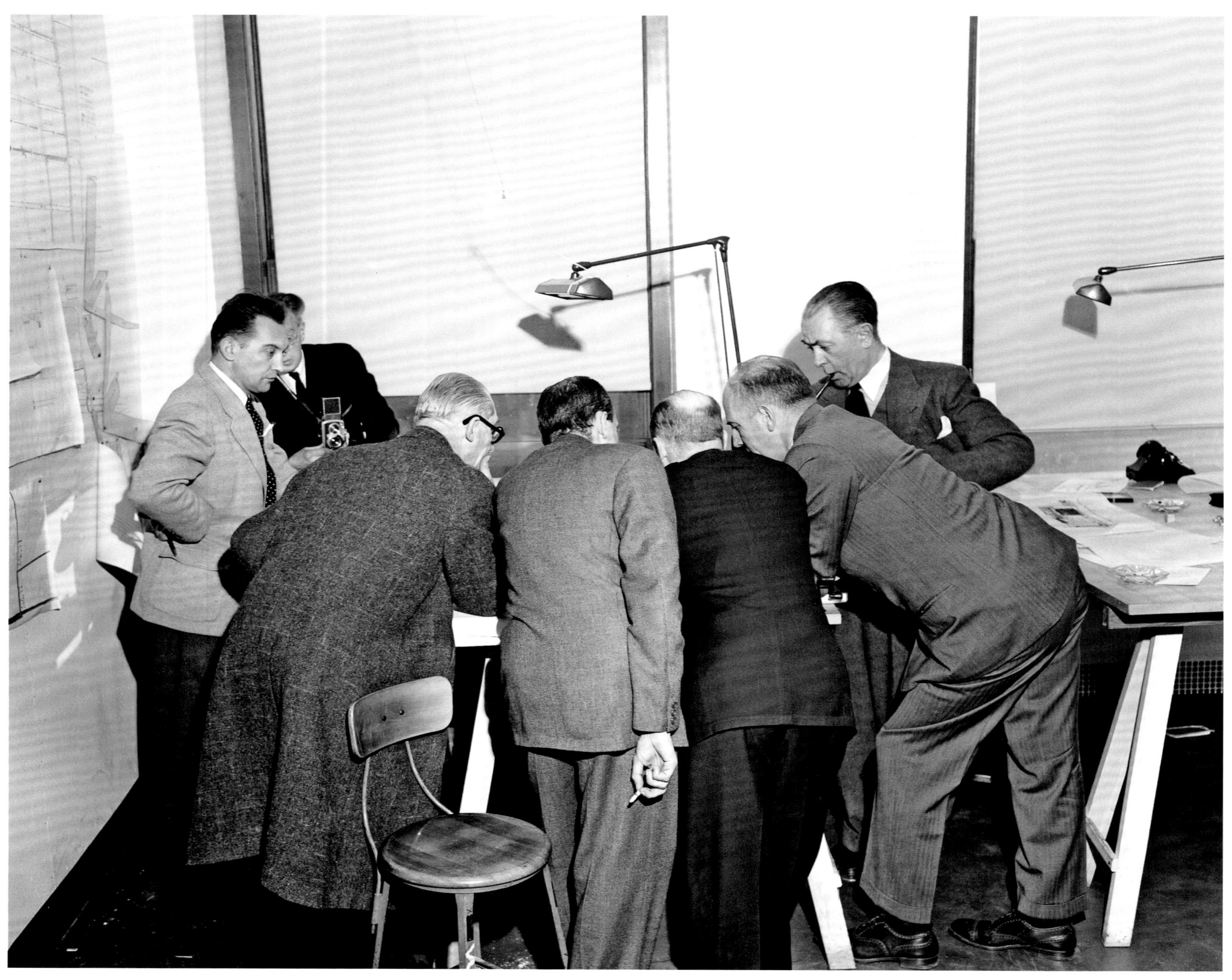

Architects from the United Nations Board of Design huddle during a press conference, 1947.

Meeting of the Board of Design, 1947.

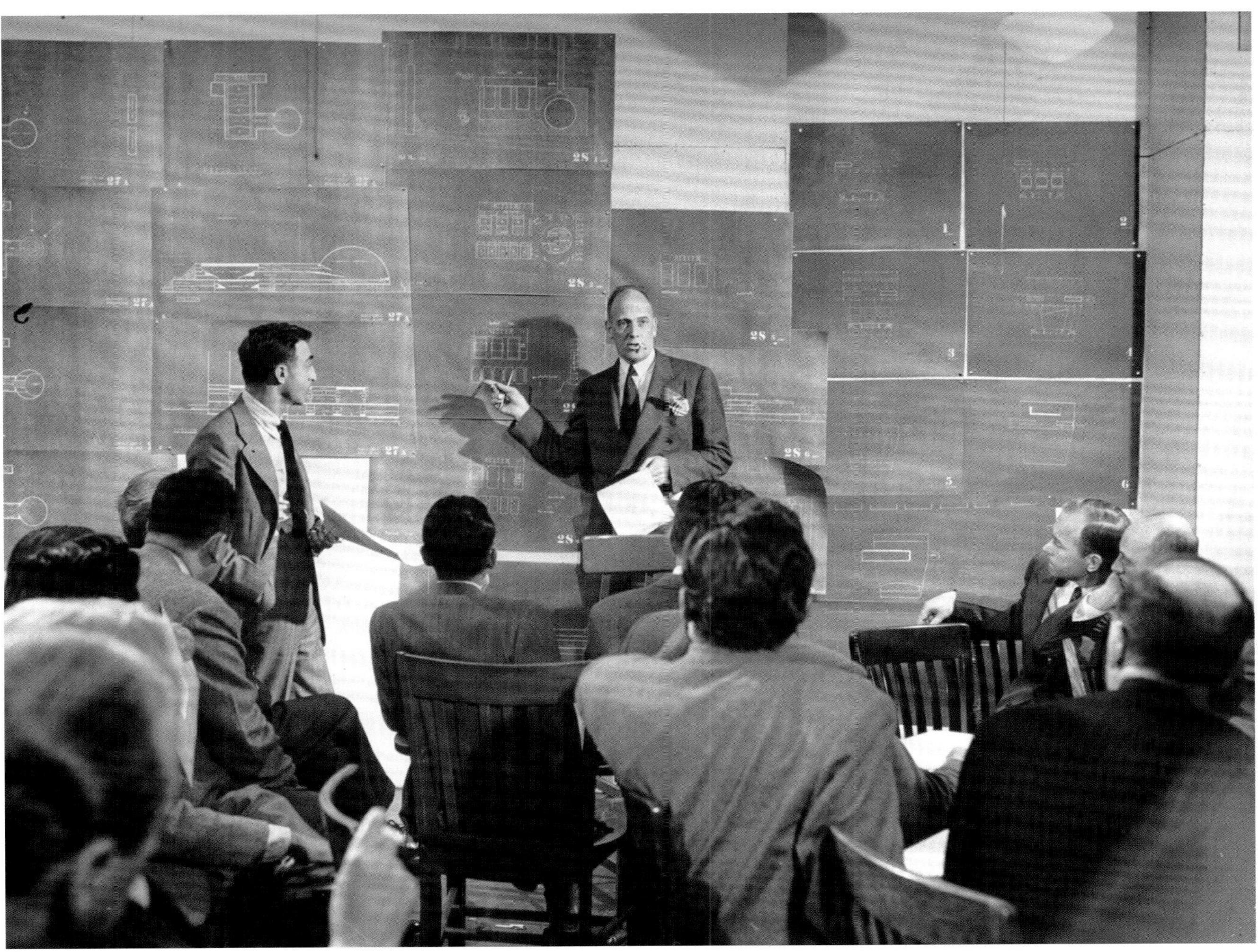

Belva Barnes, the only female architect on the staff of the United Nations Headquarters Planning Office, drawing preliminary plans of one of the architectural concepts, 1947.

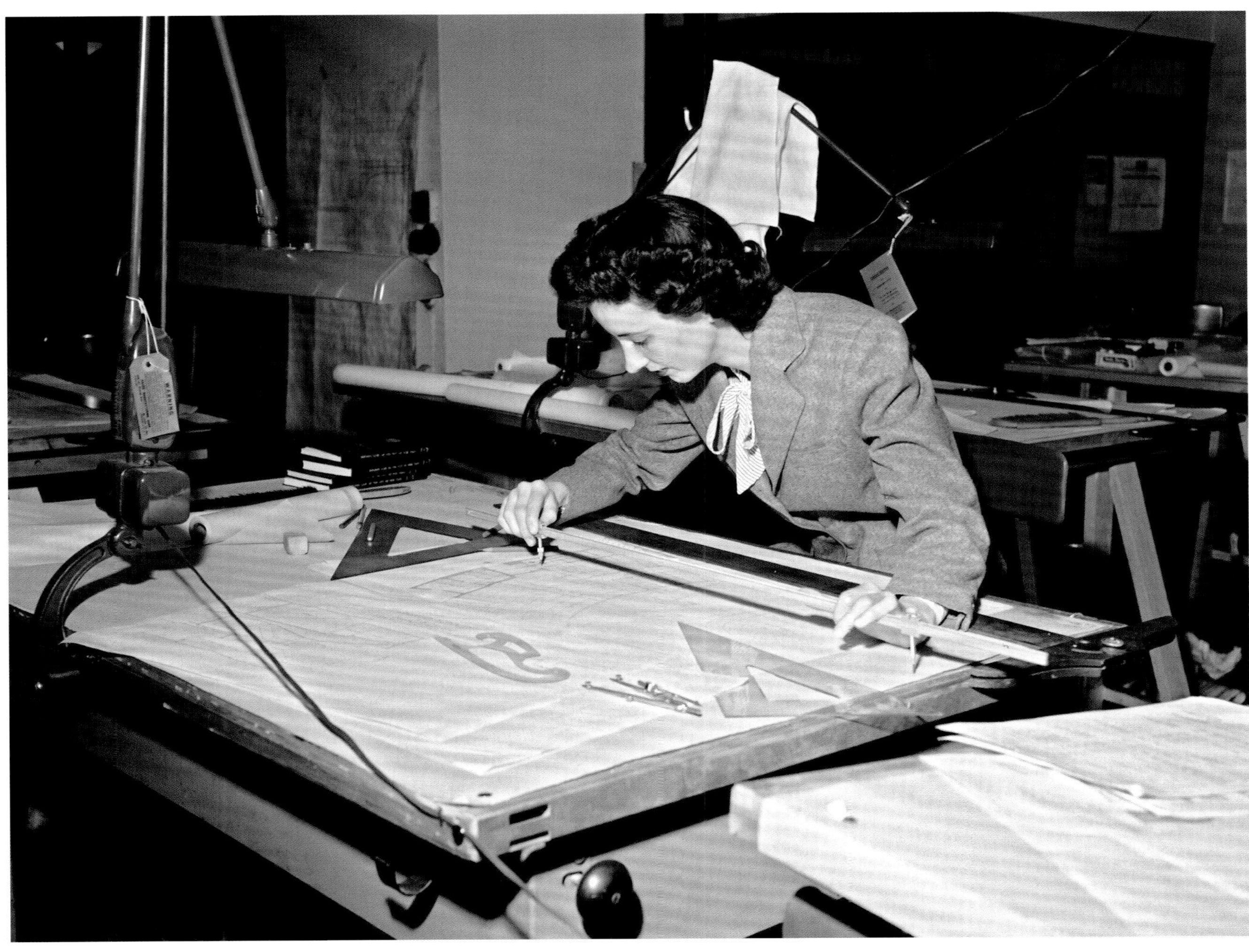

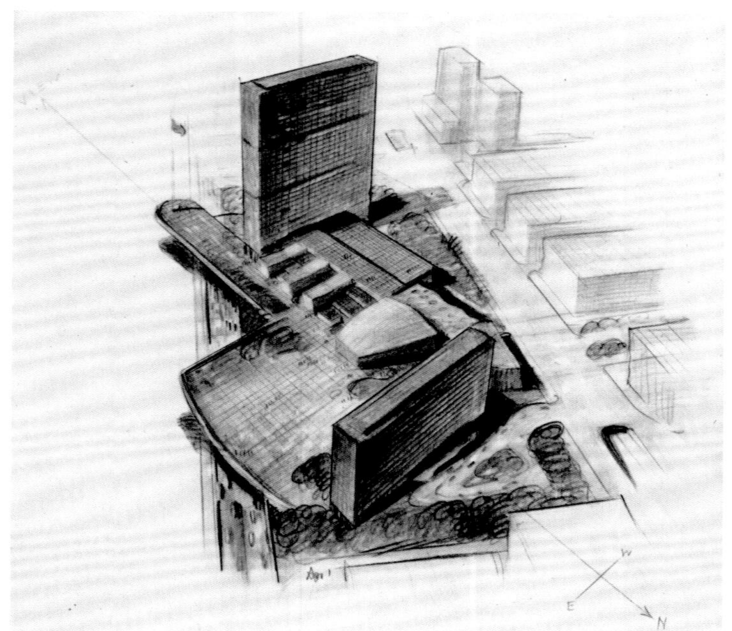

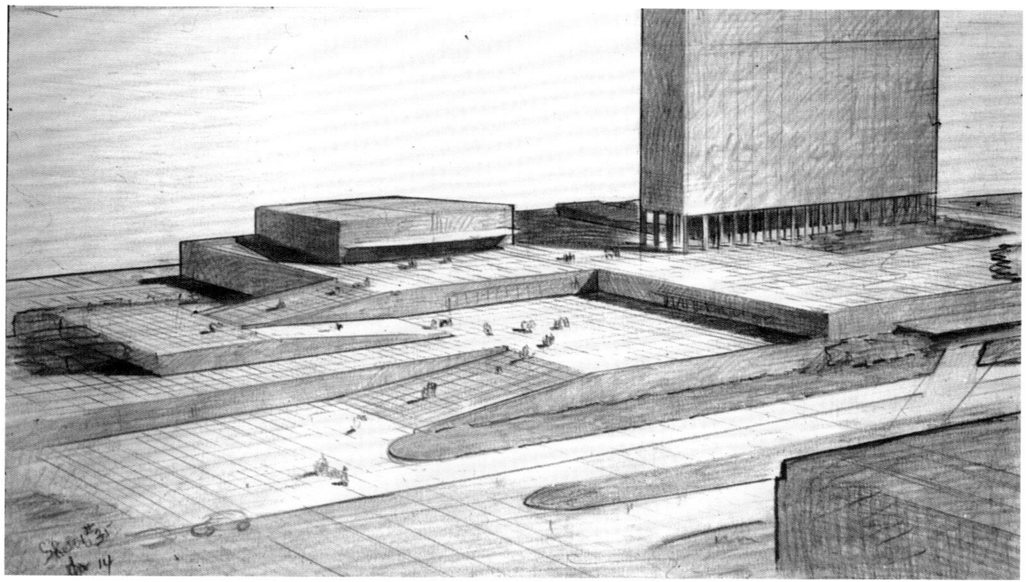

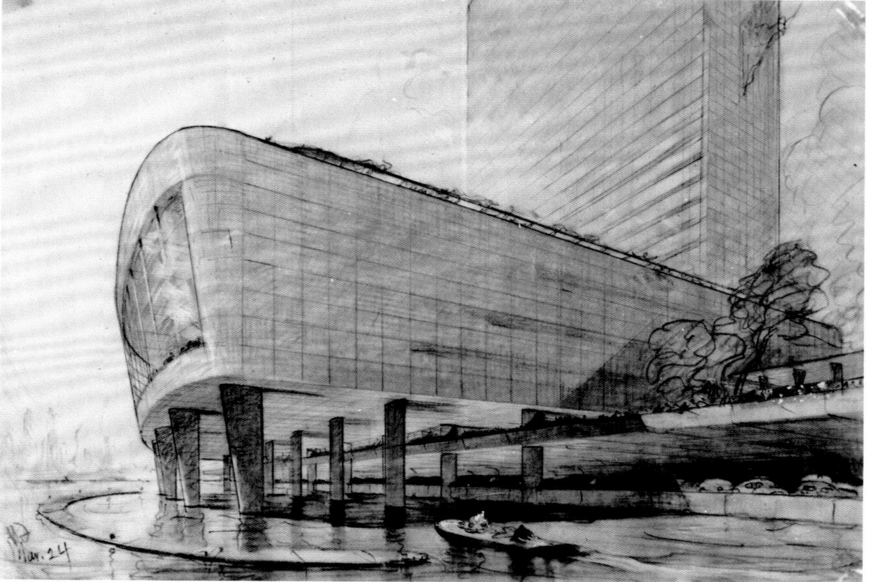

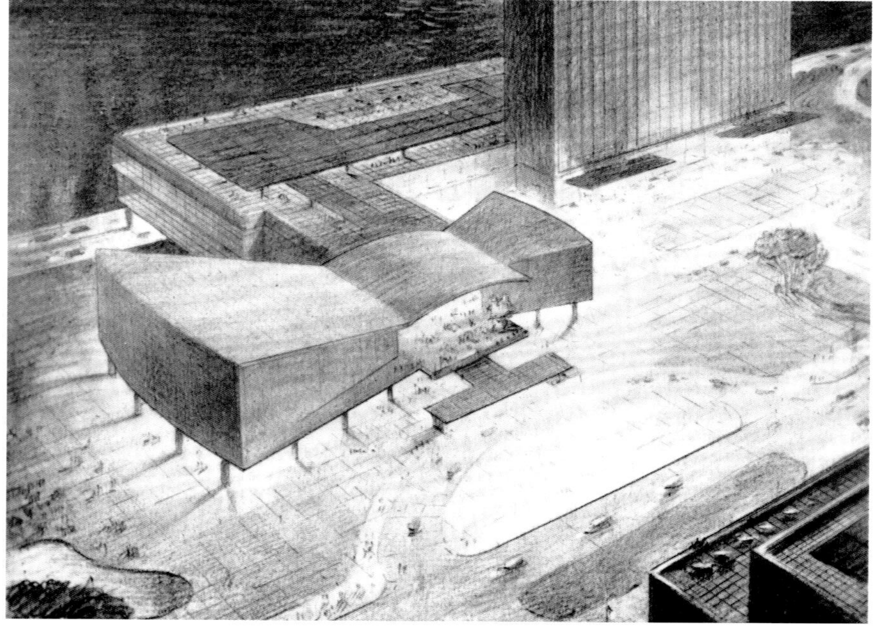

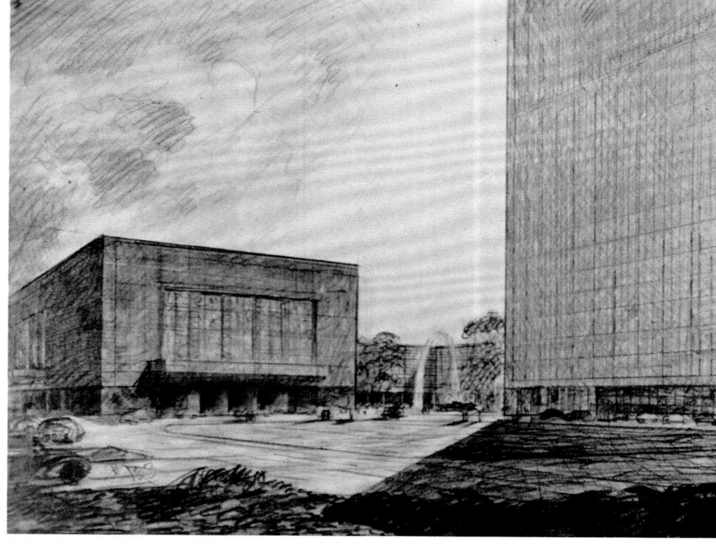

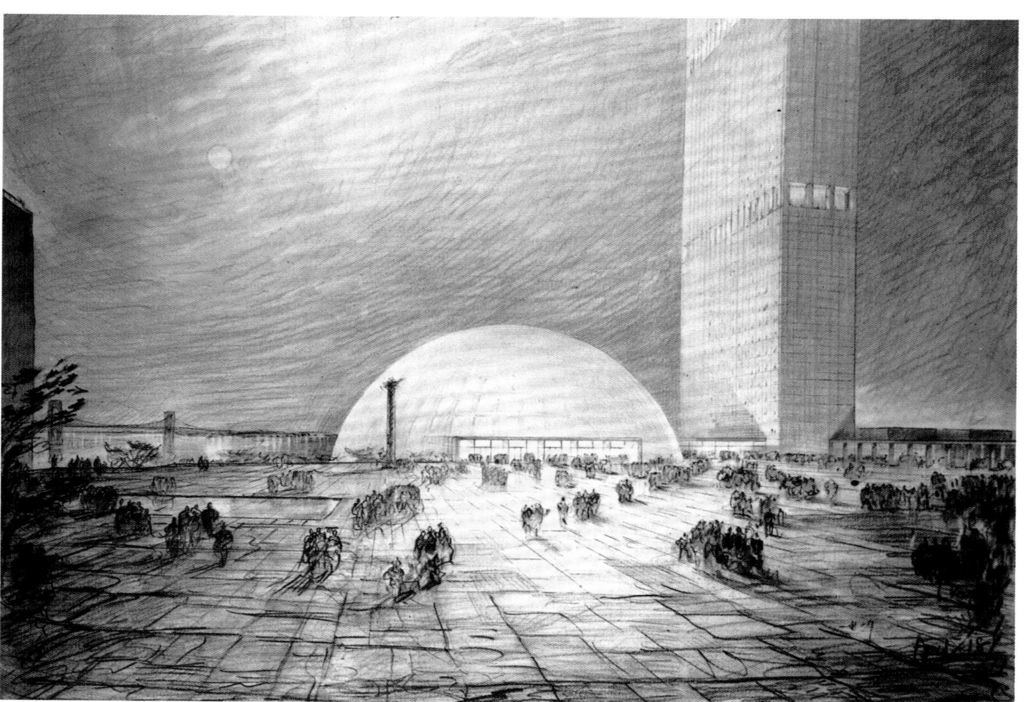

Hugh Ferriss renderings of various schemes by esteemed architects from the UN Board of Design.

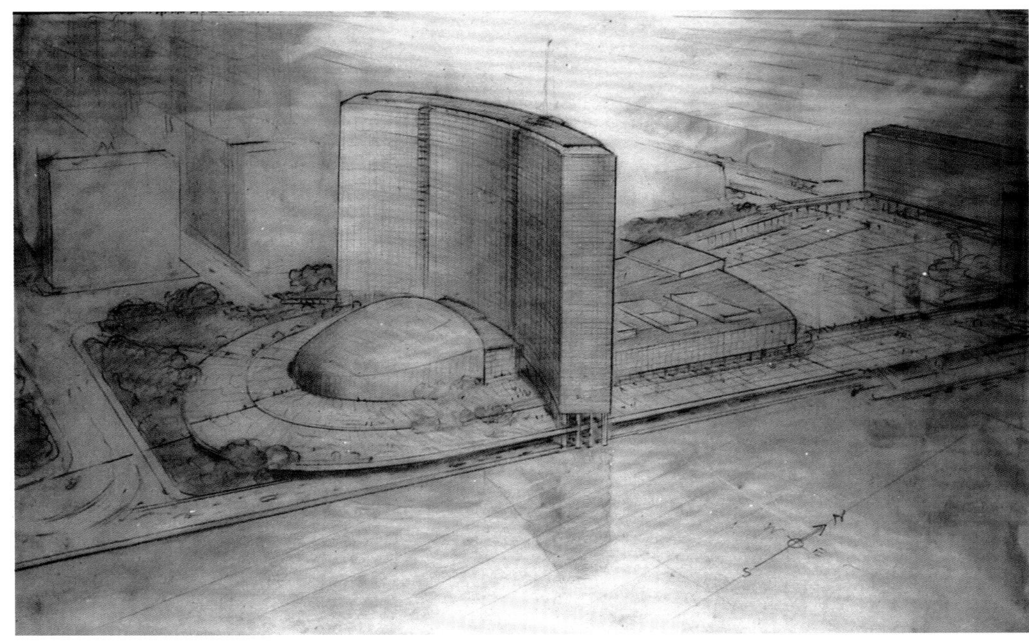

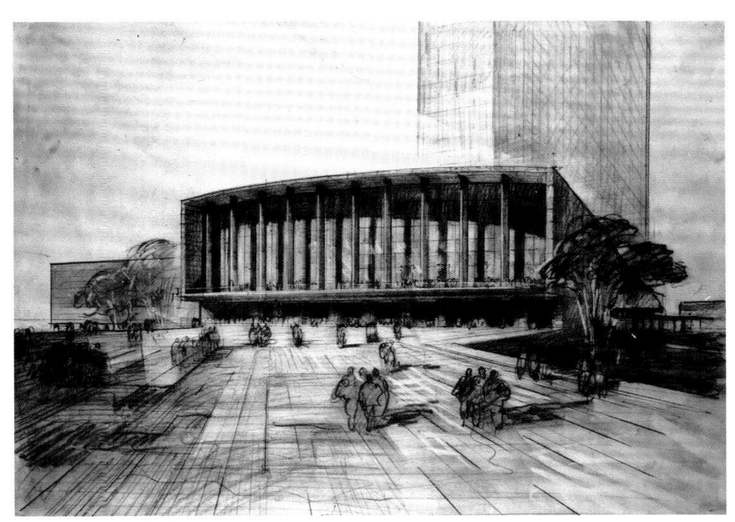

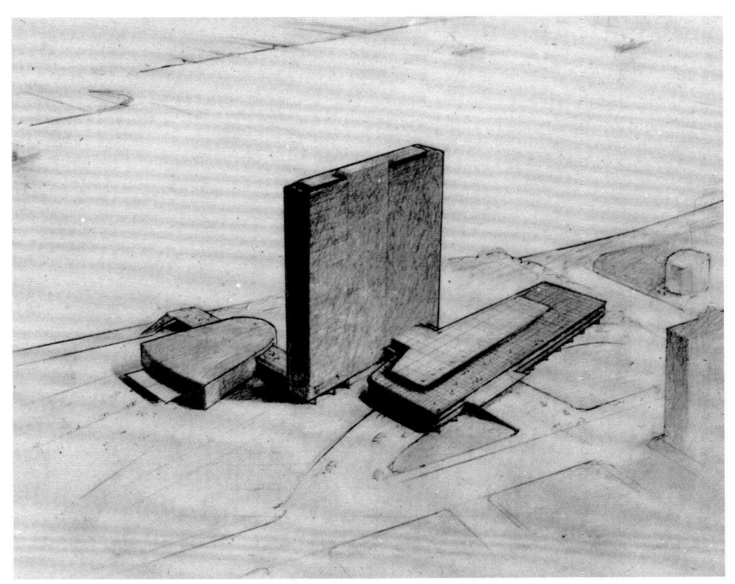

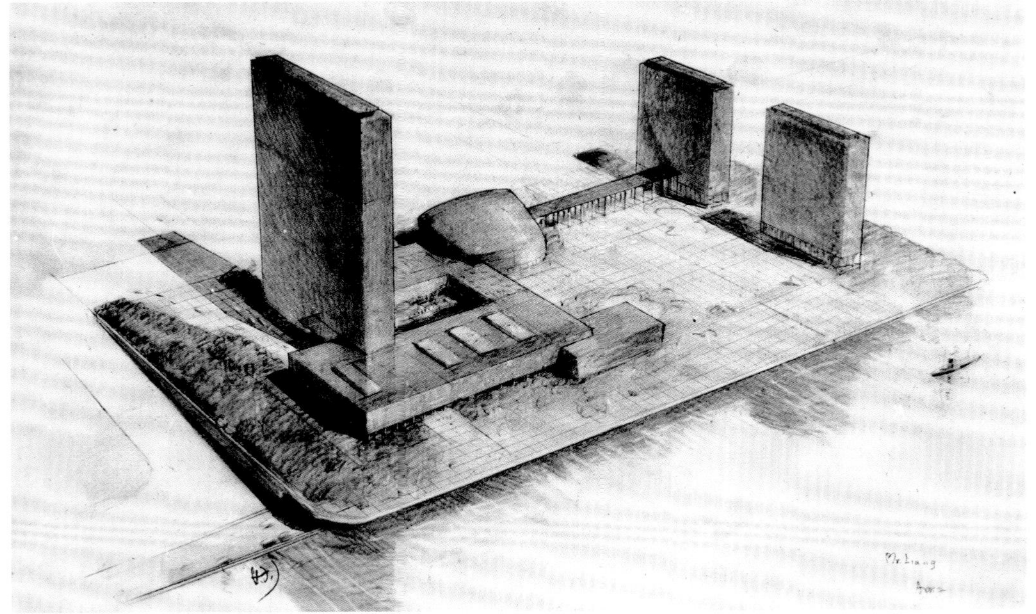

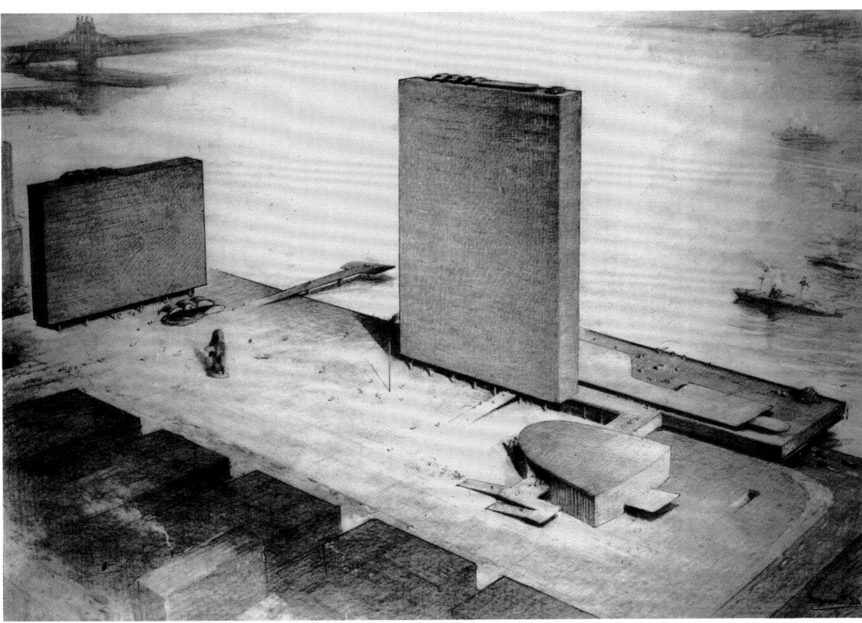

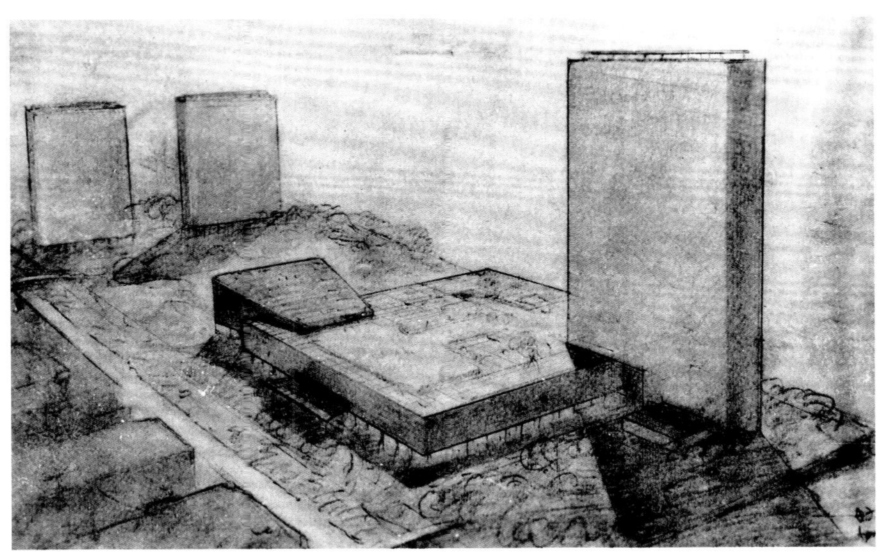

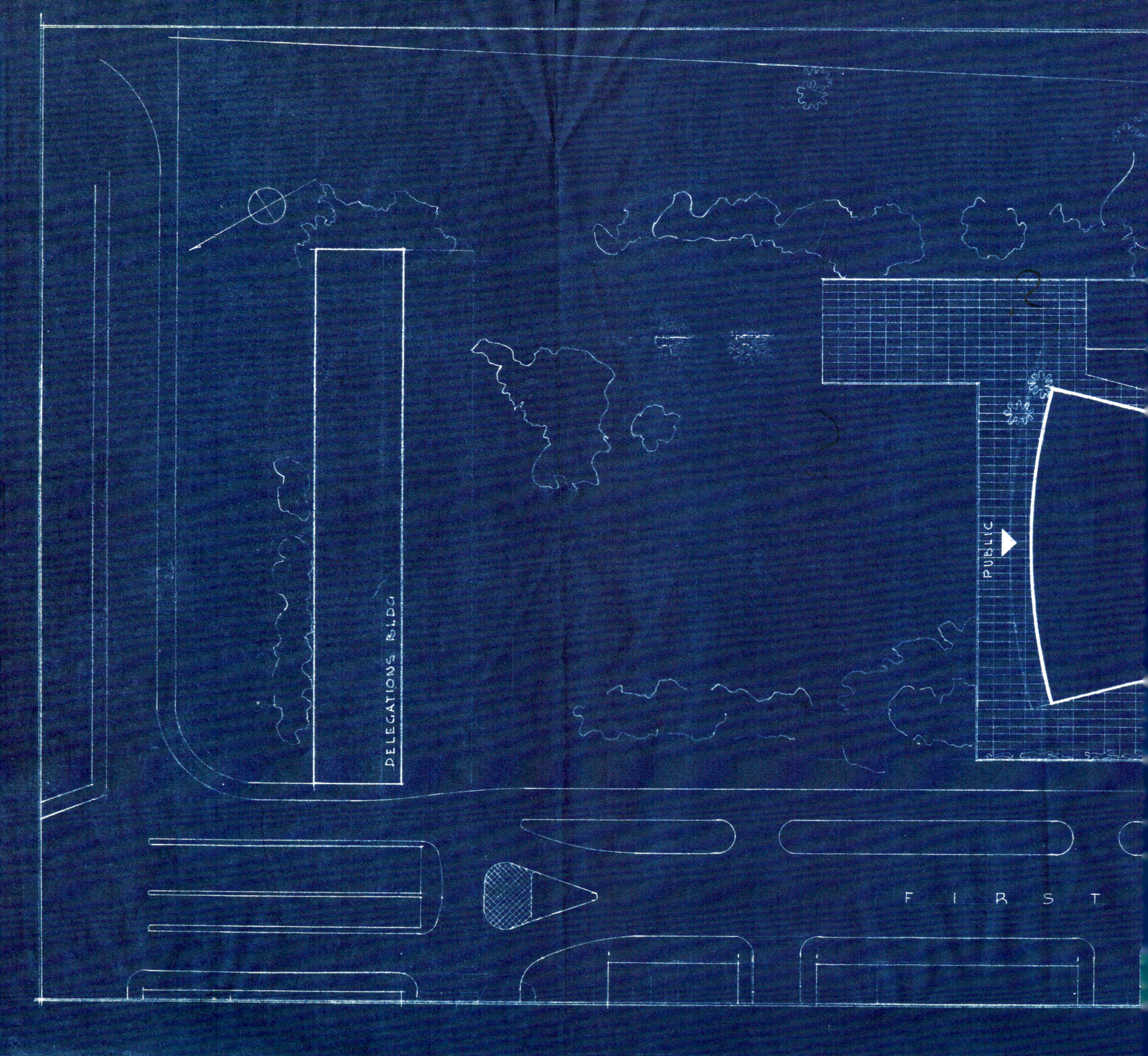

Blueprint of UN
Headquarters, 1948.

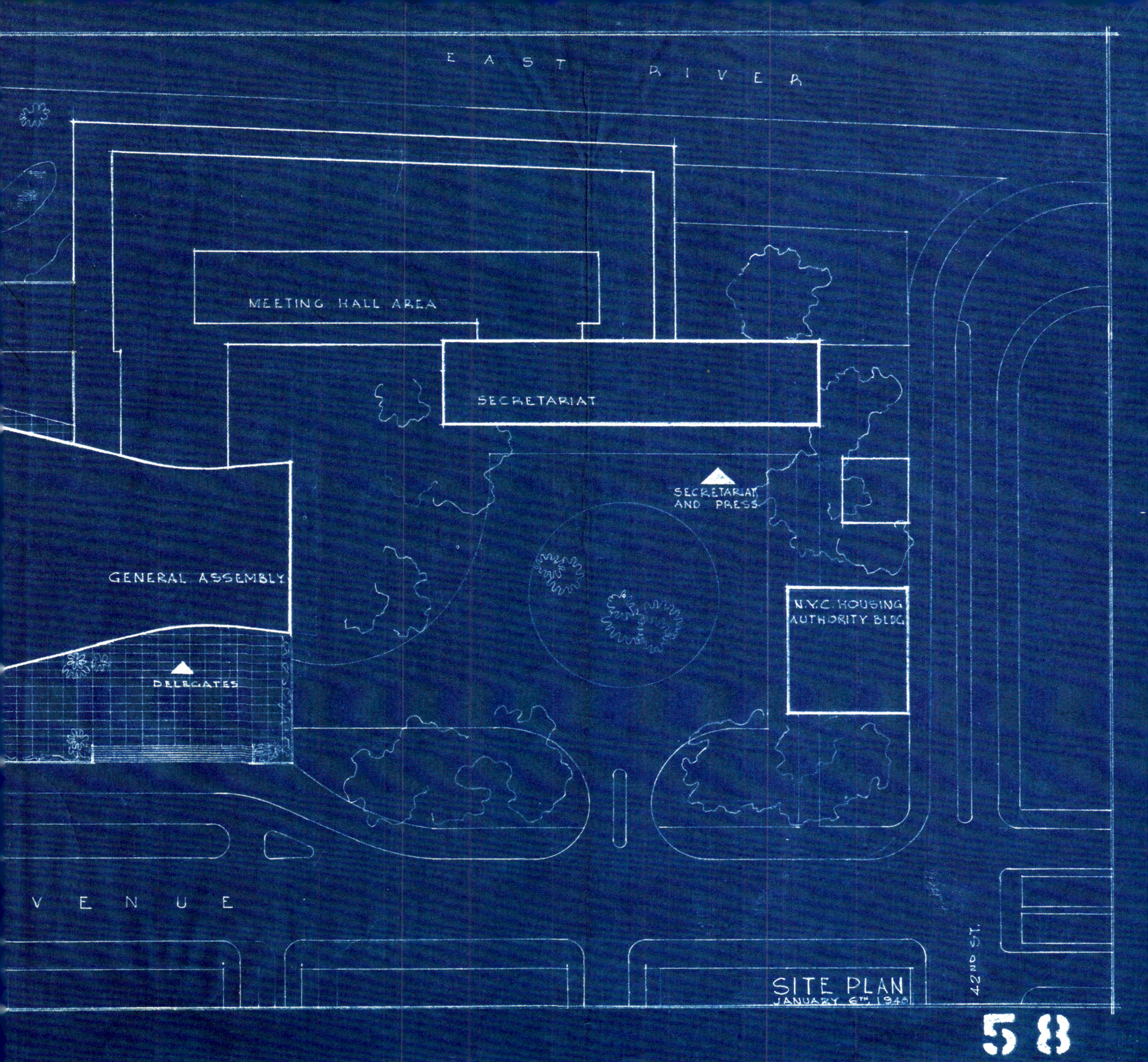
E A S T R I V E R
MEETING HALL AREA
SECRETARIAT
SECRETARIAT AND PRESS
GENERAL ASSEMBLY
N.Y.C. HOUSING AUTHORITY BLDG.
DELEGATES
V E N U E
SITE PLAN
JANUARY 6TH, 1948
42ND ST.
58

The Architecture of the United Nations

By Paul Goldberger

The United Nations is at once deeply woven into the fabric of New York, and a place apart. It was the hope of the original architects, an international team of distinguished practitioners that included Le Corbusier and Oscar Niemeyer, that the architecture of the UN buildings would integrate the dynamism of New York—unquestionably the preeminent city of the second half of the 20th century—and the aspirations of modern architecture, something that New York, for all its cultural energy, had been hesitant to embrace. And while arriving at a final design for the United Nations complex proved contentious, what finally emerged unquestionably became the architectural symbol of a new age that New York had been lacking.

The Secretariat Building was New York's first glass skyscraper, a sign to the city and to the rest of the United States that the United Nations aspired to look forward, not backward. It stood alone beside the East River, surrounded by open space, a site that itself was enough to distinguish it from every other tower in Manhattan, where skyscrapers jostle each other along crowded city blocks. The Secretariat made its mark not through height—even when it was new, it was not among the New York's very tallest buildings—but by the sense of openness and transparency that its glass walls offered to a city in which even the highest towers were built of solid masonry and topped by ornate crowns. The United Nations offered a different model: a long, elegant slab with glass walls, marble sides, and a flat top. If the prominence of the Secretariat did suggest that the administrative bureaucracy was now the most important part of government, as the critic Lewis Mumford pointed out when he observed that the Secretariat, not the domed General Assembly Building, was the landmark on the skyline, its design pointed with equal certainty to a new and more enlightened form of that bureaucracy. And the other wings of the

Paul Goldberger is a Pulitzer Prize-winning architecture critic and author.

United Nations complex, the lyrically curving General Assembly Building and the handsome, low-slung Conference Building, showed the possibility that modern architecture could present New York with images of stability, dignity, and grandeur.

It did not appear so positive to Le Corbusier, the French-Swiss architect whose studies formed much of the basis of the original design and who complained bitterly that compromises had been forced on the plan by his colleagues who worked under the guidance of Wallace K. Harrison, the New York architect who served as the overall coordinator of the design committee. Not the least of Le Corbusier's complaints was that Harrison had rejected his proposal for *brise-soleil*, or concrete grills on the west side of the tower to reduce the impact of the intense summer afternoon sun. Harrison preferred the purity of unobstructed glass, and that the east and west sides of the tower be identical, whatever the implications in terms of air conditioning. (Le Corbusier's recommendation would have been far more prudent in terms of energy use.) Still, the final design of the overall complex owes more to Le Corbusier's early proposal than to any other source, and the architecture also shows the not inconsiderable influence of Oscar Niemeyer, the Brazilian who would become, after Le Corbusier, the most famous of the international committee of architects who constituted the United Nations Board of Design.

If the political squabbles among the architects from different countries seemed to mirror the challenges their governments were facing as they also tried to find common ground, the architects did, in the end, reach consensus, negotiated by Harrison, whose diplomatic and political skills made him, in effect, the architectural equivalent of the Secretary-General. Harrison was both a committed modernist and a confirmed pragmatist, without any of the ideological baggage that weighed down many of his colleagues. And unlike Le Corbusier, he had little pride of authorship; to him, it was more important that the United Nations design reflect the creative ideas of the entire Board of Design, which also included Matthew Nowicki of Poland, Sven Markelius of Sweden, Ernest Weissmann of Yugoslavia, G. A. Seilleux of Australia, Ernest Cormier of Canada, Nikolai Bassov of the Soviet Union, Liang Sicheng of China, Vladimir Bodiansky of France, and Harrison's colleague Max Abramovitz.

It was a large and unwieldy group, and 75 years later, it is difficult not to be amazed that it produced a coherent, let alone a distinguished, result. The United Nations complex quickly became one of the city's most recognizable pieces of architecture, its unapologetic modernism an implicit rejection of New York's own history of eclecticism, not to mention conservatism, in architectural taste. The UN buildings would have been noticed under any circumstances, but their unusual open site made them even more conspicuous. While Le Corbusier, ever the contrarian, thought that the UN had been too tightly squeezed between the Manhattan grid and the East River, putting the buildings too close to the rest of the city, by New York standards the 18-acre site between First Avenue and the river was almost rural. It was a campus, albeit a small one, and thus in stark contrast to every other building site in midtown Manhattan.

The site, once a slaughterhouse, had been assembled by the developer William Zeckendorf, who sold it to John D. Rockefeller, Jr., who made it a gift to the United Nations. The Rockefeller gift clinched the decision to locate the headquarters in New York. By the end of World War II midtown Manhattan was heavily built up, and this riverfront site offered the only opportunity for the UN to be close to the heart of the city. Not everyone shared Rockefeller's belief that the United Nations should have an intimate relationship to the city; Le Corbusier was known to favor a suburban site, and many diplomats did as well, questioning whether the almost relentlessness density of New York, a strength from a commercial and cultural standpoint, made sense for a home for international diplomacy.

From the beginning, the city tried to accommodate, albeit modestly, with the desire to have the United Nations stand apart from the rest of Manhattan, even as the UN also tried to connect itself closely to the city. First Avenue, renamed United Nations Plaza for the blocks around the UN, was converted into a tunnel for several blocks so that through traffic would not clog the main artery in front of the complex; 47th Street was widened to allow a more generous approach, although compromised by being off the main axis with no view of the UN; and an elegant, small plaza was created on the east side of First Avenue to acknowledge the United Nations across the street. New York, built on a tight and continuous grid, was not a city of wide-open, Beaux-Arts style vistas, so these small planning gestures had little impact on the city at large. But they opened up the area around the UN slightly, and they underscored the idea that the addition of the United Nations to the Manhattan skyline was something more than the coming of a new skyscraper: it was a whole new kind of architecture for New York, on a whole new campus that the entire world would see.

For the first two decades after the completion of the United Nations, its neighborhood was relatively quiet, at least by New York standards, and there was a certain aura of tranquility to the complex on the east side of First Avenue, enhanced, perhaps, by the fact that the generous amount of open space around the UN meant that more sky was visible there than almost anywhere else in midtown Manhattan. By the late 1960s, however, change began to come, first in the form of a pair of glass apartment towers by Harrison & Abramovitz to the north of the UN campus, completed in 1966, which the architects, conscious of their legacy as UN planners, designed in a Miesian style to complement the Secretariat and the other buildings of the campus. Not long afterwards, it became clear that the United Nations itself had outgrown the original complex, and that additional office space would be needed. In 1968, New York State formed the United Nations Development

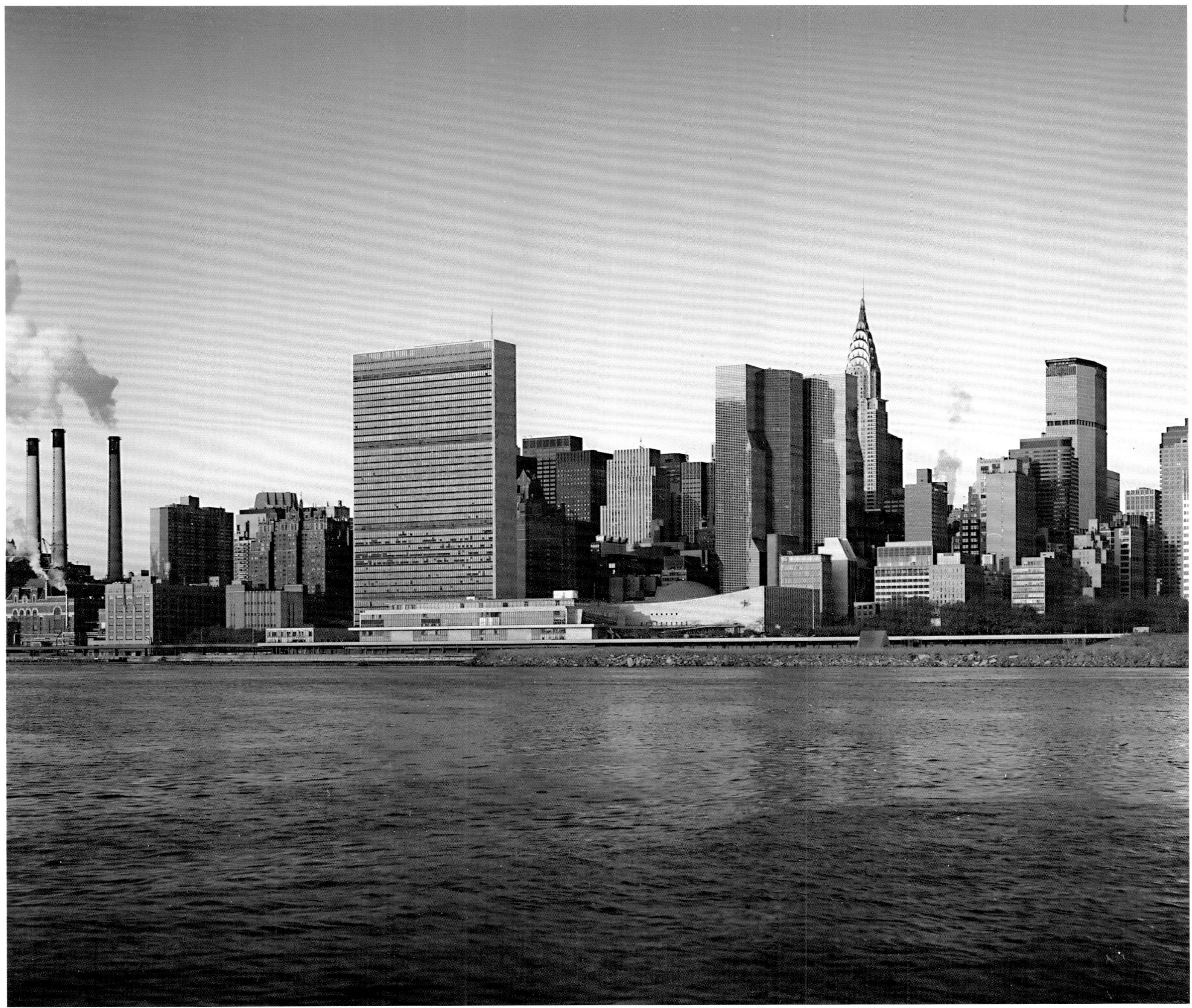

The United Nations complex.

Corporation, a public benefit corporation empowered to assist the UN by developing and operating real estate for its use in the blocks surrounding the complex. Between 1976 and 1987 the UNDC would develop three significant new buildings, named One, Two, and Three United Nations Plaza, just to the west of the United Nations, each of which would have a significant impact on the overall neighborhood.

All three of the UNDC buildings were located on East 44th Street, just across First Avenue from the United Nations complex, and they posed an unusual architectural challenge. None of the UNDC buildings was sited in open space, like the United Nations itself; they were New York City buildings on New York City streets, and yet they somehow had to distinguish themselves as different from typical commercial buildings and make clear in some way that they related to the United Nations even as they also fit into the Manhattan cityscape.

The UNDC hired Kevin Roche to do the first building, One United Nations Plaza, which was completed in 1976. Roche, an inventive modernist who at that point in his career was inclined toward abstract sculptural forms in glass, made the wise decision to create a glass tower that would allude to the Secretariat Building by loosely echoing the bluish-green color of its glass, but would be quite different in shape. Roche produced a tower that was bulkier than the thin Secretariat slab and was covered entirely by reflective glass, set in a grid pattern that was a pure abstraction, hiding both the floor levels and the window locations behind it. In his determination to make his building read as a minimalist, abstract object, Roche made a radical break with the conventions of skyscraper design. But he was not at all indifferent to his building's surroundings—the new tower's shape, as well as the color of its glass, played off the slab of the Secretariat, and invited the original United Nations into a larger urban conversation. Its refined facade paid homage to the Secretariat and offered something breathtakingly new at the same time.

The 34-story building contained a mix of offices and a much-needed hotel managed by the Hyatt Corporation, for which Roche designed interior public spaces with mirrored ceilings that would eventually win the rare status of being named interior landmarks by the New York City Landmarks Preservation Commission. In 1984, Roche completed a companion building, Two United Nations Plaza, a tower immediately to the west of the 1976 building, which he designed to adjoin the first building and which he wrapped in an identical glass facade, turning both buildings, in effect, into a larger version of his original minimalist composition. And then in 1987 Roche completed the third building, Three United Nations Plaza across the street, a headquarters for UNICEF.

This site was in the middle of the block, and the program called for a 15-story tower, so it would not have the conspicuous presence on the skyline that the combination of One and Two United Nations Plaza did. For the third building, then—perhaps motivated by the rising tide of post-modernism in architectural fashion, but more likely by his instinctive sense of how to deal with the complicated demands of difficult urban sites—Roche produced a more ornate building of granite. He gave Three UN Plaza a row of columns at its base, rectangular windows in the middle, and a mansard roof at the top, realizing that the challenge here was to blend into the streetscape, not to stand apart from it. But Roche also understood that where One UN Plaza provided a lively foil to the original United Nations complex and Two UN Plaza intensified the urban dialogue, it would have been excessive to have given the third building the same glass facade as its older siblings; this ran the risk of creating a critical mass of abstract glass structures that could have rivaled the pre-eminence of the original United Nations complex. By giving the third building a different identity, Roche allowed it to recede into the larger Manhattan cityscape.

And that, of course, has been the question all along—how much should the architecture of the United Nations stand apart, and how much should it connect to the rest of Manhattan? In the years that followed the completion of the three United Nations Development Corporation buildings, numerous other structures have been built, including tall apartment towers by Foster + Partners and Costas Kondylis, and most have attempted to continue the modernist tone set by the original United Nations, but few have shown either the inventiveness or the ability to relate to the architecture of the UN itself that Roche demonstrated in his buildings. In 2010, the United States Mission to the United Nations, designed by Gwathmey Siegel, represented one of the most ambitious attempts to keep the level of architecture in the United Nations neighborhood high: a narrow, concrete-clad tower that aspired to dignity, its design was heavily dictated by security concerns, and its appearance is more industrial than monumental.

In the end, it is the United Nations complex itself that still presides over this part of New York City, as it should. It is now more tightly surrounded by other buildings than it once was, and of the newcomers, only One and Two United Nations Plaza truly succeed at engaging the original United Nations in a larger architectural discourse. But the United Nations remains, unique and historic: a skyscraper on a campus, and a place at once monumental and open, a place that demonstrates all of the hope that modern architecture embodied in the middle of the 20th century.

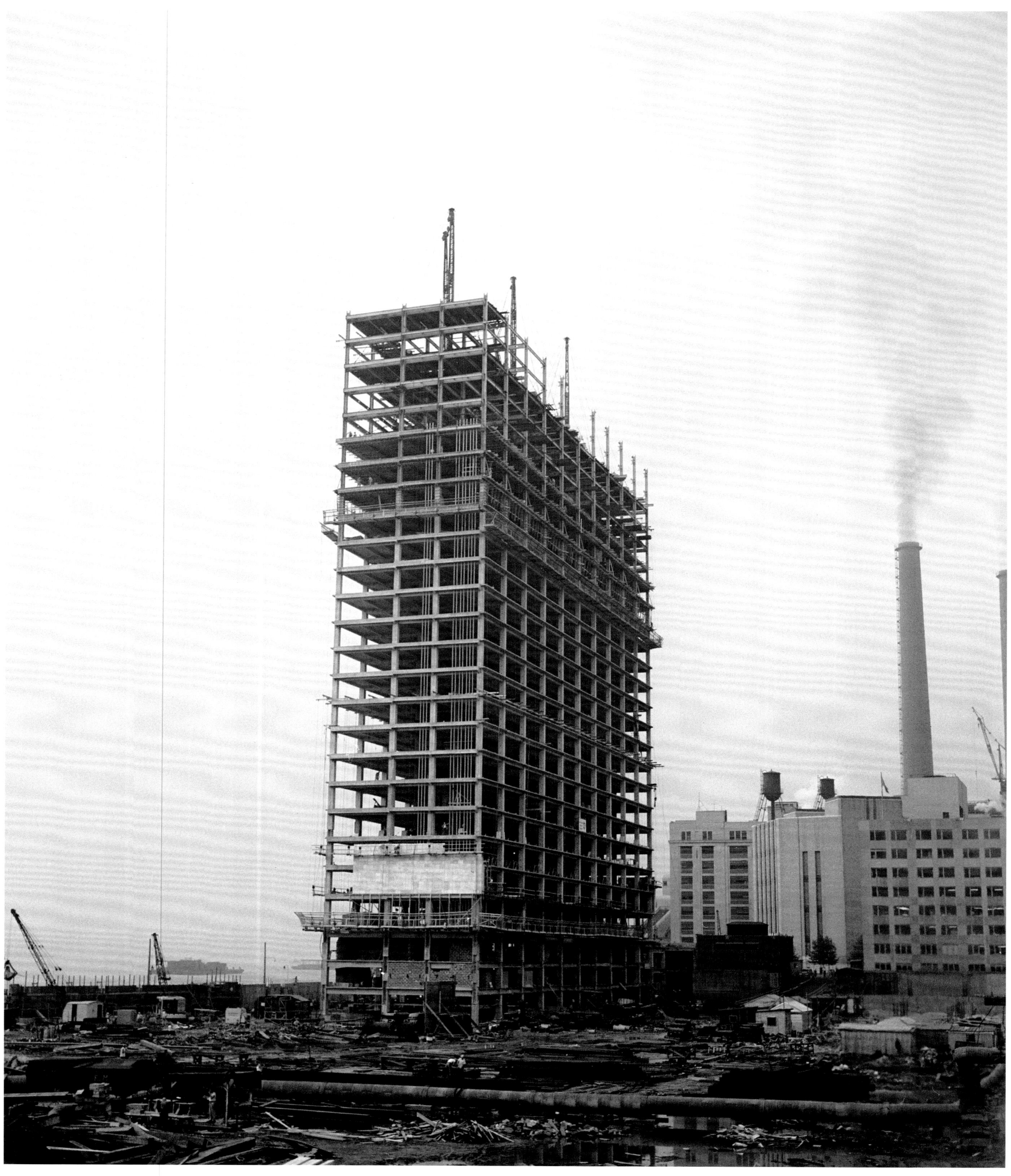

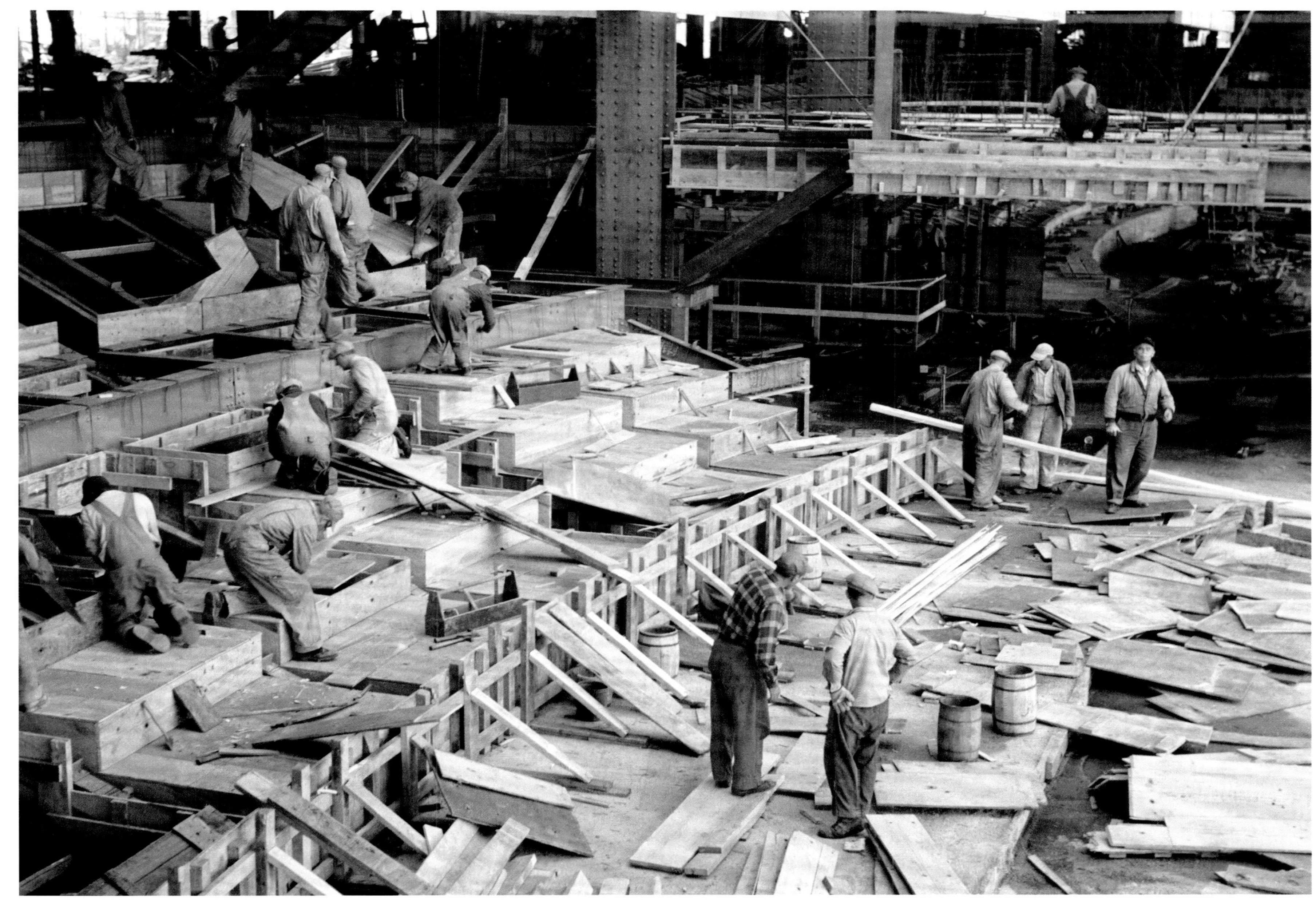

Construction proceeds rapidly in the meeting hall area, 1951.

Steelwork on 24 of the 39 stories of the United Nations Secretariat Building. August 8, 1949.

Construction worker labors on the Secretariat Building with Midtown Manhattan in the background, January 1949.

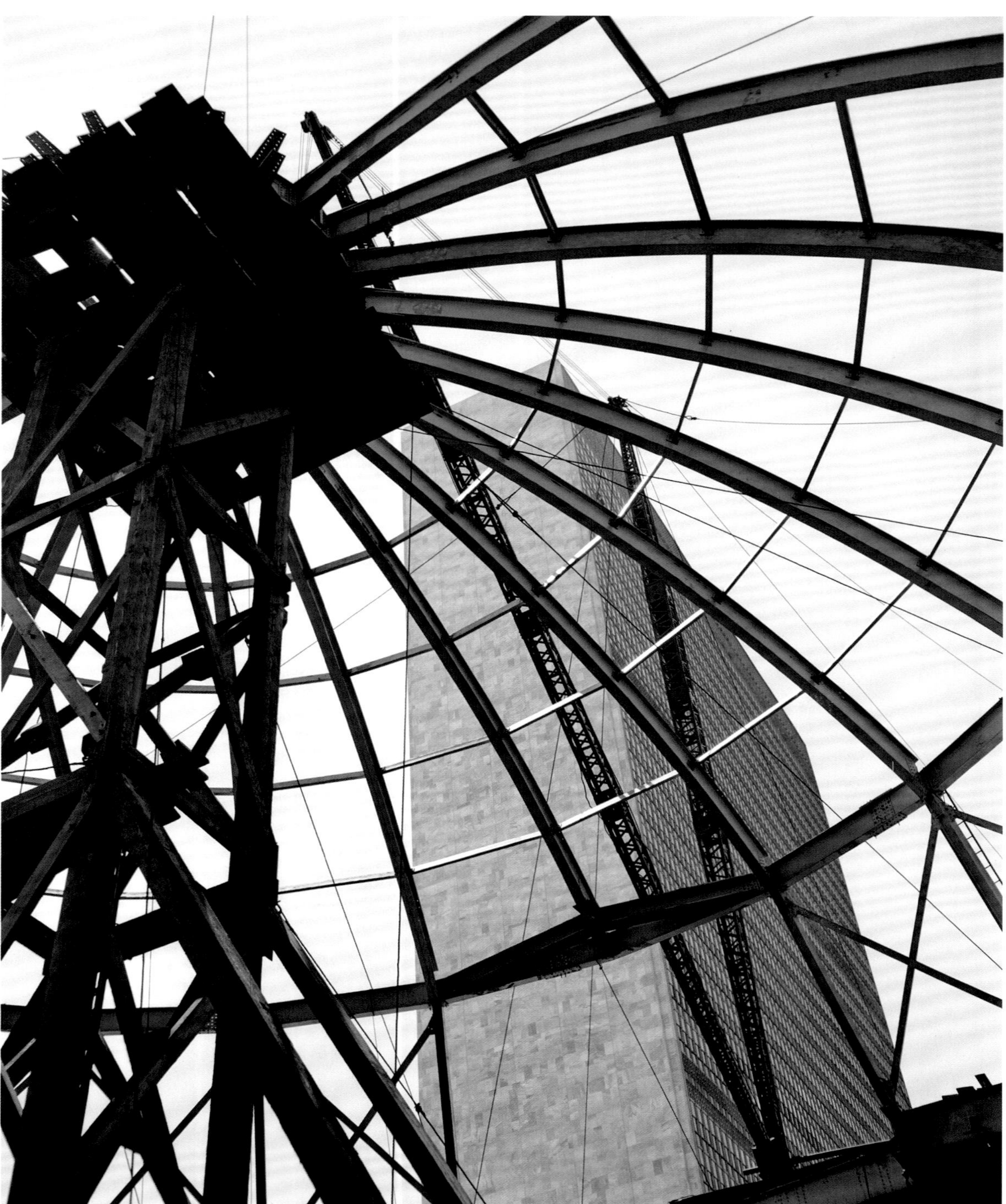

Secretariat Building as seen through the still-unfinished steel structure of the General Assembly Hall dome. August 23, 1951.

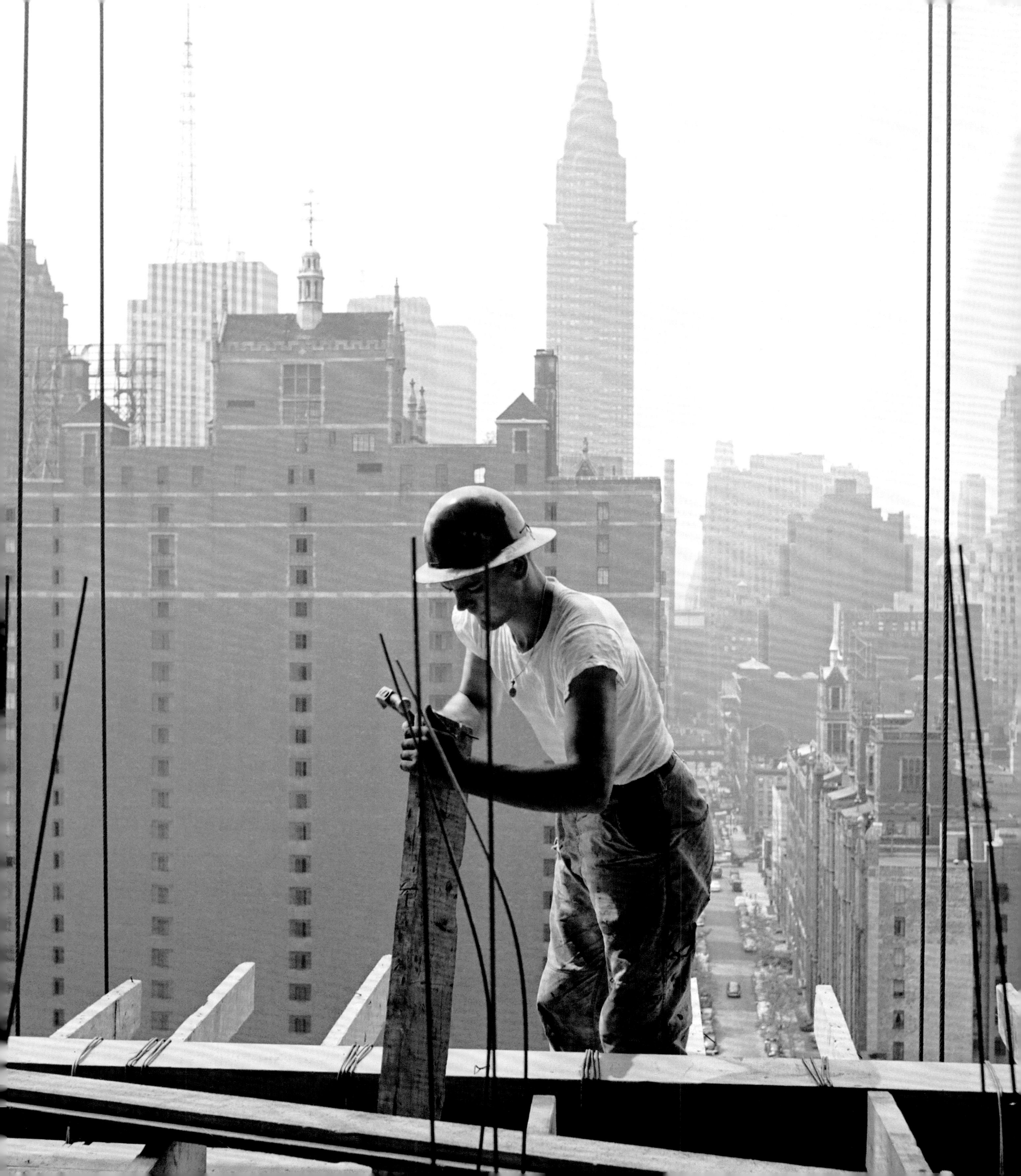

Steelworkers cheer as the UN flag is unfurled atop the completed framework for the 39-story Secretariat Building in accordance with the custom of construction workers. October 5, 1949.

The cornerstone of the United Nations Headquarters was laid on United Nations Day at a special open-air General Assembly meeting. The ceremony, marking the organization's fourth anniversary, was attended by President Harry S. Truman who was the principal speaker. Secretary-General Trygve Lie, accompanied by Wallace K. Harrison, Director of Planning, deposited in the stone copies of the United Nations Charter and the Universal Declaration of Human Rights. October 24, 1949.

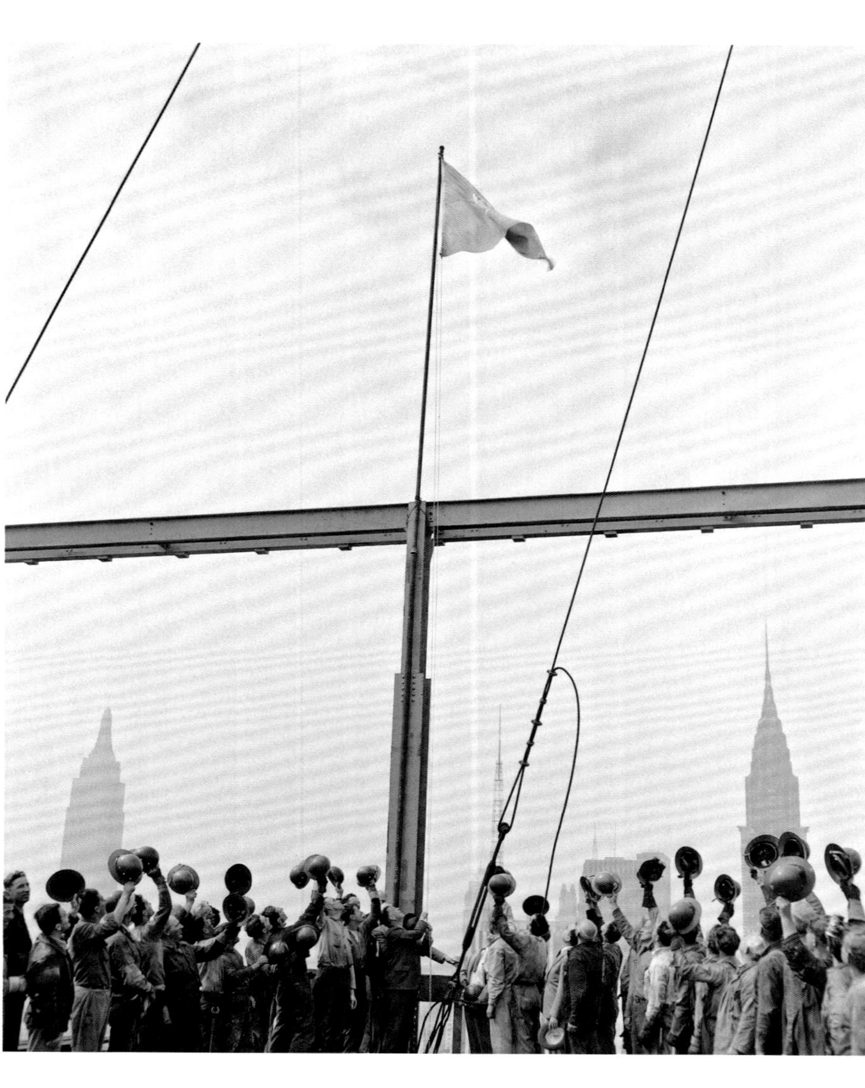

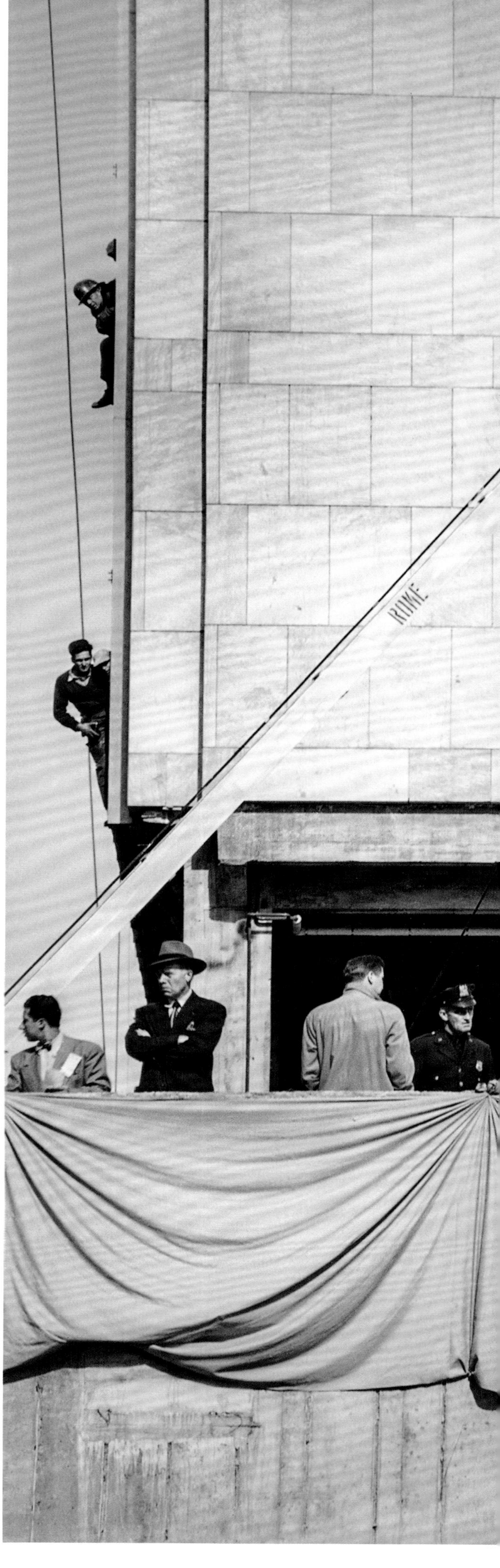

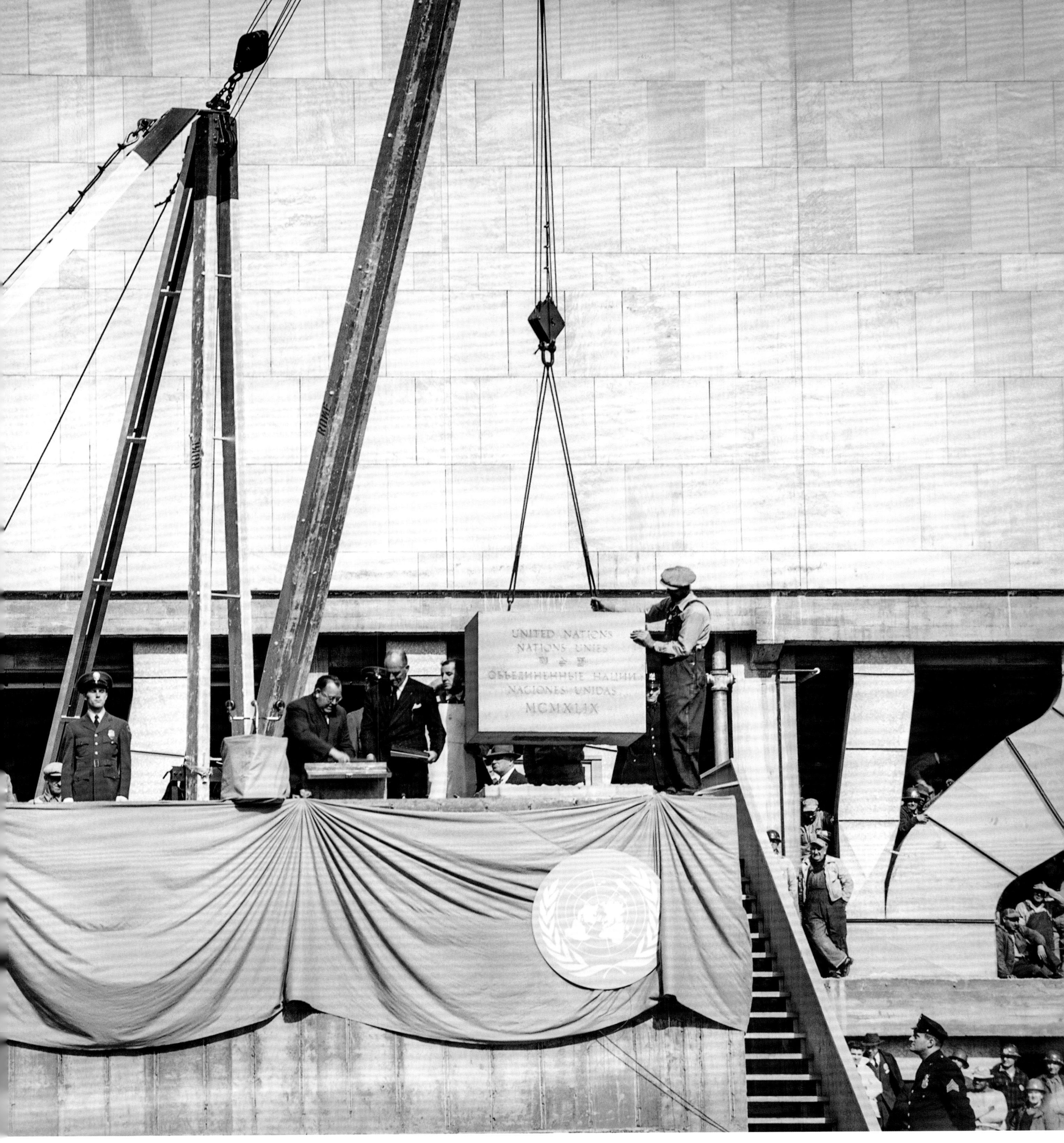
UNITED NATIONS
NATIONS UNIES
ОБЪЕДИНЕННЫЕ НАЦИИ
NACIONES UNIDAS
MCMXLIX

View of the United Nations Headquarters in New York, 1960. The General Assembly Building occupies the most prominent part of the site and is the focal point of the headquarters' composition. Its low sweeping lines stand in sharp contrast to the 39-story Secretariat Building (to which it is connected by the Conference area). The northern facade of the building is made of translucent glass set between marble columns. The concave side walls are faced with English limestone, with panels and trimmings in marble matching the narrow ends of the Secretariat Building.

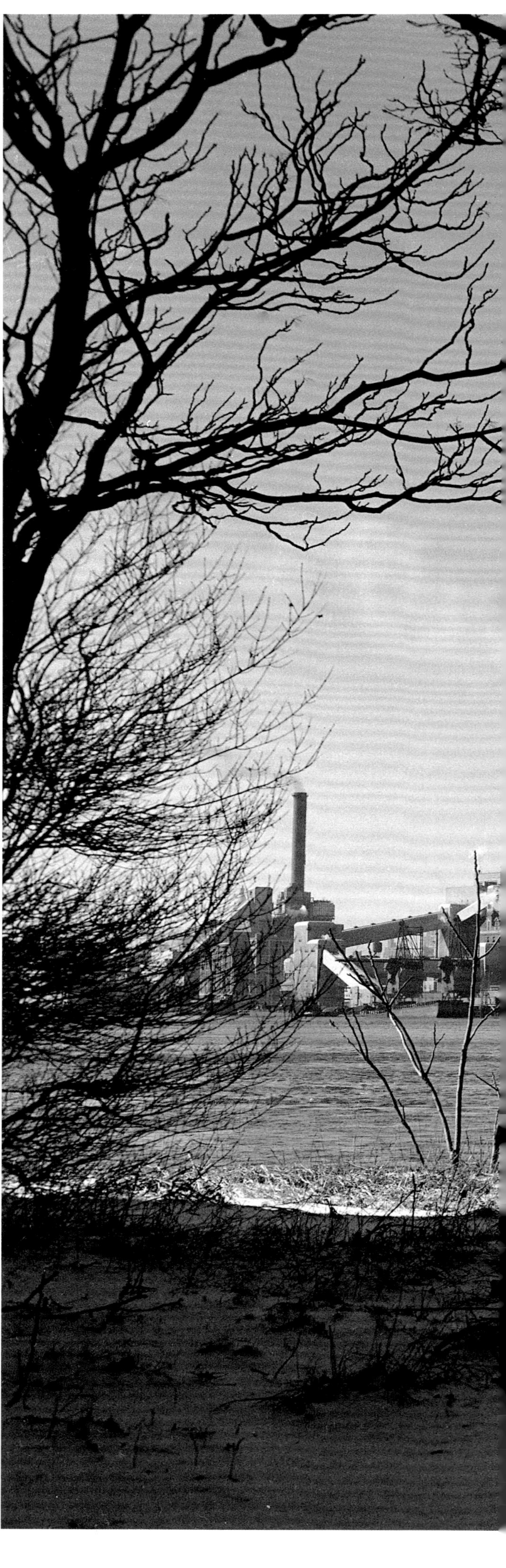

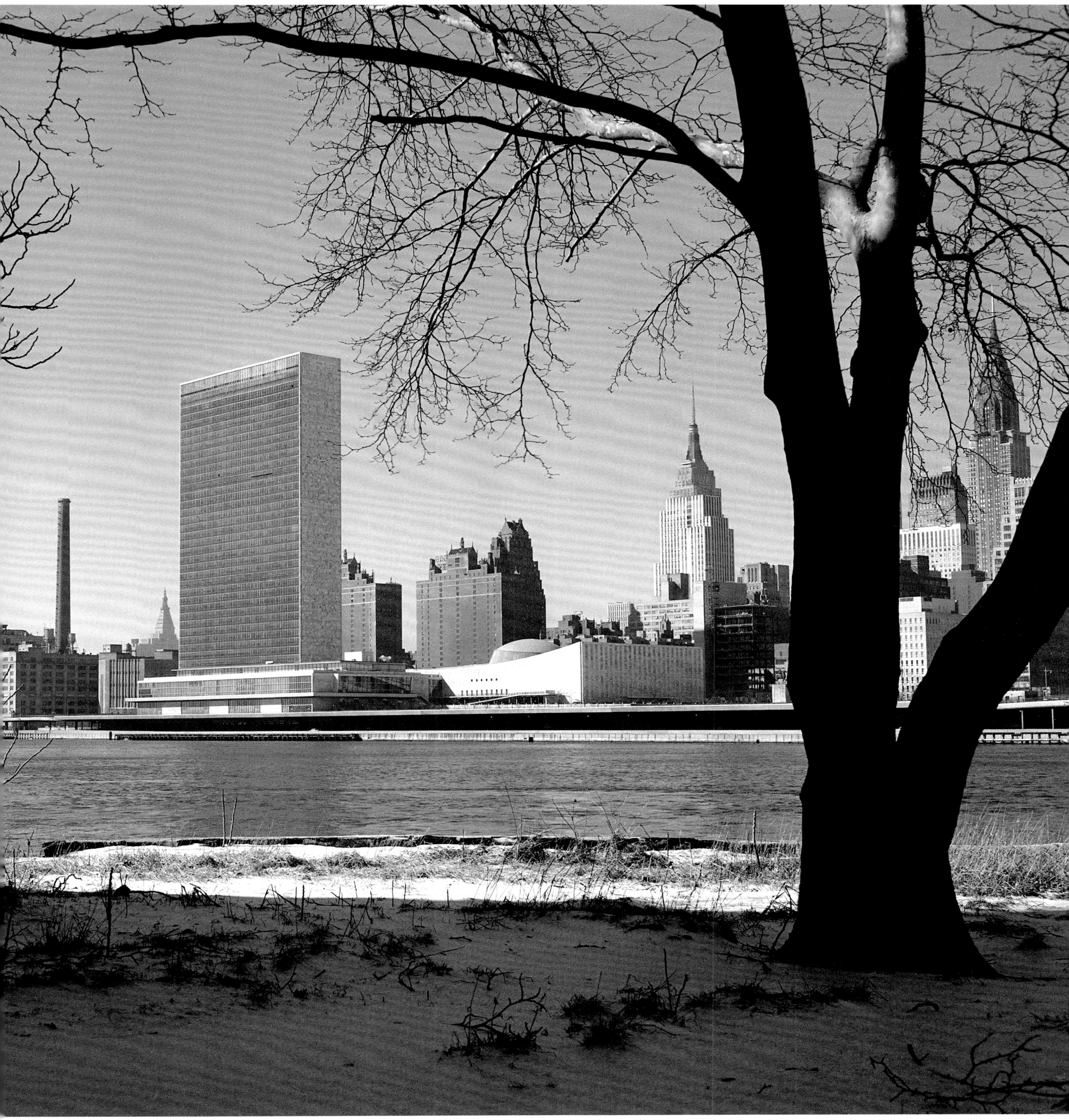

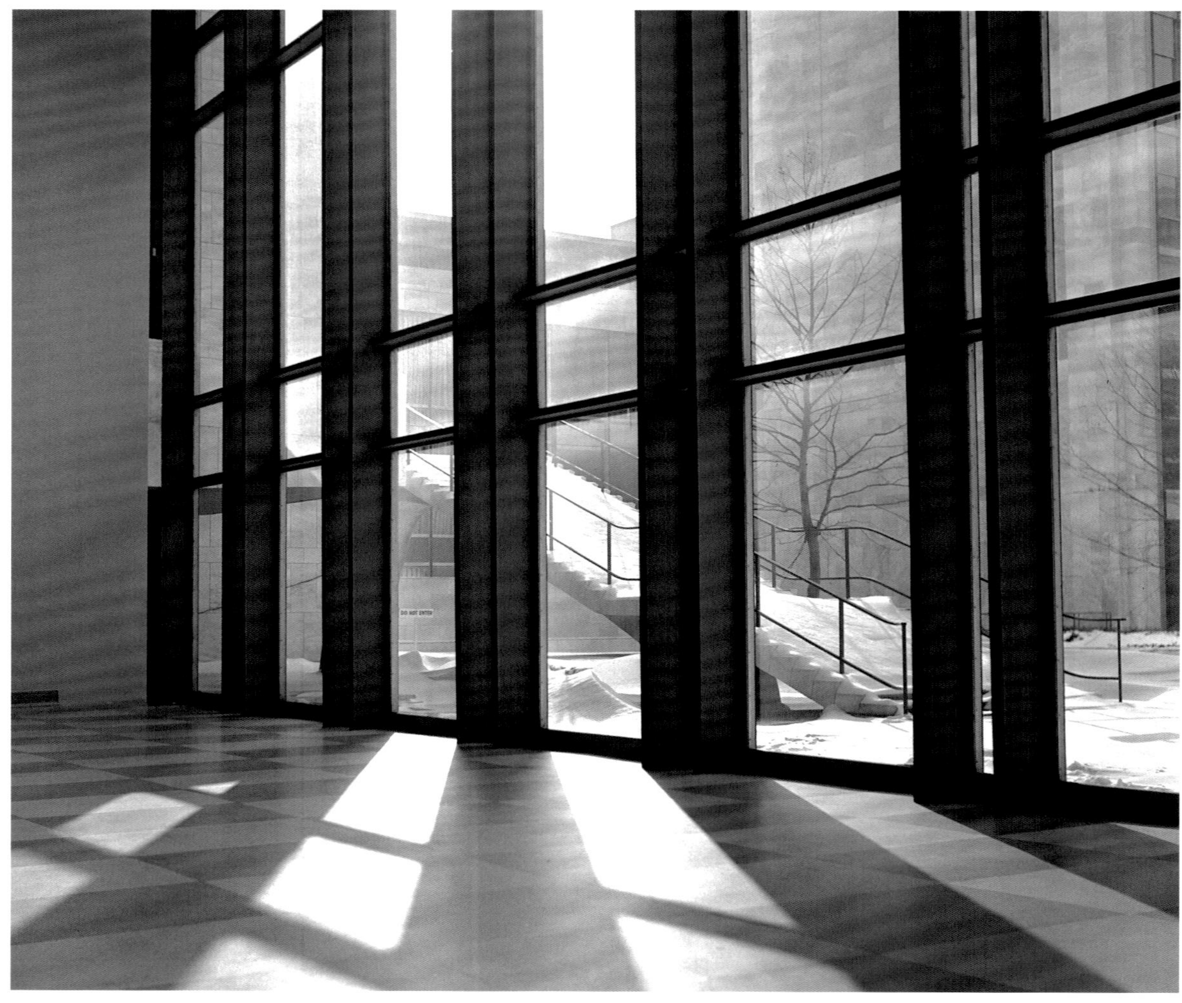

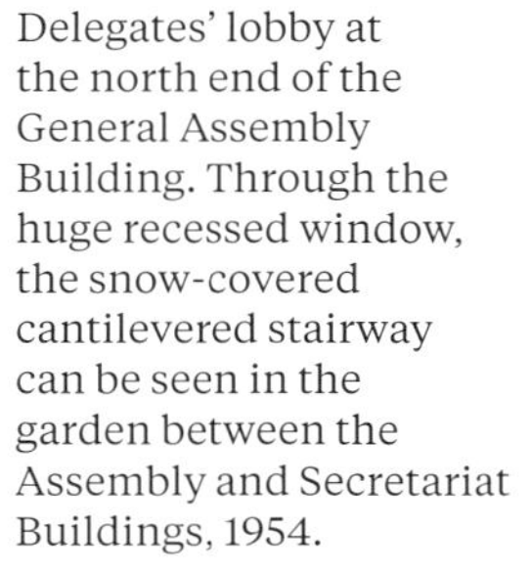

Delegates' lobby at the north end of the General Assembly Building. Through the huge recessed window, the snow-covered cantilevered stairway can be seen in the garden between the Assembly and Secretariat Buildings, 1954.

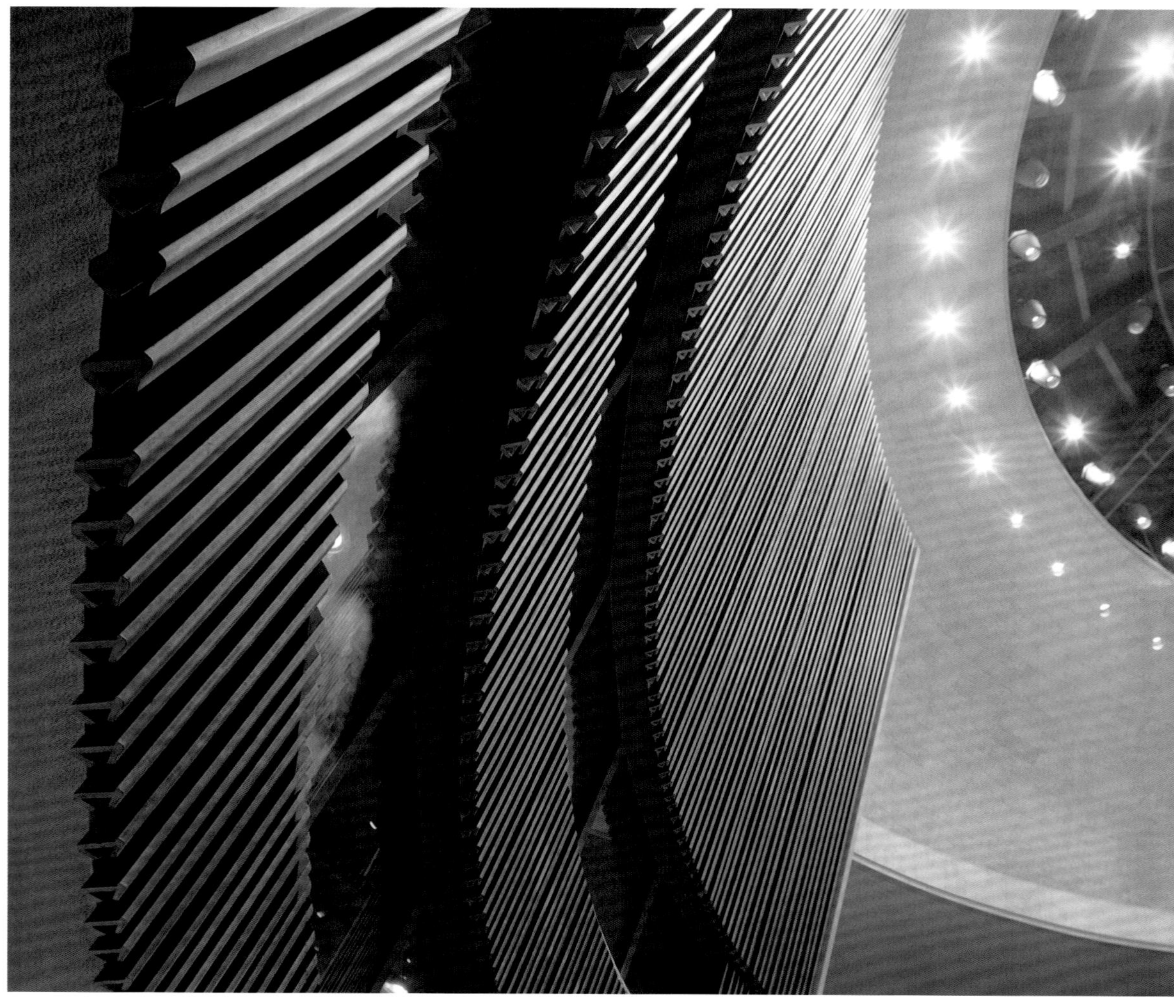

Detail of the gold wood-battens in the Plenary Hall of the General Assembly Building. They are used for acoustic and decorative purposes. This picture shows also the booths for the interpreters and photographers, and, at the top, part of the dome, 1952.

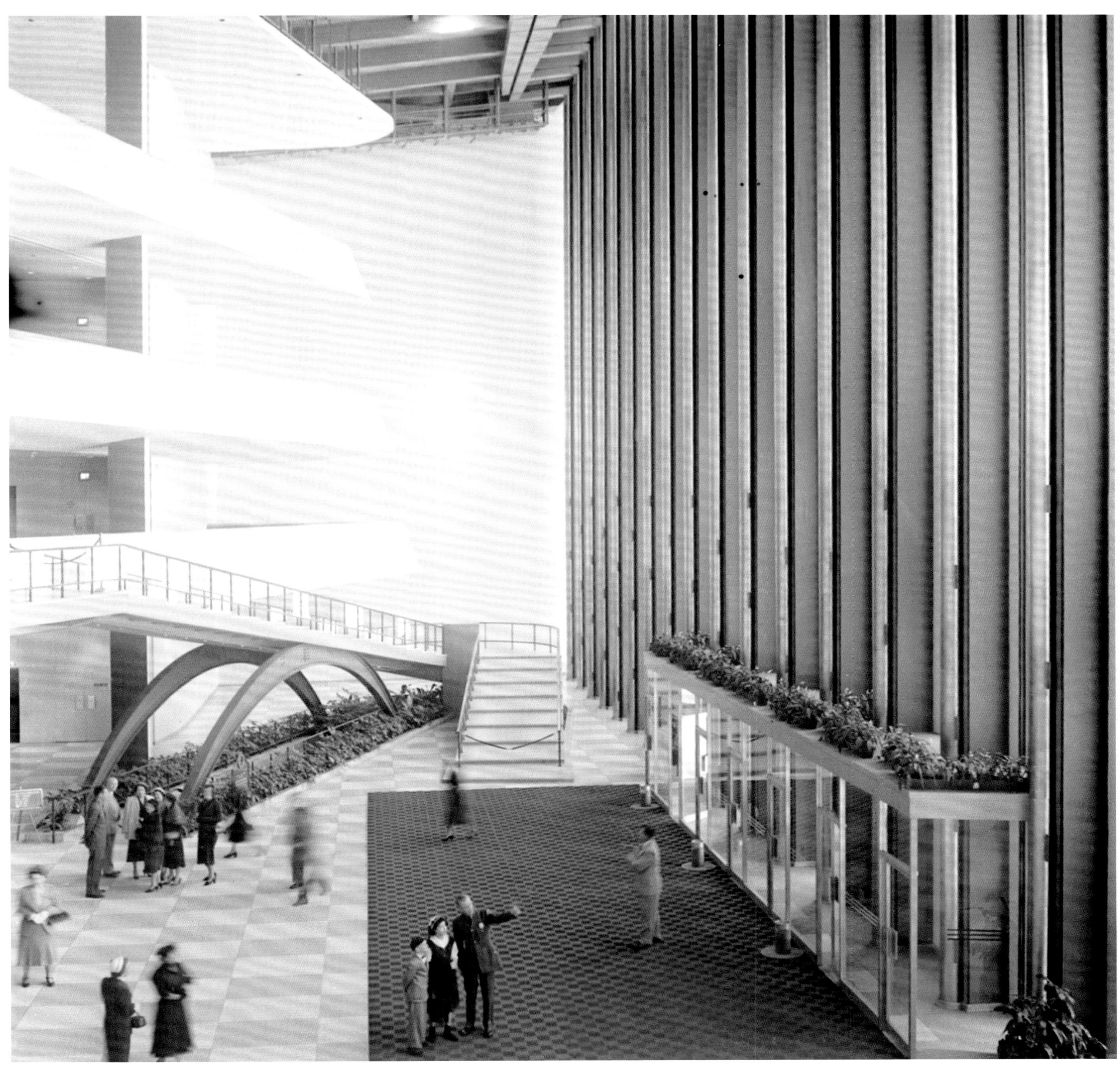

View of the main public lobby at UN Headquarters. This huge foyer, which is open to the roof (75 feet high), is located at the north end of the General Assembly Building. The large step-ramp leads up to the cantilevered balconies, public galleries, and the auditorium beyond, 1953.

Main public lobby at the north end of the General Assembly Building, showing the information desk and the seven public entrance doors, 1952.

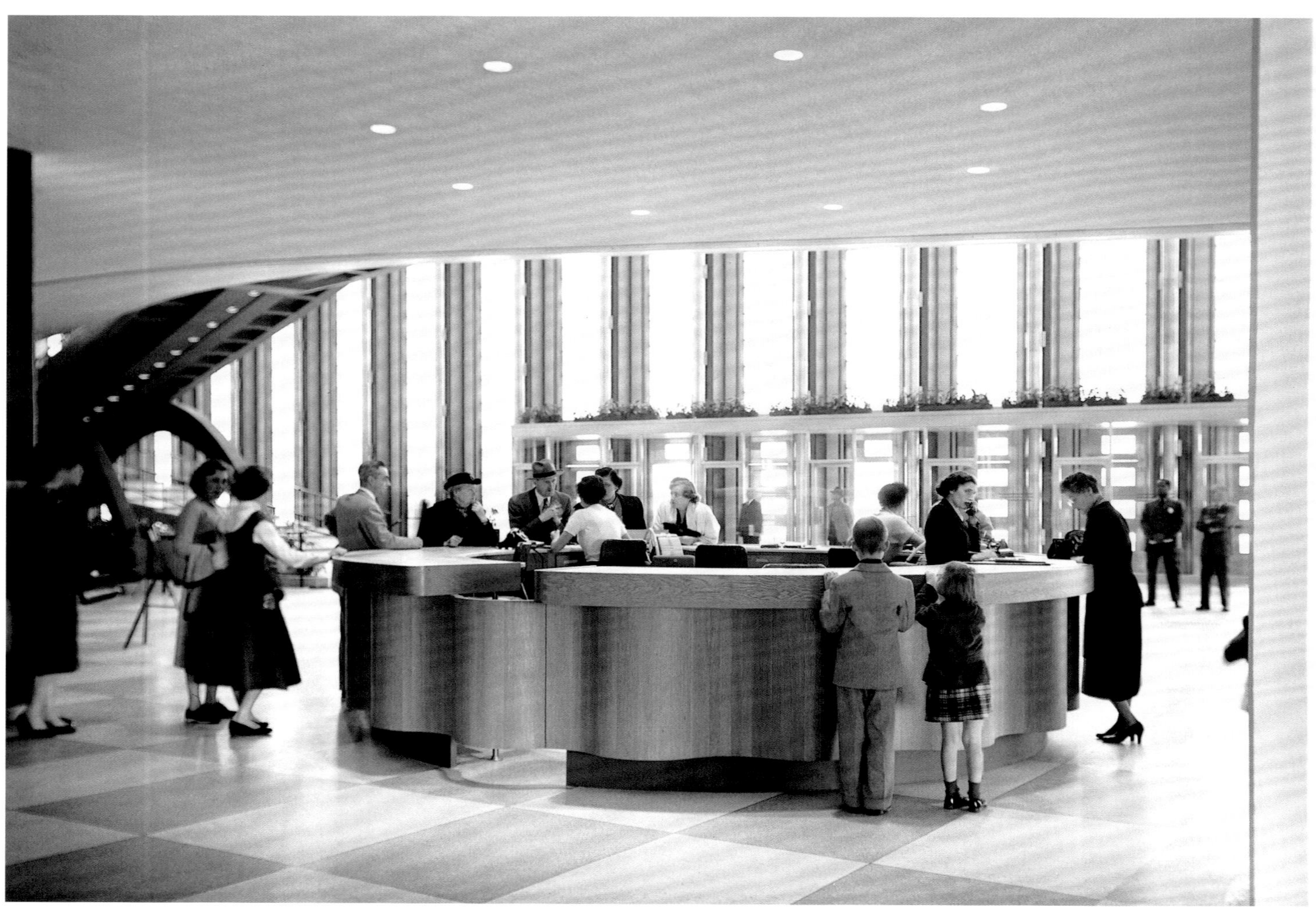

A meeting of the Third (Social, Humanitarian, and Cultural) Committee, at UN Headquarters during the seventh session of the United Nations General Assembly, as seen from the public galleries. October 29, 1952.

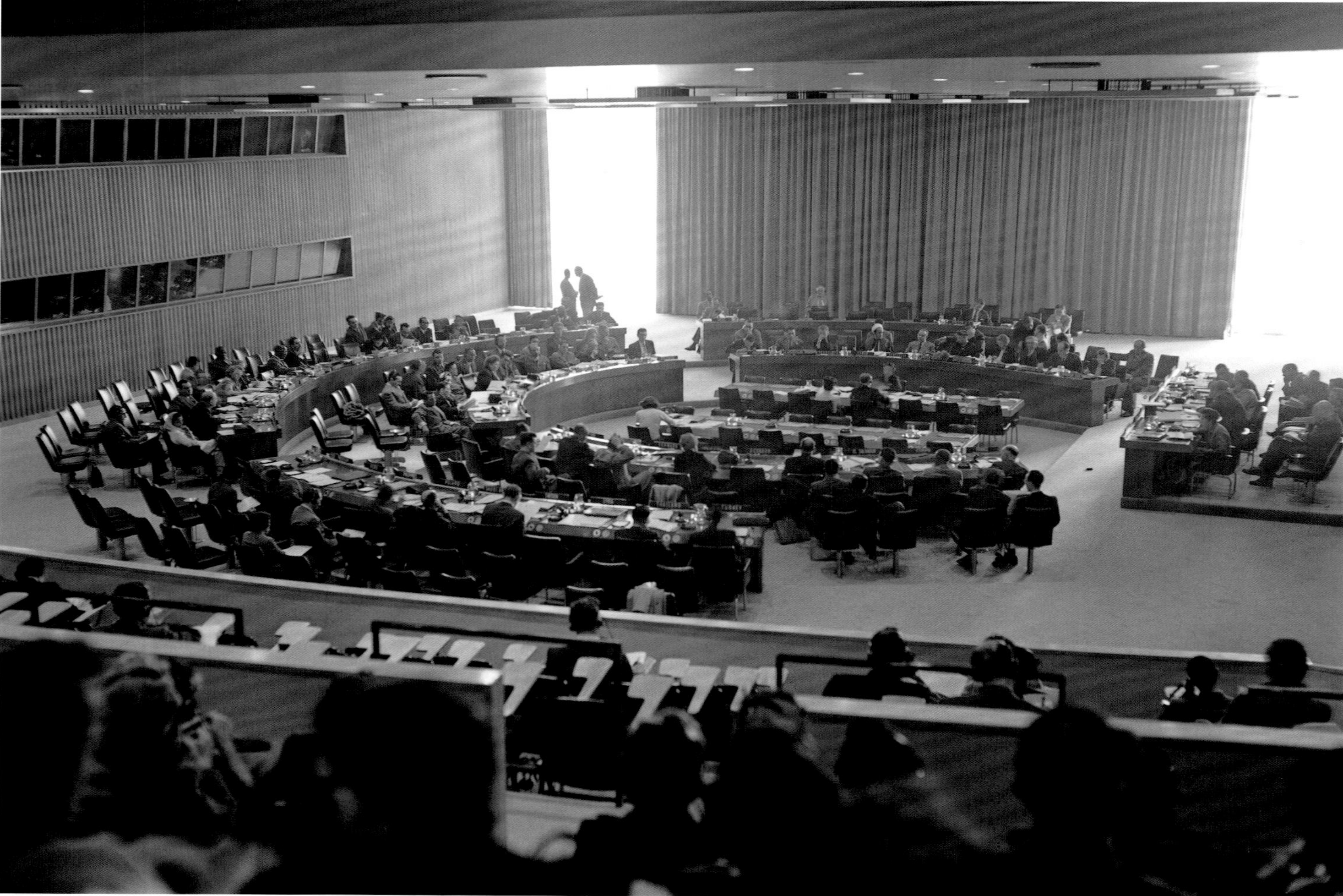

The UN printing plant located in the basement of the Conference Building. The plant, operated by Secretariat staff, produces thousands of UN documents a year. During busy periods, such as Assembly sessions, it operates on a 24-hour basis. Shown here are two of the plant's offset printing presses, 1954.

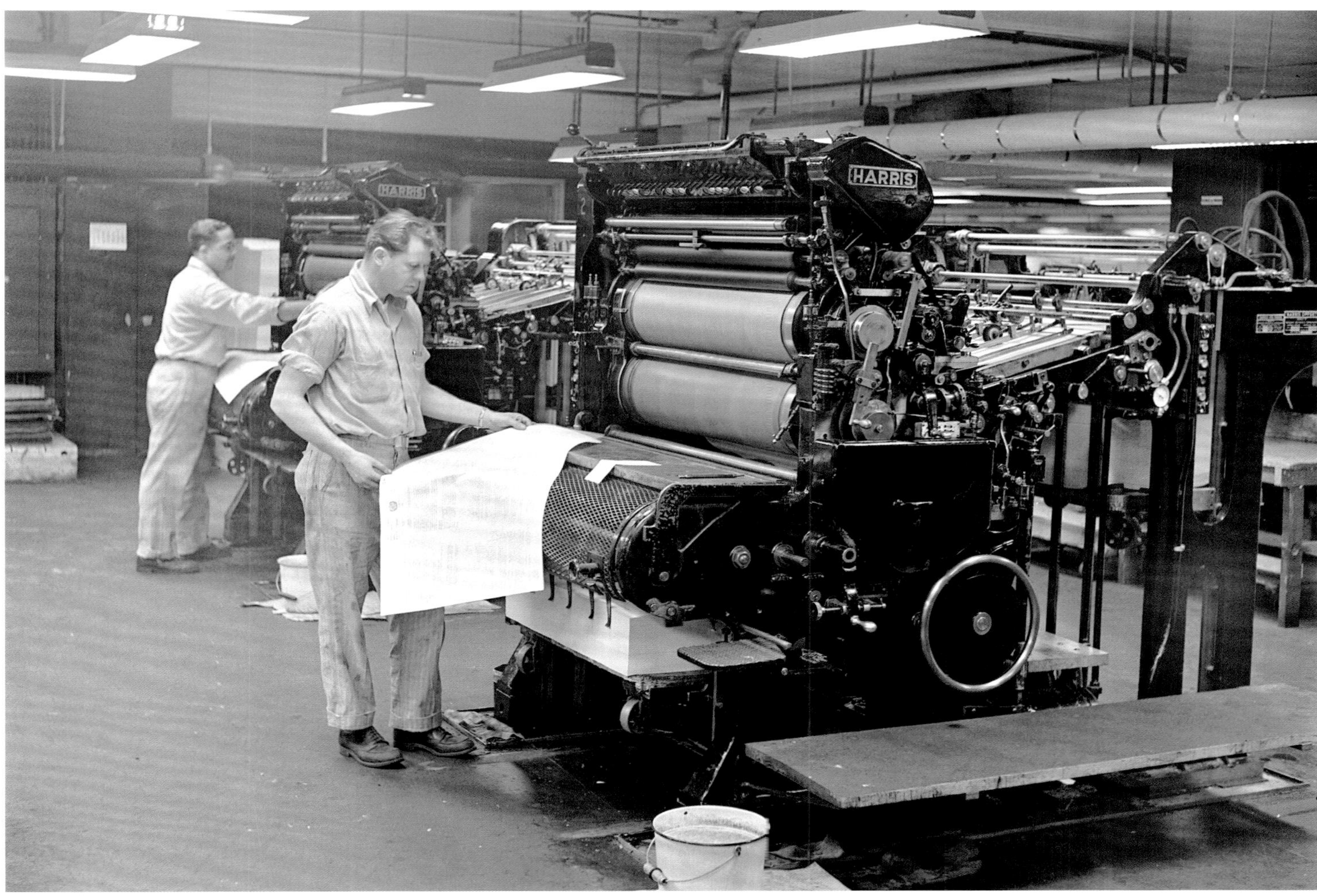

View of North Lawn with the Queensboro Bridge in the background, 1977.

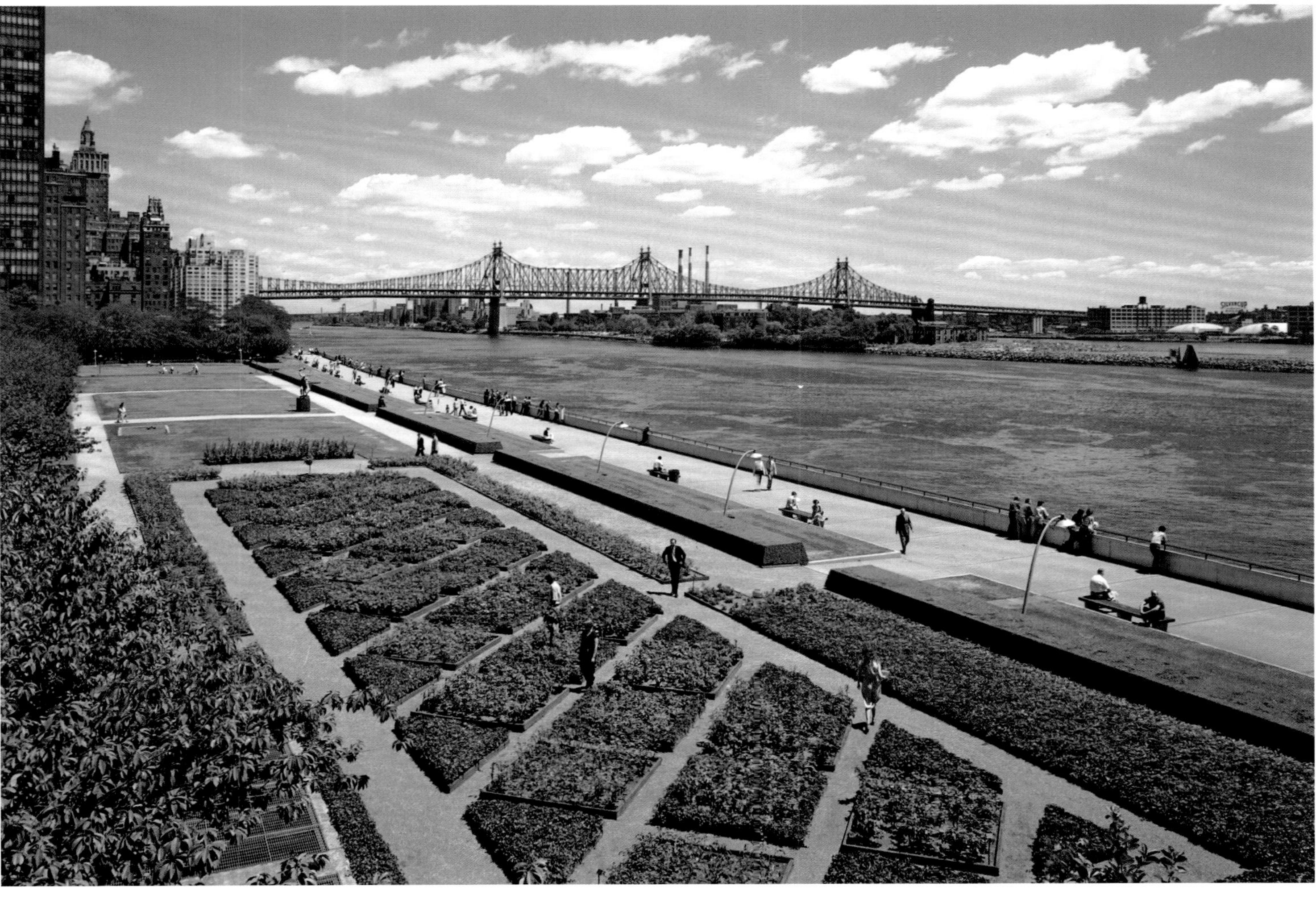

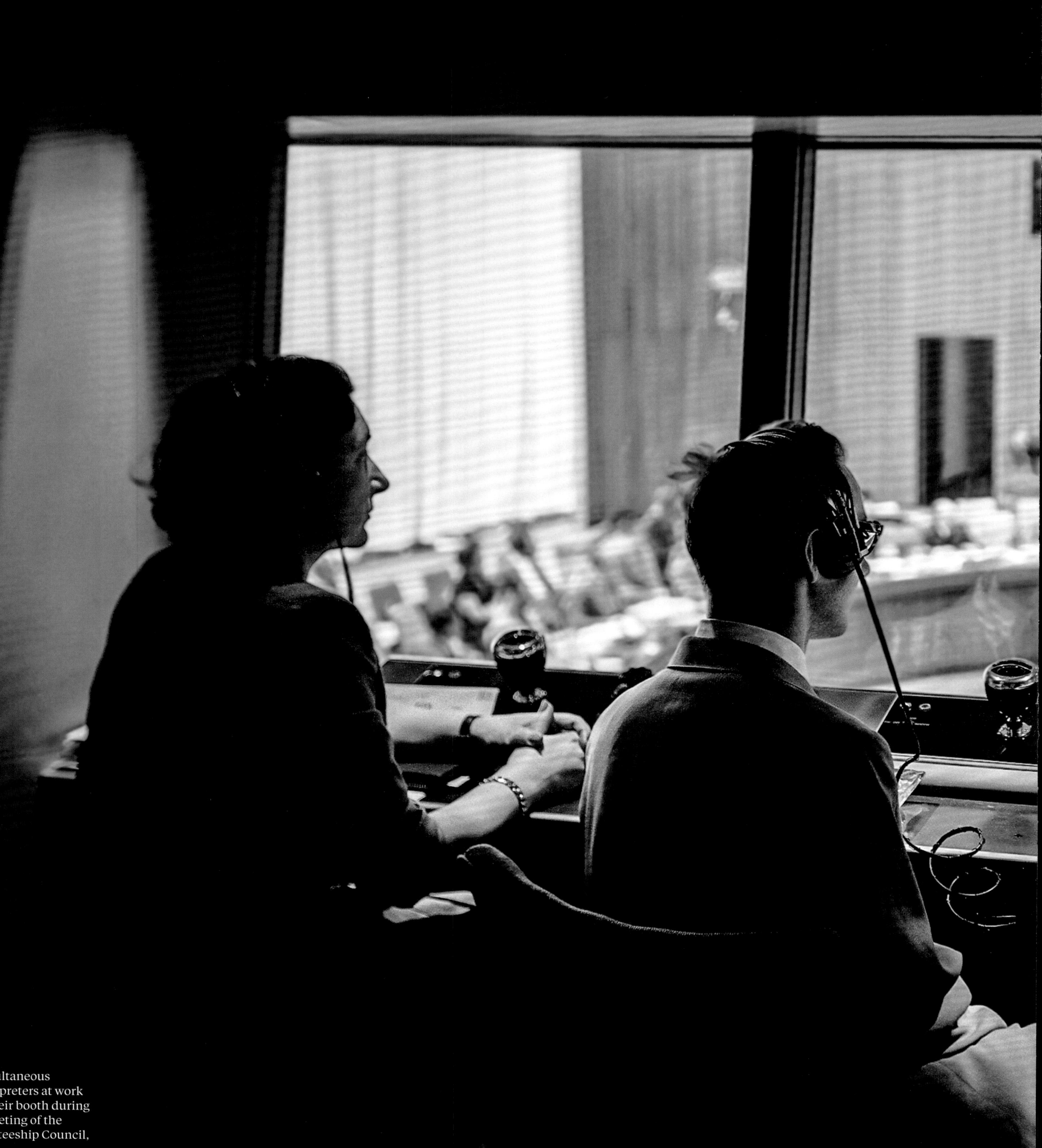

ltaneous
preters at work
eir booth during
eting of the
teeship Council,

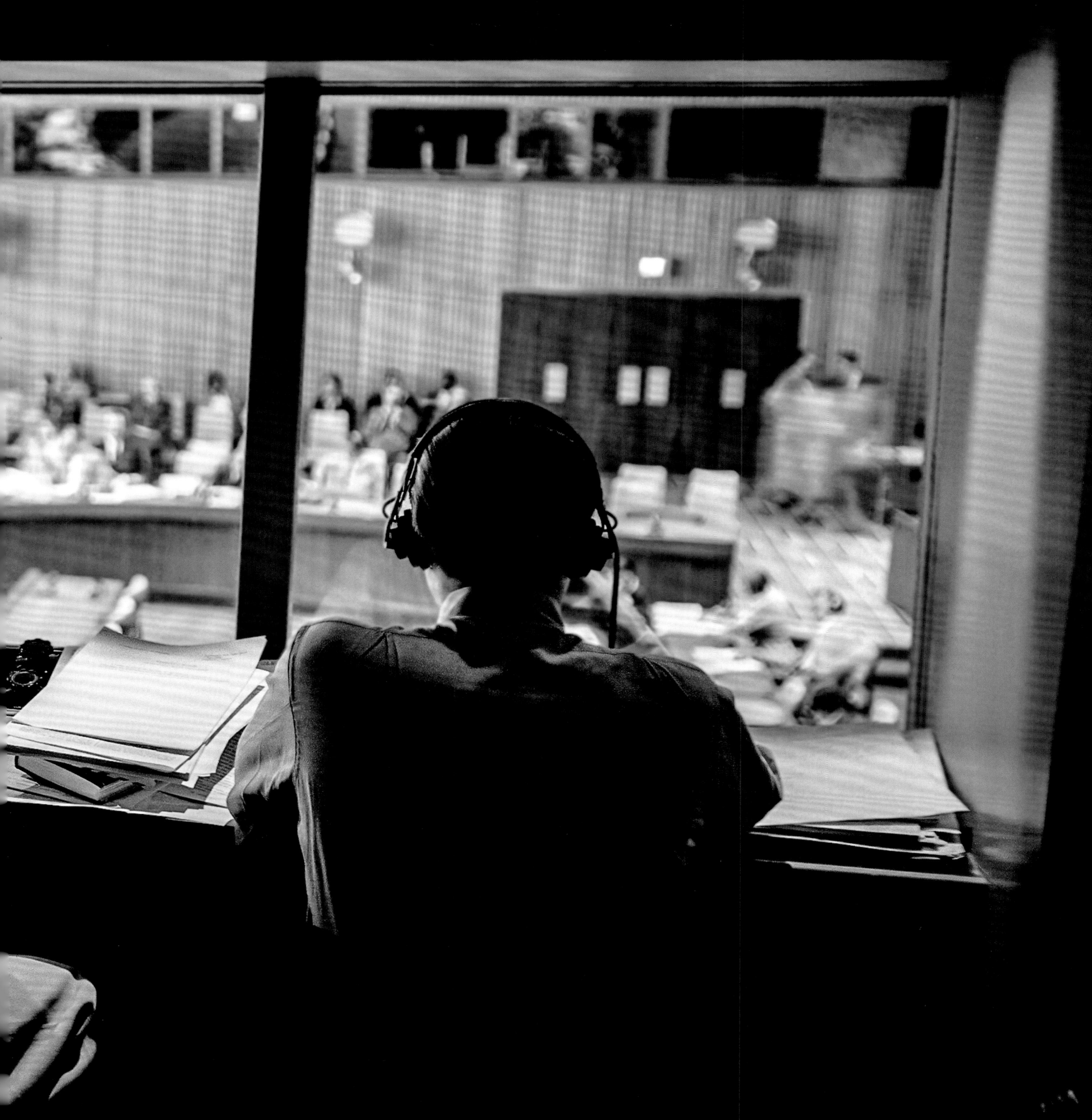

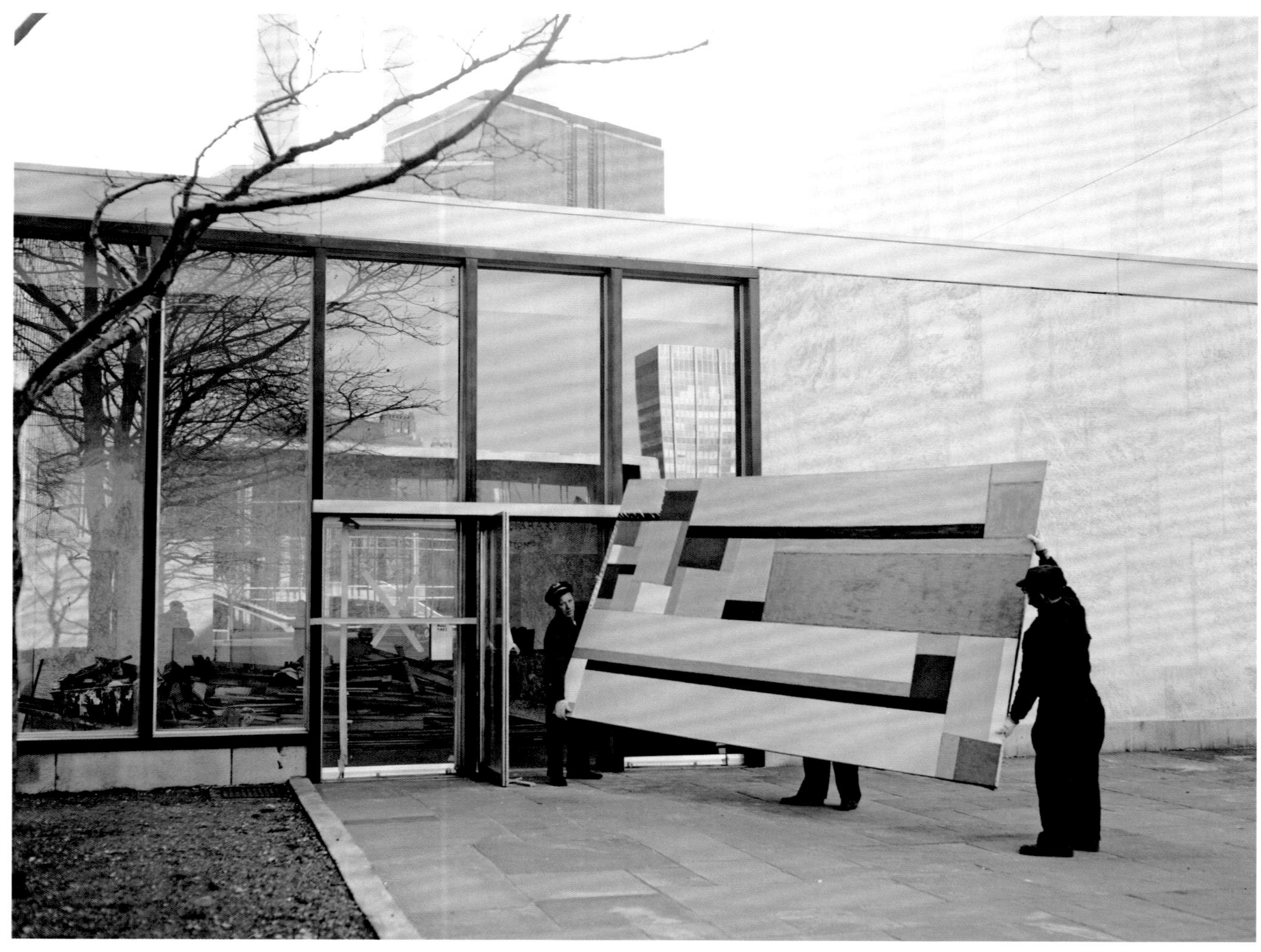

A large abstract mural (11'4" x 22'), specially executed by the well-known American artist Fritz Glarner is to occupy a wall panel facing the ornamental terrazzo marble staircase which leads from the main lobby of the Dag Hammarskjöld Library to its auditorium level, one floor below. The mural is seen here being moved into the library building. January 11, 1962.

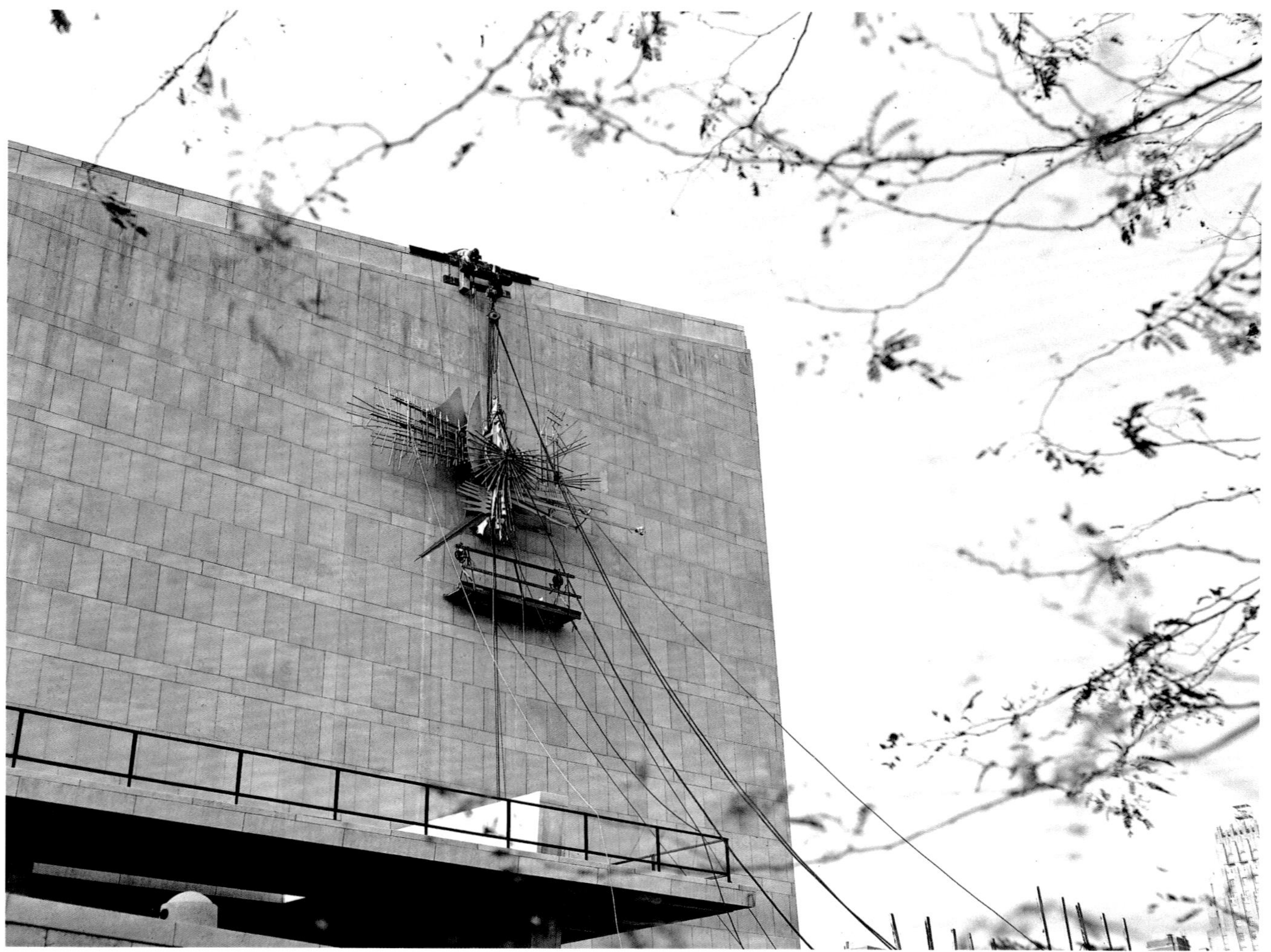

A modern sculpture by the American artist Ezio Martinelli being mounted. October 25, 1961.

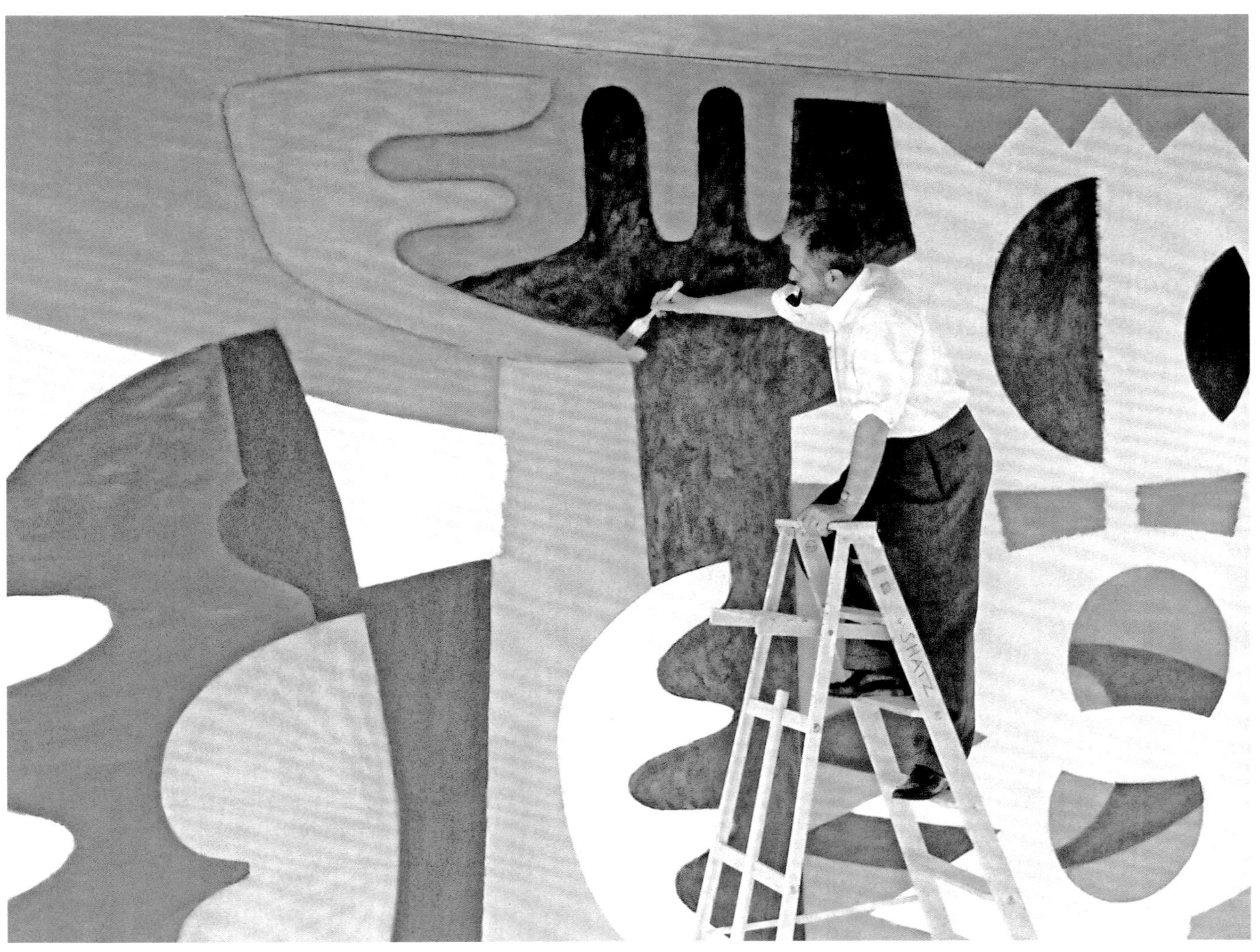

A large mural by the Swedish artist Bo Beskow on the top floor of the Dag Hammarskjöld Library. Painted in oils on canvas and mounted on the concave wall at the west end of the penthouse lounge, the mural is an abstract composition, 26 feet wide by 14 feet high. Mr. Beskow putting the finishing touches on the mural, the second work he has completed for the UN. In 1957, at the request of Secretary-General Dag Hammarskjöld, he painted the fesco in the Meditation Room on the main floor of the General Assembly Building. November 3, 1961.

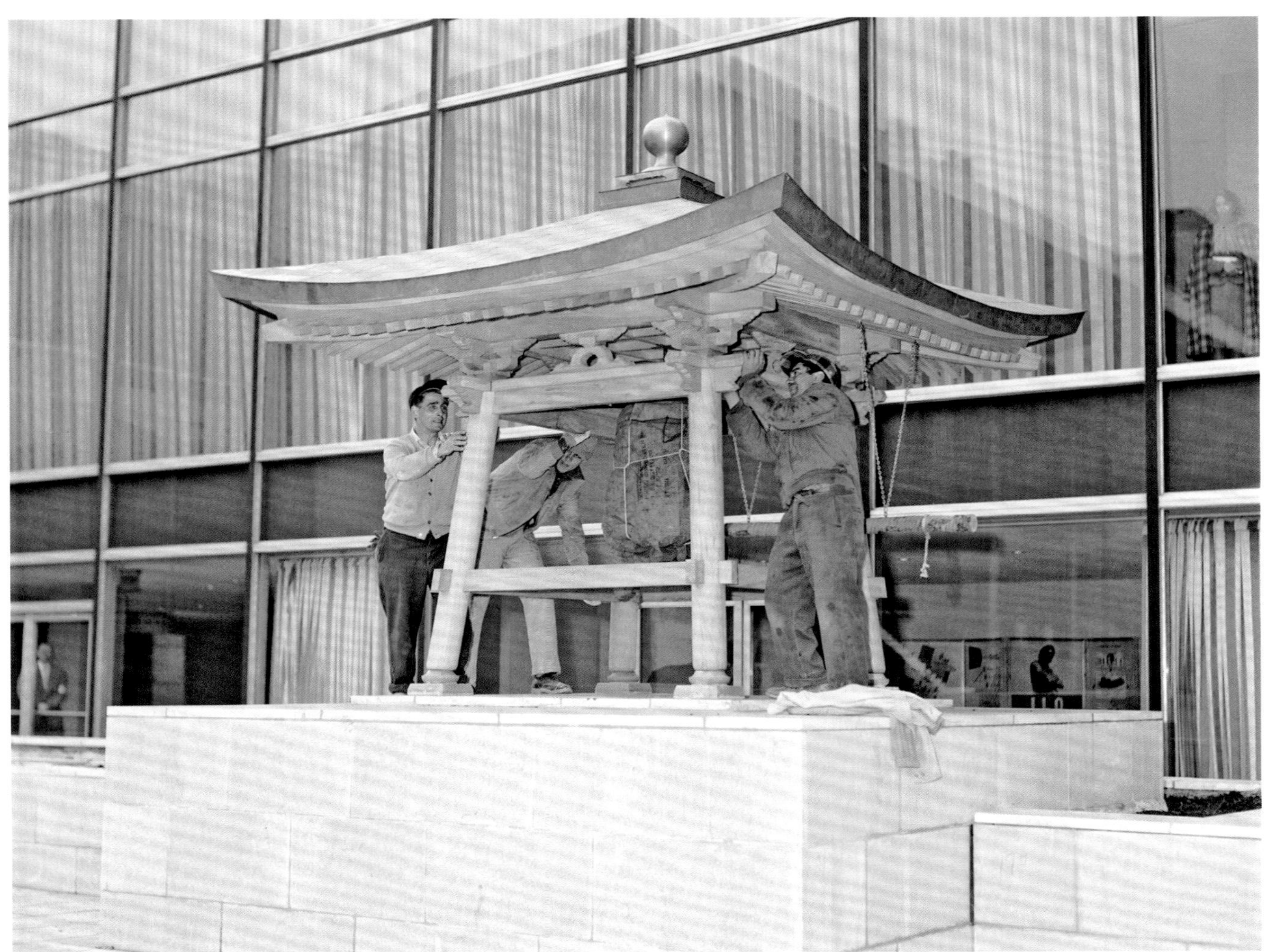

The gifts of two governments—Israel and Japan—being combined by workers at UN Headquarters for the final treatment of a small open area directly north of the Secretariat Building and west of the conference area. Cut from the hills of Jerusalem, 880 slabs of Israeli stone have been put in place to form the base and setting for the large bronze peace bell and pagoda-like enclosure donated to the UN by Japan. February 25, 1954.

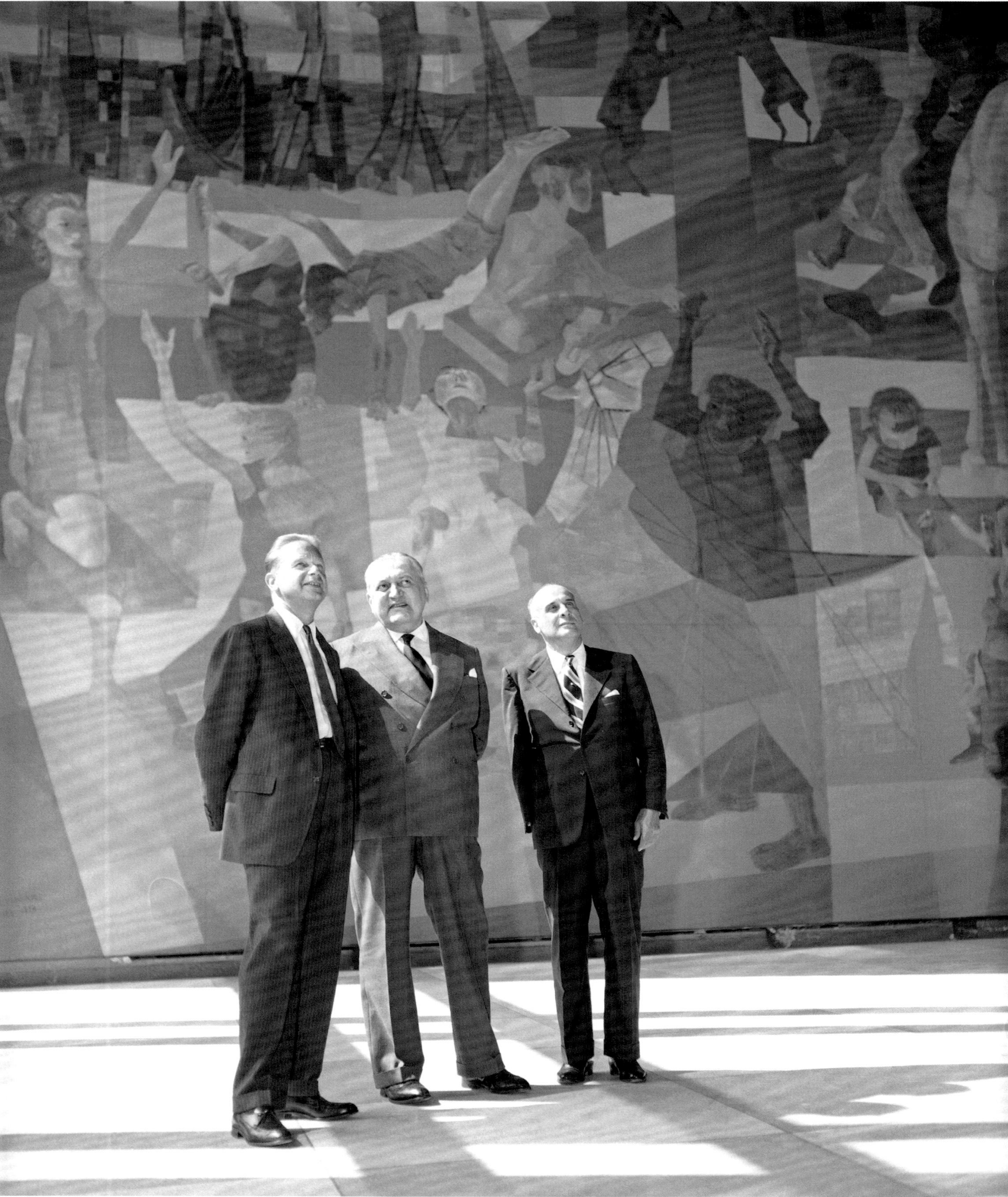

War and *Peace* murals, Brazil's gift to UN Headquarters. Seen here examining sections of the murals already mounted are (left to right) UN Secretary-General Dag Hammarskjöld, Ambassador Cyro de Freitas Valle, Permanent Representative of Brazil to the UN, and Jayme de Barros, Deputy Permanent Representative of Brazil to the UN, who proposed the subject for the murals. September 3, 1957.

Opposite page:
A view of the equestrian statue symbolizing peace, which was installed in the North Lawn of the United Nations Headquarters. The statue is a gift from the government of Yugoslavia and is the work of Antun Augustinčić, a Yugoslav sculptor. The 16-foot-high bronze statue stands on a 26-foot-high pedestal faced with blocks of rose-colored marble quarried in Yugoslavia. December 29, 1954.

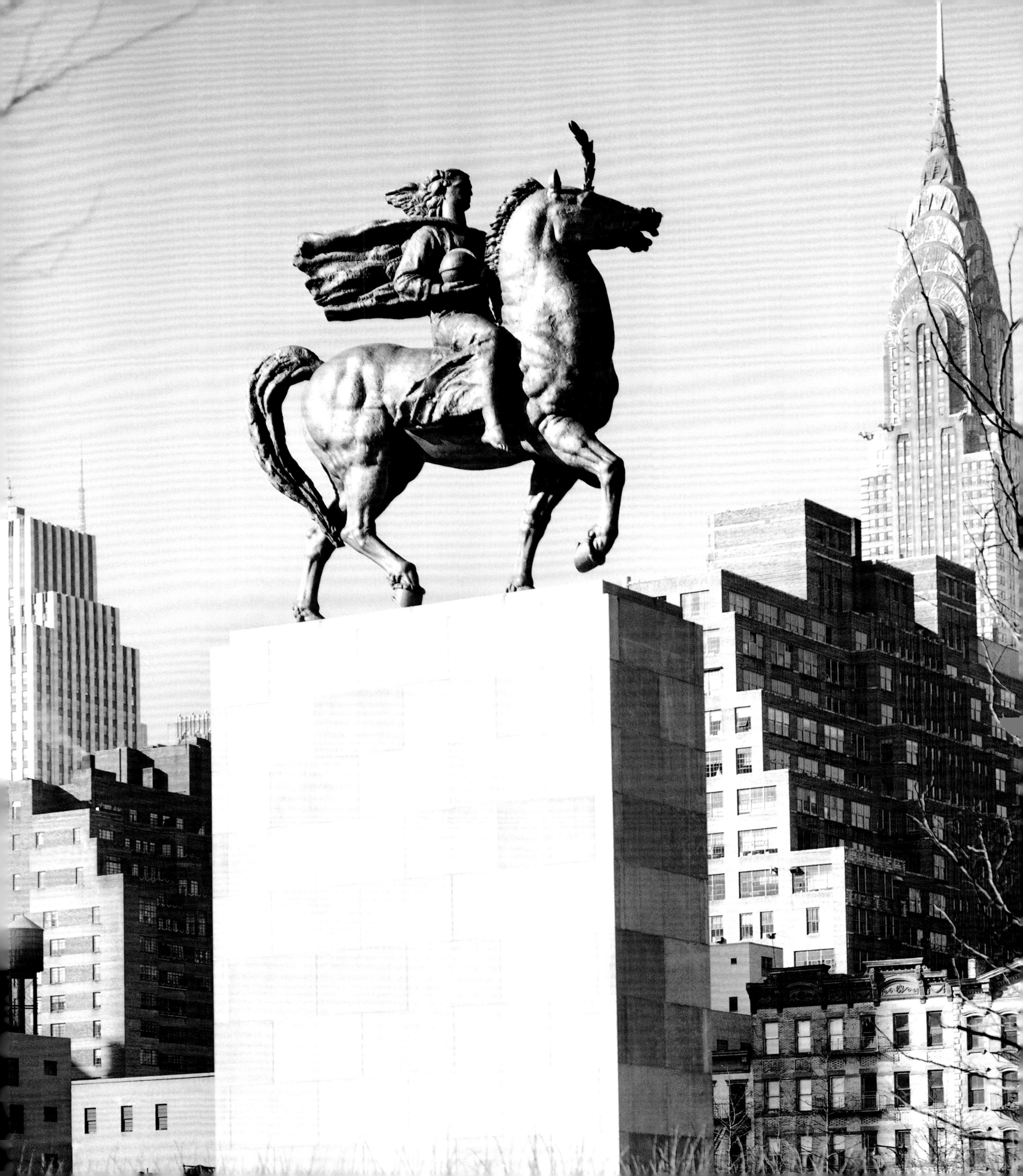

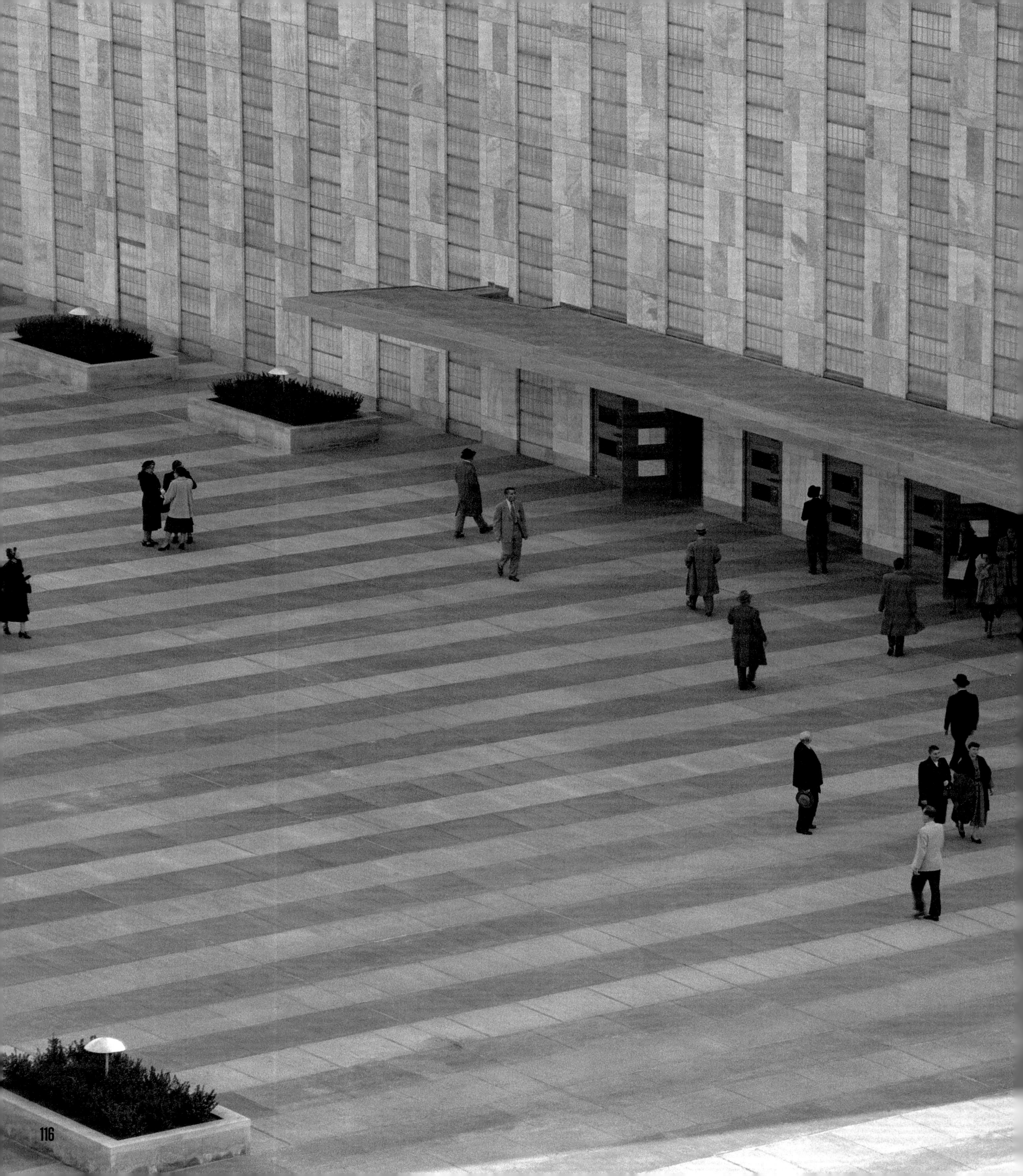

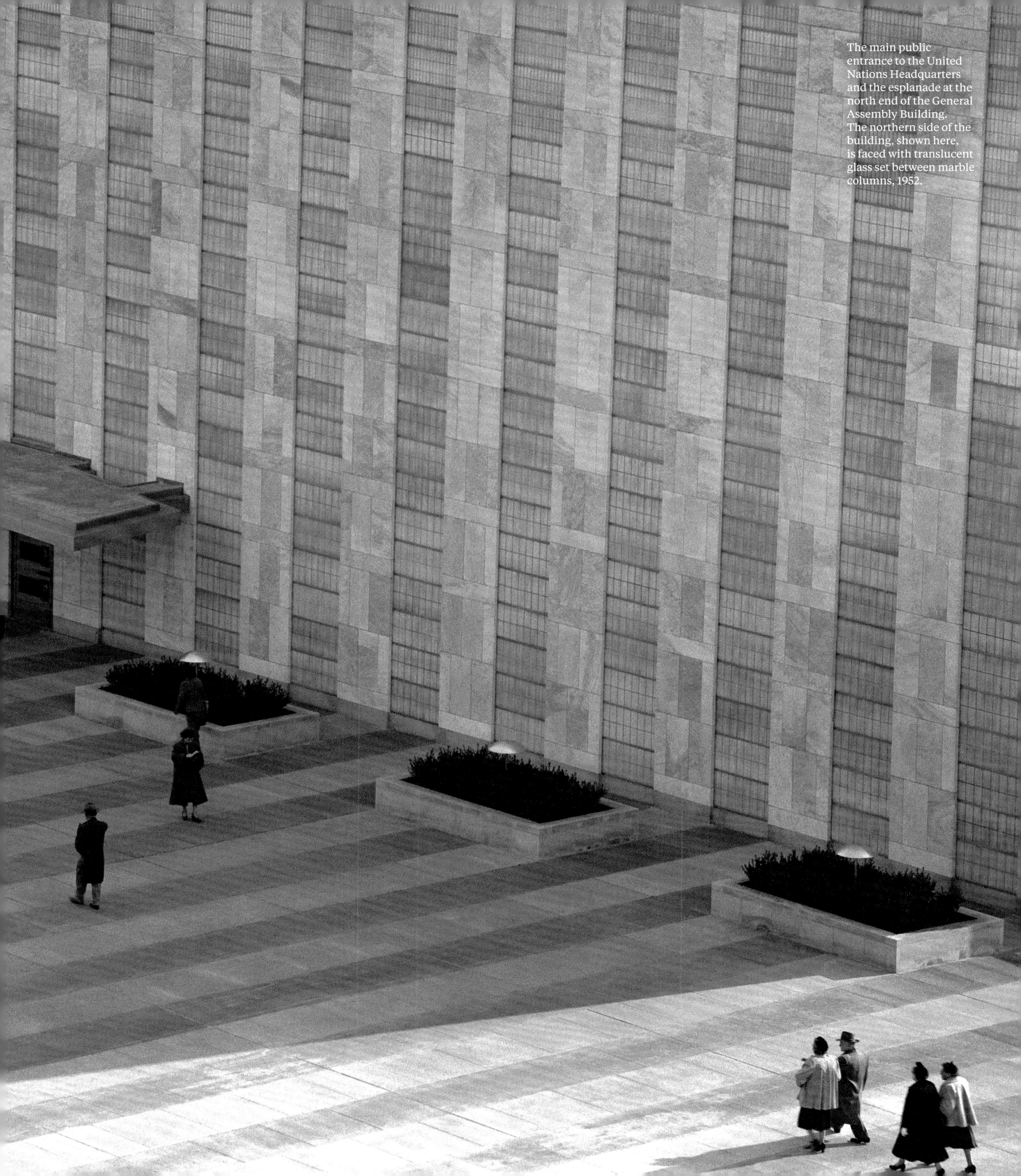

The main public entrance to the United Nations Headquarters and the esplanade at the north end of the General Assembly Building. The northern side of the building, shown here, is faced with translucent glass set between marble columns, 1952.

CHAPTER 4

THE WORLD COMES TO NEW YORK CITY

When Kevin Roche accepted the Pritzker Prize some four decades ago, he said: "To build well is an act of peace."

Roche designed many dozens of buildings well, of course. But to me, two of his most iconic are the United Nations Plaza, home to UNICEF Headquarters, and the Ford Foundation Center for Social Justice, where I am privileged to work each day.

These sister structures house sister institutions. And both fully embody Roche's radical vision: Building "well" is an act of righteousness—an affirmation of human dignity, equal rights, and social progress.

When I walk our neighborhood, I find myself often reflecting on this idea—on all that it contains and all that it unleashes. For one, Tudor City and the United Nations Plaza encompass one of the most international neighborhoods in the world's most global city. New York is a city that houses the world—in the space of a single block, our stories span seas and cross continents. As much as the United Nations Plaza is a beacon around the globe, it is also a beacon in this city —an embodiment of the profound diversity that makes us who we are.

But furthermore, this is the place where democratic aspirations meet democratic processes. This is where protesters speak their truth and where presidents and prime ministers gather in peace—where people take to the streets, but also come together in the halls of power. This is where all of humanity unites in pursuit of recognition and representation and the right to seek our own dignity and destinies.

For five decades now, the UN Development Corporation (UNDC) has ensured that the built environment is more than a neutral space or static landmark; our public spaces and places are the theaters in which justice happens. And for 75 years,

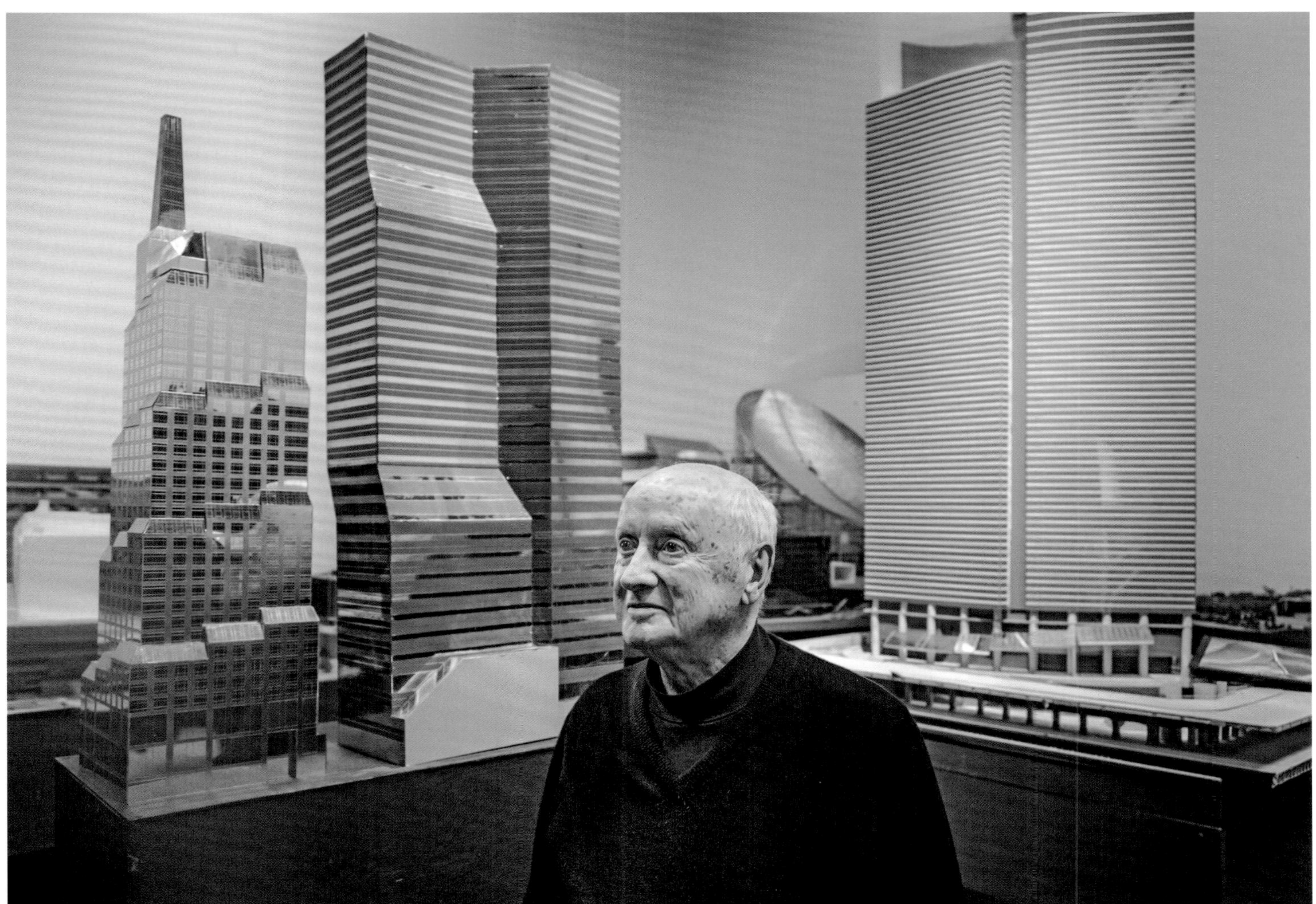

Kevin Roche, Pritzker Prize-winning architect and founding principal of Kevin Roche John Dinkeloo and Associates, at his office in Hamden, Connecticut. The firm was founded in 1966 and has completed over 200 projects in the U.S. and internationally. A scale model of One and Two UN Plaza can be seen behind him. January 13, 2015.

the United Nations itself has served a common commitment to a fairer, better world.

As we commemorate this historic anniversary during these most challenging times—right here, in our most global of communities—I'm struck with awe, admiration, and appreciation for the United Nations' mission and mandate. Together, let us continue to build common ground for a common good—and to build it well. —**DARREN WALKER**

Darren Walker is President of the Ford Foundation

New York—the first metropolis on the planet, a great melting pot embracing and nurturing representatives of all races and religions, speakers of all languages and dialects is also the breeding ground for another amazing microcosm that unites all countries: the United Nations. Despite numerous crises and tragedies that both the city and the organization have had to face during their history, their successful symbiosis continues to be an important sign of world politics and diplomacy.

At the time the construction of the UN Headquarters was completed, its design was perceived as cutting-edge. Nevertheless, the highest skills of its creators, architectural giants of the time including a representative of the Soviet Union, Nikolai Bassov, have ensured that even 75 years later the complex of this global organization in Manhattan still looks modern and is equally harmonious with the changing urban landscape. New York's genuine cosmopolitan spirit is amply incarnated in the interior designs of the UN Headquarters. It has been only a few years since the consultations chamber of the Security Council, the so-called "Russian Room," furnished and ornamented by the Russian Federation, reopened after reconstruction. It adds, along with donations, gifts, decorations, and designs from other nations, to the inherent vibe of the United Nations that keeps the space up-to-date throughout decades.

Born out of the Second World War, this unique and universal global structure for maintaining peace and security was so wisely designed by its founding fathers that it still remains a platform with no alternative, where all states can discuss and address the most pressing and acute international issues on an equal basis. —**VASSILY A. NEBENZIA**

Vassily A. Nebenzia is Permanent Representative of the Russian Federation to the United Nations.

2001

Year the United Nations was awarded the Nobel Peace Prize

71.4 MILLION

Number of people fleeing war, famine, and persecution assisted and protected by the UN

$29.8 BILLION

Amount of United Nations humanitarian aid appeals in 2019

50

Number of countries provided with UN electoral assistance every year

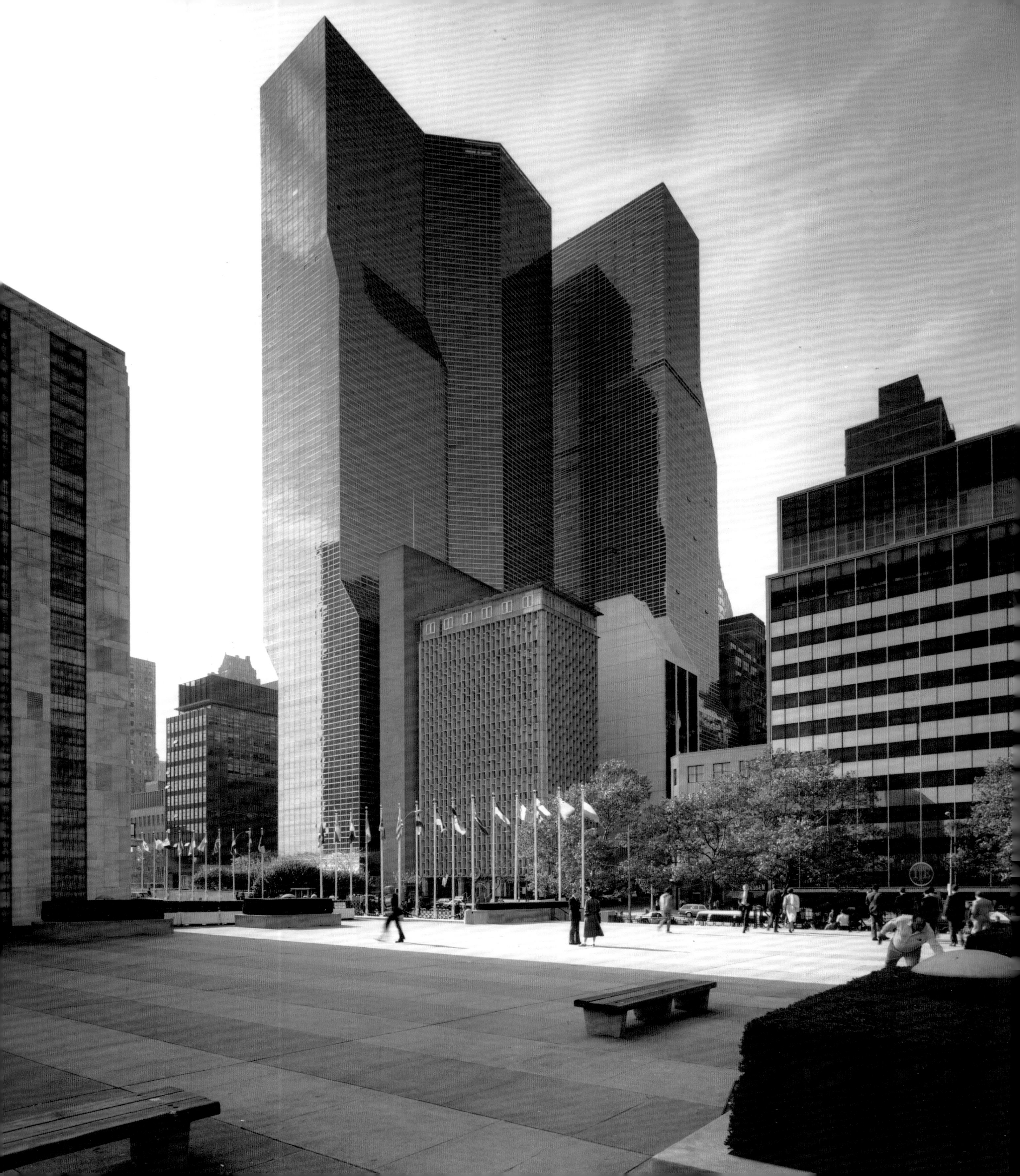

One and Two United Nations Plaza viewed from the north end of the General Assembly building.

The relationship between the United Nations and the host city to the largest diplomatic community in the world is a unique one.[22] Although the UN has made itself at home in New York for 75 years, it is not legally part of the city—nor is it extraterritorial or sovereign.[23] The 18 acres of land beneath its headquarters is owned by the UN, but still part of the United States. The UN has its own firefighting and security forces and its own post office branch, but depends on local emergency services. As host city, New York City is responsible for securing the campus and facilities and making sure that the children of UN community members have access to the city's public education system. Federal, state, and local officers and officials are banned from entering the UN Headquarters, except with the consent of and under conditions agreed to by the Secretary-General. However, the UN is bound by an agreement with its host country that prevents its territory from being used as a refuge for anyone attempting to avoid arrest under U.S. law or being extradited by the U.S. government.

As the organization has grown over the last 75 years—from 60 Member States in 1952 to 193 today—the UN campus has had to evolve and expand. In 1976, the General Assembly undertook some of the first notable alterations to the original buildings, refurbishing and expanding the seating capacity of the General Assembly Hall and all the large conference rooms. The project was completed in 1980. A printing plant, occupying two levels beneath the north lawn of the headquarters campus, opened in June 1981. It is the second-largest printing operation in the world, following the U.S. Government Publishing Office in Washington, DC.[24] In 1982, a 750-seat cafeteria for staff and delegates was opened in a two-story building adjacent to the Secretariat Building, overlooking the East River.

By 1962, it was clear that modest expansions and alterations could not accommodate the huge growth of the UN, UN-related programs such as UNICEF and the UN Development Programme, and the permanent missions of its member nations, which by then had already doubled. To ease crowding and establish an even larger foothold in New York City, the UN would have to look beyond the confines of its new campus and lease additional office space nearby.[25] The first big move took place in 1965, when two agencies signed a five-year lease at 866 United Nations Plaza on East 48th Street.

The growth of the United Nations during that time also became of interest to the Ford Foundation, which was in the midst of building a new headquarters building on East 42nd Street designed by architects Kevin Roche John Dinkeloo and Associates. The Ford Foundation had previously financed several projects in Turtle Bay, including the UN's Dag Hammarskjöld Library. It had also been quietly purchasing multiple parcels on East 43rd, 44th, and 45th Streets, between First and Second Avenue, with an eye toward improving the neighborhood surrounding the UN and its own headquarters.[26] In 1965 the foundation and the Rockefeller Brothers Fund established the East River-Turtle Bay Fund, later known as the Fund for Area

Planning and Development, to explore options that would provide more space for the UN and its groups.[27] The fund asked Roche-Dinkeloo to prepare a feasibility study for an expansion of the UN in Turtle Bay. Roche-Dinkeloo's design called for a "superblock" of multiple towers with offices, hotels, and residences, as well as a visitors' center, all surrounded by parkland.[28]

Recognizing the UN's expansion and its importance to the State and City of New York and the United States, in 1968 the New York State Legislature voted to establish the United Nations Development Corporation (UNDC), a public benefit corporation charged with developing and operating office space, hotel accommodations, housing, and other real estate needs for the UN community. Governor Nelson Rockefeller, whose support for bringing the UN to New York City helped convince his father, John, to make his foundational $8.5 million gift in 1946, signed the legislation. In 1969, the UNDC received a $3.15 million refundable grant (since repaid) from the Ford Foundation to help launch UNDC's activities. Since that time, the UNDC has issued over $1 billion of its own tax-exempt debt to finance the development, construction, and operation of its buildings.

Under its enabling statute, the UNDC is permitted to develop and operate real estate within a prescribed United Nations Development District surrounding the UN—roughly from First Avenue to the mid-block between First and Second Avenues, and from East 43rd to East 45th Streets. Those boundaries may only be altered by legislation.

The first project proposed by UNDC in 1969 was an evolution of Roche-Dinkeloo's earlier "superblock" plan for the Fund for Area Planning and Development. This time, the architects designed an office and business complex with four towers clad in reflective glass and encapsulated within a colossal glass dome rising 40 stories tall. Although the city's Board of Estimate approved the architecturally ambitious project in April 1970, continued criticism from neighbors and funding issues caused a more measured design to be adopted, with a single mixed-use hotel and office tower on the corner of East 44th Street and First Avenue. The 39-story One United Nations Plaza, financed with a $52 million bond issue, was dedicated in 1976. The tower's offices are fully leased by the UN and foreign missions, with the former United Nations Plaza Hotel (owned and operated by a private entity since 1997) occupying its top dozen floors. The hotel's amenities include a tennis court, swimming pool, and meeting facilities. *The New York Times* architecture critic Paul Goldberger celebrated the tower's abstract form and reflective materials, writing, "The building is an exquisite minimalist sculpture; its abstract form has nothing to do with any of the buildings near it, except for the allusions its blue-green glass makes to the United Nations Secretariat Building across First Avenue."[29]

In 1980, the UNDC announced plans for an adjoining 40-story Roche-Dinkeloo designed office and hotel tower, to be called Two United Nations

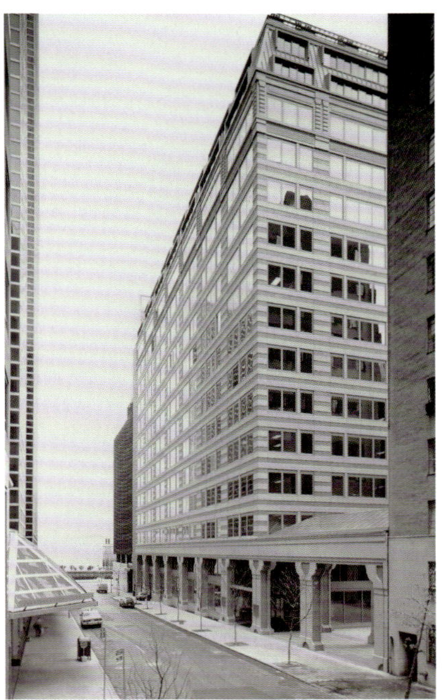

Three United Nations Plaza.

Plaza. Linked with its predecessor by an enclosed sky bridge, the second tower was designed as a complement more than a twin. The building's office space is occupied by the UN and foreign missions to the UN. The building opened in 1983, the year after Kevin Roche received the Pritzker Prize, architecture's highest honor. Paul Goldberger later called the architectural duo "arguably the best glass buildings in Manhattan since the Seagram Building" and noted that "their utterly cool, self-assured abstraction set the tone for a generation of late-modern towers."[30] In 2017, the hotel's reception area, entrance foyer, hallway, and iconic Ambassador Grill received protected status from the New York City Landmarks Preservation Commission. Roche later designed a third building for the UNDC, in a much different architectural style. Opened in 1987, the 15-story Three UN Plaza, located across East 44th Street from the earlier UNDC buildings, features a granite exterior with ground-level colonnade and a mansard roof. UNICEF occupies Three UN Plaza as its global headquarters.

In addition to this trio of buildings, the UNDC has also contributed its expertise to other UN-related building projects. A number of years ago, the UNDC led a design competition for a new structure, known as the United Nations Consolidation Building or DC-5, intended to consolidate UN staff from scattered locations in New York City. The building would be located on a site just south of the Secretariat Building and the Dag Hammarskjöld Library on East 42nd Street and First Avenue. Japanese architect Fumihiko Maki, a Pritzker Prize Laureate, won the competition with a design for a slender 36-story tower featuring a white glass facade, symbolizing peace, that would reflect the sky. The tower, which included office space, conference and meeting facilities, and a new UN cafeteria and library, would be connected to the existing UN campus via an underground pedestrian tunnel beneath 42nd Street.[31] While the UN continues to review its long-term accommodation needs, the General Assembly has not made any decision on the DC-5 project. As the UN's real estate requirements evolve, UNDC will continue to partner with the State and City of New York to look at opportunities in support of the UN's mission and goals.

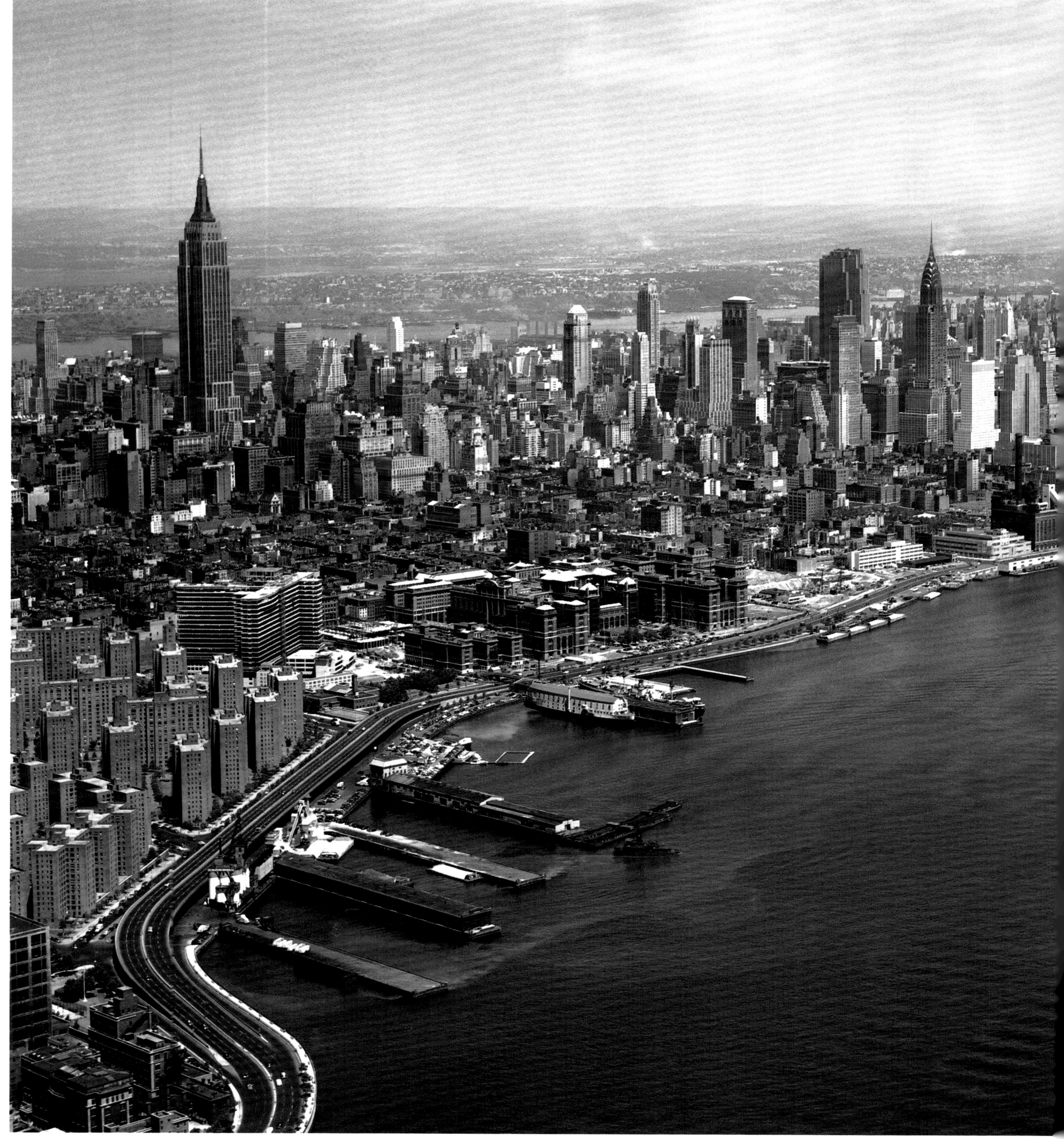

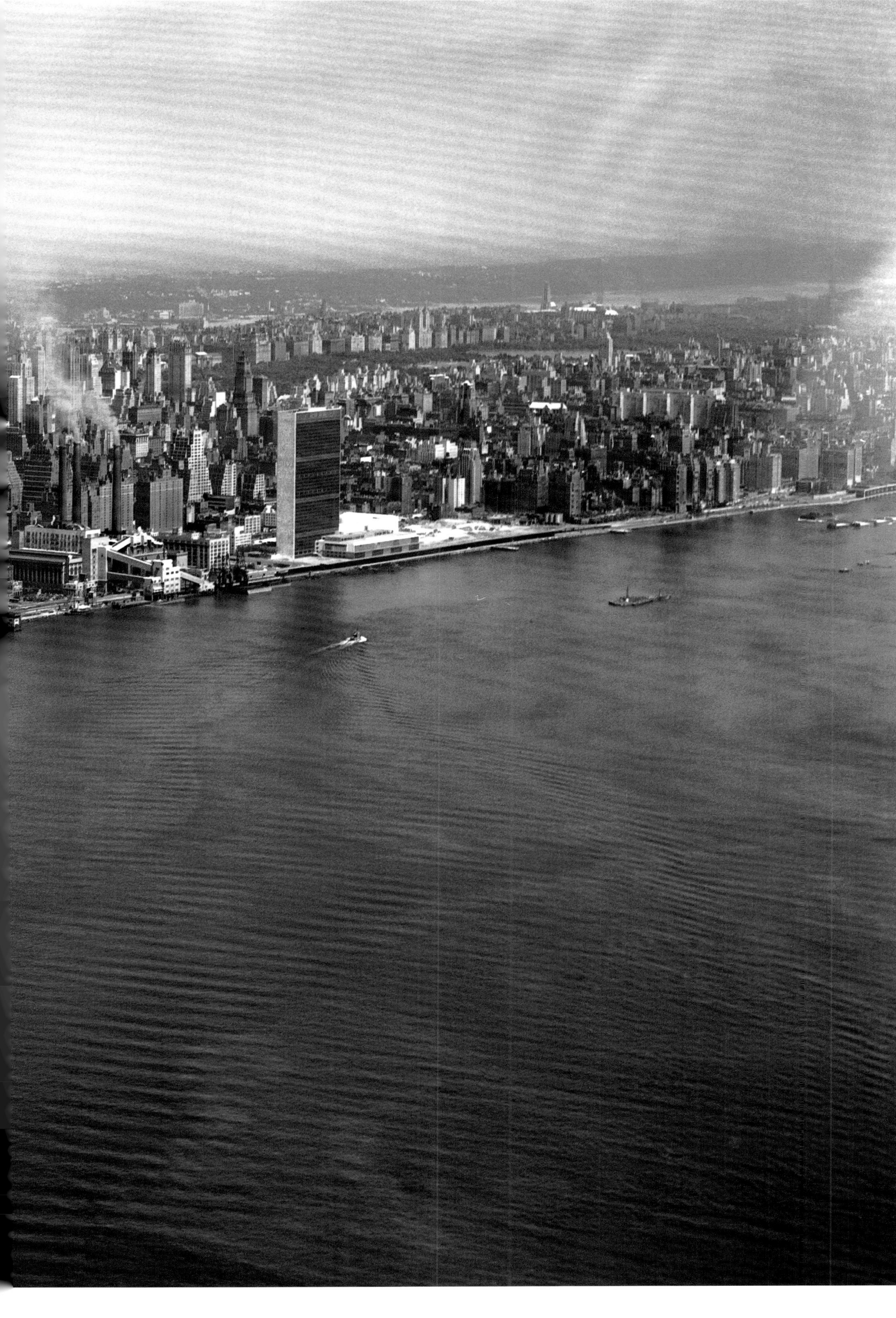

Midtown Manhattan seen from a plane flying above the East River. The United Nations Headquarters is at the far-right of the picture. In the background, the Hudson River and New Jersey, June 1952.

General view of the opening meeting of the tenth session of the United Nations General Assembly. Photo taken as Mr. Vyacheslav Molotov, Minister of Foreign Affairs of the Soviet Union, at the rostrum, was raising the issue of Chinese representation.

Seated behind him, at the presidential rostrum are (left to right) Secretary-General Dag Hammarskjöld; Joseph Luns, Foreign Minister of the Netherlands, who opened the session on behalf of Dr. van Kleffens; and Andrew W. Cordier, Executive Assistant to the Secretary-General. September 20, 1955.

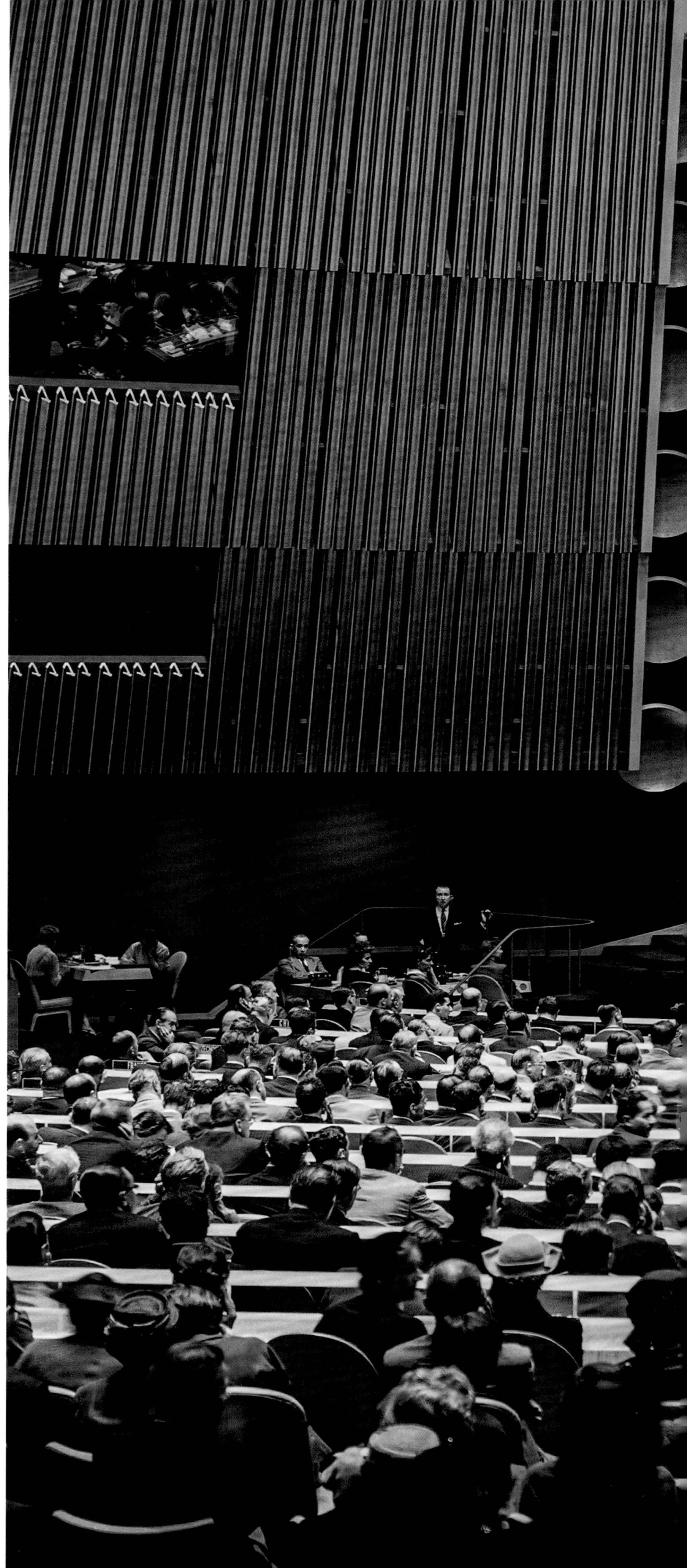

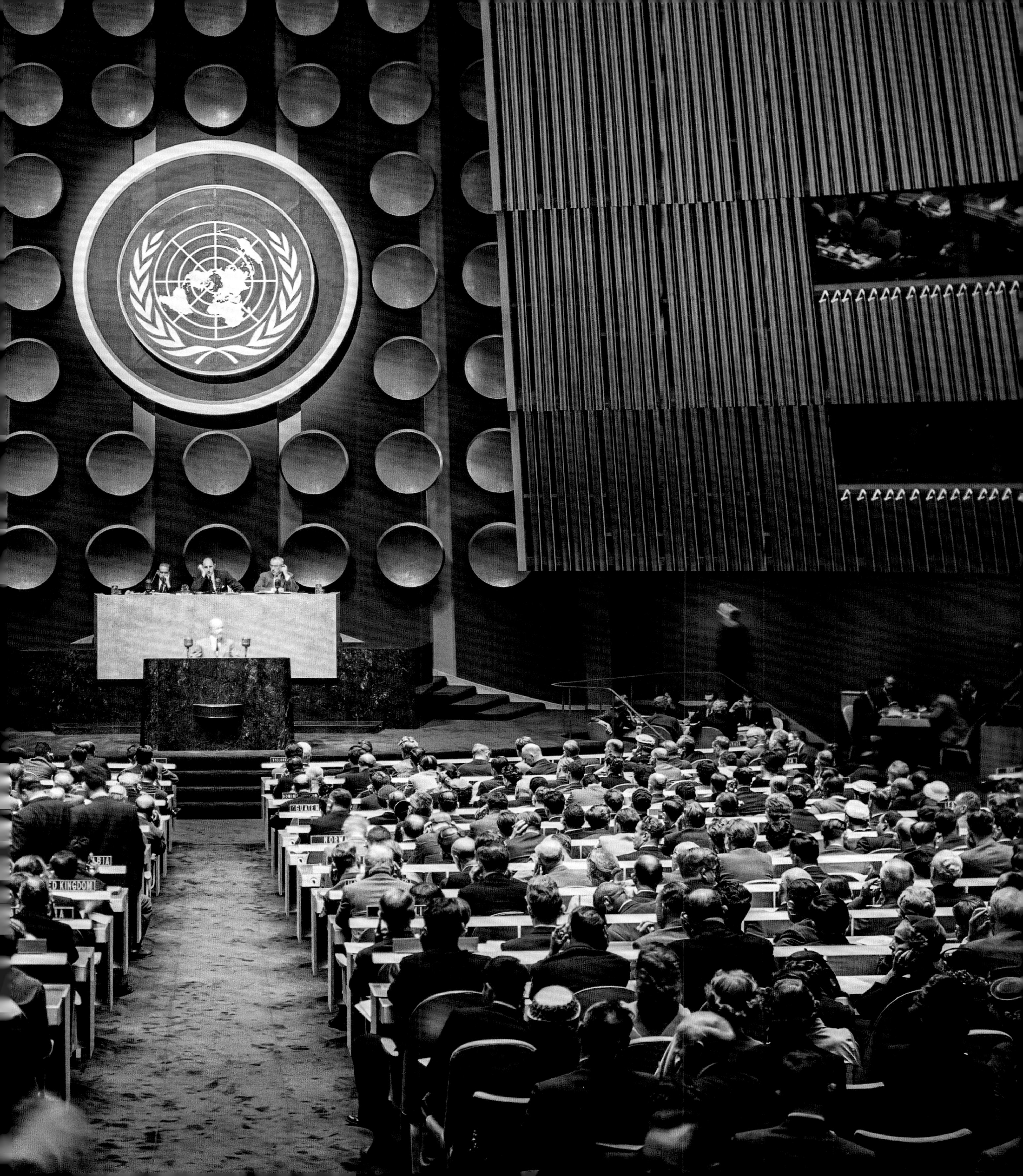

Delegates in the Assembly Building lounge, exchanging views and discussing the issues of the day, during the 15th session of the UN General Assembly, October 1960.

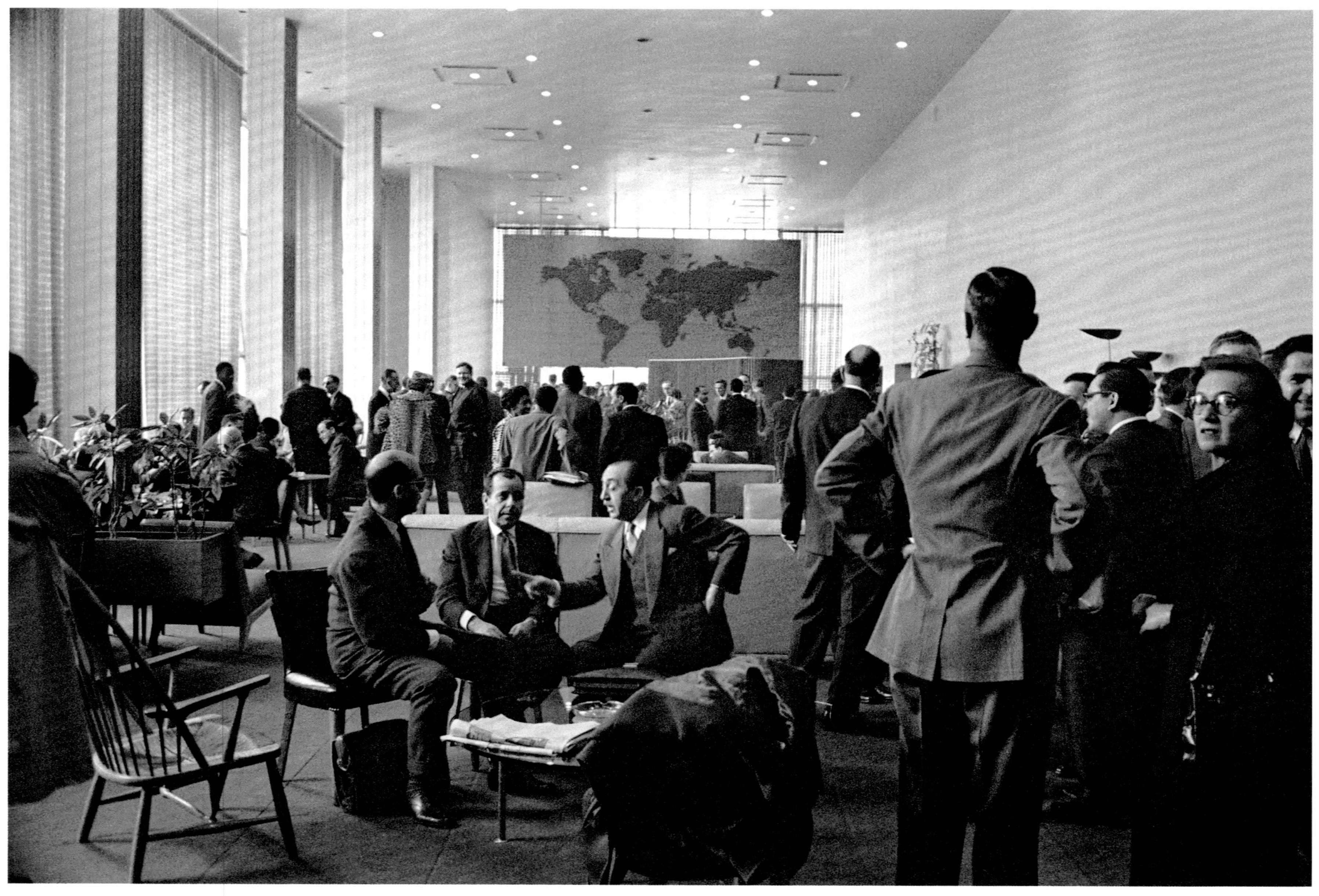

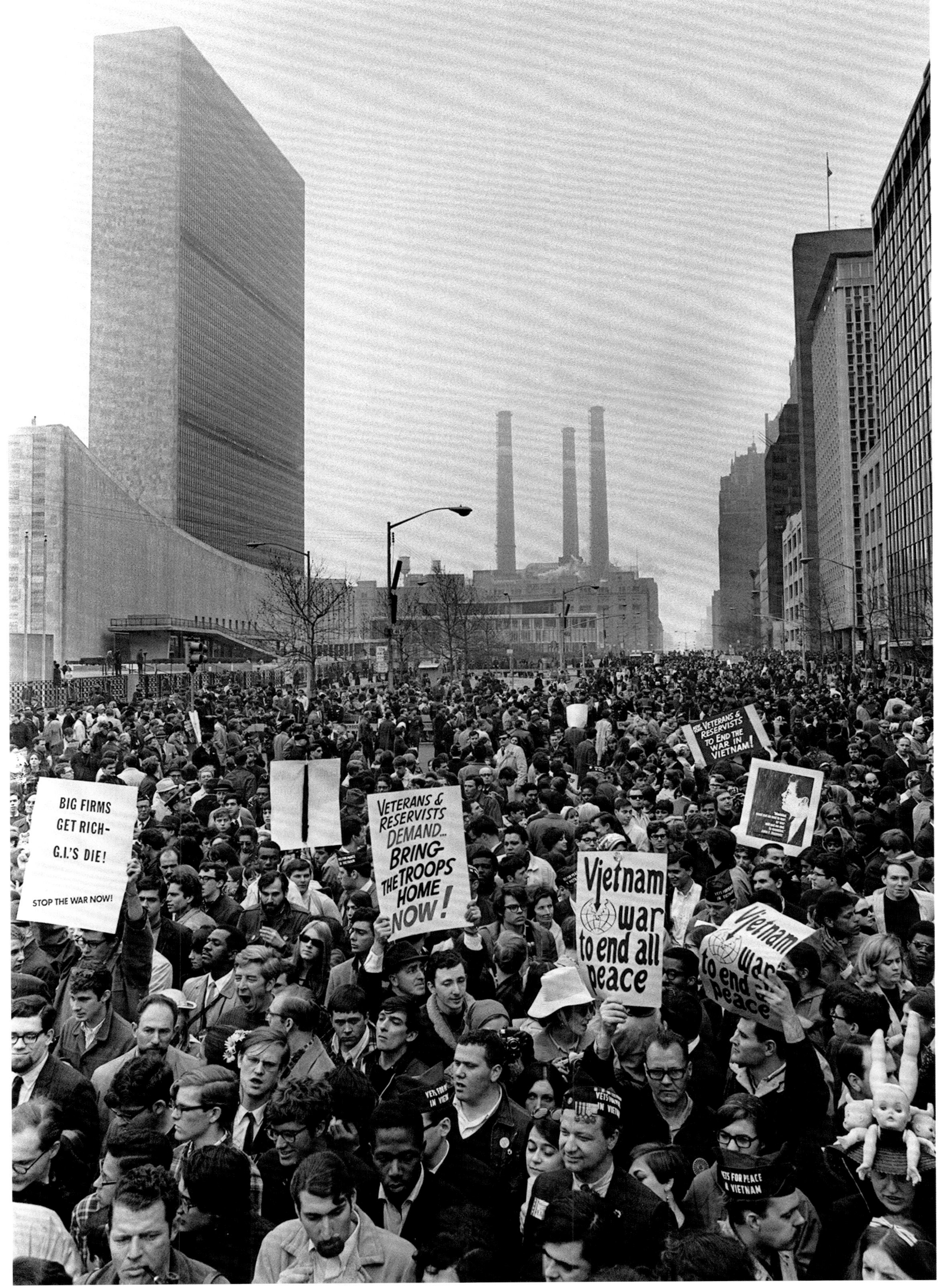

Anti-war demonstrators march outside United Nations Headquarters to protest the war in Vietnam. April 16, 1967.

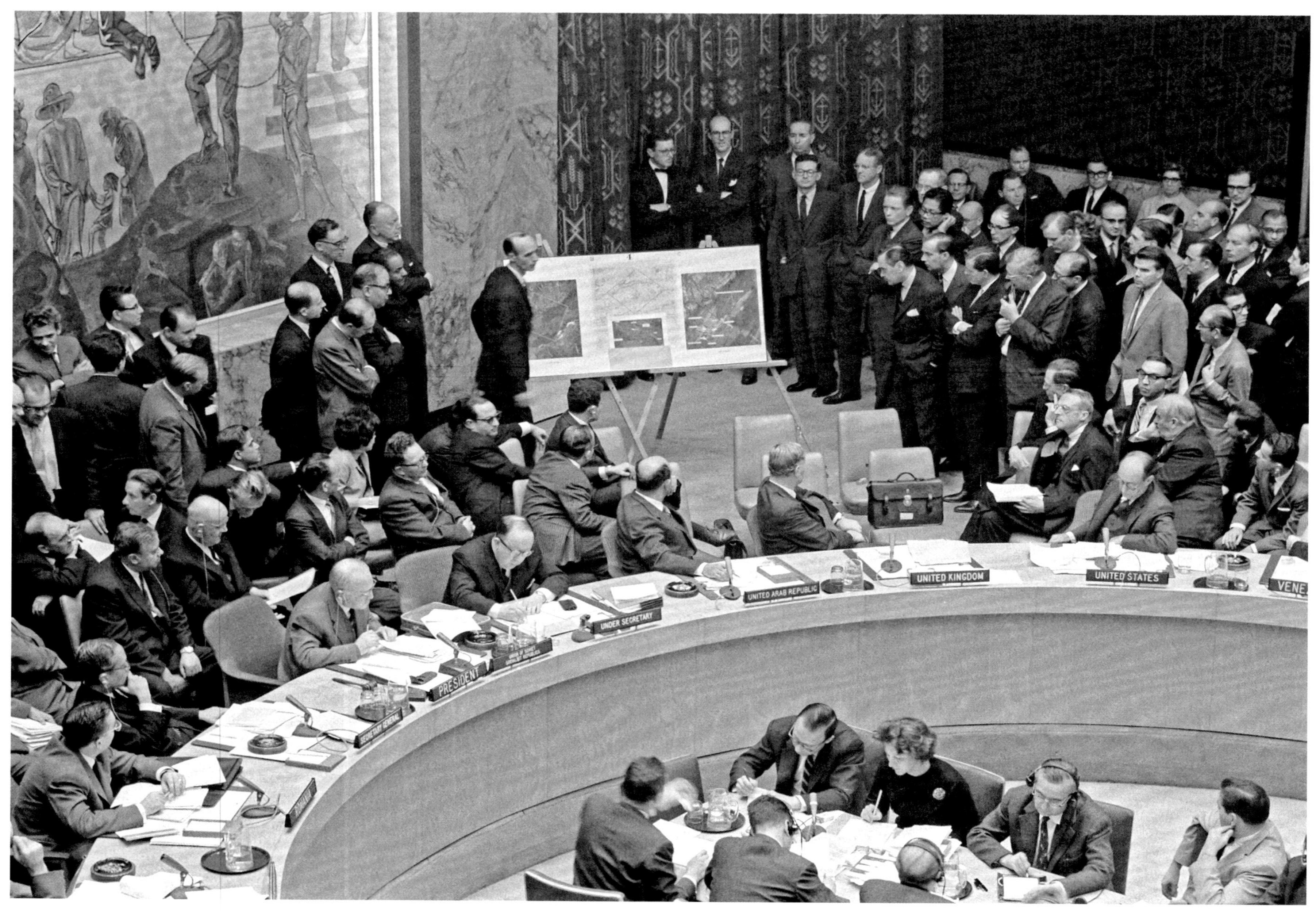

Emergency meeting of the Security Council. Ambassador Adlai E. Stevenson (2nd from right, at table) of the United States presents photographs and maps of Cuba which he said shows ballistic missile sites. The Security Council adjourns to await results of talks between parties concerned and Acting Secretary-General U Thant. October 25, 1962.

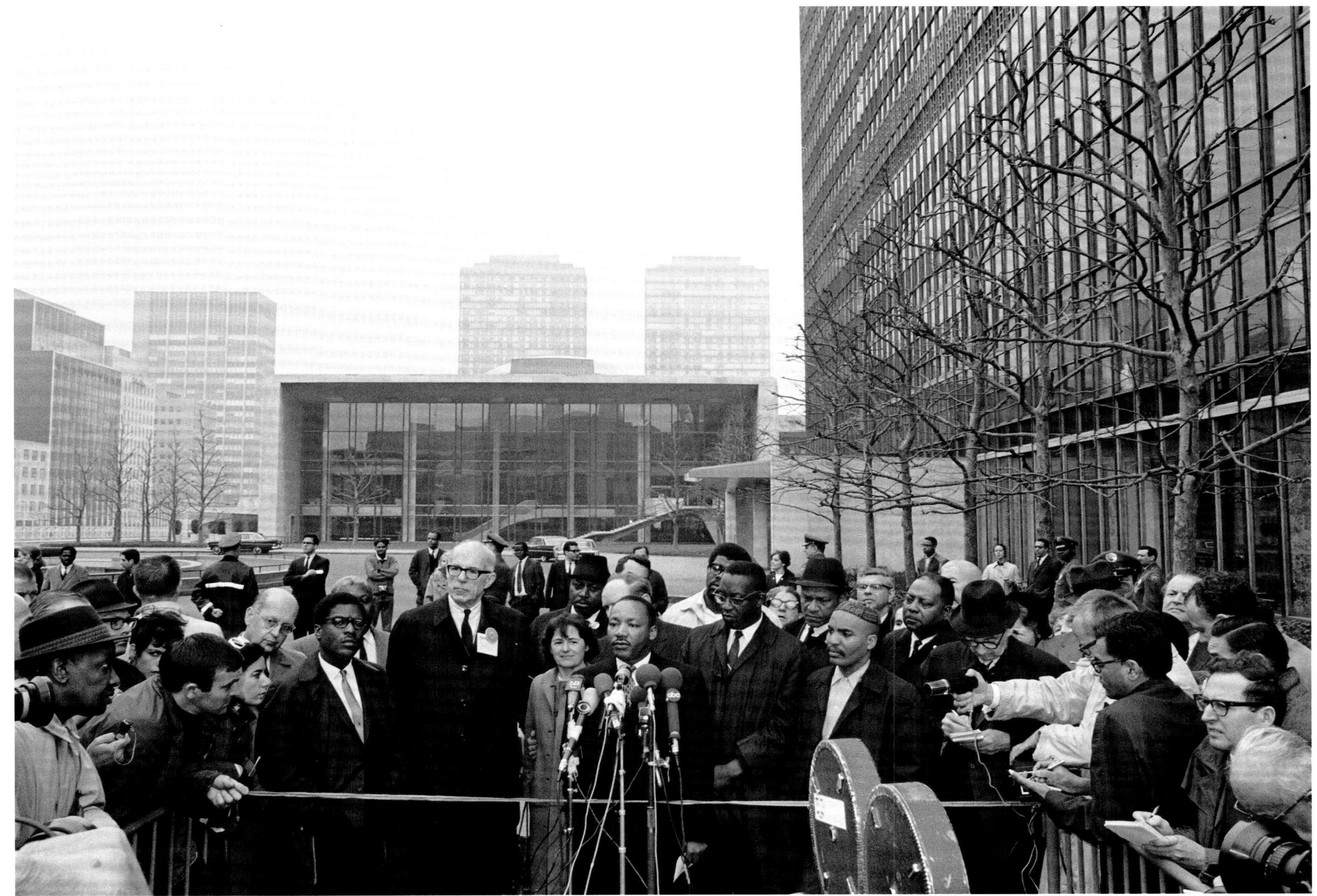

A large crowd, estimated by New York City police at 125,000 people, gathered in front of UN Headquarters to protest the war in Vietnam and the involvement of the United States. The march was led by the Rev. Dr. Martin Luther King, Jr., Dr. Benjamin Spock, and other leaders of the Civil Rights and peace movements. Dr. Martin Luther King, Jr., making a statement to the press following a meeting with Dr. Bunche. April 15, 1967.

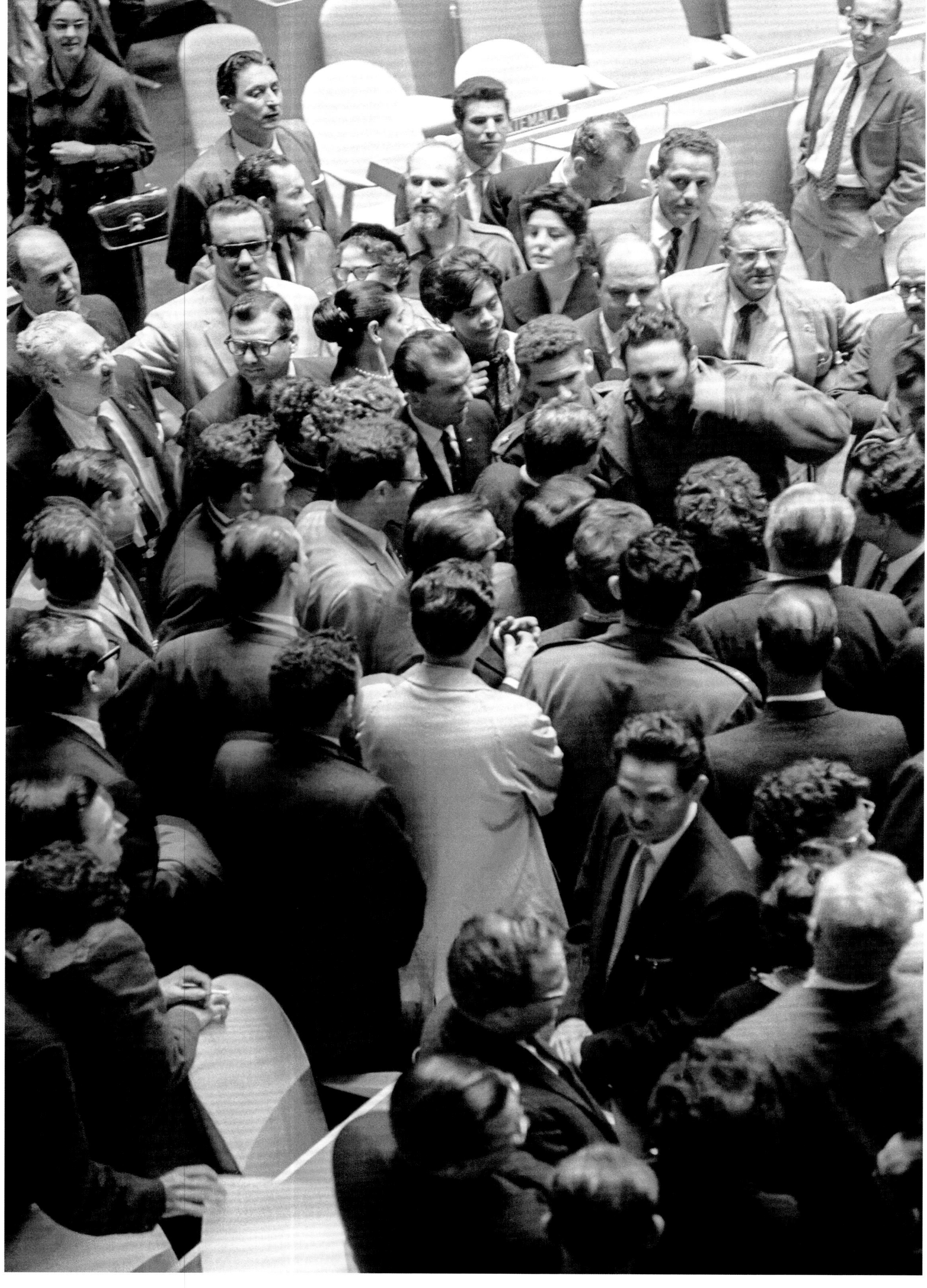

The General Assembly, holding its 15th regular session, continued its general debate. An unprecedented number of high officials attended this session which had before it an 87-item provisional agenda, the longest in its history. The afternoon's plenary meeting heard an address by Cuban Premier Fidel Castro. Here, at the conclusion of the meeting, Castro is seen on the Assembly floor surrounded by colleagues and well-wishers. September 26, 1960.

Soviet cosmonauts Yuri Gagarin and Valentina Tereshkova giving a press conference during their visit to the UN Headquarters. October 16, 1963.

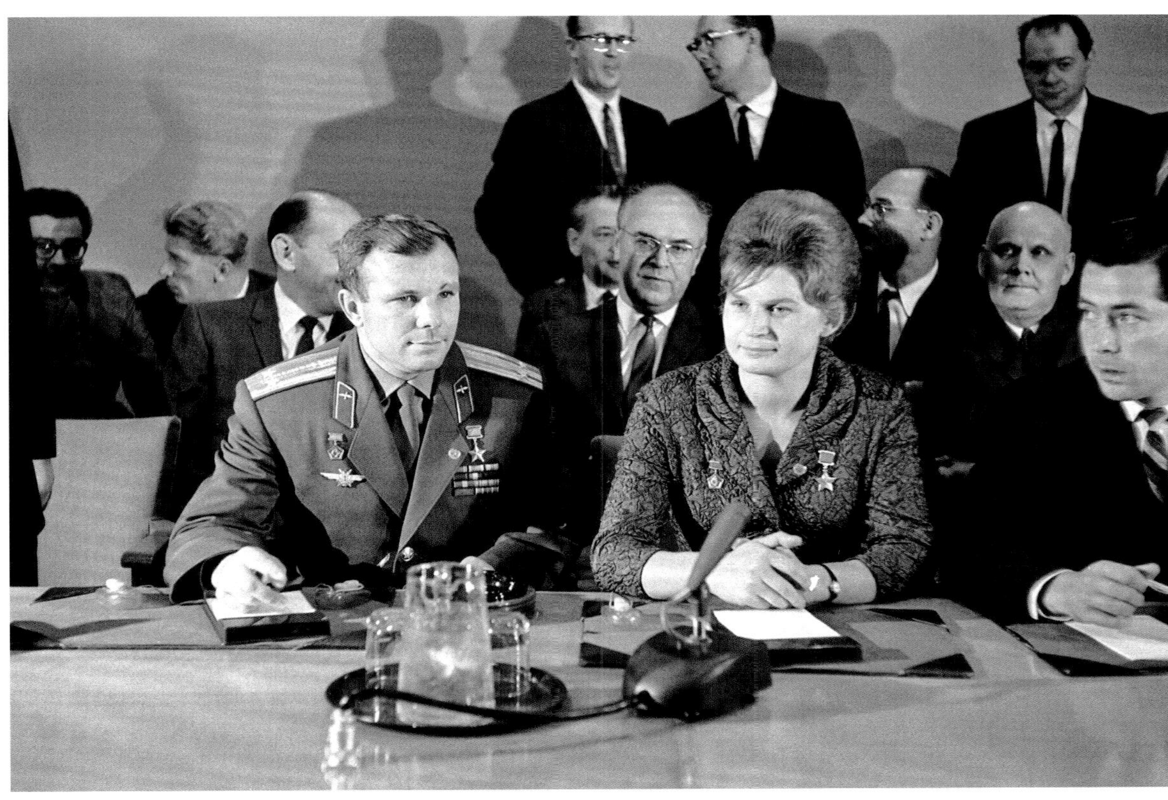

The General Assembly raised the membership of the United Nations to 135 by admitting the German Democratic Republic, the Federal Republic of Germany, and the Commonwealth of the Bahamas during its 28th regular session. Otto Winzer (right), Foreign Minister of the German Democratic Republic, conversing with Walter Scheel, Minister for Foreign Affairs of the Federal Republic of Germany, before the opening of the meeting. September 18, 1973.

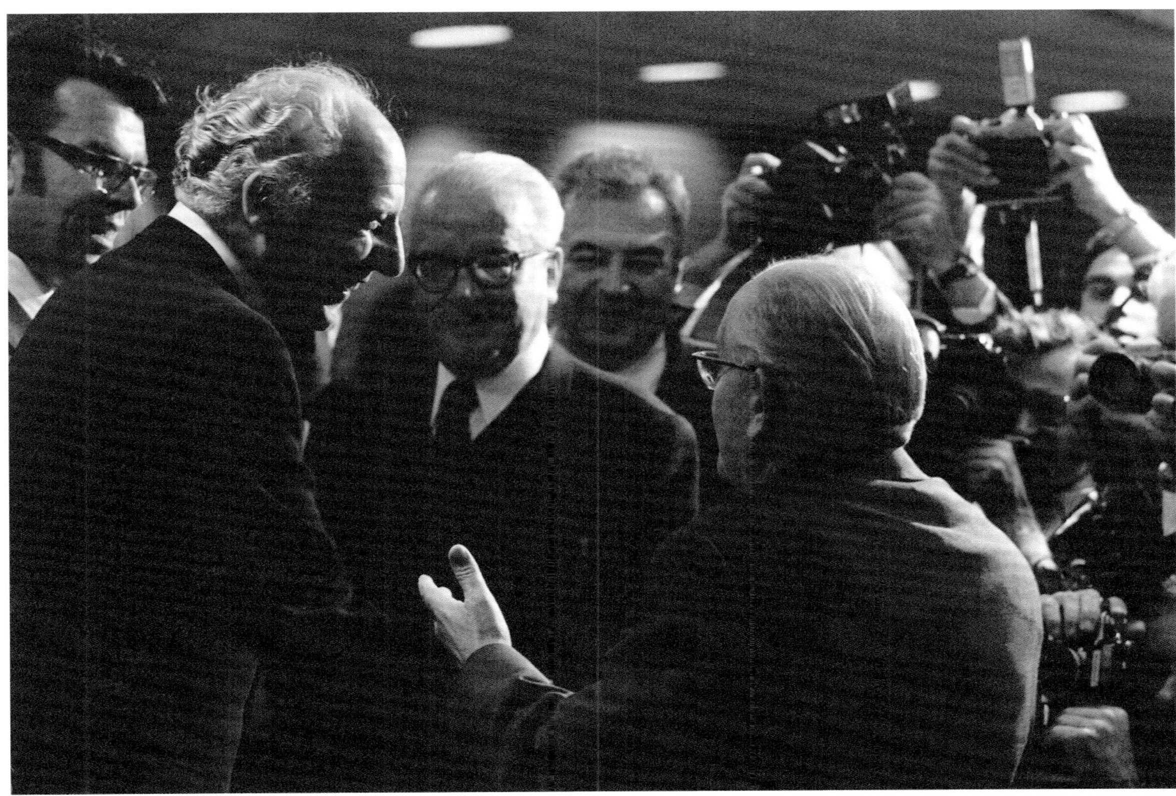

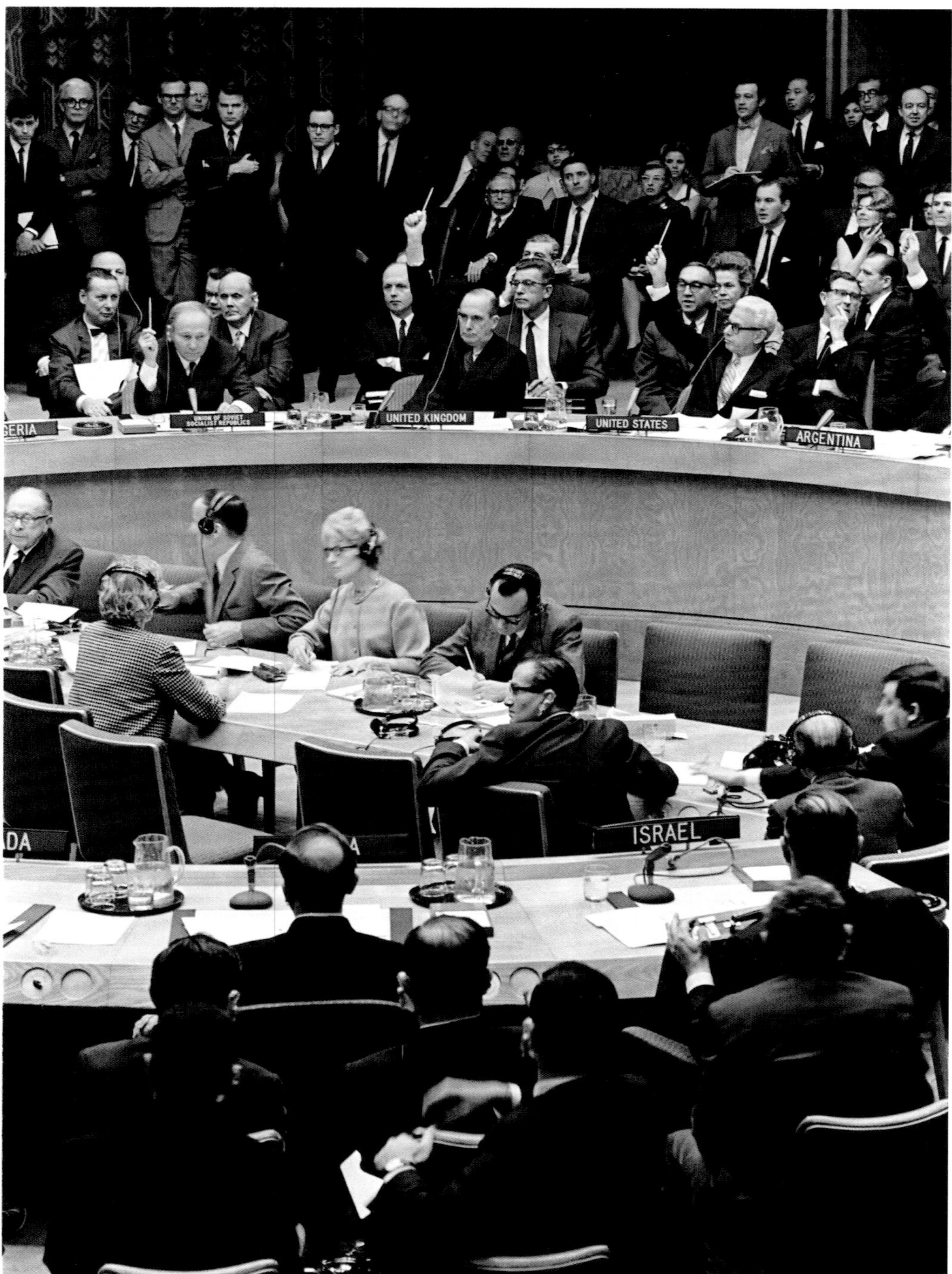

A view of the Security Council as a vote was taken unanimously adopting a resolution regarding the establishment of a just and lasting peace in the Middle East. Facing the camera with hands upraised to indicate votes in favor of the resolution are (from left to right): Vasily V. Kuznetsov, First Deputy Foreign Minister of the Soviet Union; Lord Caradon, Permanent Representative of the UK; and Arthur J. Goldberg, Permanent Representative of the United States. November 22, 1967.

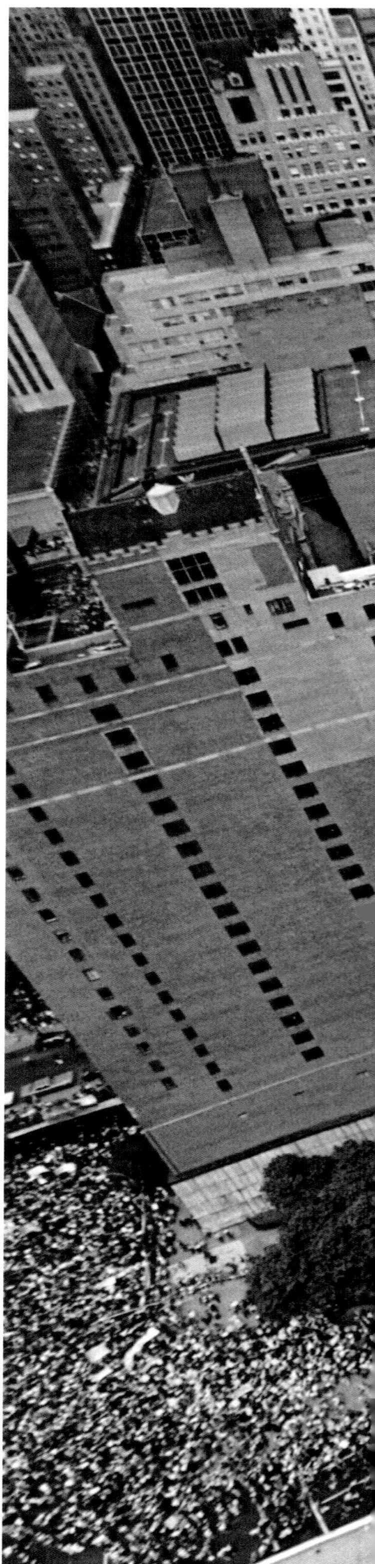

An aerial view of thousands of demonstrators filing past United Nations Headquarters on their way to a peace rally in Central Park. The rally was timed to coincide with the UN General Assembly's second Special Session on Disarmament. An estimated three-quarters of a million people gathered in the cause of world nuclear disarmament, making it the largest demonstration of its kind ever to take place in the U.S. In the background, Two United Nations Plaza is under construction. June 12, 1982.

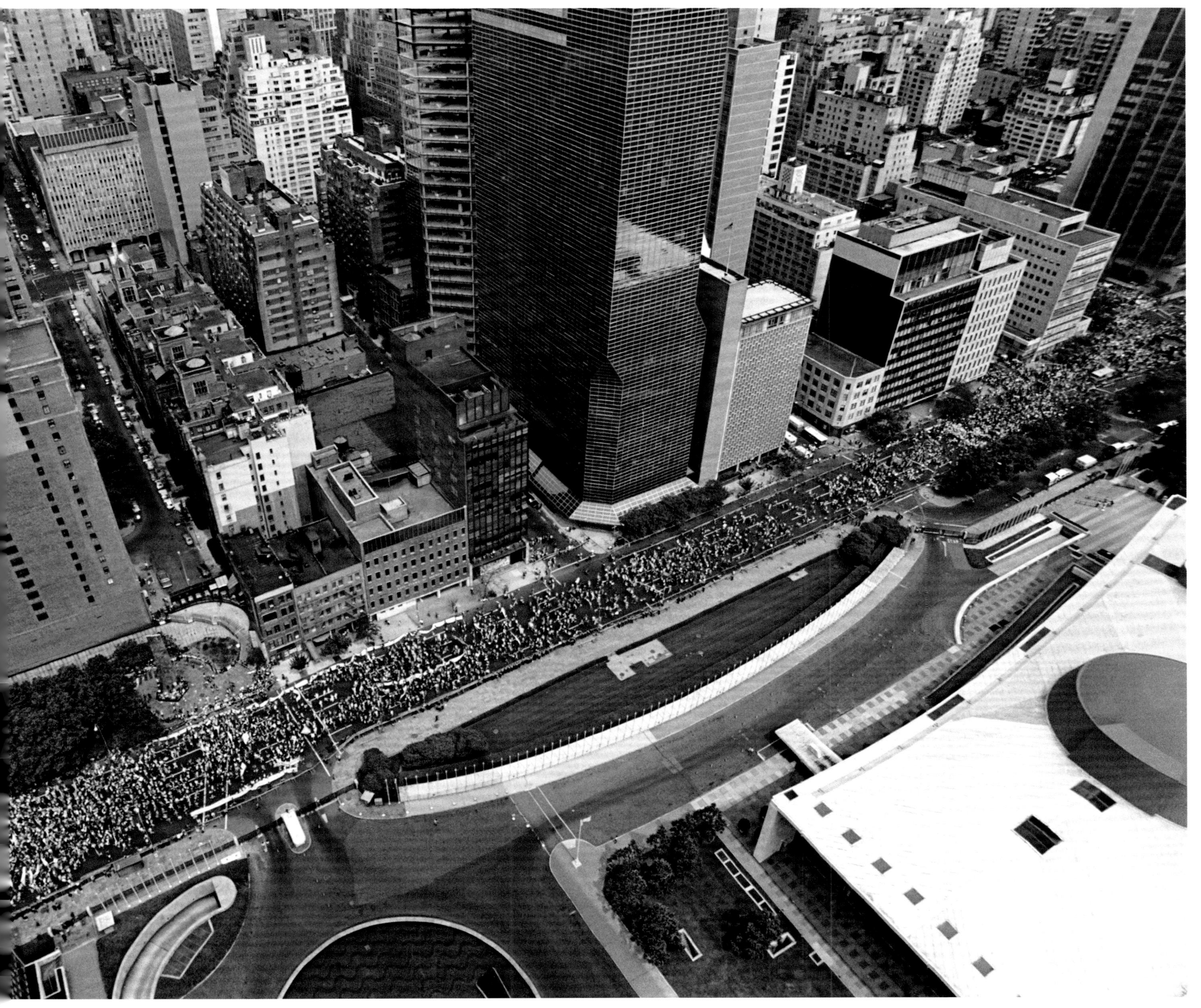

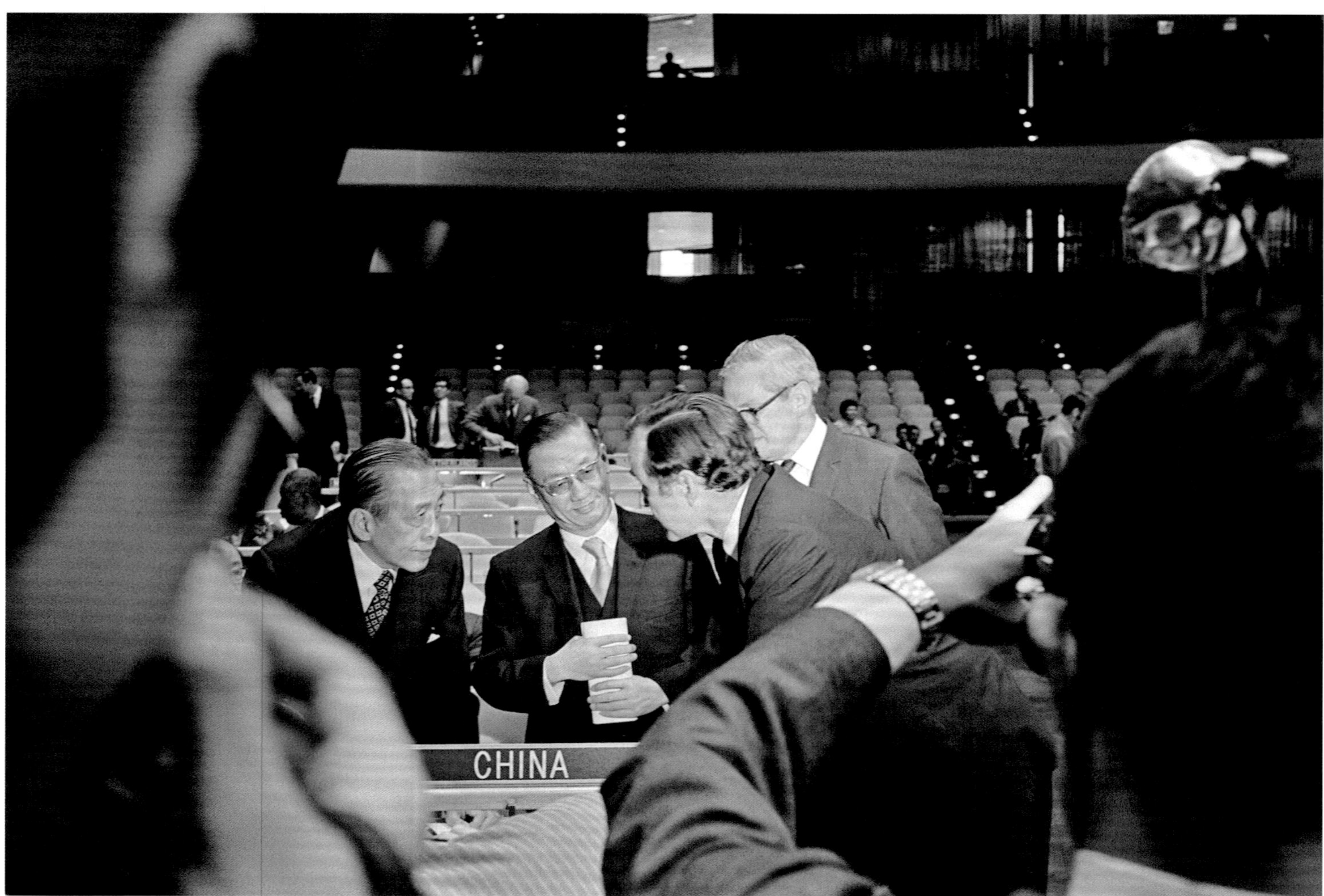

The General Assembly began consideration of the item entitled Restoration of the lawful rights of the People's Republic of China in the United Nations. Conferring before the meeting began are, from left: Liu Chieh, Permanent Representative of China; Chow Shu-Kai, Minister for Foreign Affairs of China; and George Bush, Permanent Representative of the U.S. October 18, 1971.

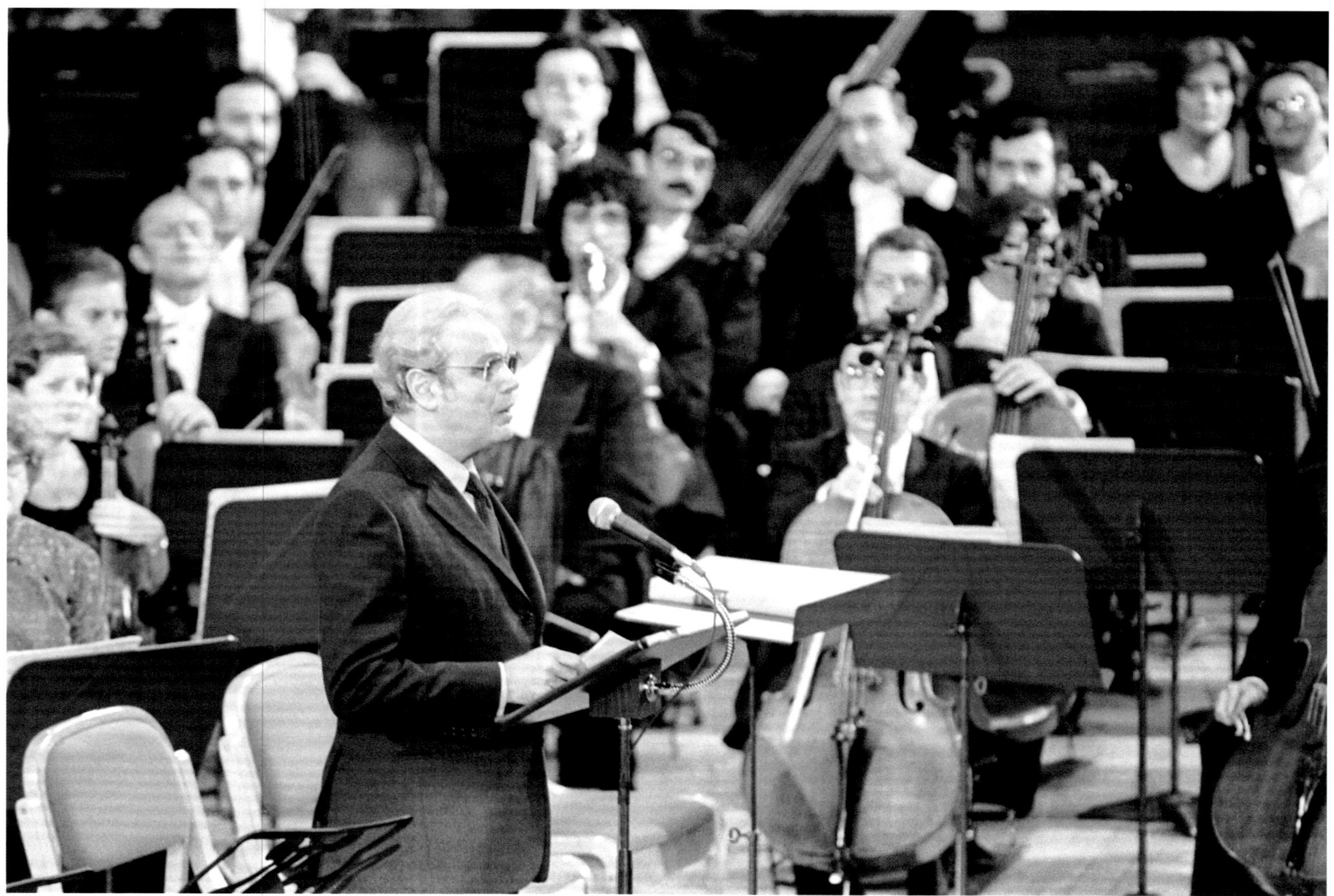

National Orchestra and Chorus of Spain performs on United Nations Day. Secretary-General Javier Pérez de Cuéllar addresses the audience in the General Assembly Hall. October 24, 1983.

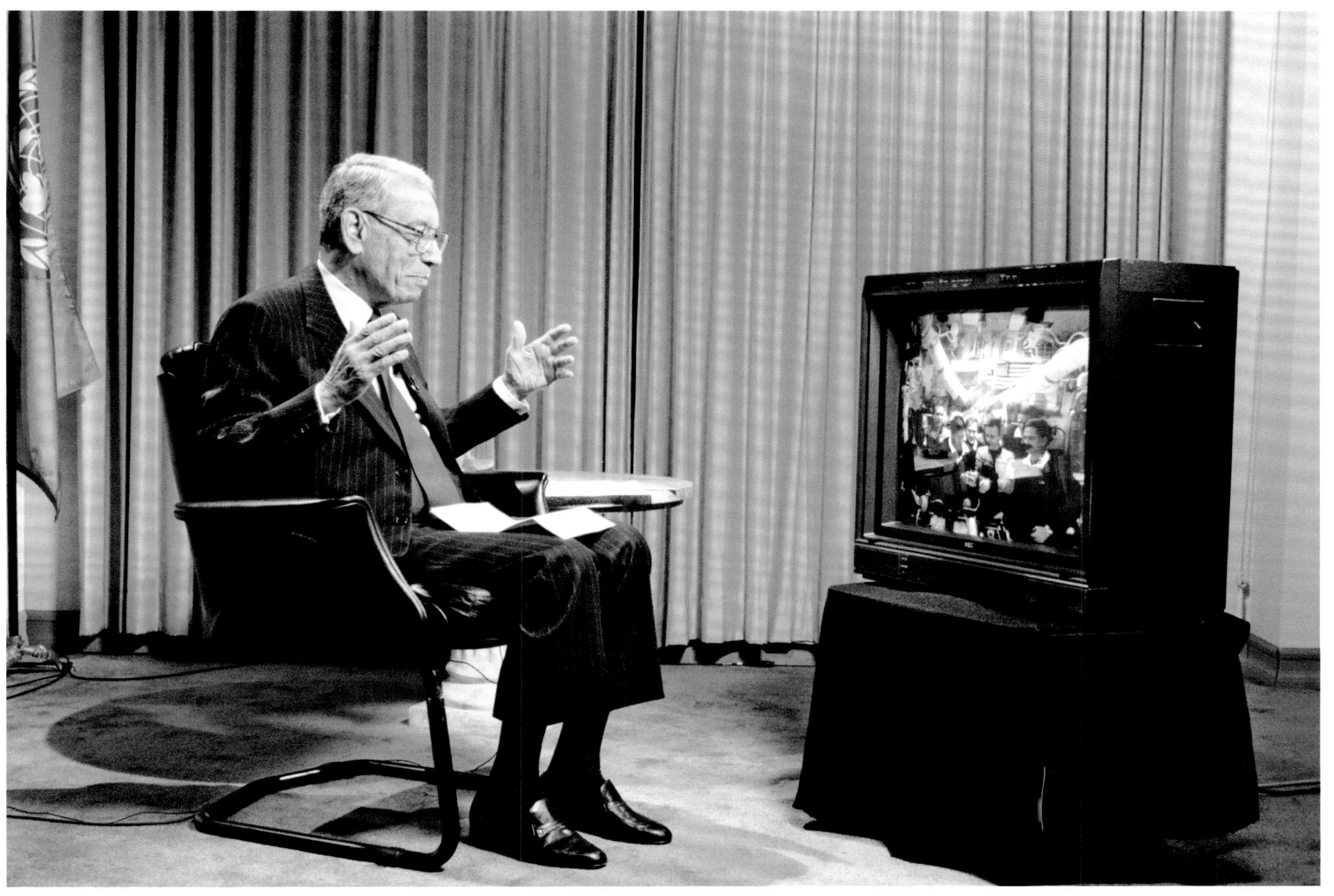

Secretary-General Boutros Boutros-Ghali holds a video-conference with the crew of the second Shuttle-Mir Docking mission, STS-74/Atlantis, shown seated in the Core Module of the Mir space station. The crew, comprised of representatives from Canada, the Russian Federation, the United States, and the European Space Agency (Germany), was the largest international crew to date. November 17, 1995.

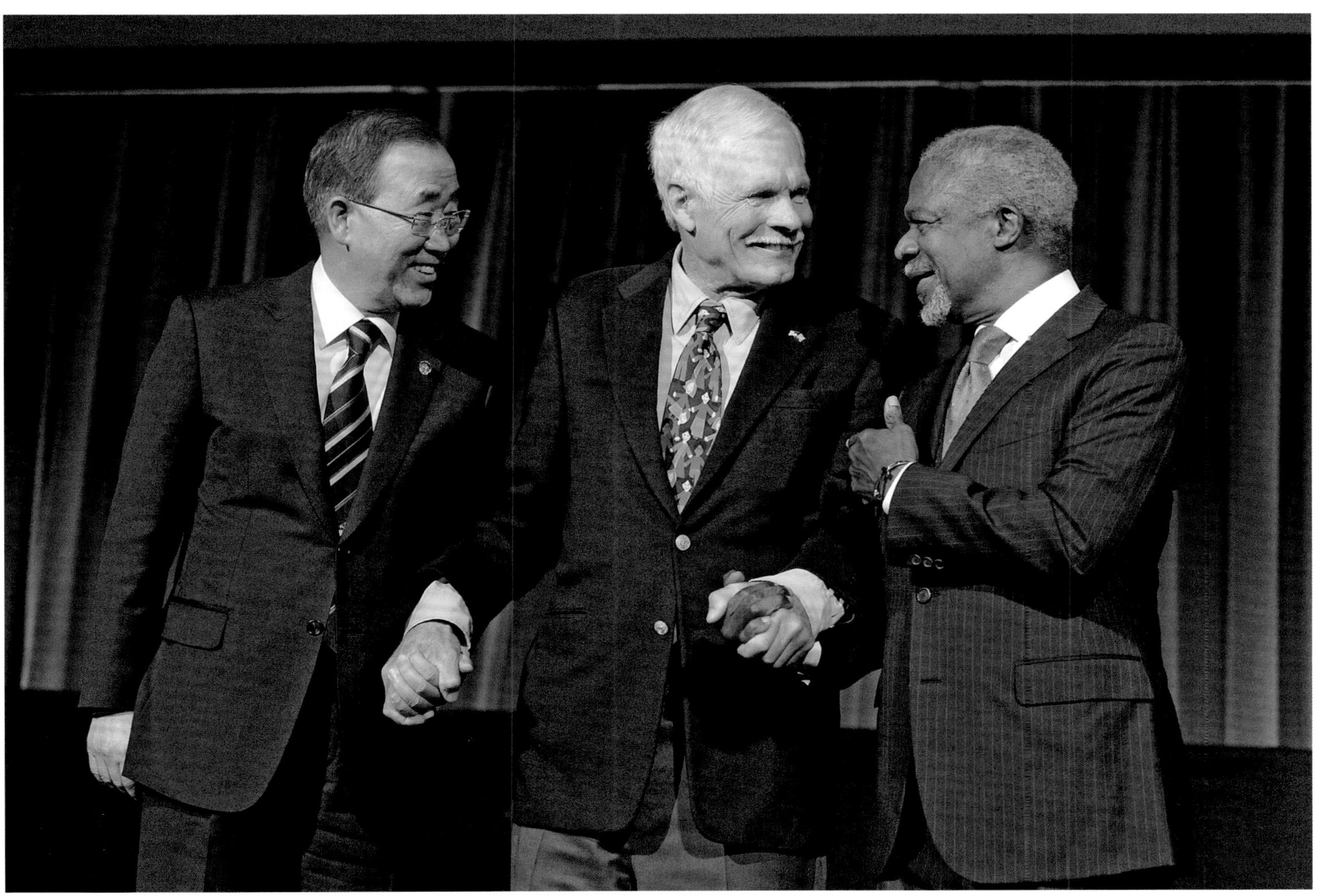

Ted Turner with former Secretaries-General Ban Ki-moon and Kofi Annan. A passionate advocate of the UN and its unique role in advancing global solutions and achieving international peace and progress, Turner created the UN Foundation in 1998 with a $1 billion investment. The foundation supports the work of the UN on sustainable development, climate, and other issues. October 16, 2012.

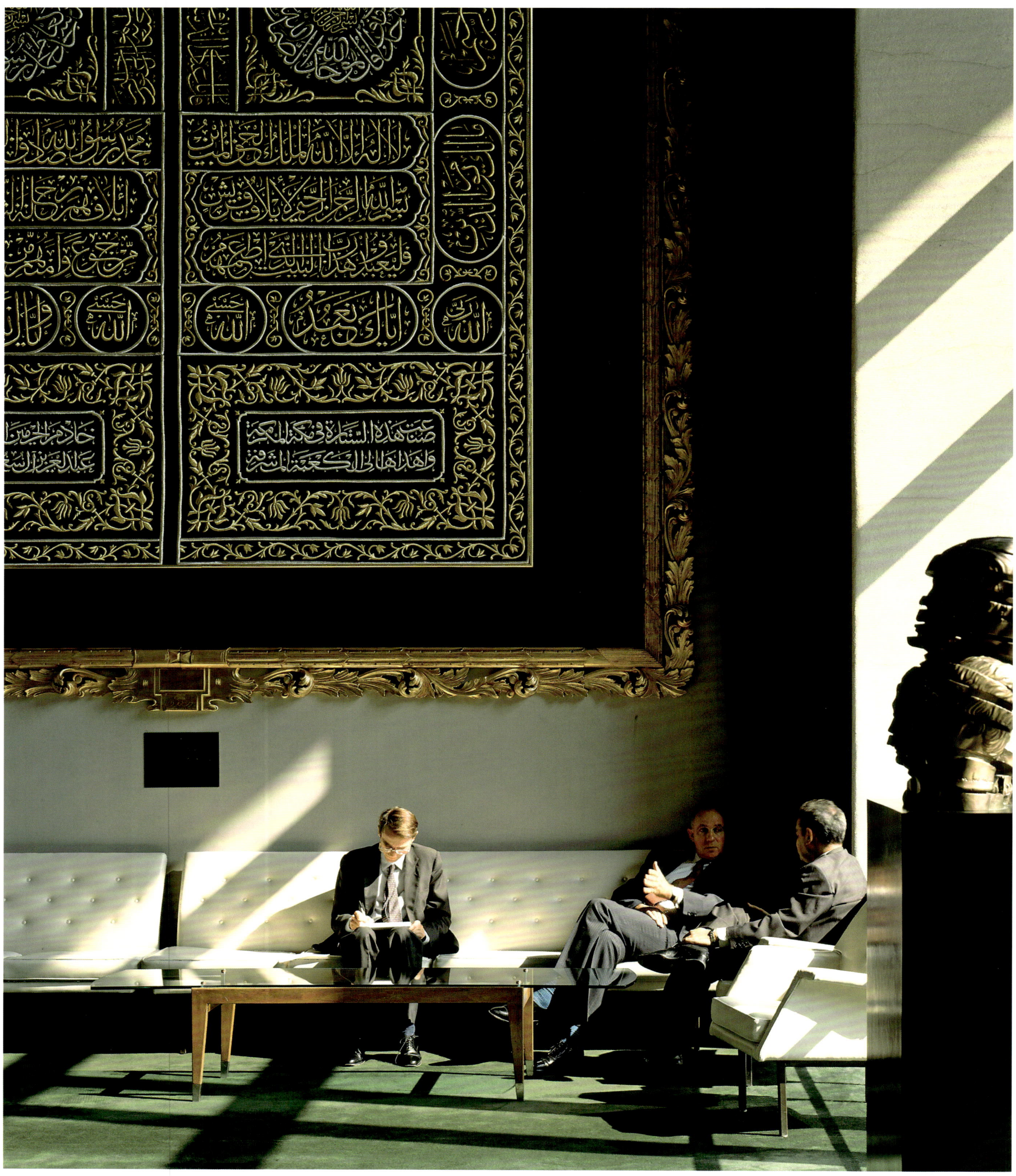

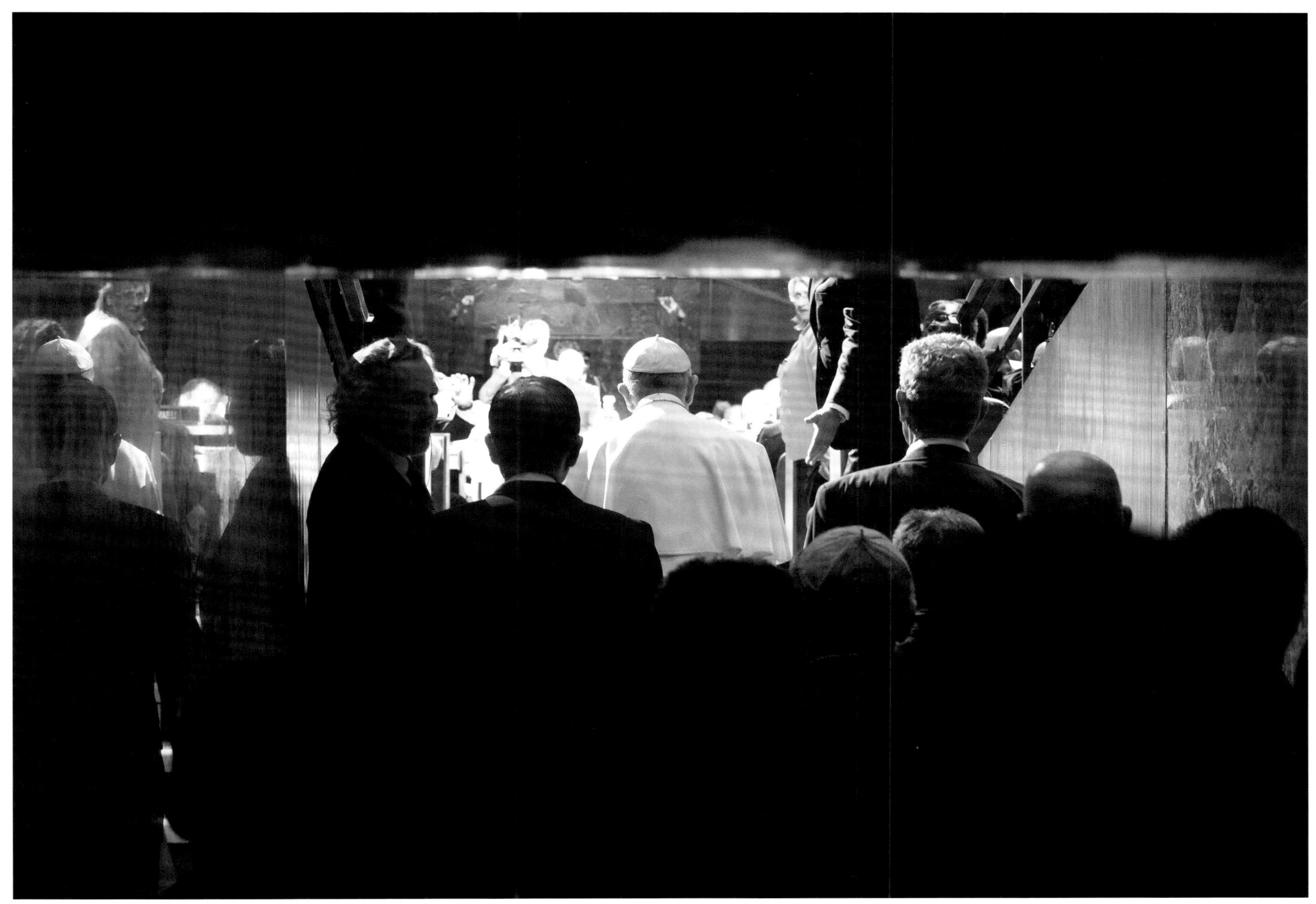

Pope Francis arrives in the General Assembly Hall to deliver an address. September 25, 2015.

Delegates confer in a lounge on the second floor near the General Assembly Hall. Above them is the Kiswa of the Holy Kaaba, a gift to the UN from the Kingdom of Saudi Arabia, January 1993.

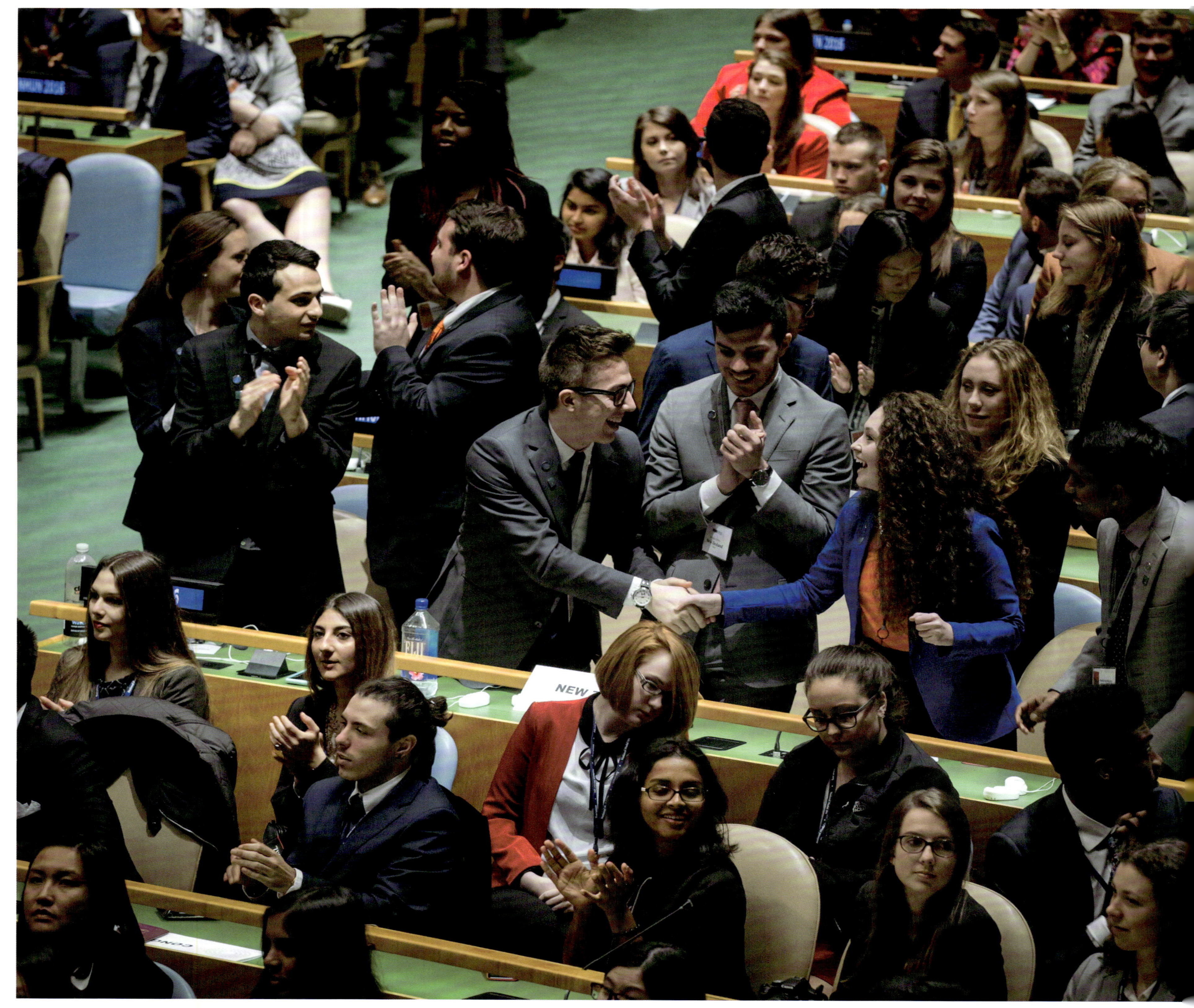

Participants of the 2016
National Model United
Nations Conference
in the General Assembly
Hall. March 31, 2016.

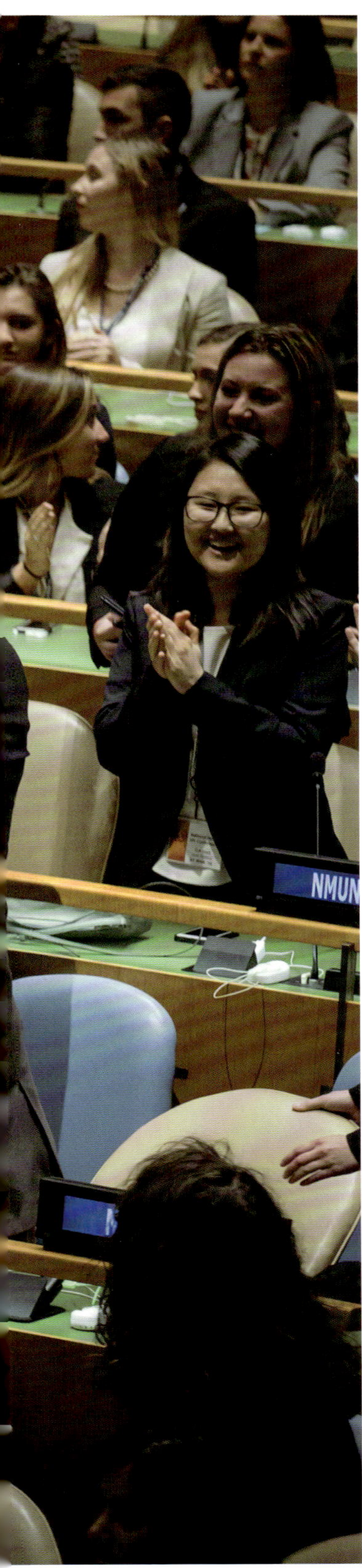

Making her first high-level public appearance since a Taliban attack on her life, Pakistani activist Malala Yousafzai delivers a powerful speech on education and girls' rights at the UN on her 16th birthday—also dubbed "Malala Day." As the youngest recipient of the Nobel Peace Prize, Malala today continues to advocate for the right to education and, among other achievements, opened a school through the Malala Fund for Syrian refugee girls in Lebanon in 2015. July 12, 2013.

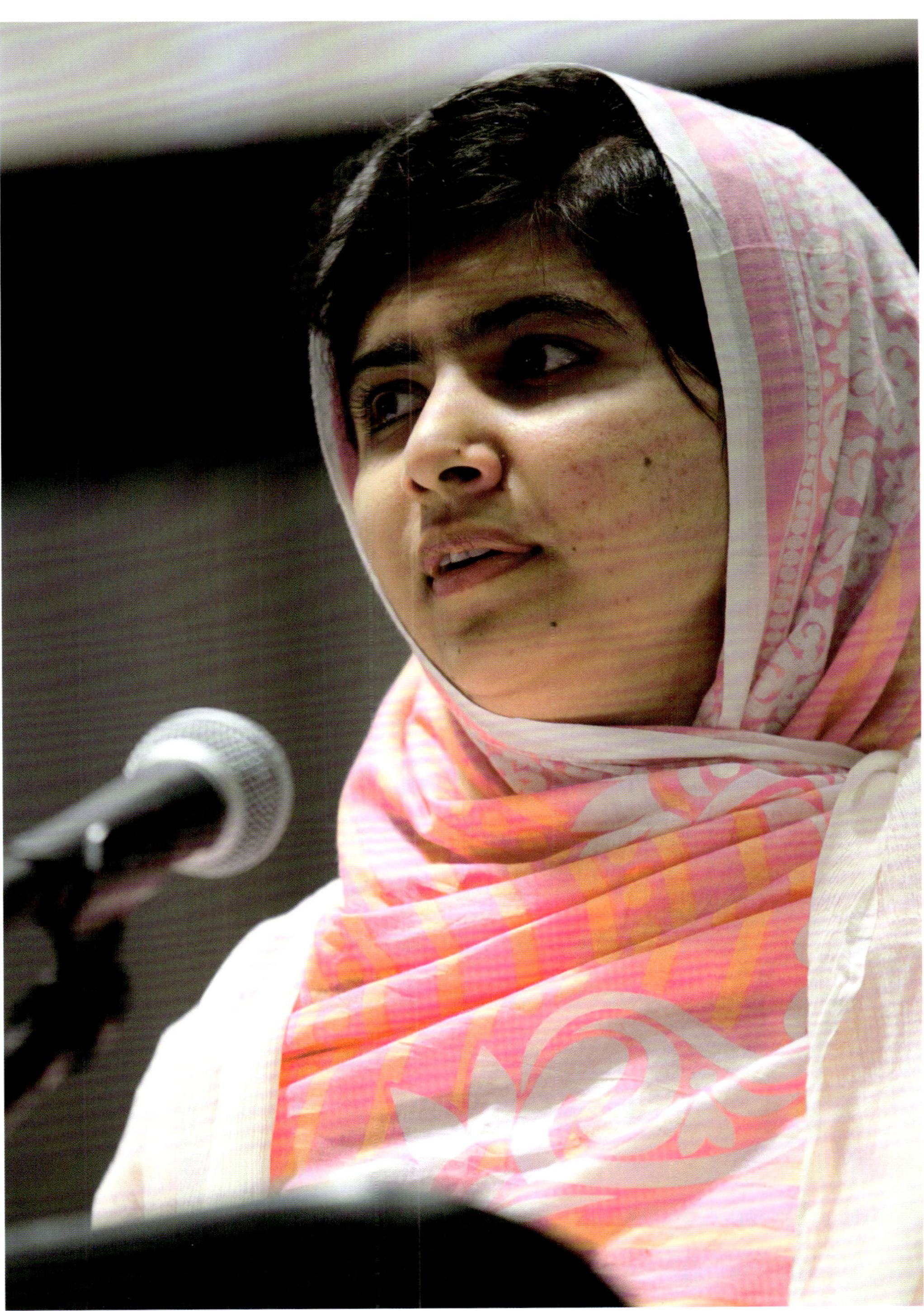

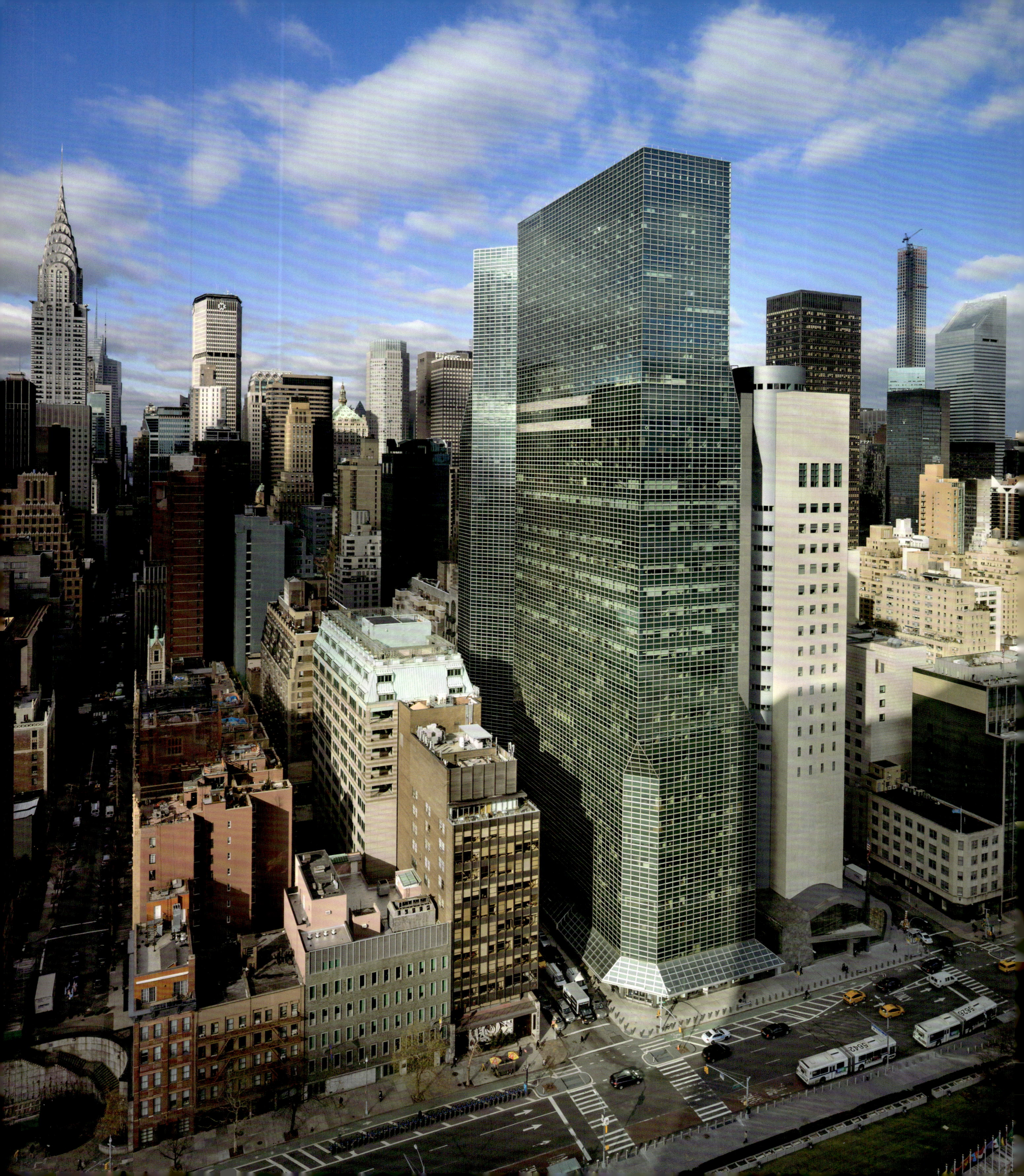

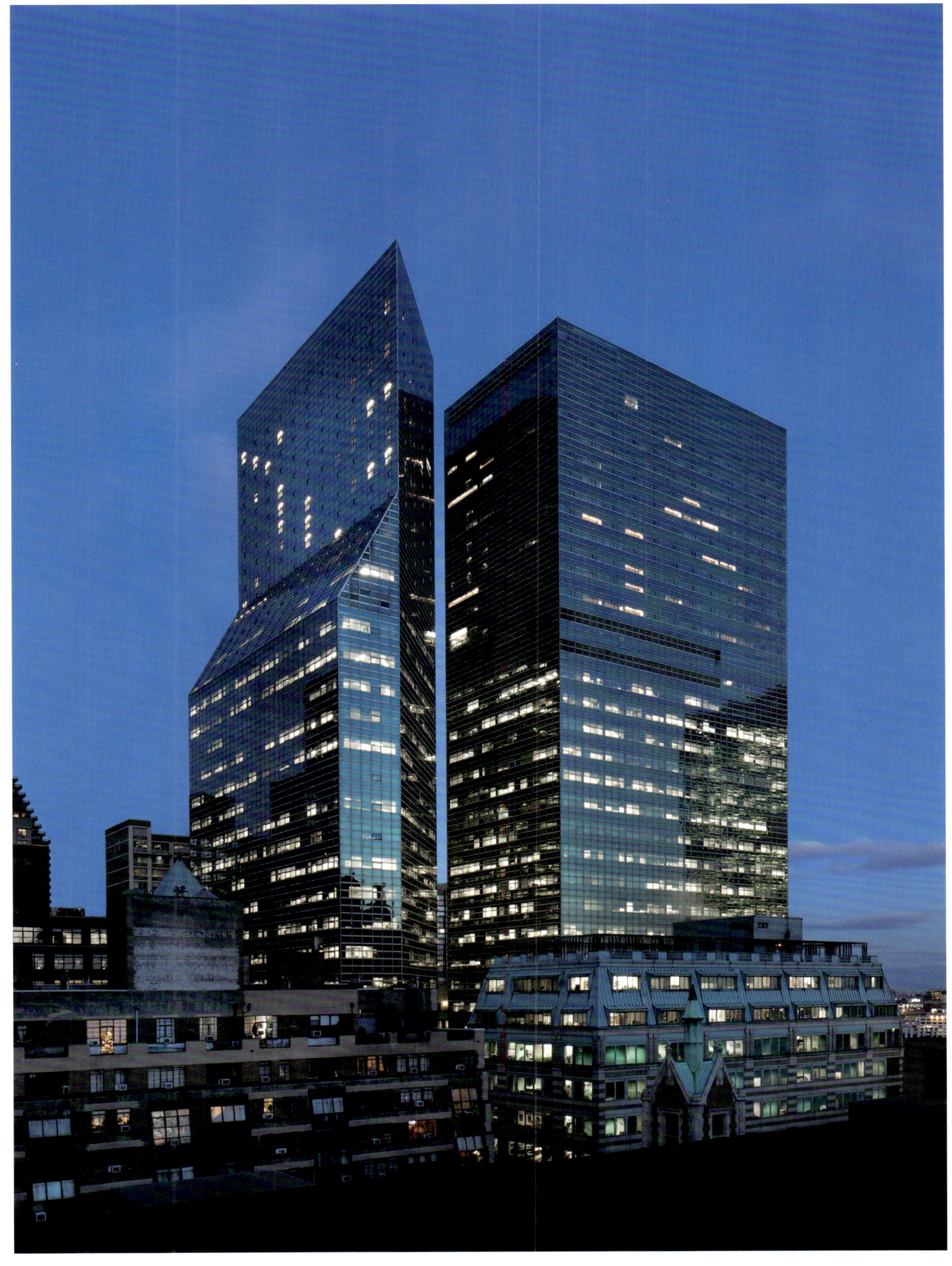

One and Two UN Plaza.

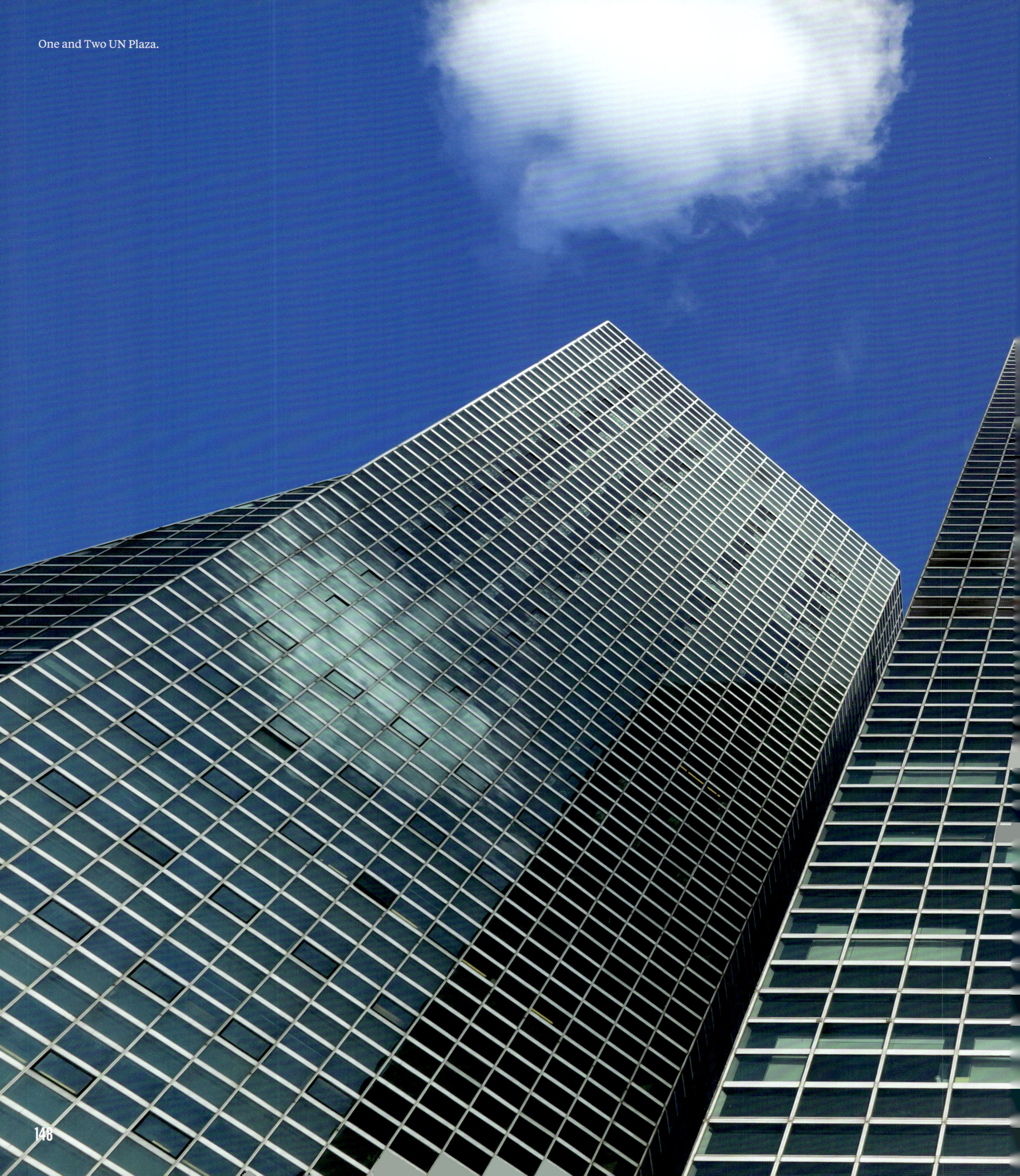

One and Two UN Plaza.

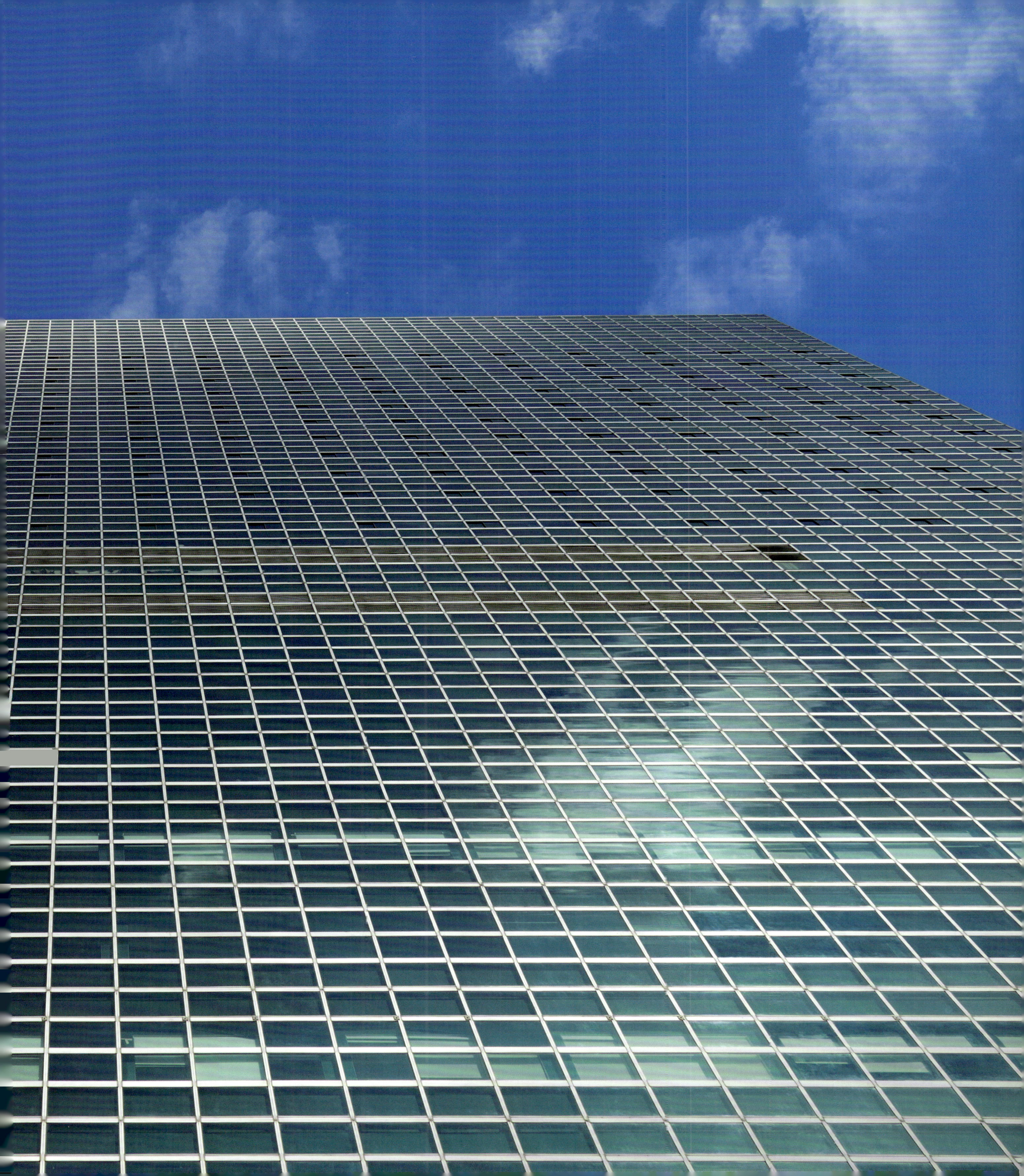

CHAPTER 5

THE UNITED NATIONS IN THE 21ST CENTURY

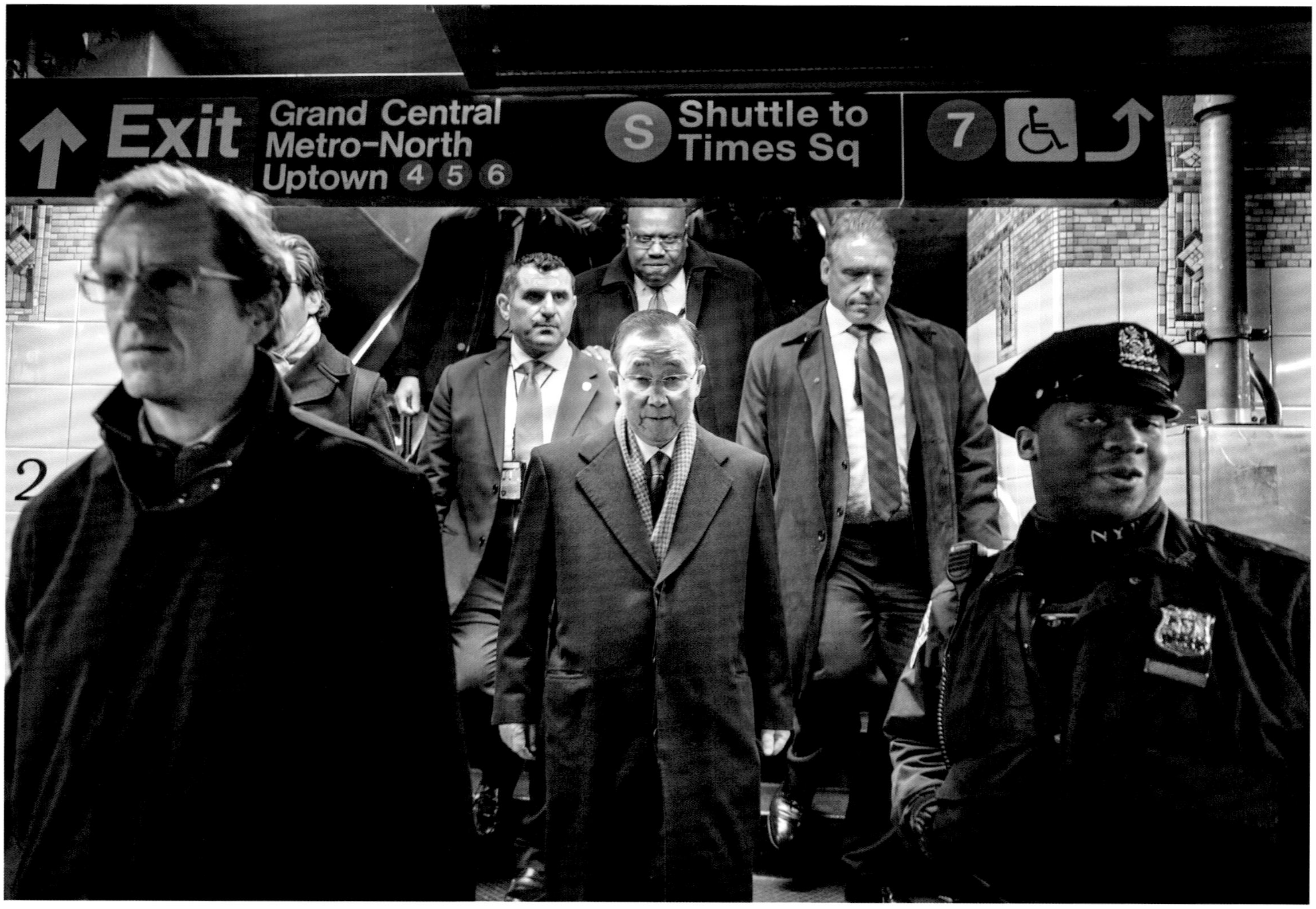

Secretary-General Ban Ki-moon takes the subway from Grand Central for his meeting with New York City Mayor Bill de Blasio at City Hall, 2016.

New York City is a living, breathing embodiment of the United Nations Charter and its guiding vision "to practice tolerance and live together in peace with one another as good neighbors." This world capital was, is, and will continue to be the most fitting choice to serve as the UN's host city following its conception 75 years ago. From its temporary humble beginnings at the Hunter College gym in the Bronx to Flushing Meadows Park in Queens to, finally, its majestic permanent home overlooking the gleaming East River in Manhattan, the UN and New York City have formed an unshakable and symbiotic bond that is mirrored in their unique, dynamic, and forward-thinking characters.

The UN is the bedrock of multilateralism, where its Member States pursue the common goals of peace and security, sustainable development, and human rights for all people and our planet. And New York City is the cornerstone of multiculturalism and diversity; the world's preeminent global city where nearly 40% of its residents are foreign born. Where daily newspapers at bodegas can be found in Spanish, Korean, Arabic, Yiddish, Haitian Creole, and so many more languages spoken by the suited professionals, delivery drivers, construction crews, municipal servants, street performers, diplomats, waitstaffs, teachers, medical workers, and artists vibrantly filling the streets and subways and cafes at nearly all hours.

As the world collectively celebrates the landmark 75th anniversary of the UN, a debt of gratitude is owed to its colossus host city who has helped the organization grow, brought the world together to solve the great challenges that we face, and forged key relations between nations and peoples. The UN is New York City. At the same time, New York City is the UN. Indeed, the famous first words of the UN Charter, "We the peoples of the United Nations determined," could just as easily describe the raison d'etre of New York City as well. Here's to the next 75 years and beyond. —**BAN KI-MOON**

Ban Ki-moon was United Nations Secretary-General from 2007 to 2016.

I would like to extend my heartfelt congratulations to the United Nations and United Nations Development Corporation on their 75th and 50th anniversaries, respectively. These are impressive milestones that deserve to be celebrated and honored.

Having served 12 years as governor of this extraordinary state, I was fortunate to witness firsthand the importance of the United Nations with its iconic building to New York City and State. The fact that the world's top leaders all converge on New York every year is a tremendous asset to our city, and one of the reasons New York remains the "Capital of the World." I was also personally privileged to meet many of these leaders while serving as governor. I was honored to have been appointed by President George W. Bush as United States Delegate for the UN 62nd General Assembly. There, I was able to experience and see firsthand the value the UN provides as a common meeting place for global diplomacy. I continue to treasure the international friendships I made within the UN community.

Just as important, my time as New York State governor allowed me to witness the positive relationship shared by UNDC and the UN. The UNDC plays a critical role in building and maintaining the facilities needed by the UN and its personnel to undertake their crucial work.

I know that once the current COVID-19 crisis passes, the international community will once again return to the UN and New York City to build on the tradition that has now lasted 75 years. It will be an exciting time. And I know that the UNDC will continue to ensure that the UN feels welcome and at home here, as the UN continues its ongoing efforts to promote peace and equality for future generations. —**GEORGE E. PATAKI**

George E. Pataki was Governor of New York State from 1995 to 2006.

91.4 MILLION

Number of people receiving food and assistance from the United Nations

83

Number of countries that the United Nations provides food and assistance to

45 PERCENT

Percentage of the world's children receiving vaccinations from the United Nations

3 MILLION

Number of lives saved each year by UN-provided vaccinations

2020

Year the Nobel Peace Prize was awarded to the UN World Food Programme

New York City is the proud home of the United Nations. Over the past 75 years, New York and the UN have been exemplars of diversity, inclusiveness, vitality, and prosperity. It can be learned from their stories that different races and cultures can coexist in harmony and forge a common future together.

The UN plays an irreplaceable role in promoting multilateral cooperation and addressing global challenges. This is especially true when our world is witnessing significant changes unseen in a century. As the UN marks its 75th anniversary amid the devastating COVID-19 pandemic, it is all the more urgent for the UN to promote unity, cooperation, and mutual benefit, and reject division, confrontation, and zero-sum game.

As a founding member of the UN and the first country to put its signature on the UN Charter, China bears witness to the extraordinary journey the UN has traveled. In its 75 years of history, the UN has stood multiple tests and emerged with renewed vigor and vitality. As President Xi Jinping said, China will remain a true follower of multilateralism, firmly uphold the UN-centered international system, and defend the UN's central role in international affairs. China will always stand firm with the UN in building a better future shared by all.

As a diplomat, I have a special bond with New York City. I was first posted to the UN in the 1990s and returned here last year. Living and working in New York is an amazing experience. I love the city and feel so proud of being a diplomat and a New Yorker. —**ZHANG JUN**

Zhang Jun is Ambassador and Permanent Representative of the People's Republic of China to the United Nations.

UNITED NATIONS SUSTAINABLE DEVELOPMENT GOALS

1. NO POVERTY
2. ZERO HUNGER
3. GOOD HEALTH AND WELL-BEING
4. QUALITY EDUCATION
5. GENDER EQUALITY
6. CLEAN WATER AND SANITATION
7. AFFORDABLE AND CLEAN ENERGY
8. DECENT WORK AND ECONOMIC GROWTH
9. INDUSTRY, INNOVATION, AND INFRASTRUCTURE
10. REDUCED INEQUALITIES
11. SUSTAINABLE CITIES AND COMMUNITIES
12. RESPONSIBLE CONSUMPTION AND PRODUCTION
13. CLIMATE ACTION
14. LIFE BELOW WATER
15. LIFE ON LAND
16. PEACE, JUSTICE, AND STRONG INSTITUTIONS
17. PARTNERSHIPS FOR THE GOALS

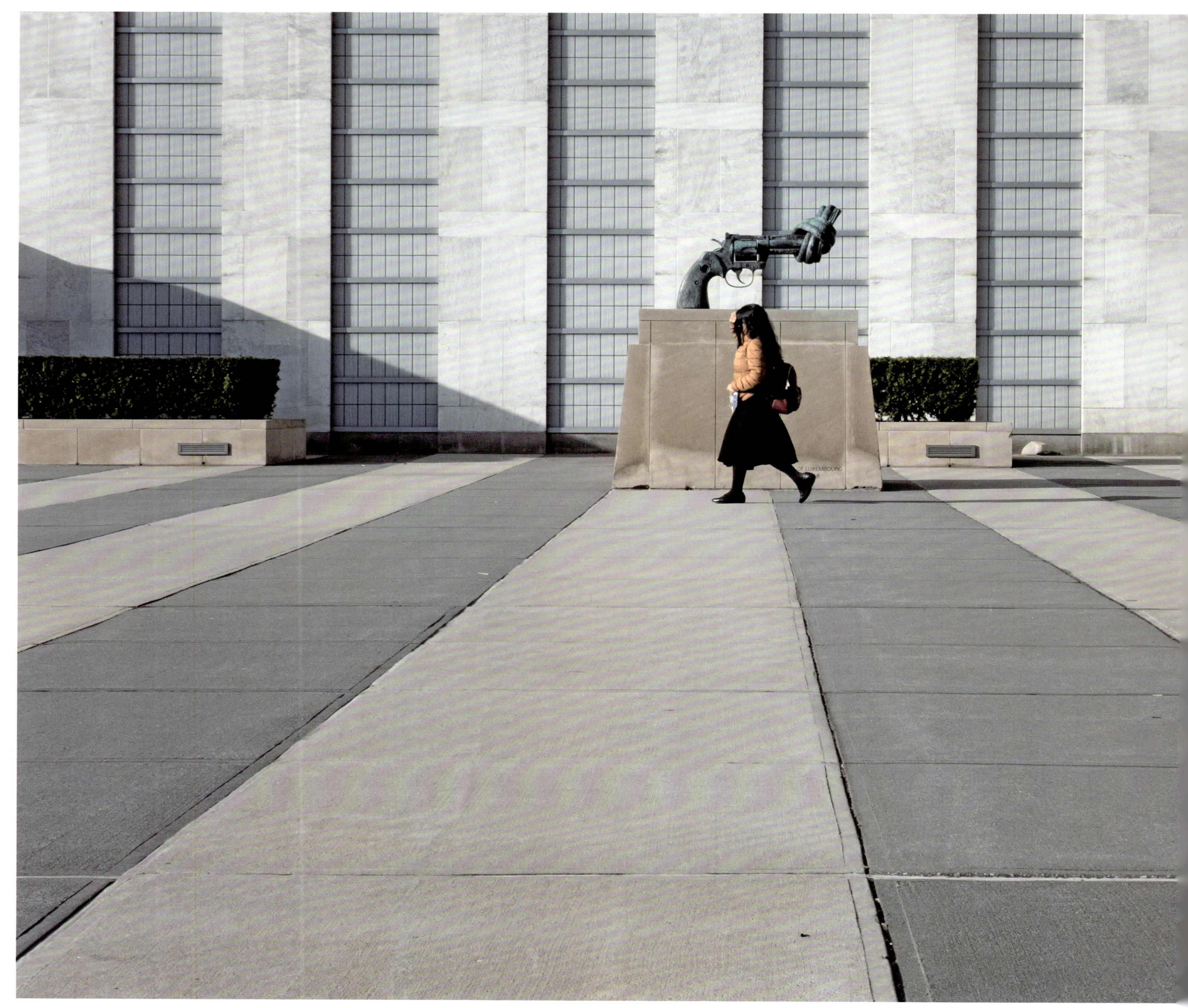

A UN staff member enters UN Headquarters through the visitors entrance. Behind her is the *Non-Violence* (or *Knotted Gun*) sculpture by Swedish artist Carl Fredrik Reuterswärd. April 10, 2019.

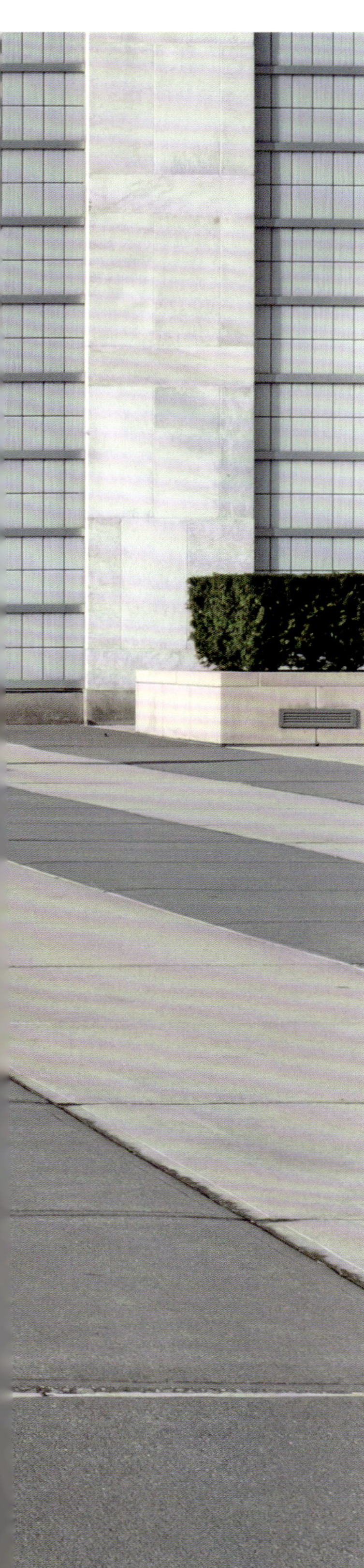

As it has across the globe, the new century has brought evolution and change to the United Nations and New York City. The numbers of people working for and associated with the UN have grown larger than ever. Delegations now send more than 5,000 persons to New York each year for the annual sessions of the General Assembly in late September. The Secretariat's staff in the city numbers about 4,900 persons. To cover the events of the organization, 2,000 journalists are permanently accredited—a figure that swells to 6,000 during major meetings. And although security is tighter than ever, there are still an average of one million annual visitors to the UN campus.[32]

Physically, the UN campus has struggled to keep up with the times. The headquarters found itself in a difficult state as the 21st century dawned over New York City. Due to its age as well as oft-deferred maintenance, the glass facades of the Secretariat Building and the roof of the General Assembly—the symbolic heart of the UN where delegates ceremoniously gather each year before the eyes of the world—had become structurally unstable and were leaking air and water. (One ambassador reportedly sat through a meeting with an umbrella over his head.[33]) Numerous structures, including the Conference Building and its meeting halls, had fallen below current fire and safety standards and were full of dangerous asbestos. And generally security was in need of upgrading.[34] The organization faced an existential crisis: to renovate its headquarters at great financial cost and institutional inconvenience, or outright replace its facilities, perhaps in another city.

With opposition to both relocating the UN Headquarters and a full-scale reconstruction overcome, planning for a massive rejuvenation of the existing campus began in 2000. In 2003, the United Nations Capital Master Plan was launched with architect Michael Adlerstein appointed as its Executive Director in 2007.[35] The mandate of the project was to make the UN campus "modern, safe, secure, sustainable, and accessible while respecting the architectural integrity of the original design." The cost of achieving such goals would come with a final price tag of $2.15 billion. Funding was to be secured by an assessment on the Member States.[36] As host nation, the United States contributed an additional $100 million to the renovation and restoration efforts.

The Secretariat Building was completely gutted starting in 2010, leaving only the existing concrete floor slabs. All of the tower's cladding —some 5,000-plus single glass panes—were replaced with new insulated, double-paned, blast-proof glazing that closely replicates the look of the tower upon its completion in 1951. The interiors were reconfigured with more fluid and less-hierarchical open-plan workspaces and informal meeting areas. Work on the Conference Building combined large-scale structural enhancements for increased safety and security with painstaking restoration and redesign of interior spaces originally designed by noted architects from the Member States. The 16-month renovation of the General Assembly Building, the final phase of the master plan, restored original design features such as the dome exterior, which had been painted brown with attempts at waterproofing, to its 1950s silver finish. It also added up-to-date infrastructure including its electronics.[37] The Plenary Hall was also redesigned to accommodate potential future increases in membership. Work on all three buildings was essentially complete by 2015.

During the multiyear construction, the Security Council moved into a temporary chamber within the General Assembly Building. The General Assembly and other conference functions were accommodated in a new, temporary building erected on the north lawn of the complex. In all, more than 6,000 employees were moved to temporary spaces both on and off the UN campus.[38]

The renovation's focus on new energy-efficient LED lighting, water-reduction measures, and other sustainable measures—which reduced energy consumption of the entire compound by half—not only met Secretary-General Ban Ki-moon's vision of the refreshed campus as a "globally acclaimed model of efficient use of energy and resources," they also align with the United Nations' broader embrace of the environment in the 21st century.[39] Also known as the Global Goals, the UN's Sustainable Development Goals, adopted in 2015, are a blueprint to achieve a better and more sustainable future for all, and call for action by all countries—poor, rich, and middle-income—to promote prosperity while protecting the planet. They recognize that ending poverty must go hand-in-hand with strategies that build economic growth and address a range of social needs including education, health, social protection, and job opportunities, while tackling climate change and environmental protection.[40]

With a target timeline of eliminating global inequalities by 2030, the campaign's 17 objectives include humanistic goals that have long been part of the UN's mission, including quality education and healthcare, clean water and sanitation, and eliminating poverty and hunger. The program also includes aggressively pro-environment goals including affordable and clean energy, sustainable cities and communities, responsible consumption and production, and climate action.[41]

As the UN evolves its relationship with the planet and our environment, New York City continues to strengthen and redefine its ties with the UN. During his tenure, from 2002 to 2013, New York Mayor Michael Bloomberg expanded the role of the city's liaison to the UN with Marjorie Tiven as Commissioner. The Mayor's Office for International Affairs continues to build on that success with Commissioner Penny Abeywardena, appointed by Mayor Bill de Blasio in 2014. Indeed, as an impact report issued by Abeywardena's office and the New York City Economic Development Corporation states, "We share more than a city —we share a vision for a more equitable world.[42]

The UN's architectural renewal has put a renewed focus on these shared aspirations between the United Nations and its host city, which have grown deeper over the last 75 years. The connection between the

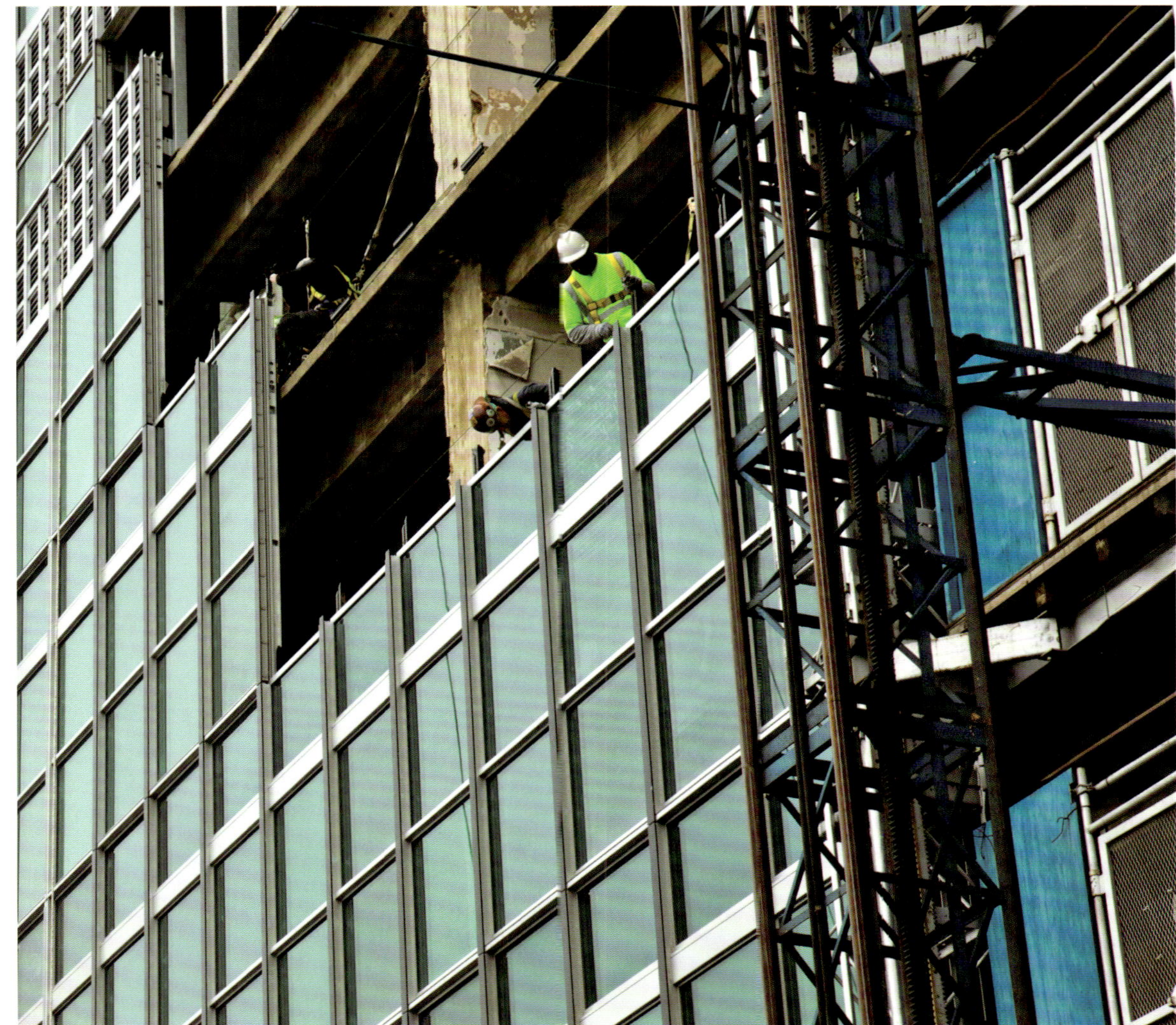

Construction workers remove the curtain wall from the Secretariat Building as part of the Capital Master Plan. The plan's state-of-the-art strategy addresses complex issues involving architecture and technology, building systems, and landscaping as well as the historic preservation and sustainable design challenges posed by this classic International Style complex. November 16, 2011.

UN and the city is not just one of proximity and interdependence, but also an emotional bond. At a 50th anniversary gala dinner hosted by Mayor Rudolph Giuliani in 1995, then Secretary-General Boutros Boutros-Ghali spoke of the relationship between the UN and its host city as a "love affair." "Sharing 50 years together has made this marriage strong. The marriage of New York City and the United Nations is destined to endure. We have been together for half a century. Half a century from now we will, I am confident, celebrate our 100th anniversary in the midst of a bright and beautiful future."[43] As author and architecture critic Carter Wiseman has written, "[T]he United Nations remains a shrine to hope."[44] And New York City will remain the proud home of this beacon to the world and its "workshop for peace."

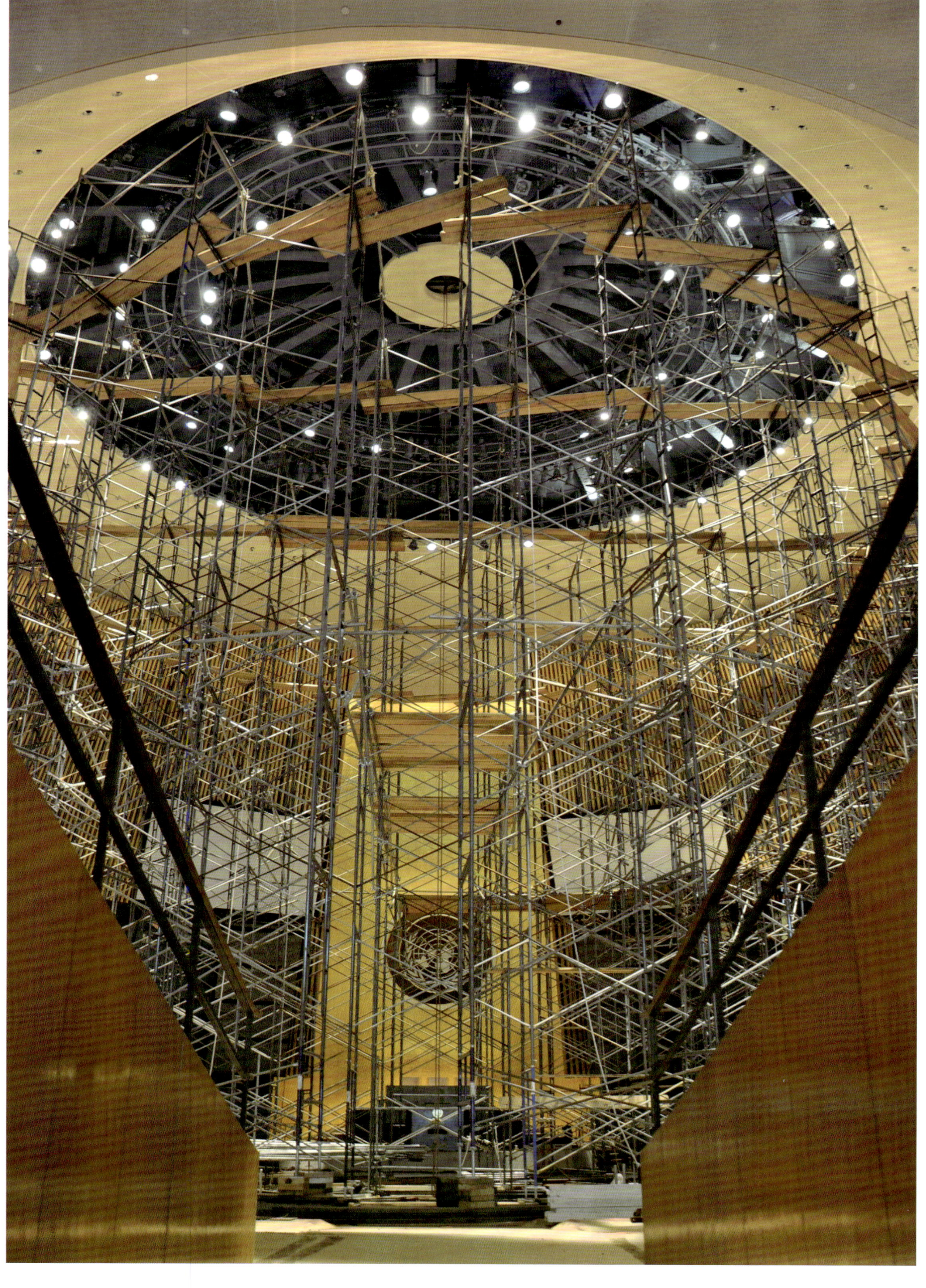

A large scaffolding has been erected in the General Assembly Hall. The General Assembly Building has been closed for construction as part of the renovation of the UN Headquarters under the Capital Master Plan. August 22, 2013.

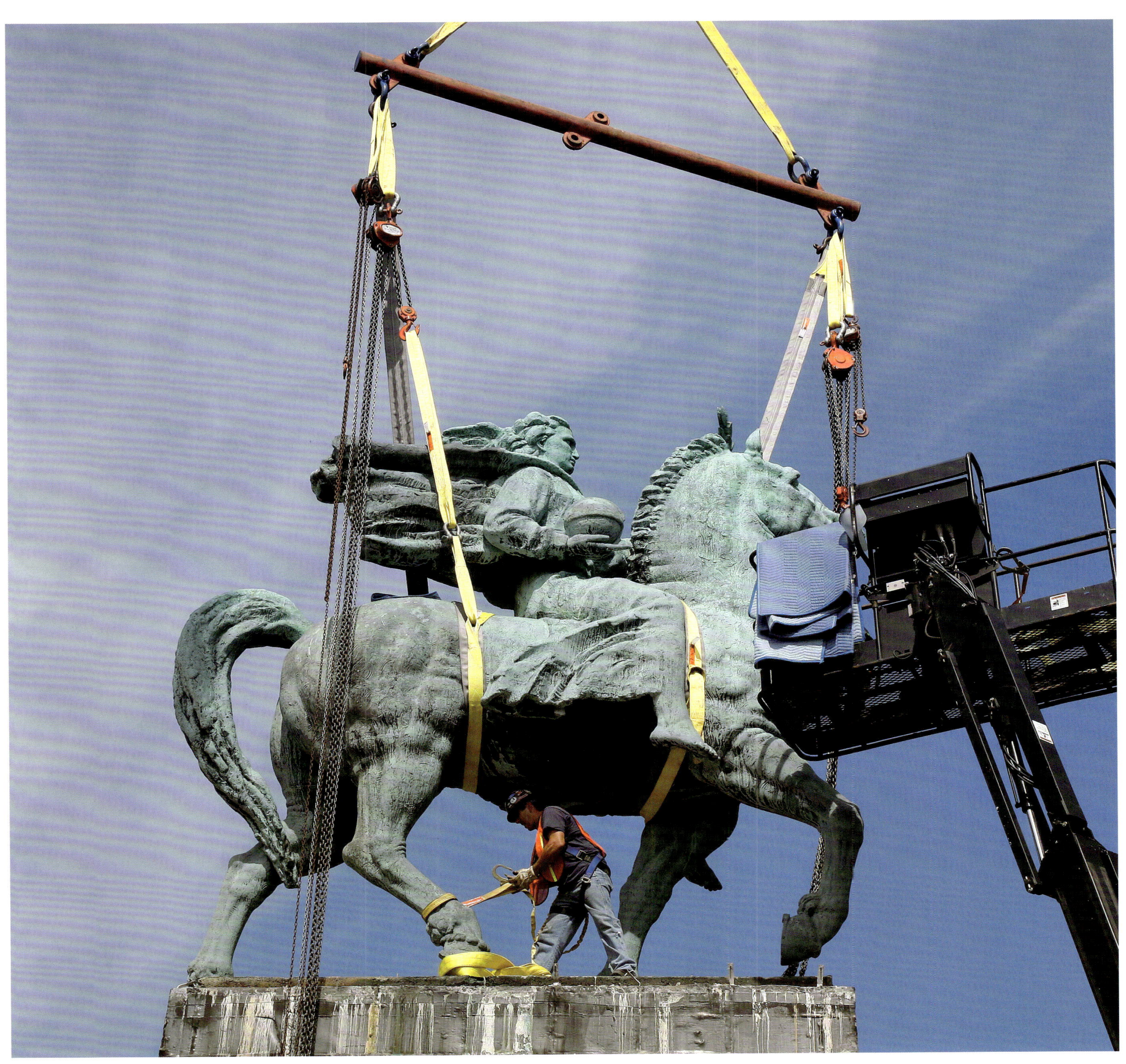

Construction workers move the *Horsewoman Monument of Peace* sculpture as construction for the Capital Master Plan begins in the North Lawn of the United Nations Headquarters. August 13, 2008.

A view of the General Assembly Hall. November 8, 2018.

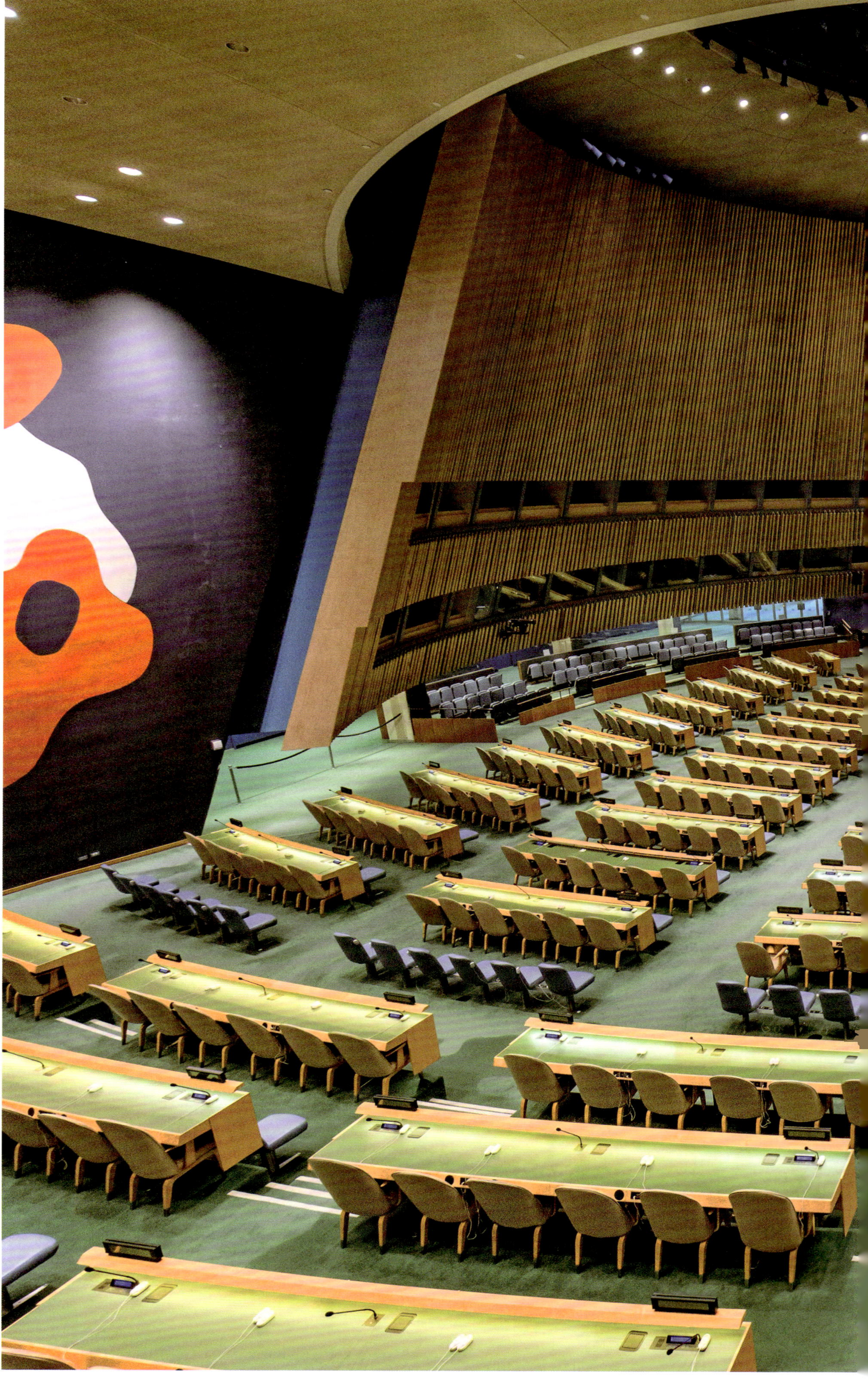

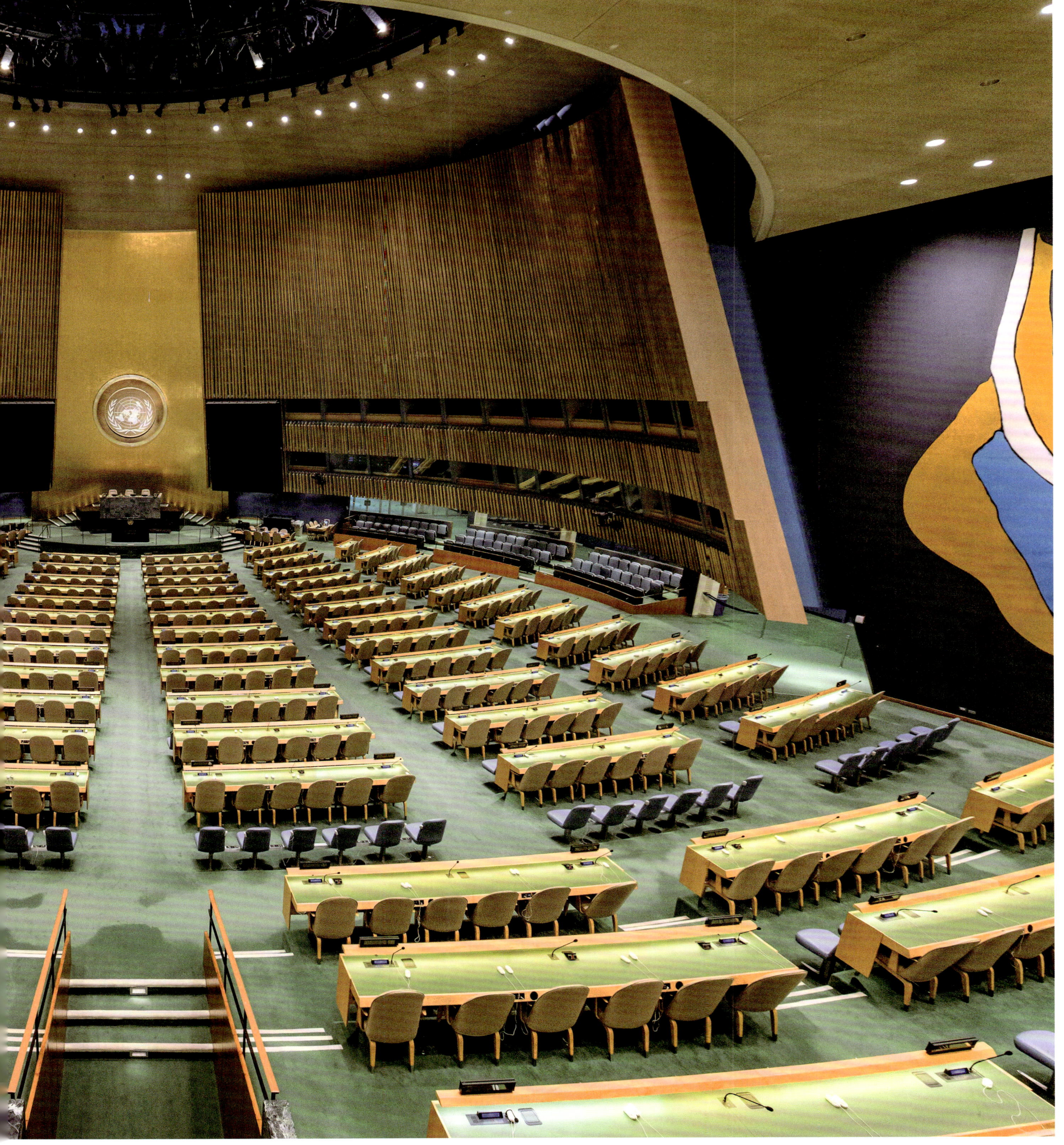

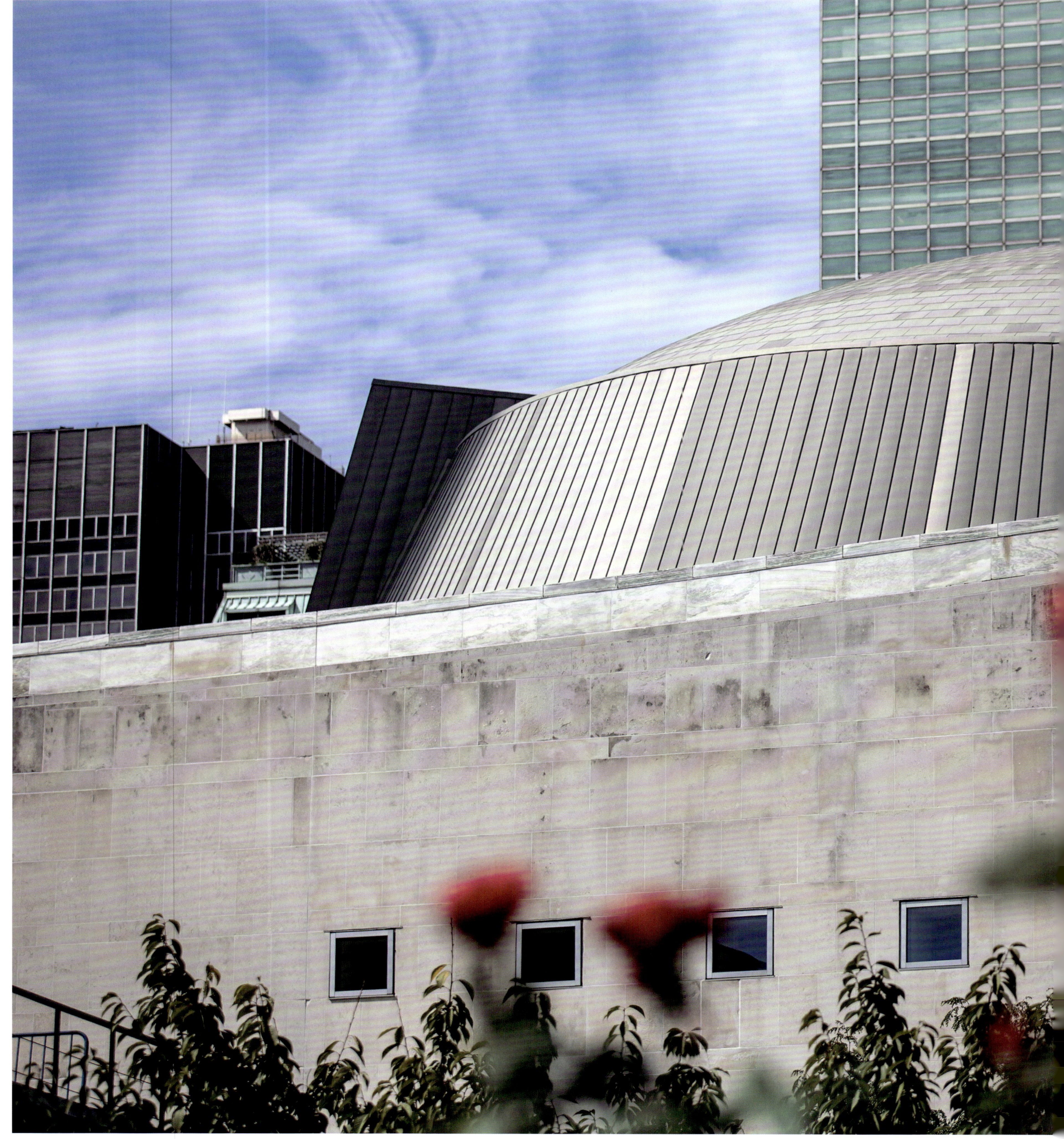

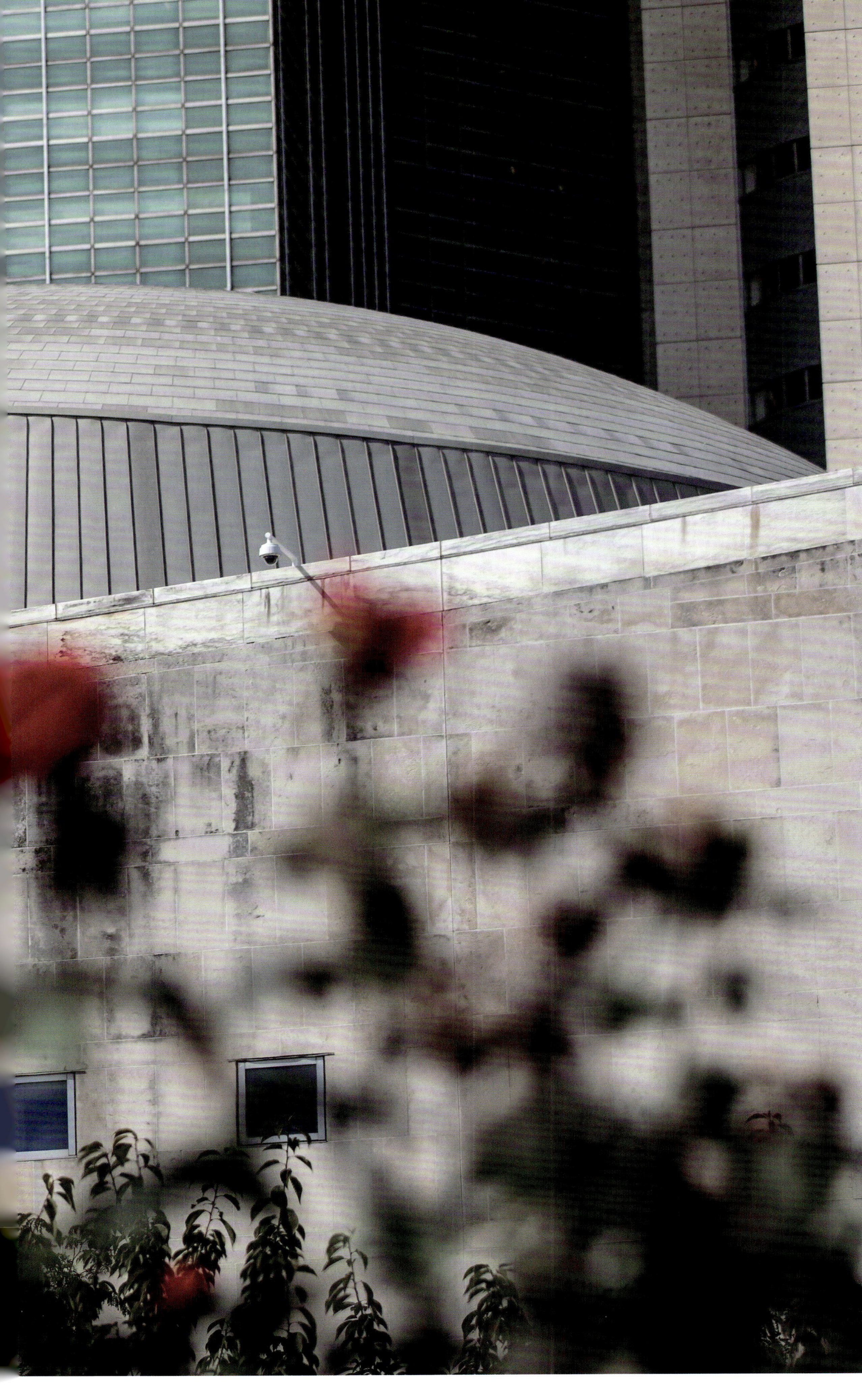

The General Assembly Building as seen from the United Nations Rose Garden during the General Assembly's seventy-third general debate. September 27, 2018.

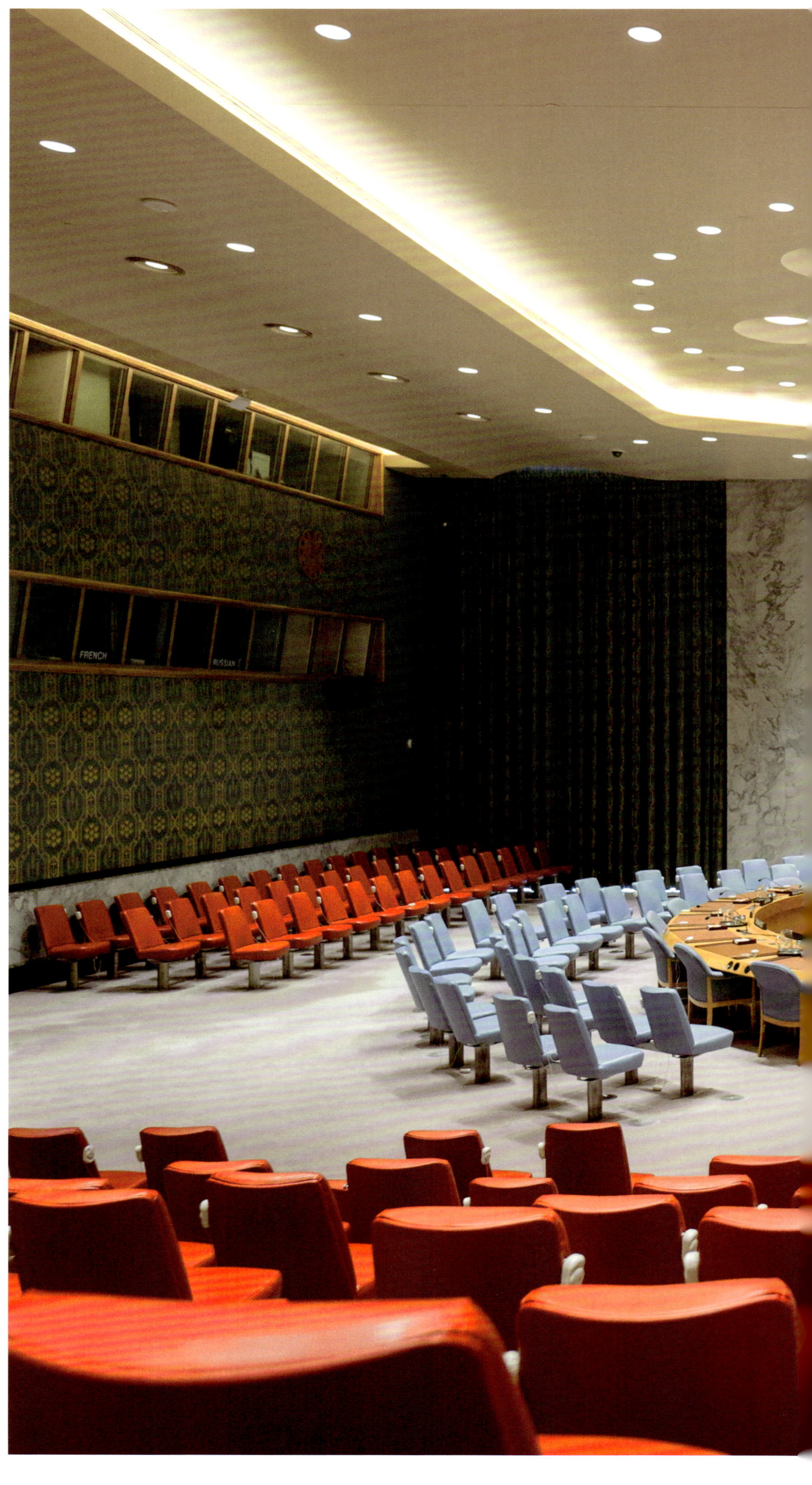

The Security Council Chamber designed by Norwegian architect Arnstein Arneberg and decorated with a mural painted by Norwegian artist Per Krohg. Most of the Chamber's original 1952 furnishings, as well as those for the 2013 Capital Master Plan renovation, are gifts from Norway. February 14, 2017.

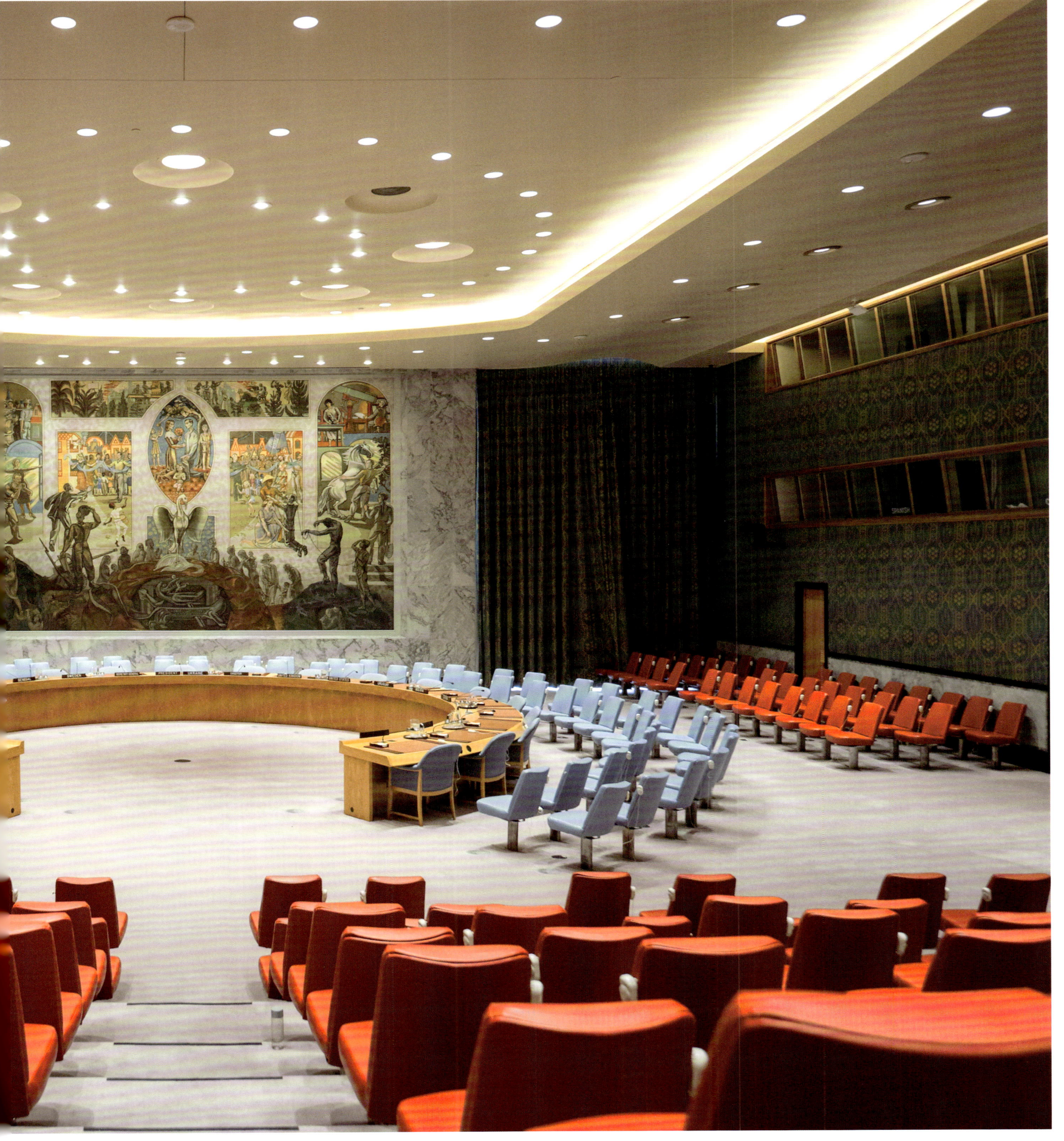

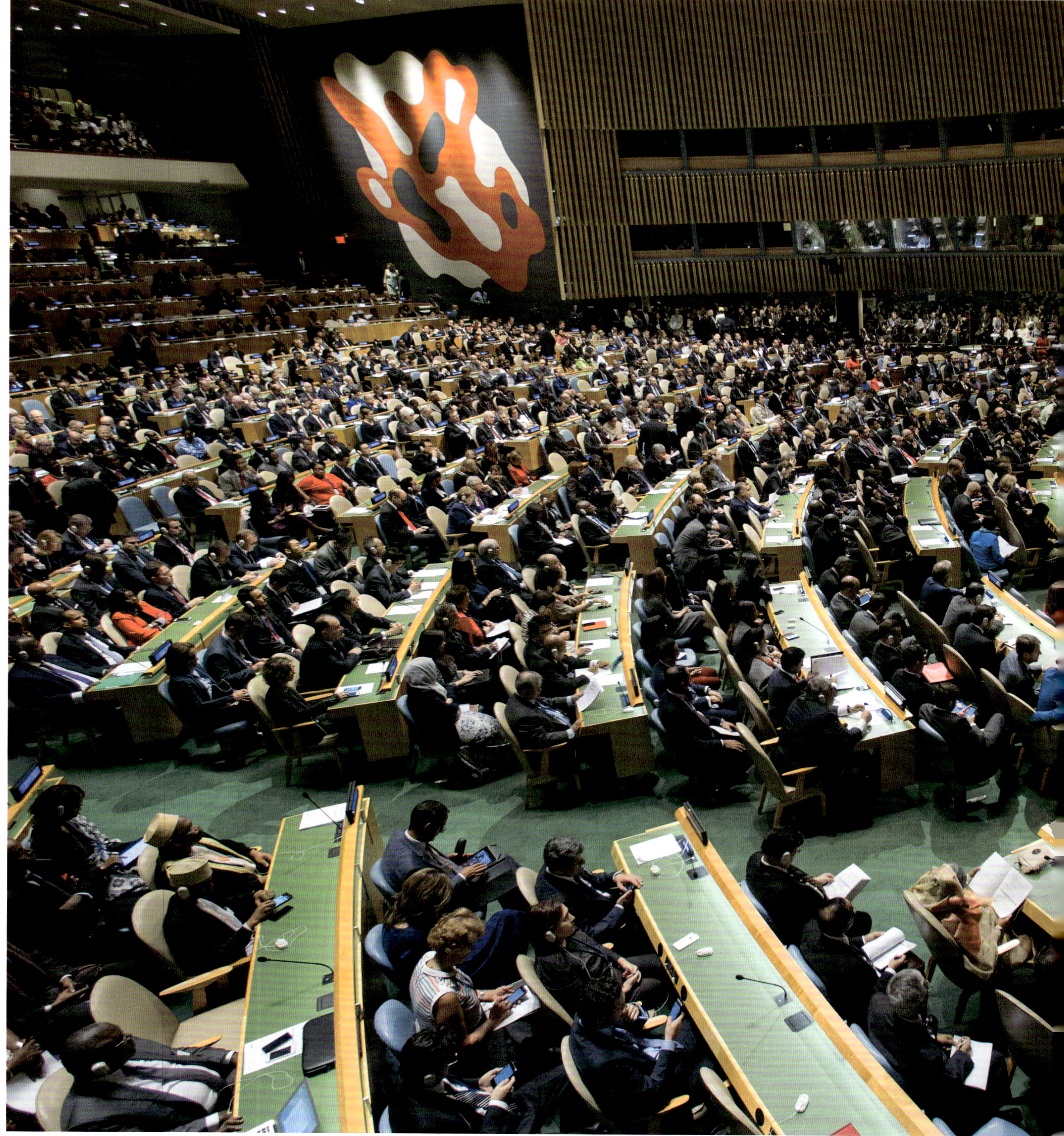

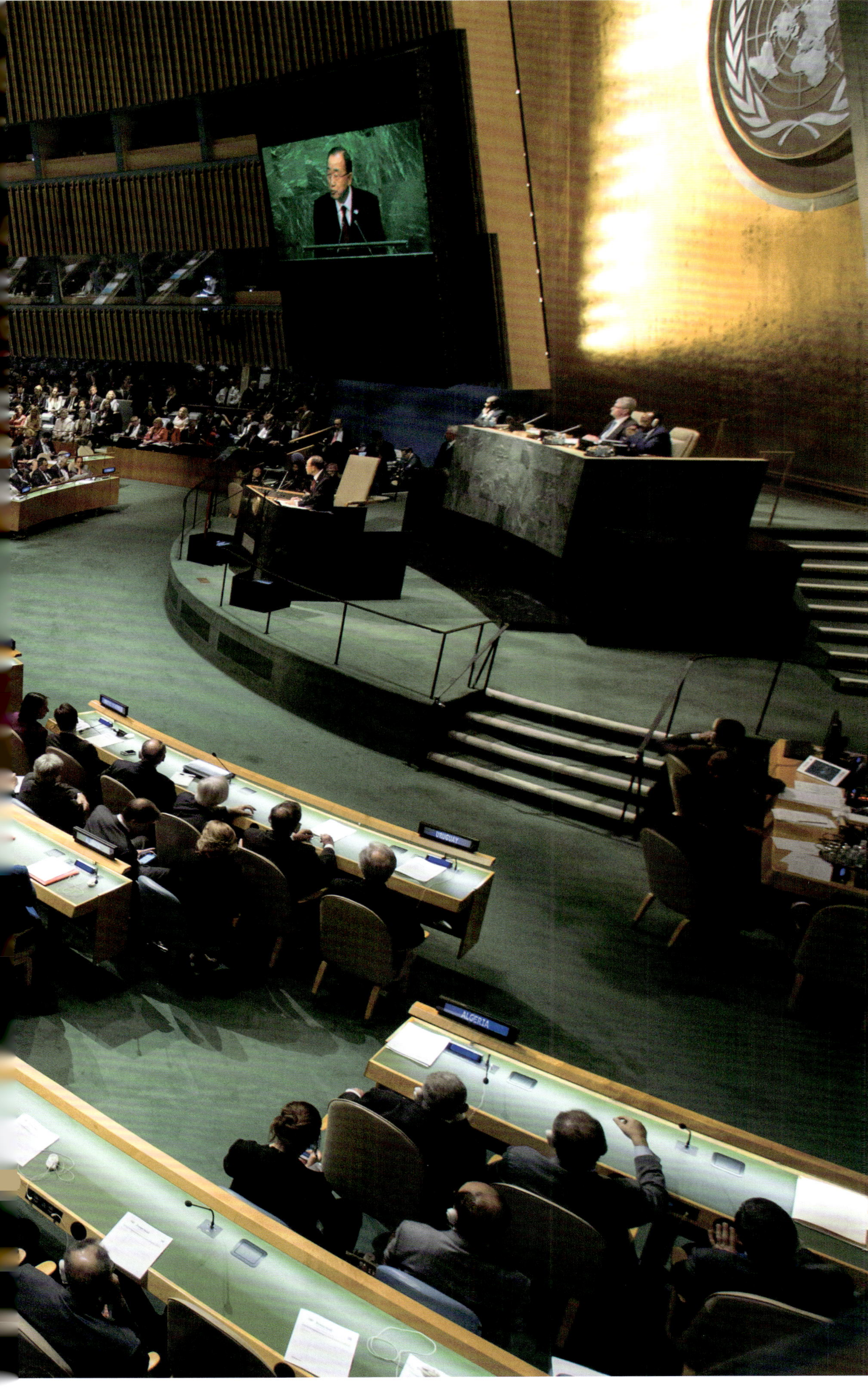

A view of the General Assembly Hall as Secretary-General Ban Ki-moon presents his annual report on the work of the organization. Each of the 193 Member States is required to pay a percentage of both the UN's regular operating budget and its peacekeeping budget. Mandatory payments and voluntary contributions, including a substantial amount of private donations, also fund UN-related organizations such as UNICEF and the World Food Programme. September 25, 2015.

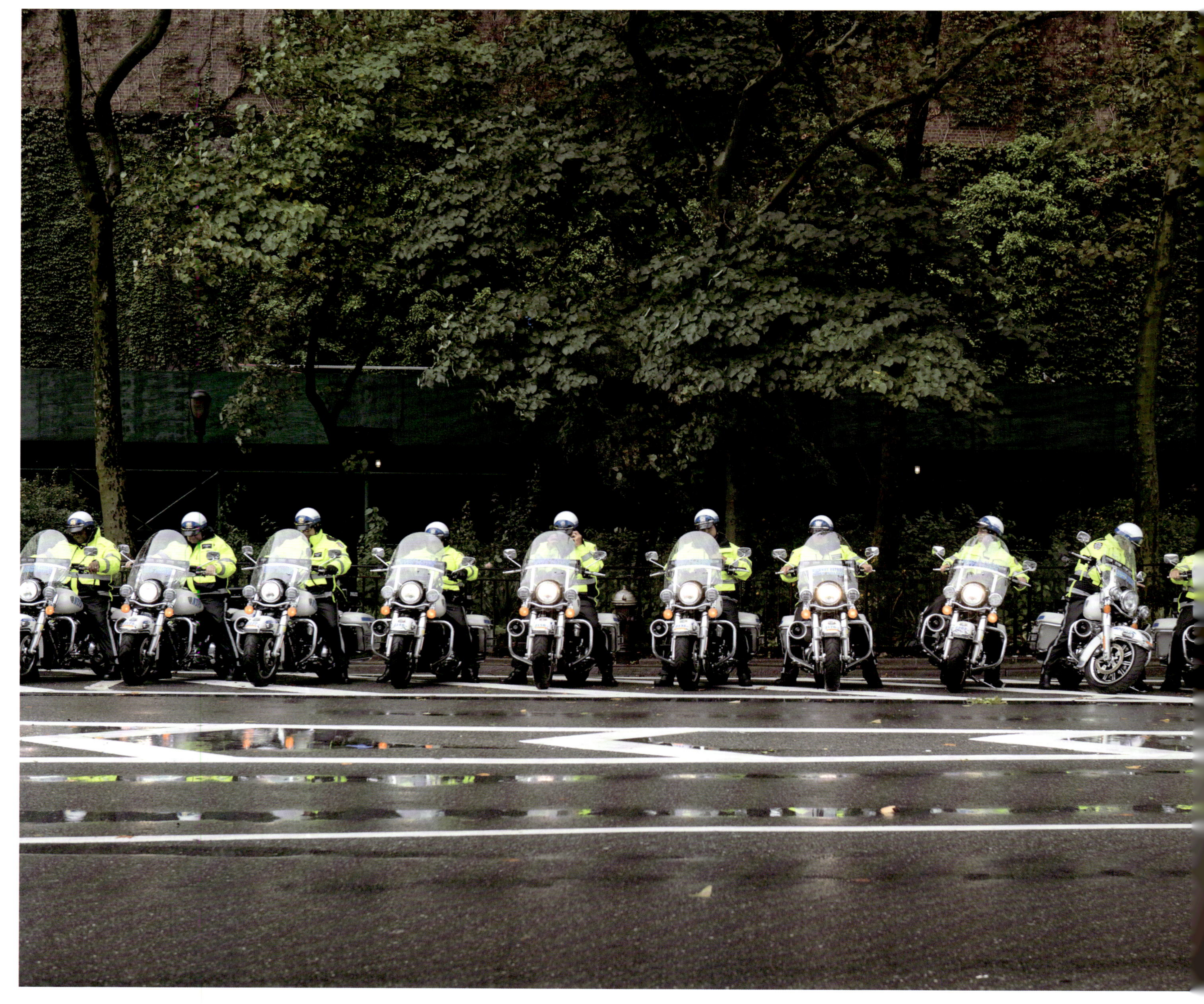

New York Police Department line up on First Avenue, outside of UN Headquarters, on the first day of the General Assembly's seventy-third general debate. September 25, 2018.

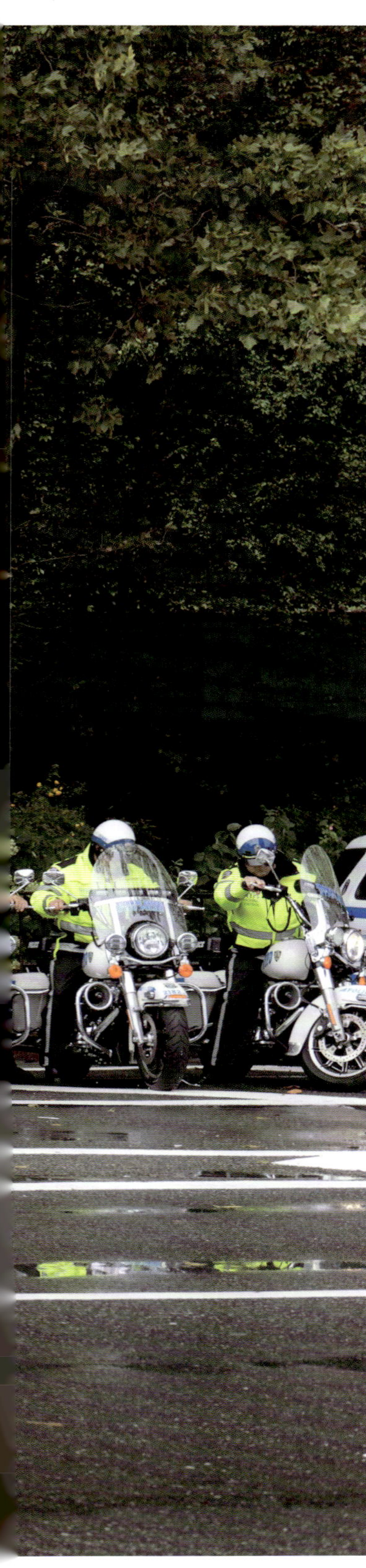

Below: Secretary-General António Guterres on his way to the opening of the UN Climate Action Summit 2019. The summit aims to deliver new pathways and practical actions to shift global response into higher gear on confronting climate change. September 23, 2019.

Bottom: Hillary Rodham Clinton, Secretary of State of the U.S. and President of the Security Council for September, addresses the Security Council. The Council adopted a resolution demanding the immediate and complete cessation of acts of sexual violence in situations of armed conflict. September 30, 2009.

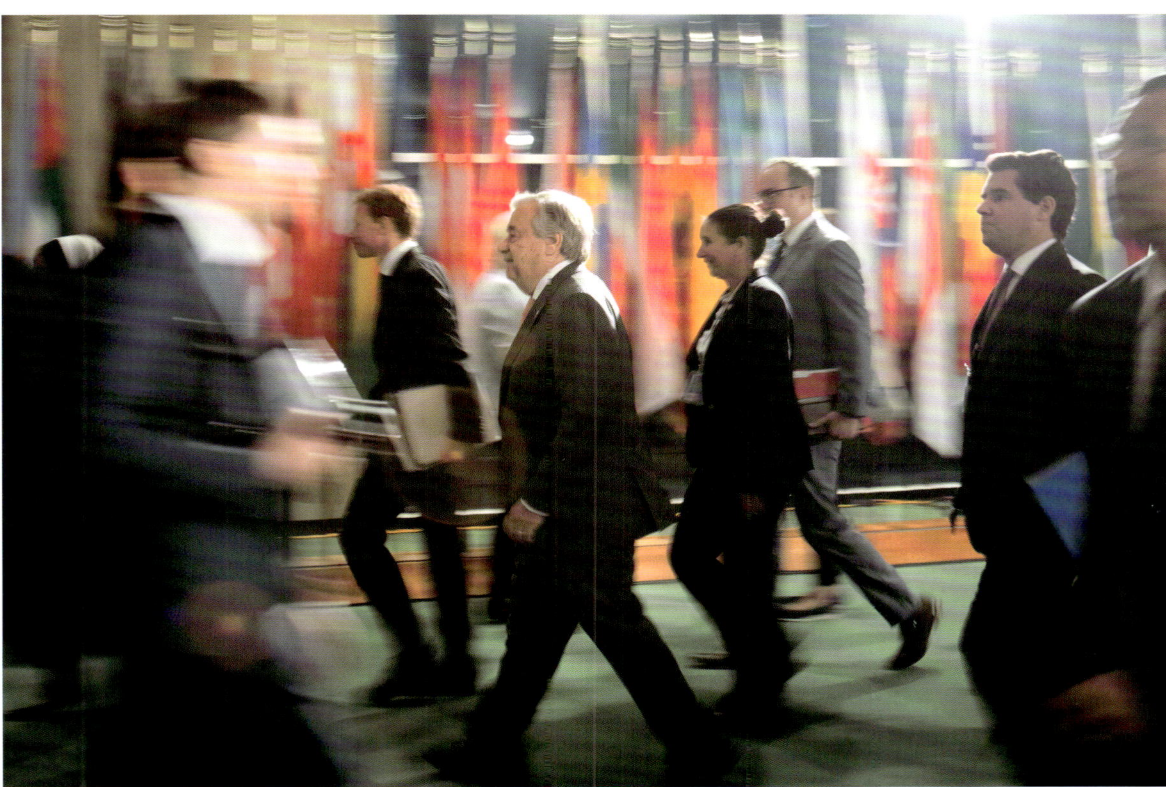

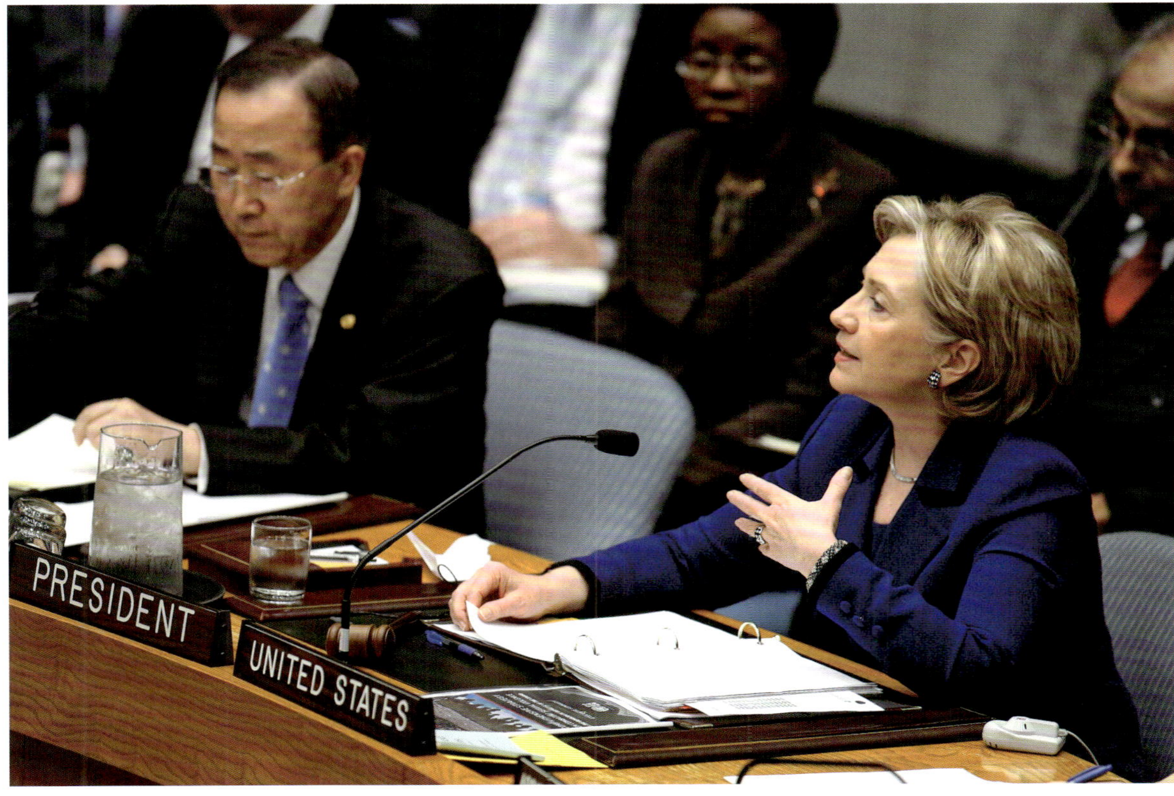

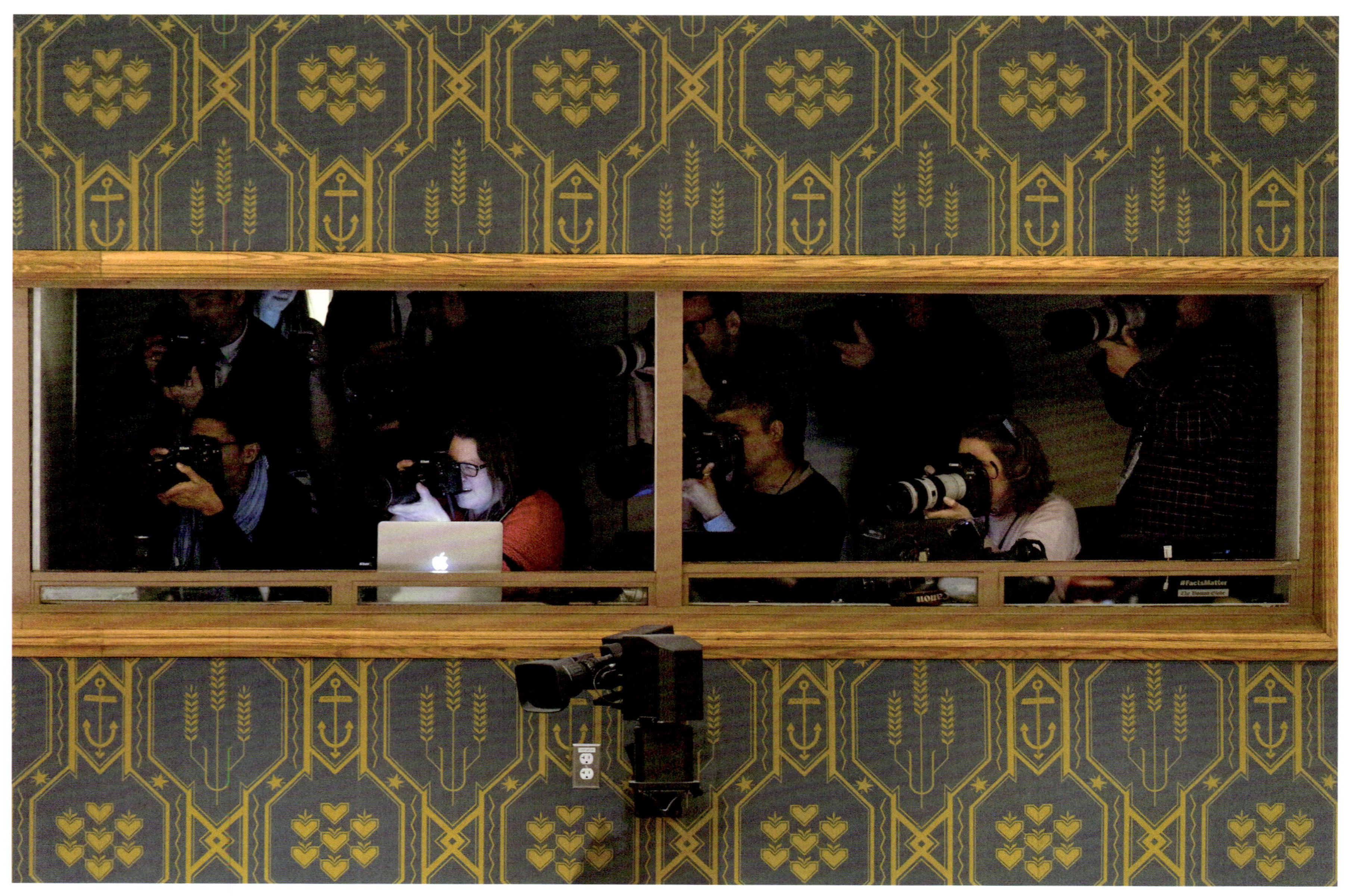

The Security Council holds an emergency meeting on the situation in Syria, following reports of air strikes against the Shayrat Airbase in Syria conducted by the United States. Photojournalists covering the meeting. April 7, 2017.

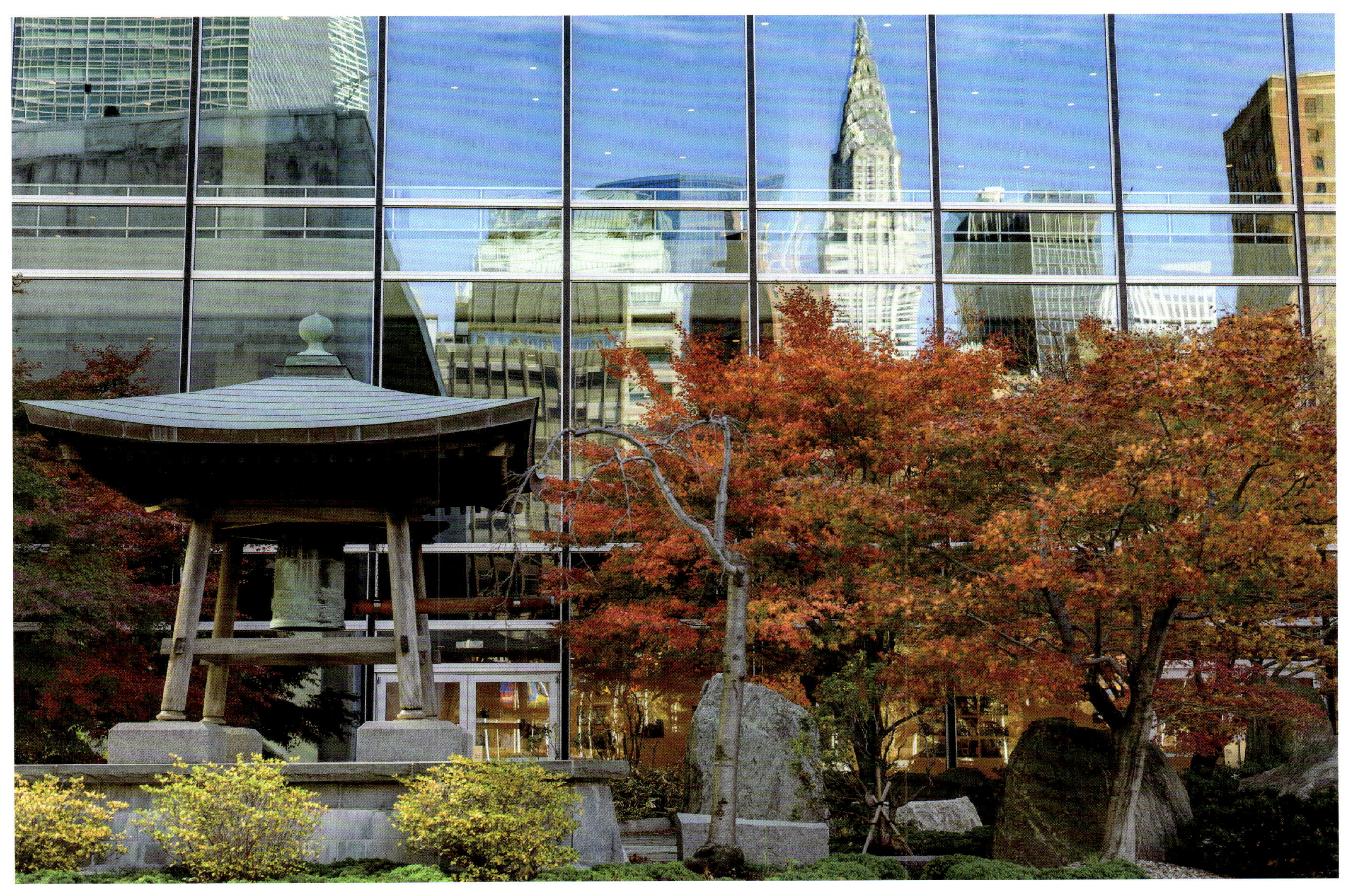

A view of fall foliage by the Japanese Peace Bell, a gift from the UN Association of Japan. The Chrysler Building is reflected in the windows. November 7, 2018.

Solar panels, a gift from India, are installed on the roof of the United Nations. The panels are designed to reach the max of 50 KW of generation power. August 27, 2019.

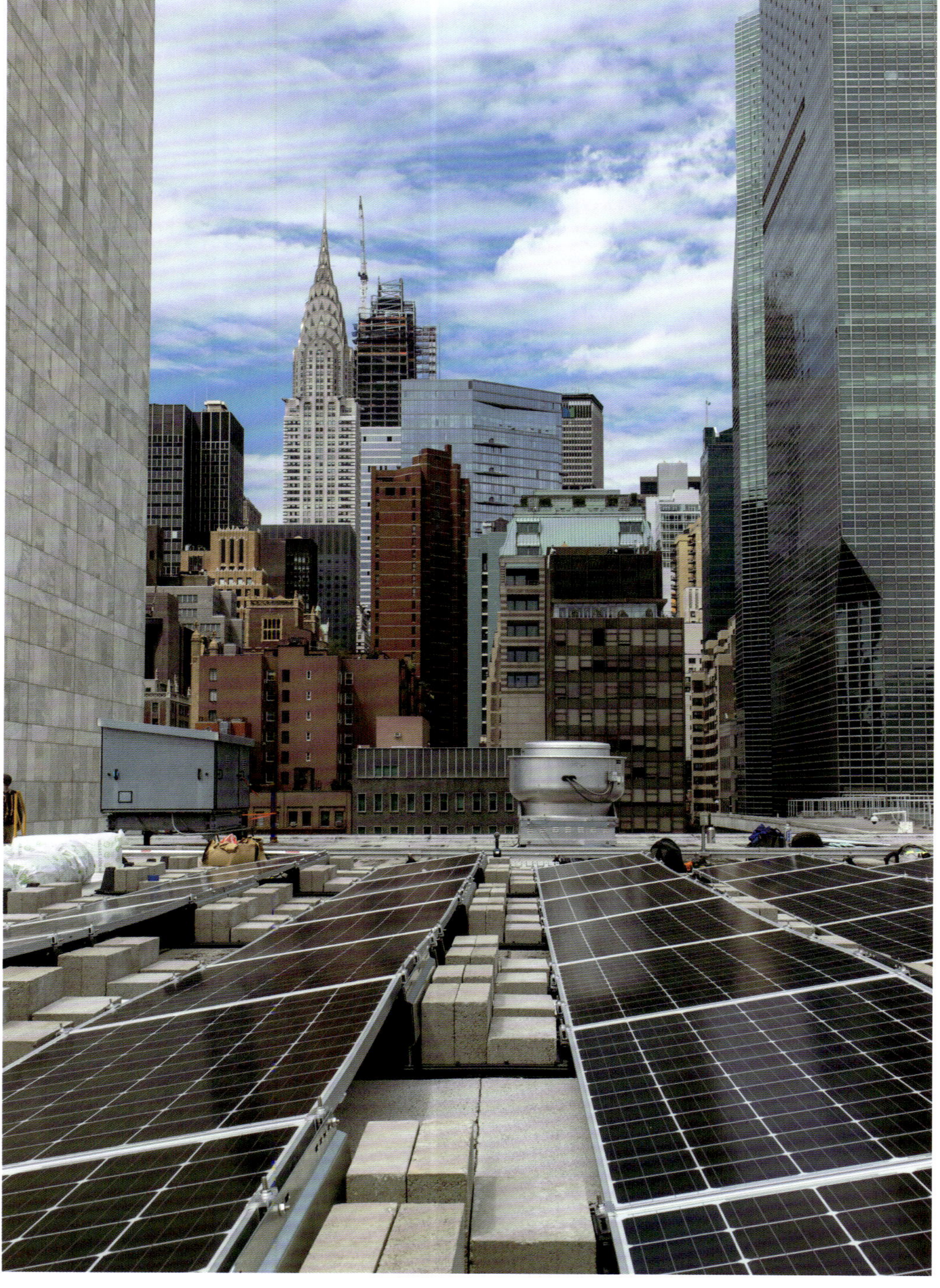

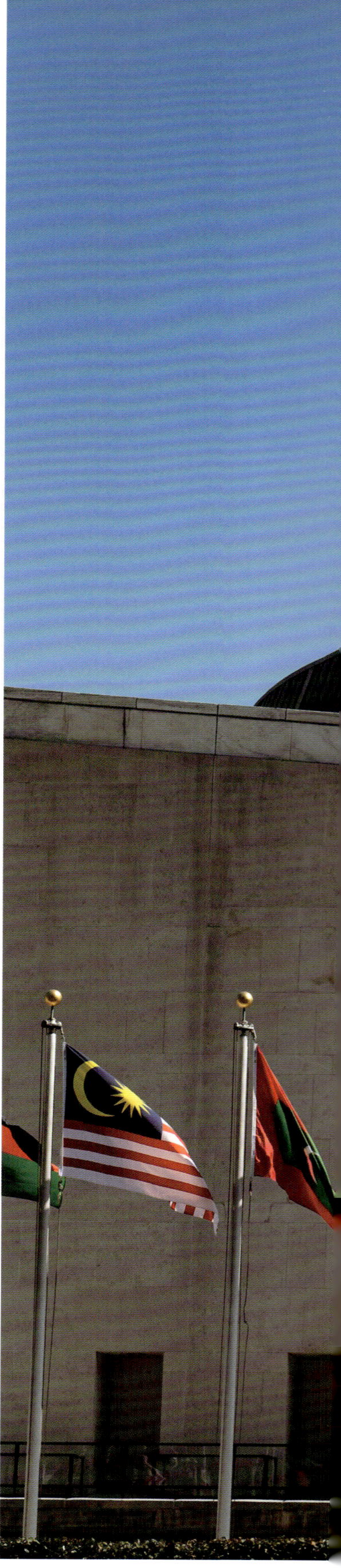

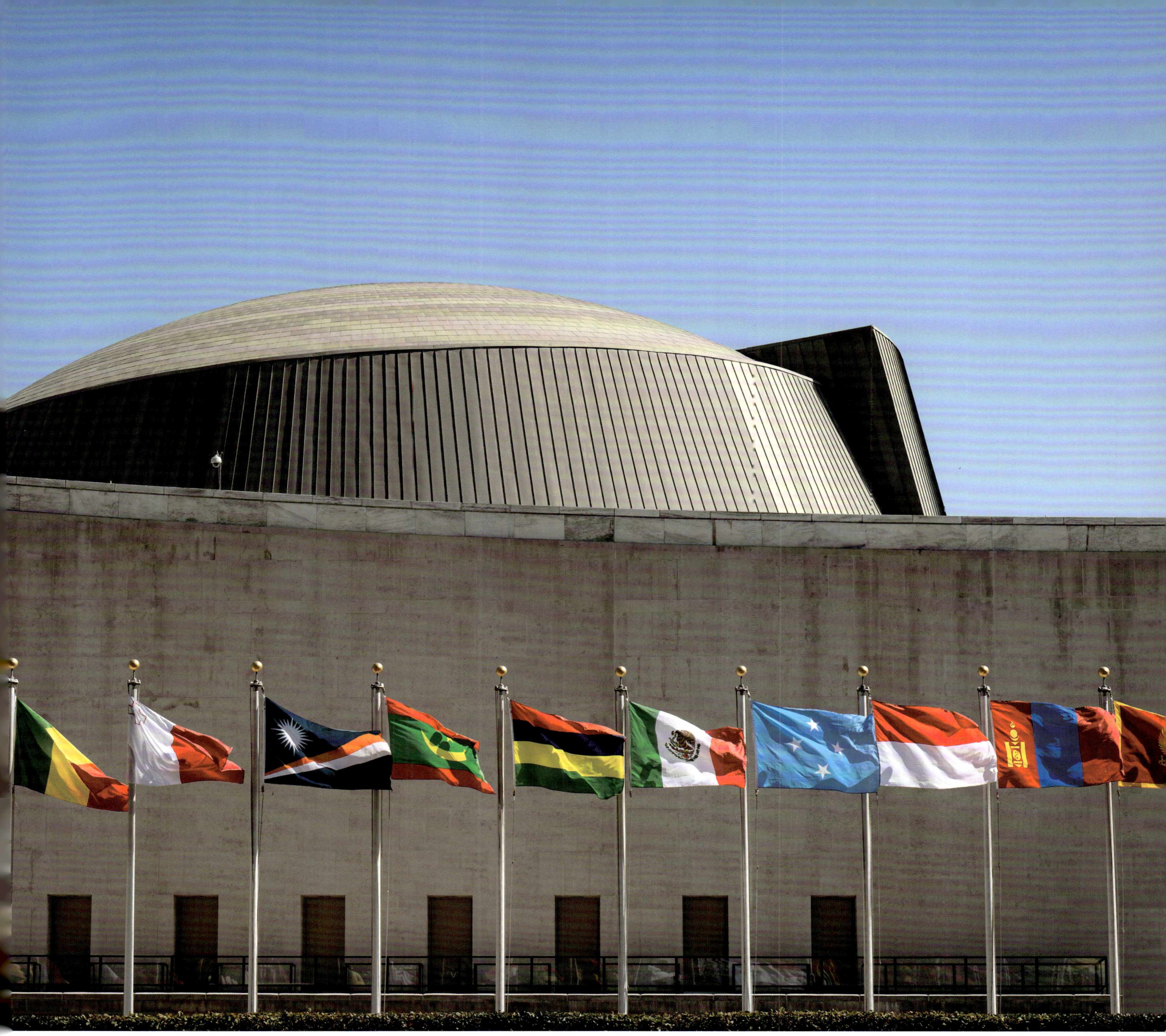

A view of the flags outside the General Assembly Building during the General Assembly's 75th session. September 23, 2020.

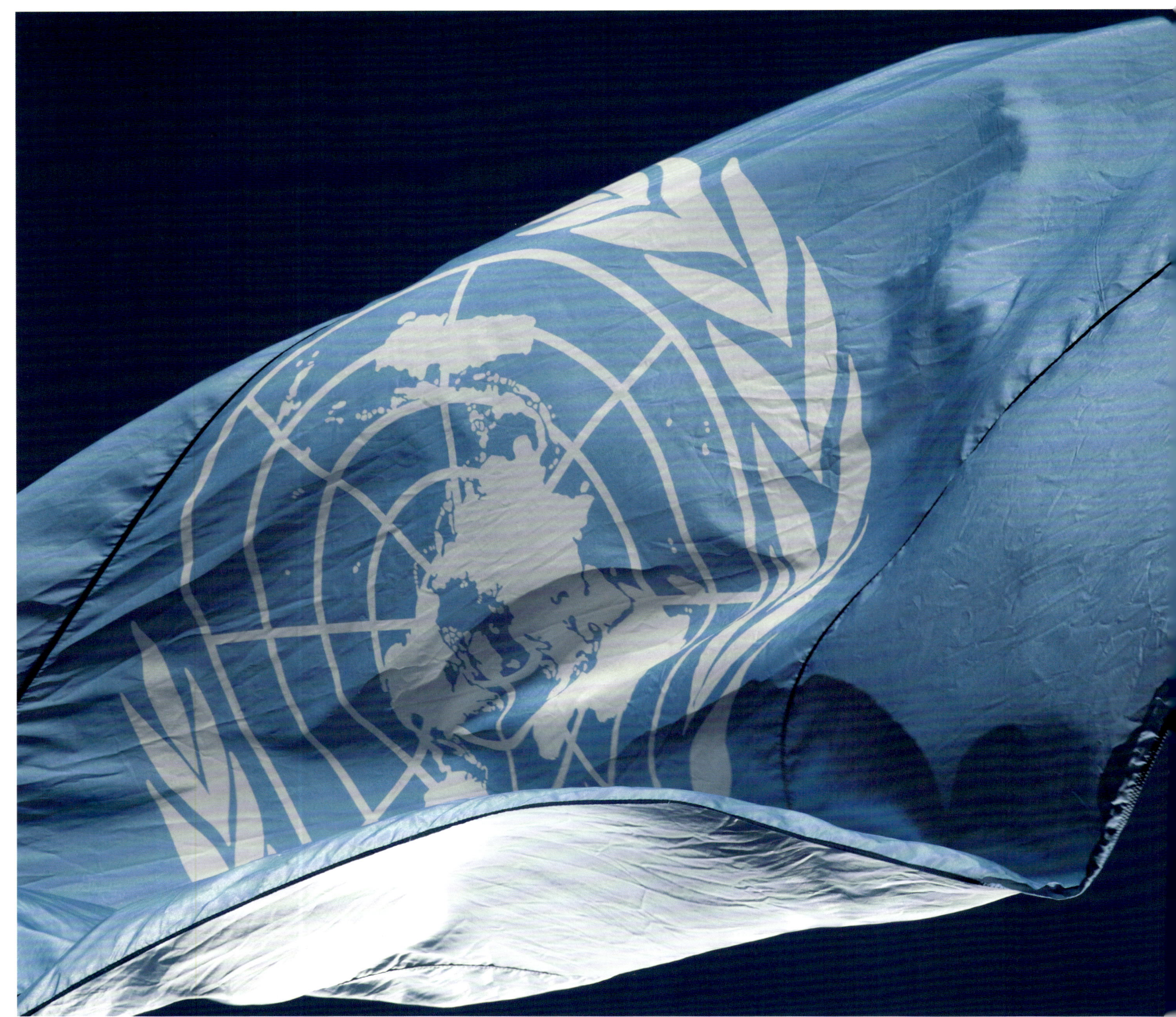

The United Nations flag in front of the organization's headquarters. The flag symbolizes the union of all people in search of a permanent, durable peace. December 27, 2018.

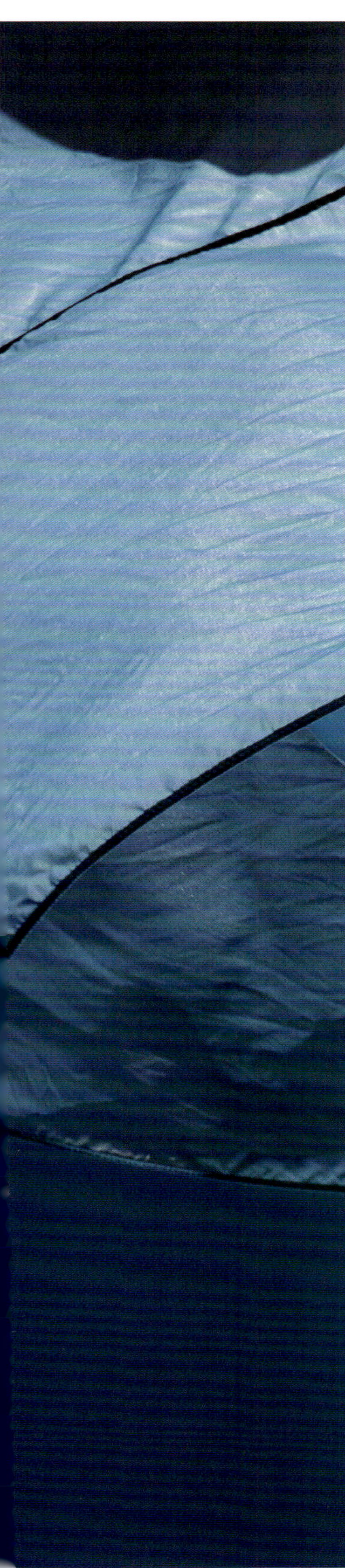

The Common Meeting Ground

Hillary Rodham Clinton

Back in 1948, Eleanor Roosevelt—one of my favorite Americans—described the United Nations as "the common meeting ground for nations, where we can consider together our mutual problems and take advantage of our differences in experience."

Given that pithy yet aspirational description, it is no mistake that the United Nations found its home in New York, making official the city's moniker as a "crossroads of the world" where people from every nation can gather.

The visionary idea of the United Nations as a platform for global cooperation dedicated to peace, dignity, and equality on a healthy planet has proved its worth with each passing year. That's particularly true now, as we mark the 75th anniversary of the United Nations and honor the special place it holds in the fabric of the City of New York.

In my own life and career as First Lady, U.S. Senator for New York, and U.S. Secretary of State, I have participated in countless gatherings under the auspices of the United Nations. Whether declaring publicly that "human rights are women's rights and women's rights are human rights" at the Fourth World Conference on Women in Beijing or working to convince the UN Security Council to act or hosting meetings during the General Assembly annual gathering, I have seen firsthand the success and failures of the UN. And, despite the ups and downs, I have never doubted the importance of its mission.

At its core, diplomacy is about relationships, and the physical space in which those relationships are formed and sustained is an oft-underappreciated aspect of their success or failure. I am grateful to the United Nations Development Corporation for providing safe, hospitable real estate for the United Nations to do its business in New York.

This is an unprecedented moment shaped by daunting challenges, from climate change to the COVID-19 pandemic. The need for a "common meeting ground for nations"—both as an idea and as a literal place—has never been more urgent. Together, as we commemorate 75 deeply impactful years, let us celebrate the United Nations' home in the City of New York and in the hearts of people around the globe.

Hillary Rodham Clinton was First Lady of the United States from 1993 to 2001, Senator from New York from 2001 to 2009, and Secretary of State from 2009 to 2013.

Below: Secretary-General Kofi Annan (right) meets with former South African President Nelson Mandela in Houghton, Johannesburg, South Africa. March 15, 2006.

Bottom: Former mayor of New York City and special envoy to the United Nations for climate change Michael Bloomberg (center left) attends a press conference during the One Planet Summit in Boulogne-Billancourt, France. December 12, 2017.

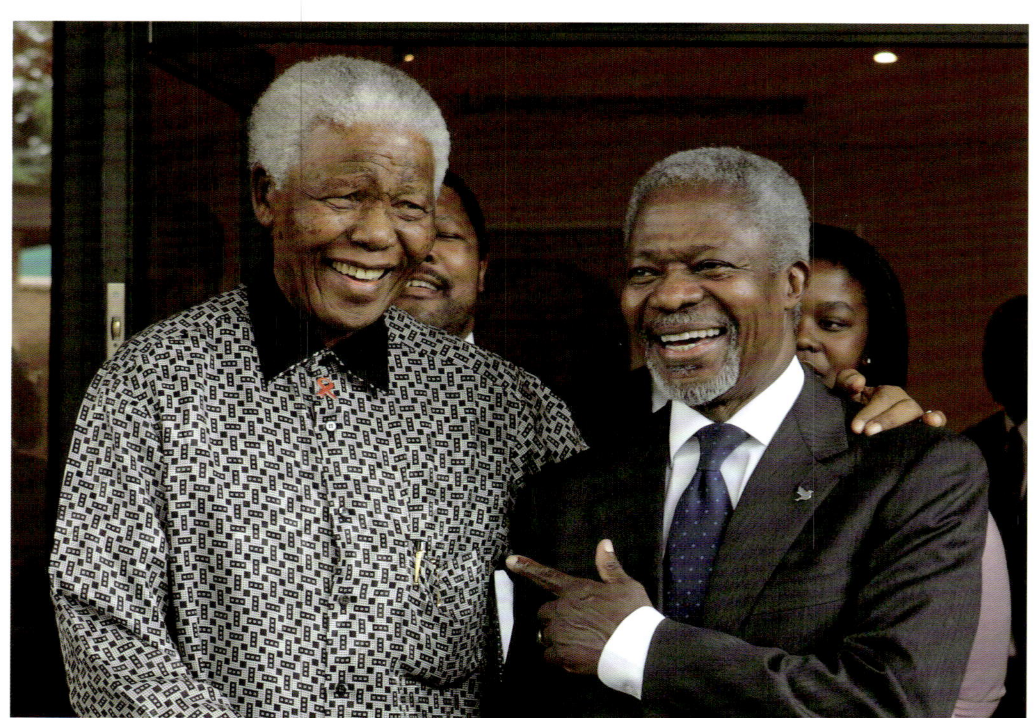

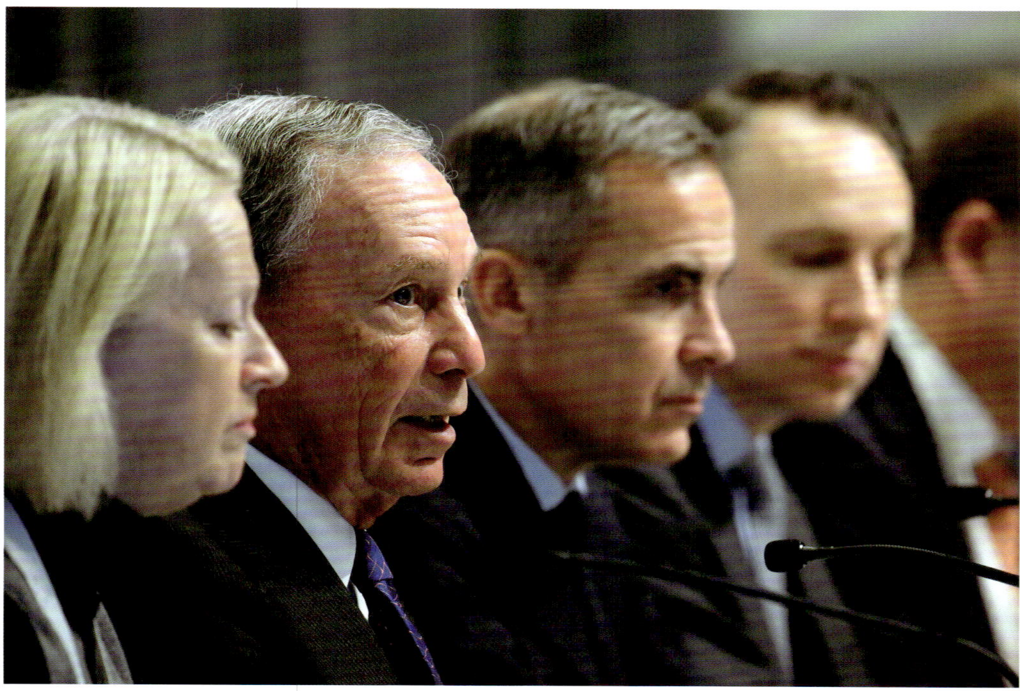

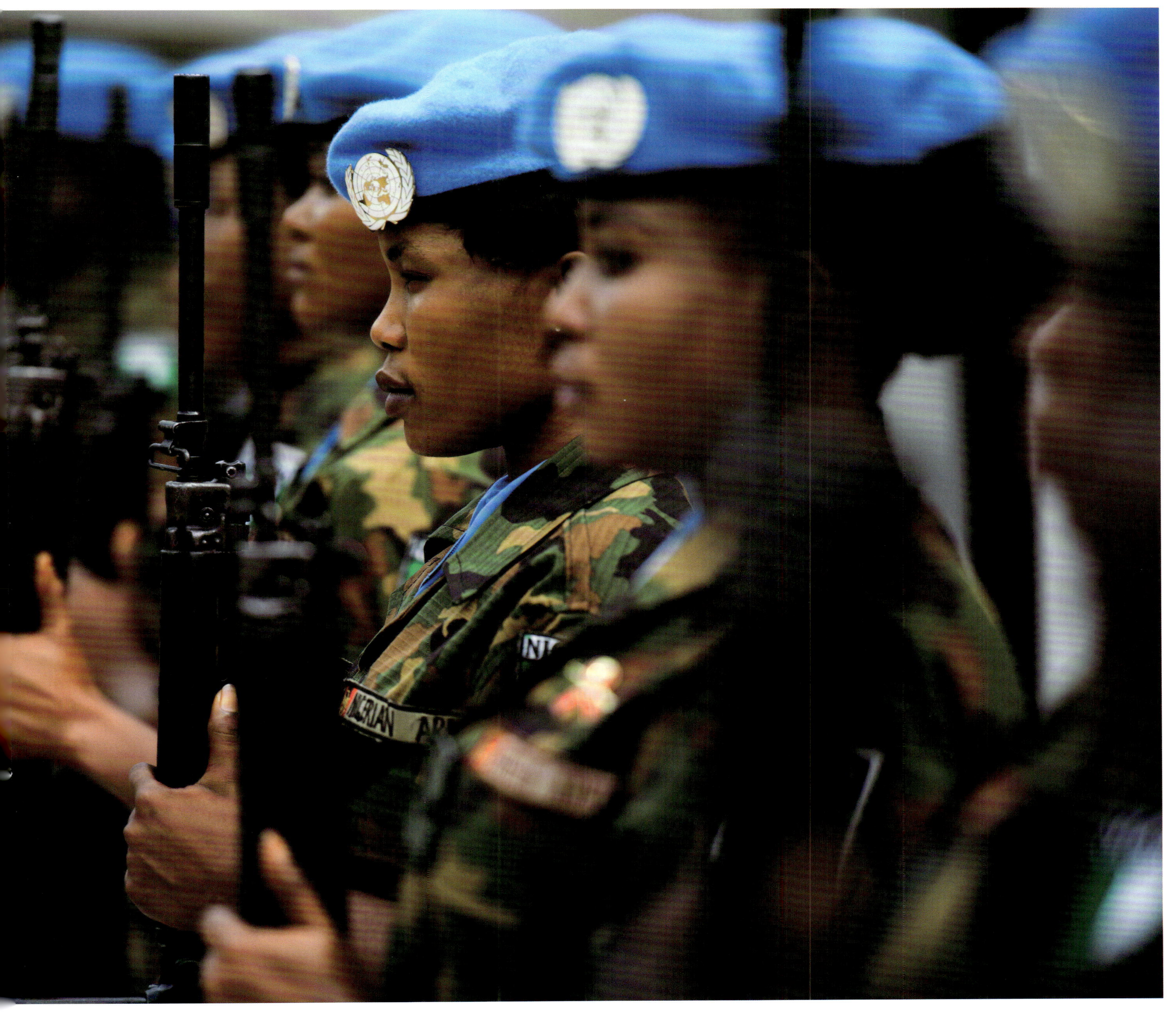

Nigerian peacekeepers serving with the United Nations Mission in Liberia (UNMIL) stand in formation during an inspection of their base. UNMIL was established in September 2003 to monitor a ceasefire agreement in Liberia, following the conclusion of the Second Liberian Civil War. January 12, 2018.

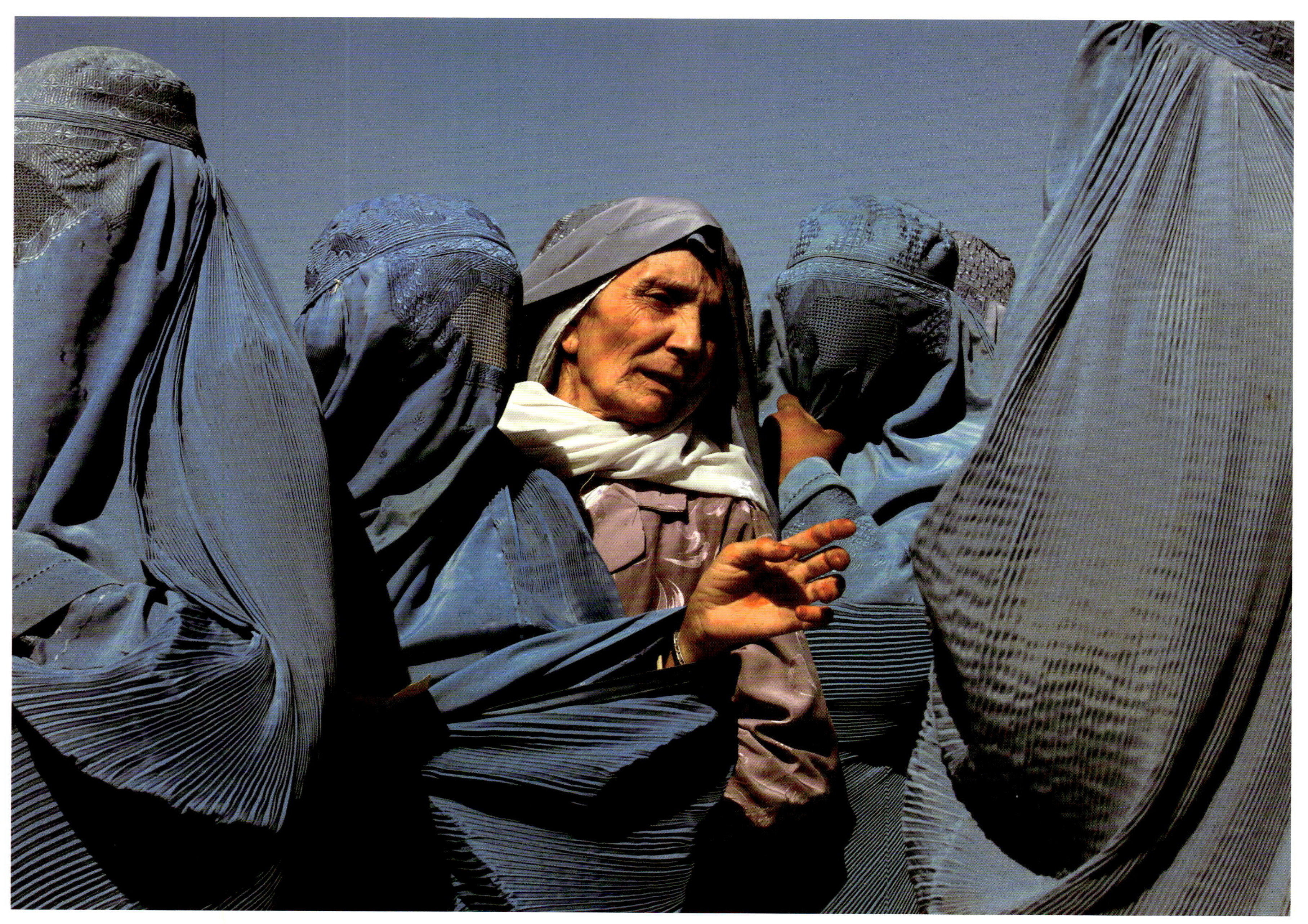

In Herat, Afghanistan, women queue to collect bags of split chickpeas, wheat, and cooking oil being distributed by the World Food Programme. June 29, 2012.

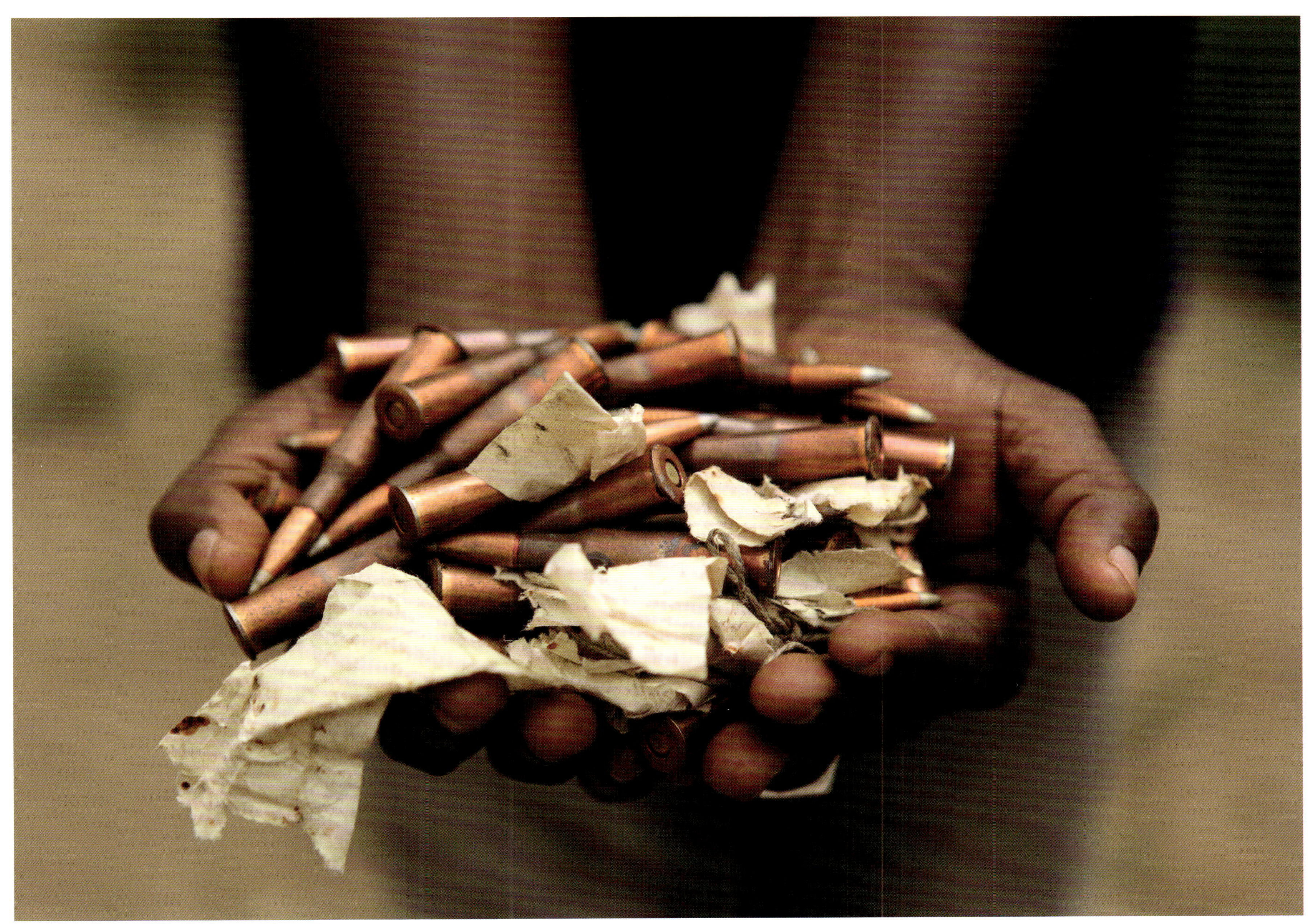

An ex-combatant holds up munitions in Attécoubé, Abidjan, Côte d'Ivoire. He is one of several to have participated in a Disarmament, Demobilization, and Reintegration (DDR) operation conducted in the area by the UN mission UNOCI. February 8, 2012.

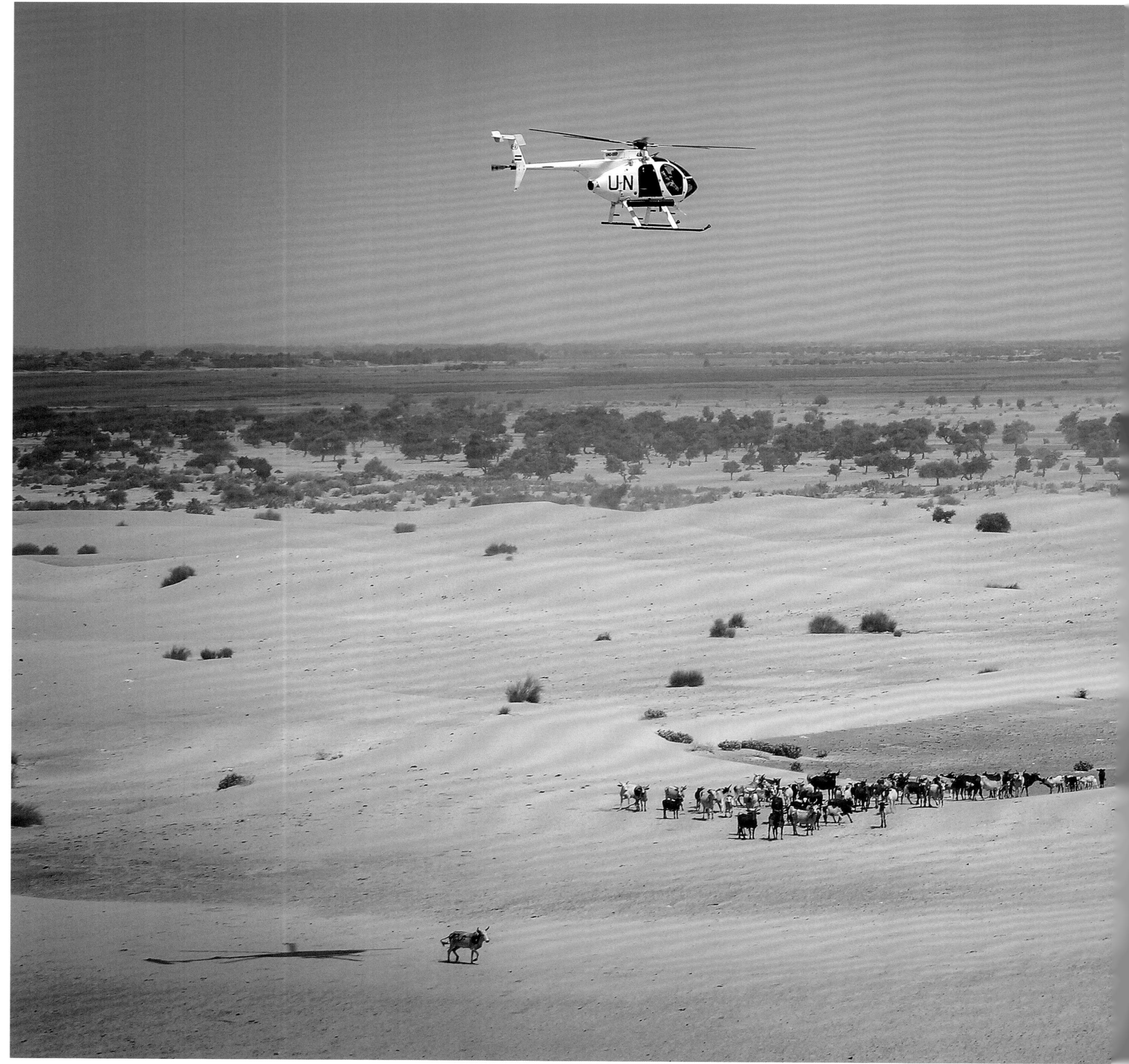
UN

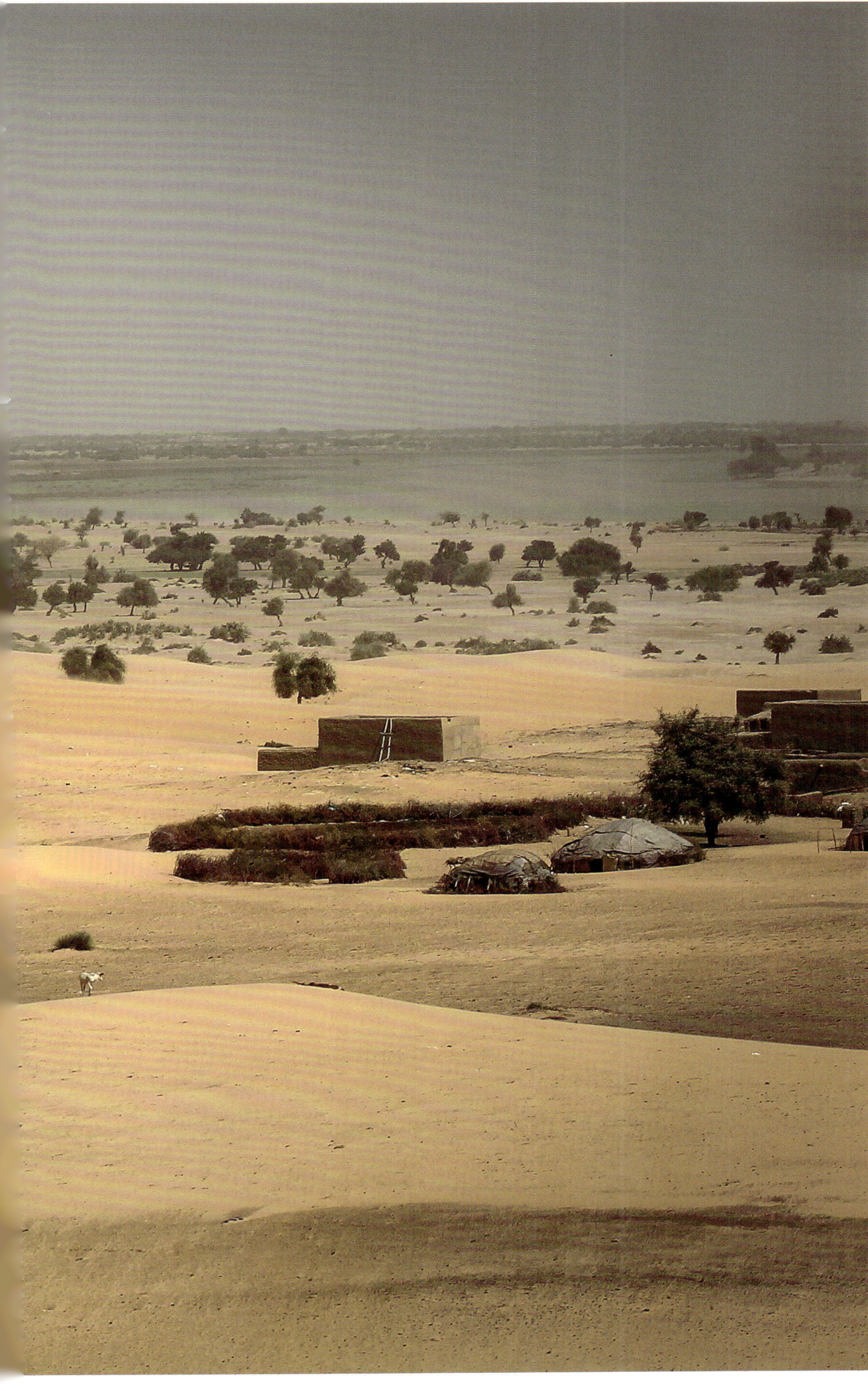

The Quick Reaction Force Unit (QRF) of the United Nations Multidimensional Integrated Stabilization Mission in Mali (MINUSMA) is composed of 90 members, including 13 pilots, air support unit (ASU) maintenance teams, medical personnel, and marines. Its mission is to conduct day and night patrols and provide support to convoys and troops on the ground. The QRF Salvadorian armed helicopter unit conducts a patrol to provide air support to a MINUSMA convoy in the Timbuktu region. The unit is named Torogoz after an emblematic bird in El Salvador. August 31, 2017.

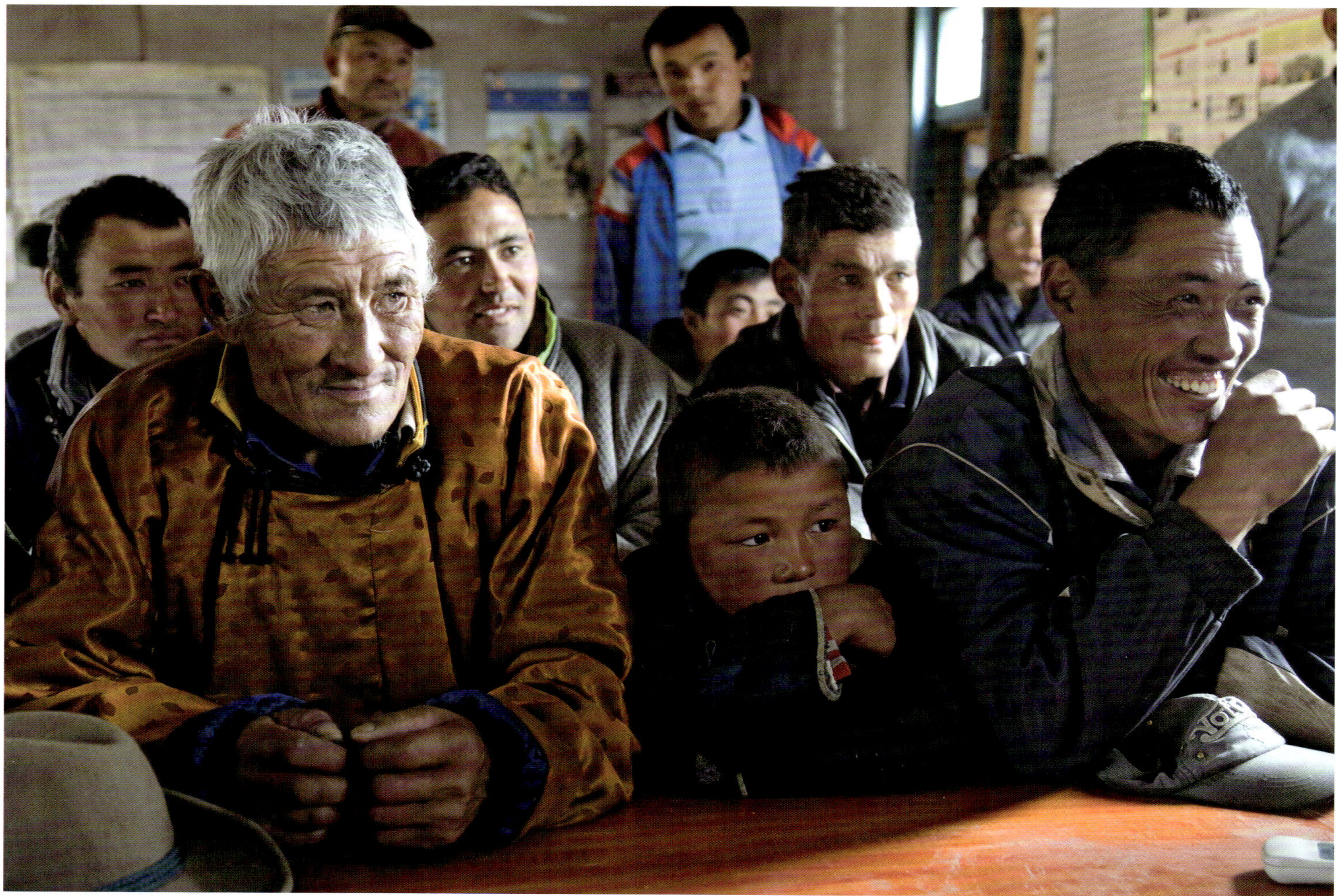

Mongolian herders in Tarialan, Uvs Province, Mongolia. The United Nations Development Programme (UNDP) supports community centers for herder groups that develop their own land-use plans, conservation maps, and sustainable practices for water, forest, and pasture management. July 28, 2009.

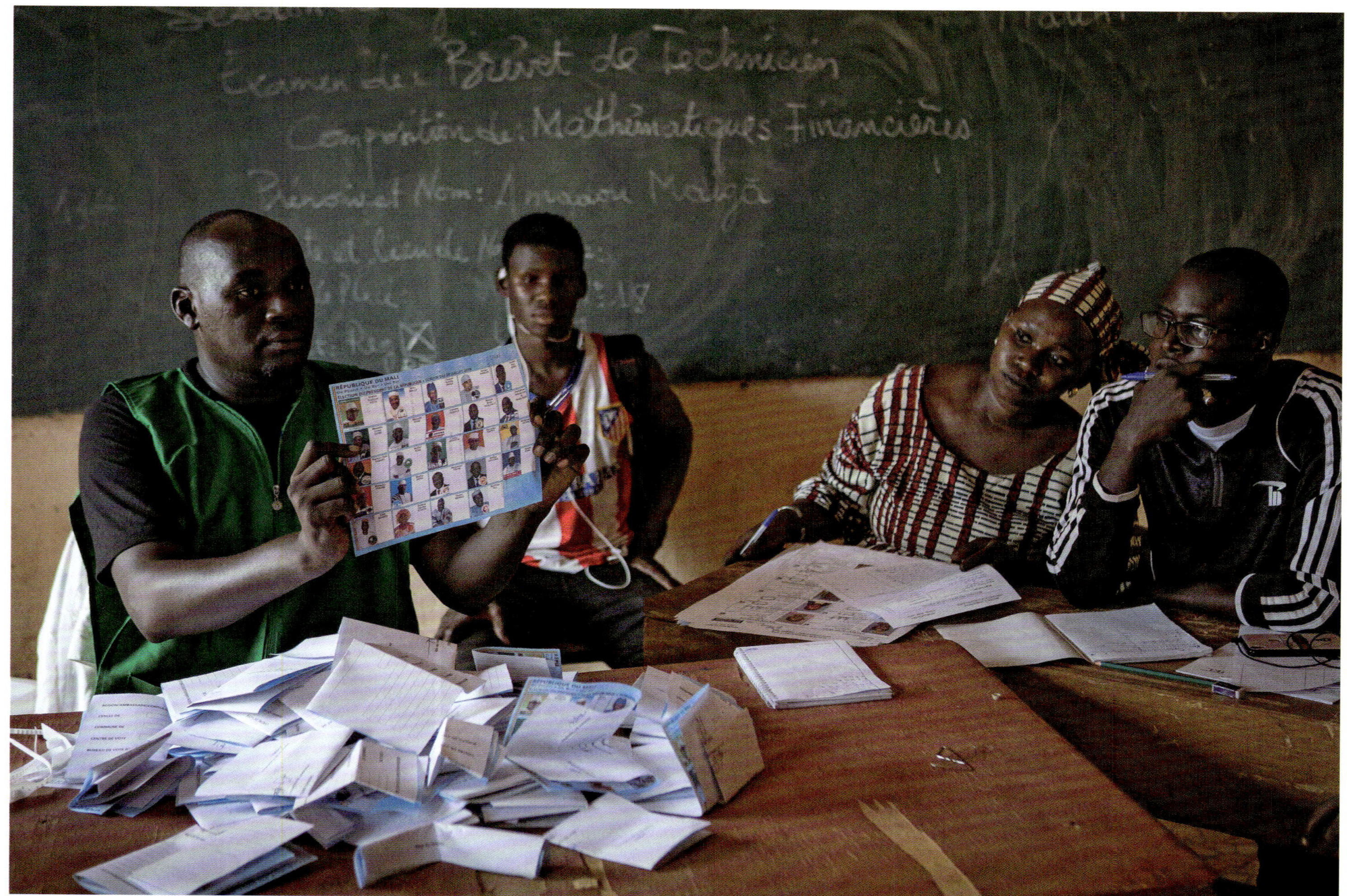

The United Nations Multidimensional Integrated Stabilization Mission in Mali (MINUSMA) Electoral Affairs Division deploys election officers and logistical assistants throughout the country in order to support local and administrative authorities in the proper organization of the vote. Ballots are counted at a polling station in Mopti after the closing of the polls, in the presence of representatives from political parties. July 29, 2018.

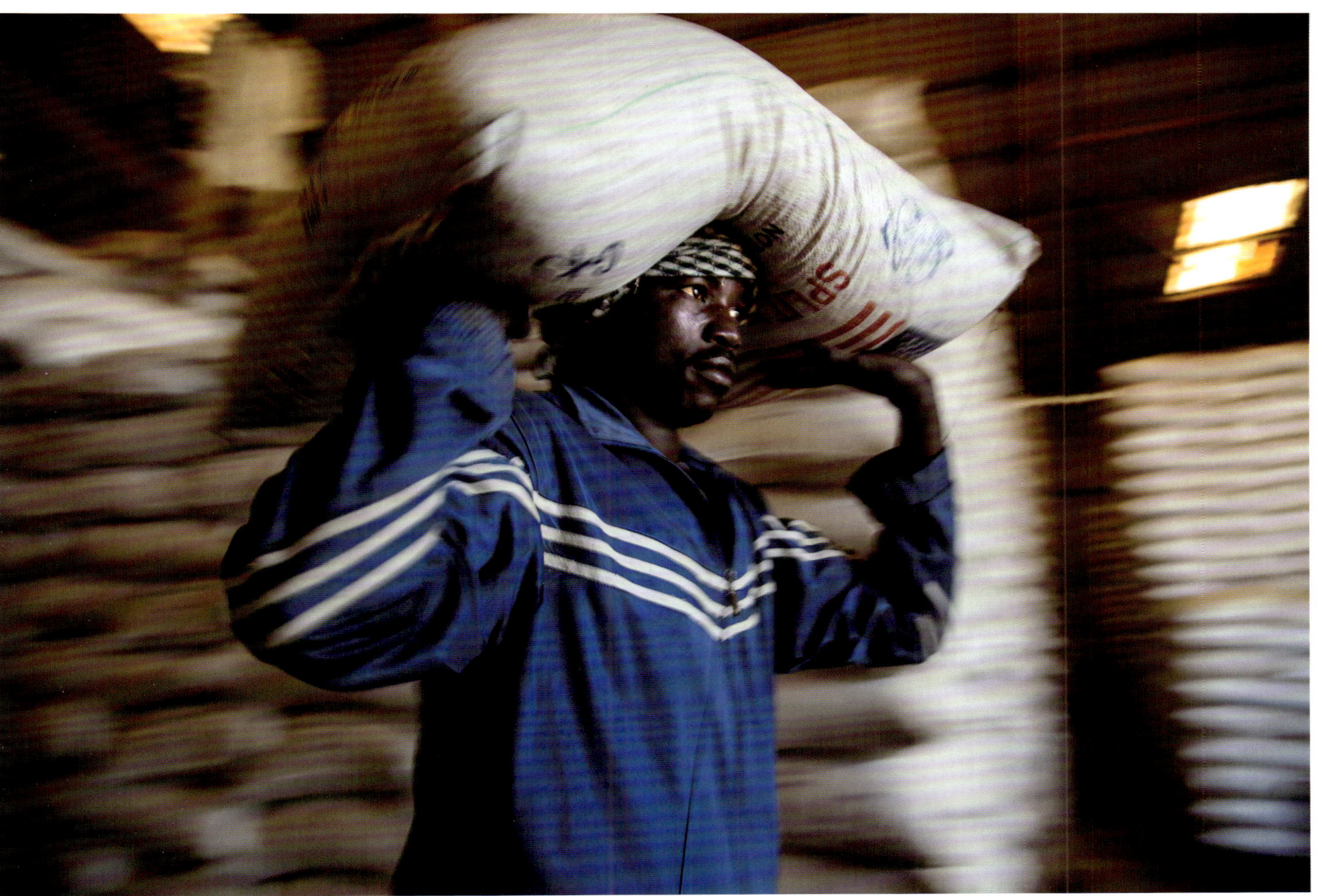

A World Food Programme (WFP) staff member loads bags of split yellow peas into a truck in a WFP warehouse based in El Fasher, North Darfur, for delivery and distribution at camps for displaced persons (IDPs) in Shangil Tobaya, North Darfur. February 9, 2014.

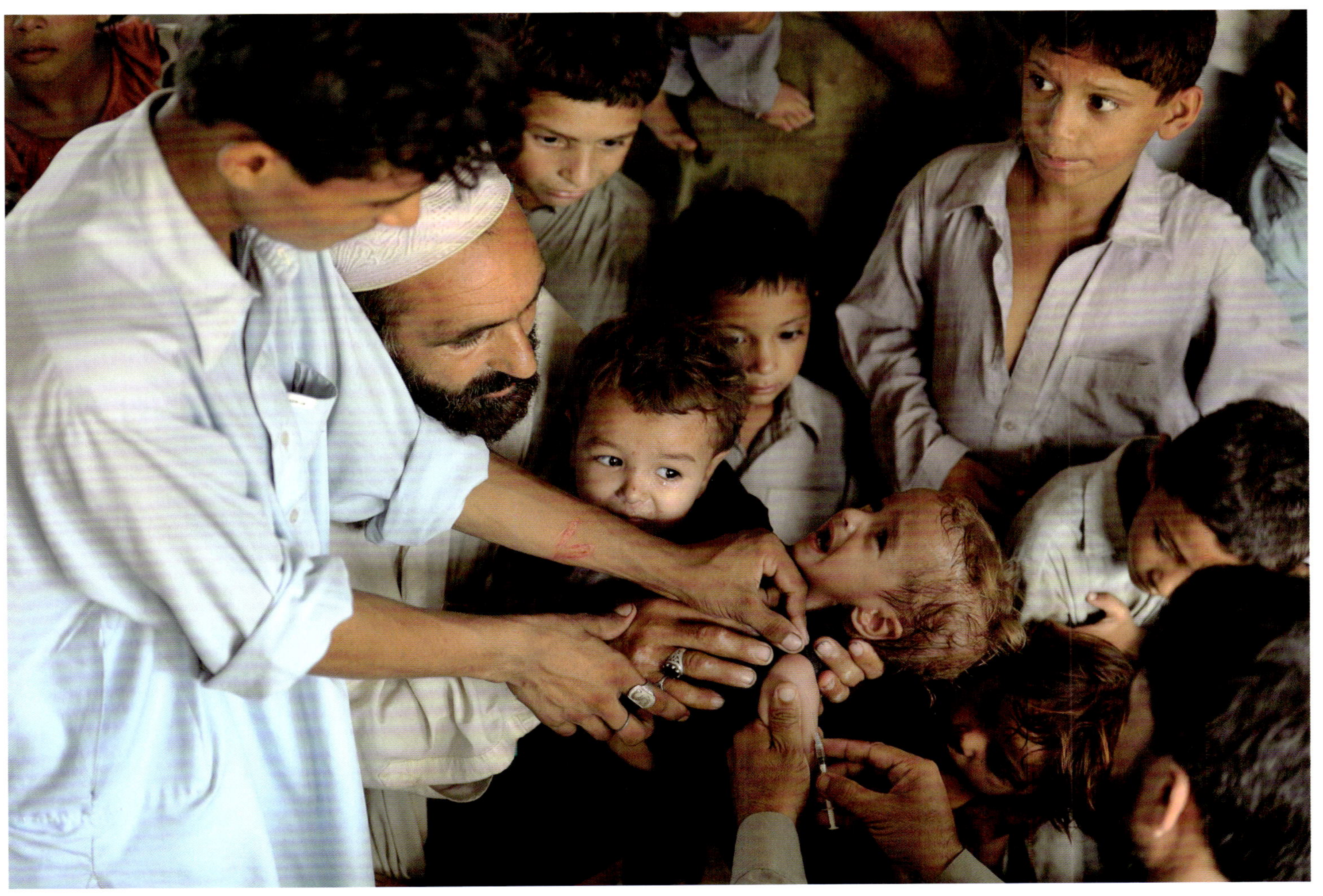

A child grimaces as he receives a measles vaccination at a school in Charsadda District in Pakistan's northwestern Khyber-Pakhtunkhwa Province. The school is housing thousands of people displaced by heavy monsoon floods. Fourteen million Pakistanis have been affected by the disaster, including many women and children at risk of waterborne and other diseases. August 11, 2010.

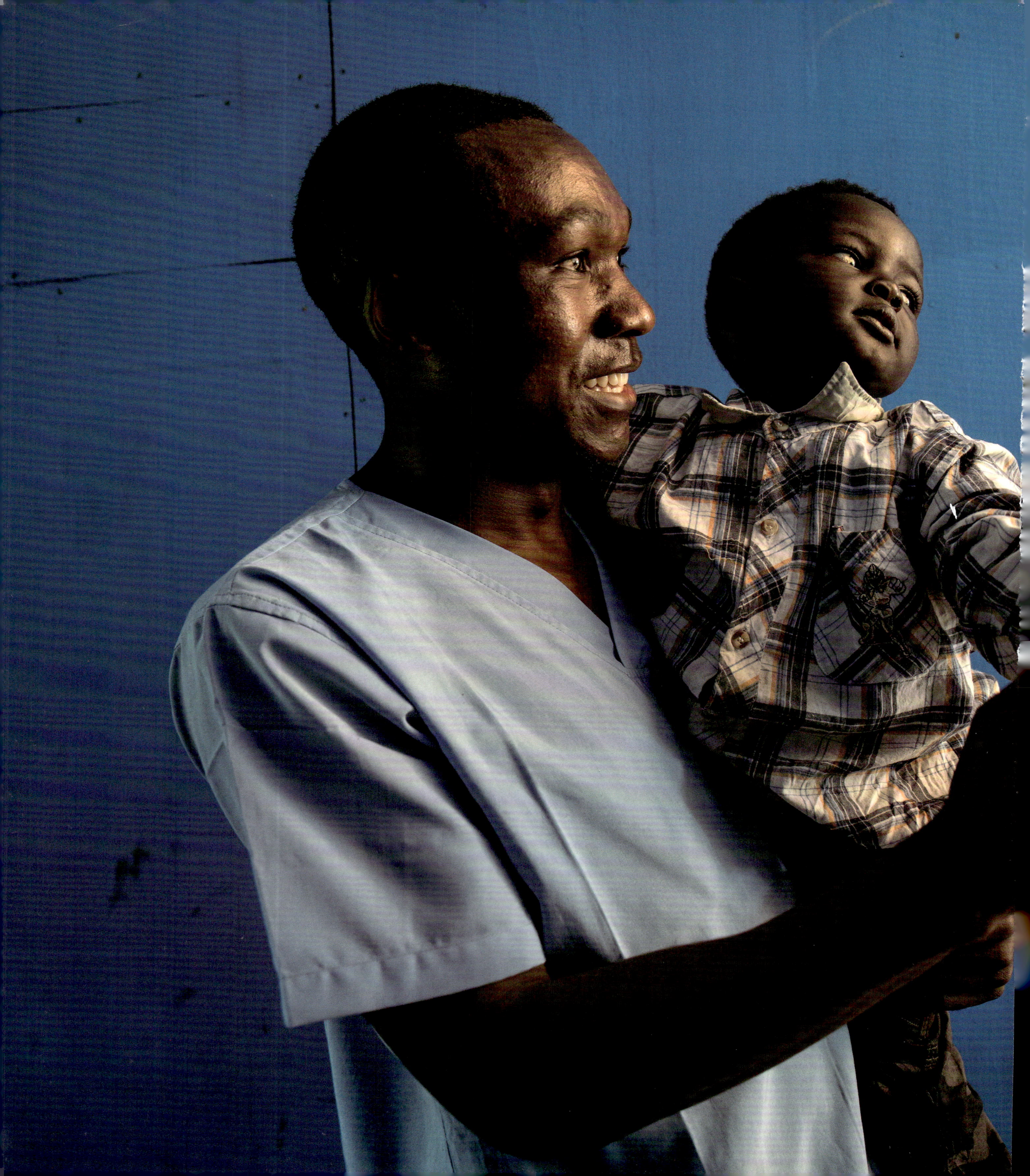

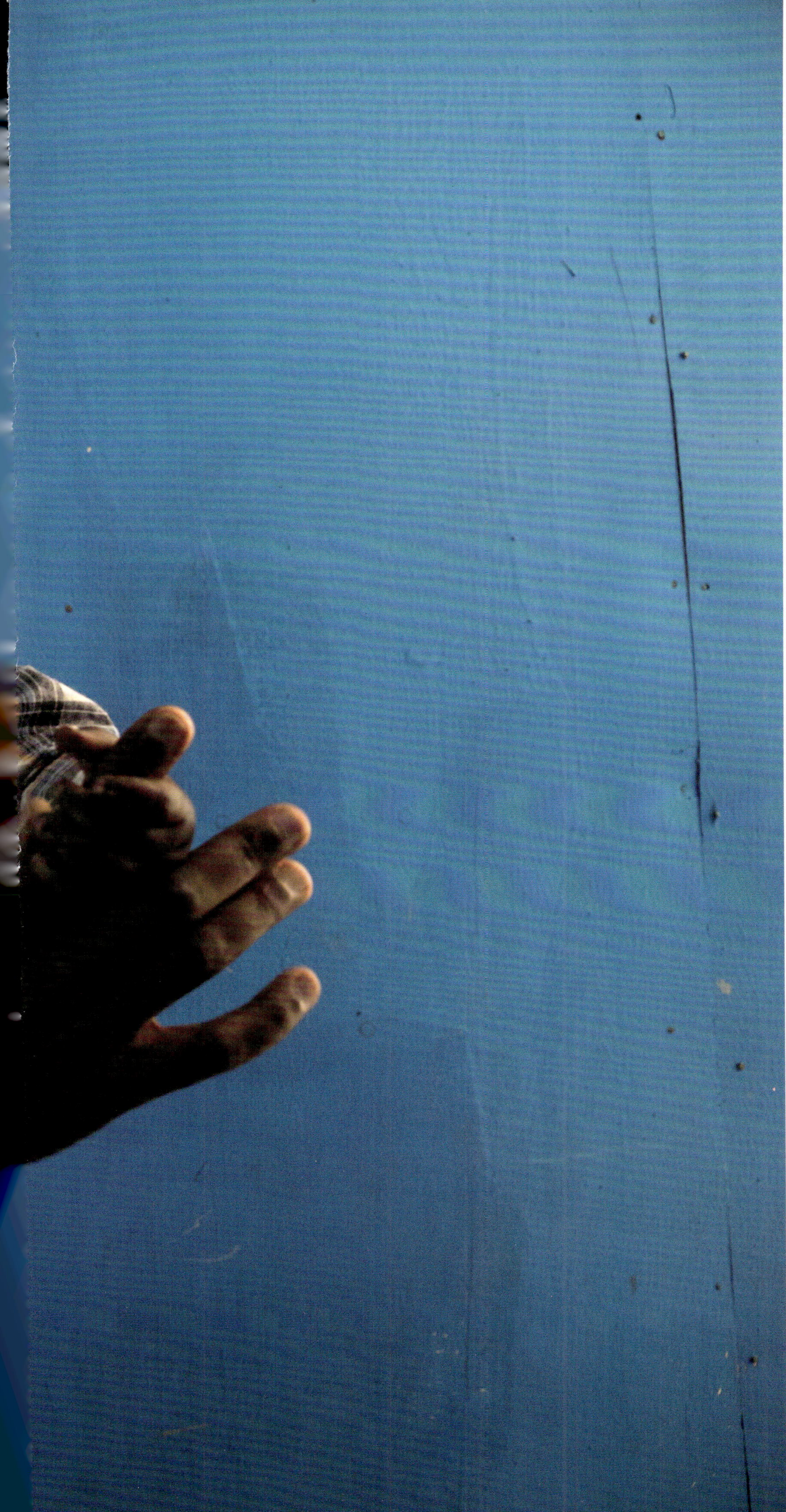

The child care center in Butembo, North Kivu, in the Democratic Republic of the Congo (DRC) cares for children whose parents are receiving care in the Butembo Ebola treatment center. Children separated or orphaned by Ebola in the country have received care and support from the UN Children's Fund (UNICEF) and its partners. August 13, 2019.

Afterword
George Klein

October 1945 marked a historic moment for the world. Following the end of World War II, the United Nations was established as a global organization committed to fostering international peace and human rights for all. But such an organization, representing different nations from around the world, needed a headquarters—one that would serve as a home and an anchor for its many Member States.

It was not a guarantee that the UN would plant its members' flags in New York City. The Charter was signed in San Francisco and the UN considered many locations for a suitable headquarters. However, New York's history and character set it apart, sharing forward-thinking leaders and residents who reflected and embraced the UN's mission and goals. New York is a place where all are welcome—a city like no other that could truly serve as a home to the world.

The United Nations Development Corporation (UNDC), founded 50 years ago, has played an integral role in the story of the UN in New York City. It recognized that to be successful, the UN would require more than just a headquarters, it would need support facilities to enable the UN's growth, to further its critical work, and to maintain itself as a symbol for world peace. In fulfillment of its mission to assist the United Nations with its real estate needs, the UNDC developed for the UN and related entities over one million square feet of office, hotel, and residential facilities which were designed to respect the Secretariat Building, the rest of the UN complex, and the surrounding neighborhood.

We owe sincere gratitude to the visionaries behind the UNDC—Governor Nelson Rockefeller and Mayor John Lindsay, who understood the importance of the UN not only to the world, but also to New York City and New York State. With the assistance of governmental officials over the last five decades, UNDC's mission has been carried out with diligence by the members of the UNDC Board and by the chairmen who have preceded me.

The UNDC has always been a steadfast partner to the UN and remains committed to serving the United Nations for generations to come.

George Klein is Chairman of the United Nations Development Corporation.

Former UNDC Chairmen

John J. McCloy
Cyrus Vance
Robert Benjamin
Ernest A. Gross
Matthew Nimetz

The UNDC pays special tribute to those serving as Governor of the State of New York and Mayor of the City of New York during the past fifty years:

Nelson A. Rockefeller
Malcolm Wilson
Hugh L. Carey
Mario M. Cuomo
George E. Pataki
Eliot Spitzer
David Paterson
Andrew M. Cuomo

John V. Lindsay
Abraham D. Beame
Edward I. Koch
David Dinkins
Rudy Giuliani
Michael Bloomberg
Bill de Blasio

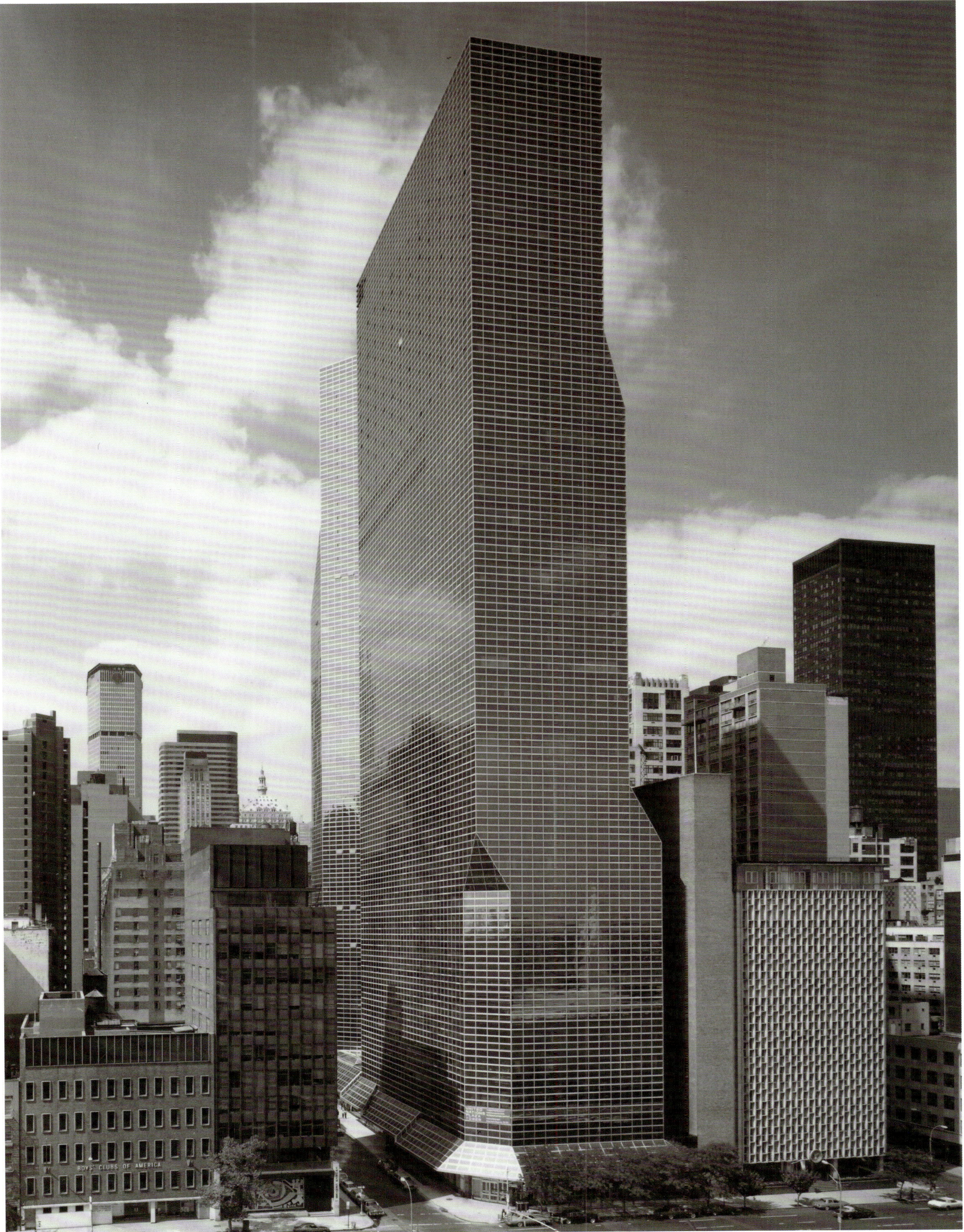

One and Two UN Plaza.

NOTES

1 Steven Heller, "Oliver Lincoln Lundquist, Designer, Is Dead At 92," *The New York Times*, January 3, 2009.
2 Julie Lasky, "Living In: Turtle Bay," *The New York Times*, January 14, 2018.
3 Turtle Bay Association, "Turtle Bay History," www.turtlebay-nyc.org.
4 Lou Goudy, ed., *The WPA Guide to New York City* (New York: Random House, 1939).
5 Ezra Stoller, *The United Nations* (New York: Princeton Architectural Press, 1999), vii.
6 www.un.org
7 George A. Dudley. *A Workshop for Peace: Designing the United Nations Headquarters* (Cambridge, MA: The MIT Press, 1994).
8 Charlene Mires, *Capital of the World: The Race to Host the United Nations* (New York: NYU Press, 2013).
9 Original documents in The Rockefeller Archive Center, Sleepy Hollow, New York.
10 Ibid.
11 Ibid.
12 Morris Kaplan. "UN Breaks Ground for Its Capital; O'Dwyer Welcomes 'Plan for Peace,'" *The New York Times*, September 15, 1948.
13 Pamela Hanlon. *A Worldly Affair: New York, the United Nations, and the Story Behind Their Unlikely Bond* (New York: Empire State Editions, 2017), 59.
14 Stoller, 4.
15 Ibid, 6.
16 Hanlon.
17 Ibid, 61.
18 Ibid.
19 Stoller, 11.
20 Hanlon.
21 Hanlon.
22 *United Nations Impact Report 2016*. NYC Mayor's Office for International Affairs; New York City Economic Development Corporation.
23 Hanlon, 66.
24 Clifford J. Levy. "Resolved: Less Paper. Any Seconds?" *The New York Times*, September 24, 1991.
25 Thomas J. Hamilton. "Crowded U.N. Seeks More Office Space," *The New York Times*, May 7, 1962.
26 New York City Landmarks Preservation Commission, Designation List 493, LP-2588, United Nations Hotel, January 17, 2017.
27 Hanlon, 120.
28 Ibid, 122.
29 Paul Goldberger. "Kevin Roche Finishes a Trio and Changes His Tune," *The New York Times*, November 27, 1987.
30 Ibid.
31 undc.org
32 *Fact Sheet: History of United Nations Headquarters*, visit.un.org.
33 United Nations, *The United Nations at 70: Restoration and Renewal* (New York: Rizzoli International Publications, 2015), 51.
34 Ibid, 42.
35 Ibid, 51.
36 Ibid, 52.
37 Ibid, 106.
38 Ibid, 62.
39 Ibid, 66.
40 un.org
41 Ibid.
42 NYC Mayor's Office and New York City Economic Development Corporation, *United Nations Impact Report 2016*, 2.
43 United Nations Press Release SG/SM/5779, 22 October 1995.
44 *The United Nations at 70*, 55.

CREDITS

Endpaper: UN Photo/Chester Price
Title spread: UN Photo/Mark Garten
Book sleeve interior: David Leventi
P. 6: UN Photo/Harandane Dicko
P. 8: UN Photo/Manuel Elías
P. 14: UN Photo/Mark Garten
P. 16: Hulton Archive/Getty Images; The U.S. National Archives and Records Administration; UN Photo
P. 17: Keystone/Getty Images; UN Photo; UN Photo
P. 18: LLNL/Science Source; UN Photo/MB; A. Barrington Brown/Science Source
P. 19: Howard Sochurek/The LIFE Picture Collection/Getty Images; NASA/Science Source; UN Photo/Yutaka Nagata
P. 20: New York Public Library/Science Source; UN Photo/Yutaka Nagata
P. 21: UN Photo; Bettmann/Getty Images; NASA
P. 22: UN Photo/Yutaka Nagata; UN Photo
P. 23: UN Photo/B. Lane; UN Photo/Teddy Chen
P. 24: UN Photo/Grant McLean; UN Photo/John Isaac; Hank Morgan/Science Source
P. 25: UN Photo/Oleg Veklenko; UN Photo/Patricia Esteve; Tom Stoddart Archive/Getty Images
P. 26: UN Photo; UN Photo/Staton Winter
P. 27: UN Photo/Evan Schneider; Philippe Plailly/Science Source; UN Photo/UNHCR/Roger LeMoyne
P. 28: NASA/Science Source; Library of Congress; José Carlos Casimiro; UN Photo/Stephenie Hollyman
P. 29: UN Photo/Jean-Marc Ferré; UN Photo/Mark Garten; UN Photo/Sylvain Liechti
P. 30: Jean-Marc Charles/Getty Images; Lionel Bonaventure/AFP/Getty Images; UN Photo/H. Arvidsson
P. 31: UN Photo/Mark Garten; Francois Lo Presti/AFP/Getty Images; UN Photo/Mark Garten
P. 38, 39: The Miriam and Ira D. Wallach Division of Art, Prints and Photographs: Print Collection, The New York Public Library
P. 40: Percy Loomis Sperr ©Milstein Division, The New York Public Library
P. 42–43: The Miriam and Ira D. Wallach Division of Art, Prints and Photographs: Print Collection, The New York Public Library
P. 44: Skyviews Survey
P. 46, 47: Percy Loomis Sperr ©Milstein Division, The New York Public Library
P. 48: Milstein Division, The New York Public Library
P. 49: Percy Loomis Sperr ©Milstein Division, The New York Public Library
P. 50: Keystone/Hulton Archive/Getty Images
P. 51: MCNY/Gottscho-Schleisner/Getty Images
P. 52: Alfred Eisenstaedt/The LIFE Picture Collection/Getty Images
P. 53: FPG/Getty Images
P. 54: Irving Browning/The New York Historical Society/Getty Images
P. 55: John Spencer Fay/FPG/Getty Images; Gjon Mili/The LIFE Picture Collection/Getty Images
P. 56: Michael Ochs Archives/Getty Images
P. 57: Three Lions/Hulton Archive/Getty Images
P. 61, 66, 68: UN Photo
P. 70: Hugh Ferriss architectural drawings and papers, 1906-1980, Avery Architectural & Fine Arts Library, Columbia University
P. 71, 72, 73: UN Photo
P. 74, 75: UN Photo/Kari Berggrav
P. 82, 84–85, 86: UN Photo
P. 87: Frank Scherschel/The LIFE Picture Collection/Getty Images; UN Photo
P. 88–89, 90–91: The United Nations Archives and Records Management Section
P. 98: UN Photo/MB
P. 99, 100, 101, 102, 103, 105: UN Photo
P. 106: UN Photo/G.; UN Photo/MB
P. 107: UN Photo
P. 108: UN Photo/MB
P. 109: UN Photo/MB; Ezra Stoller/Esto
P. 110–111: UN Photo/MB
P. 112: UN Photo/MMB; UN Photo/Teddy Chen
P. 113: UN Photo/Yutaka Nagata; UN Photo/MB
P. 114: UN Photo/MB
P. 115: UN Photo/AB
P. 116–117: UN Photo/MB
P. 121: Jesse Neider for the Wall Street Journal
P. 128–129, 130–131, 132: UN Photo
P. 133: AFP/Getty Images
P. 134: UN Photo/MH
P. 135: UN Photo/Teddy Chen
P. 136: UN Photo/Yutaka Nagata
P. 137: UN Photo/Yutaka Nagata; UN Photo/Teddy Chen
P. 138, 139: UN Photo/Yutaka Nagata
P. 140: UN Photo/Yutaka Nagata; UN Photo/Saw Lwin
P. 141: UN Photo/Milton Grant
P. 142: UN Photo/Andrea Brizzi; Jamie McCarthy/WireImage/Getty Images
P. 143: UN Photo/Evan Schneider
P. 144: UN Photo/Loey Felipe
P. 145, 152: UN Photo/Rick Bajornas
P. 158: UN Photo/Manuel Elías
P. 161: UN Photo/Rick Bajornas
P. 162: UN Photo/Werner Schmidt
P. 163: UN Photo/Eskinder Debebe
P. 164–165: UN Photo/Manuel Elías
P. 166–167: UN Photo/Laura Jarriel
P. 168–169: UN Photo/Rick Bajornas
P. 170–171: UN Photo/Loey Felipe
P. 172: UN Photo/Rick Bajornas
P. 173: UN Photo/Ariana Lindquist; UN Photo/Marco Castro
P. 174: UN Photo/Rick Bajornas
P. 175: UN Photo/Manuel Elías
P. 176: UN Photo/Mark Garten
P. 177: UN Photo/Rick Bajornas
P. 178: UN Photo/Evan Schneider
P. 180: UN Photo/Eskinder Debebe; Chesnot/Getty Images
P. 181: UN Photo/Albert González Farran
P. 182: UN Photo/Eric Kanalstein
P. 183: UN Photo/Patricia Esteve
P. 184–185: UN Photo/Christian Jonathan Guevara Reyes
P. 186: UN Photo/Eskinder Debebe; UN Photo/Harandane Dicko
P. 187: UN Photo/Albert González Farran; UN Photo/UNICEF/ZAK
P. 188–189: UN Photo/Martine Perret

Typeface:
The display type used throughout this book is based on a condensed sans-serif font designed by the United Nations' Presentation Services department for use at the UN Headquarters complex. No exact date is available for the creation of this unnamed font, but records indicate that it was completed prior to 1950. This typeface was redrawn and extended in 2020 by Julian Morey.

The body copy is set in Tiempos, designed by Kris Sowersby; and Atlas Grotesk by Kai Bernau and Susana Carvalho with Christian Schwartz.

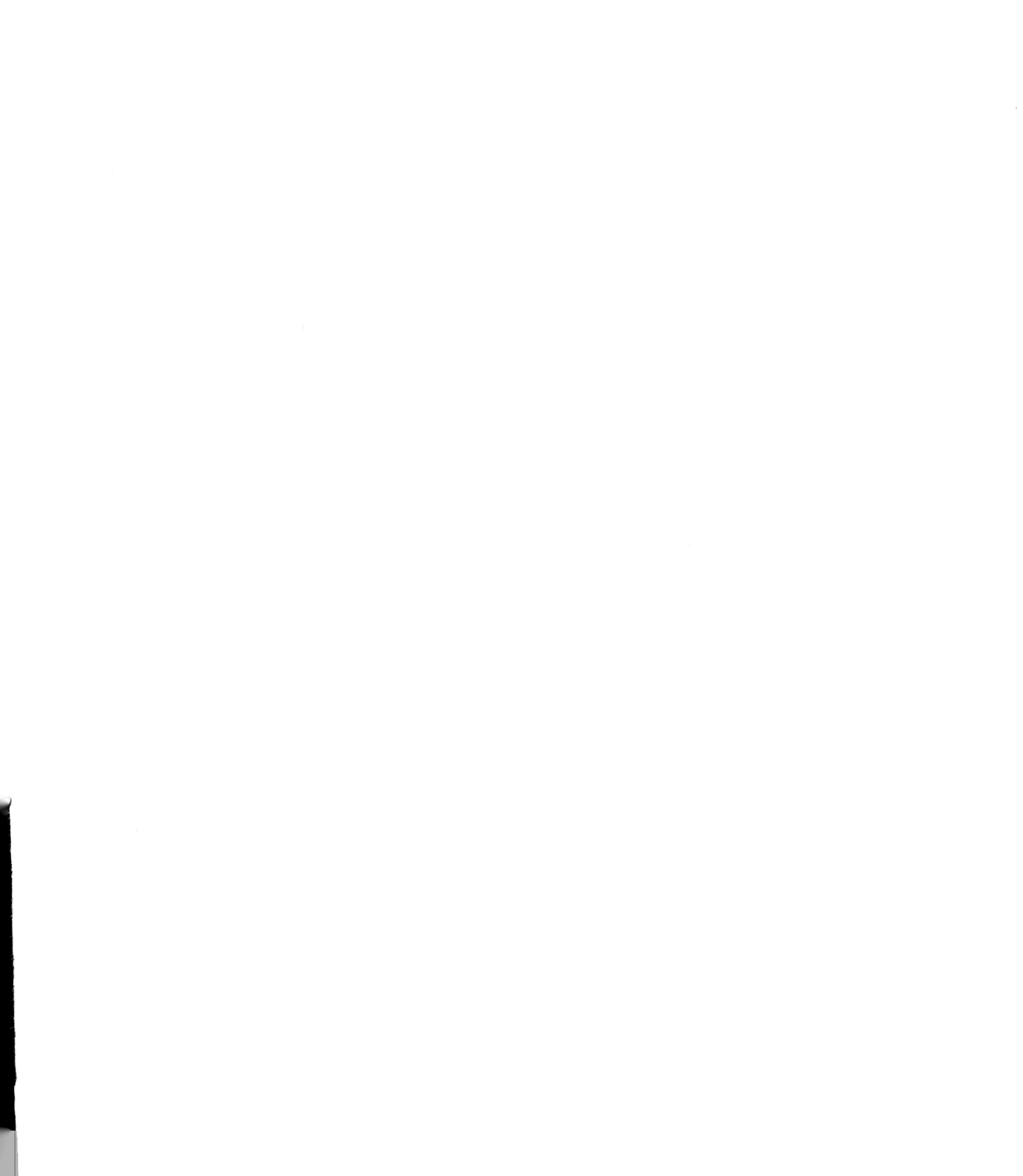

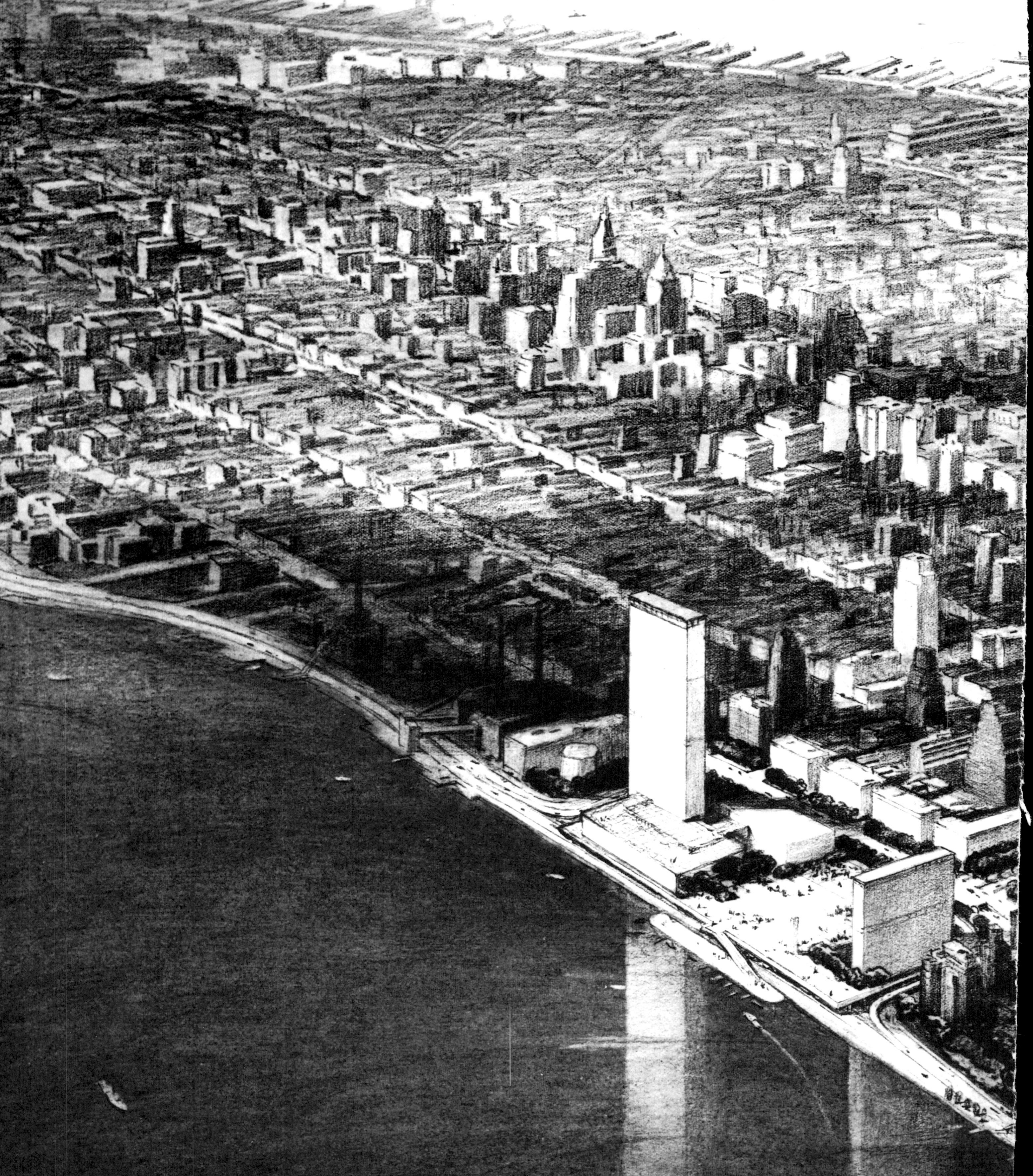